Cinderella across Cultures

New Directions and Interdisciplinary Perspectives

EDITED BY
Martine Hennard Dutheil de la Rochère,
Gillian Lathey, and Monika Woźniak

Wayne State University Press
Detroit

20 19 18 17 16 5 4 3 2 1

ISBN 978-0-8143-4155-1 (paper) | ISBN 978-0-8143-4156-8 (e-book)
Library of Congress Control Number: 2015958995

Published with the assistance of a fund established by Thelma Gray James of Wayne State University for the publication of folklore and English studies.

Designed and typeset by Keata Brewer, E.T. Lowe Publishing Company
Composed in Minion Pro

Contents

List of Color Plates

Foreword

The Walt Disney Studios' "Cinderella Countdown to #Midnight" Official Tease was released just before midnight on New Year's Eve 2014 (eastern USA time). While in it the fairy godmother (Helena Bonham Carter) cautions, "Remember the magic only lasts so long!," the glamorous vision of Lily Adams in her starry blue dress is clearly meant to live on, firing the public's desire to see the movie. Similarly titillating is the double-tongued warning—Disney's acknowledgment that the success of its 1950 animated film cannot last forever and the Studios' simultaneous promise that their 2015 live-action adaptation will renew the magic. Anticipation was already being sparked with the news that Richard Madden from *Game of Thrones* would play Prince Charming, another preview that featured the crystal shoe, and the tease of a reflective, postmodern Cinderella (Anna Kendrick) presented in *Into the Woods*, another Disney production that in North America opened on December 25, 2014. With the "Countdown" trailer, the commercial hype harnessed the liminal power of midnight to further flaunt the wish fulfillment in the Cinderella story being turned into a capitalist-patriarchal consumer fantasy.

To consider Cinderella as a text of culture requires that we understand the Disneyfication of the tale to be symptomatic of a globalized popular culture that capitalizes on a "rags-to-riches" interpretation of the tale, one that for women instrumentalizes marriage as a form of mere acquisition. But considering Cinderella as also, and perhaps more importantly, a cultural text implies that we realize Cinderella has not been reduced to this one type of story or fantasy, and that its variable meanings have continued to live, adapt, and translate in and across cultures. Raised bilingual in Italy, I watched the animated Disney *Cinderella* as a child in the early 1960s, but I also read an abbreviated translation of Charles Perrault's Cinderella in a book of fairy tales illustrated by Adrienne Ségur—where the round-eyed girl in gray rags made as much of an impression on me as the lavishly dressed images of Donkeyskin and the Queen Cat, and my grandmother in Ravenna would tell me a story that (I would later learn) combined elements of Cinderella and Donkeyskin and was very clear about the heroine's agency concerning when and by whom she wanted to be recognized. Later, I came to know other homegrown Cinderella tales. In "Grattula-Bedattula," a Sicilian tale translated by Italo Calvino, the protagonist Ninetta is an explorer more than a fashion maker: she finds the garden of the King of Portugal hidden behind the wall of the well in the courtyard of the house "with the doors sealed" where the father had confined his three daughters during his business trip. There is no stepmother or lost shoe in this version, but plenty of disguises and surprises at the ball. In contrast, Giambattista Basile's Zezolla, in "La Gatta Cenerentola," has two stepmothers, and she murders the first one only to discover that her manipulative teacher-turned-stepmother number two has seven daughters of her own and no love for her. The lost slipper—a patten with cork heels, further eroticized by its popularity with courtesans in Basile's time—is clearly a fetish in the Neapolitan prince's baroque soliloquy, presented here in Nancy Canepa's translation: "Oh lovely candlestick that held the candle that consumes me! O tripod of the charming cauldron in which my life is boiling! O beautiful corks, attached to the fishing line of Love used to catch this soul!" (2007, 87). As scholars, whatever our disciplinary home is, we ought not only to enjoy the diversity and richness of the many Cinderellas but also accept the responsibility to put the historical and current multiplicity of fairy tales at play in our discussions.

Published in 1982 and edited by Alan Dundes, *Cinderella: A Casebook* was a pathbreaking volume that continues to be useful, even foundational, if getting to know Cinderella beyond Disney's 1950 animated film is our goal. What the volume achieved over thirty years ago was to contextualize various versions of the popular tale as well as critical approaches to them, all within the scope of folklore studies. In particular, I remember my delight with the "Cinderella Variant in the Context of a Muslim Women's Ritual" and my realization of how insightful Margaret Mills was in her analysis, and careful but bold in her feminist ethnographic methodology. Whether the tales are fictional or scholarly, the trick, or meaning, is in their telling as well as in the cultural conventions by which we agree to receive them. The foot maiming and blinding of the selfish stepsisters in the Grimms' nineteenth-century version is to be understood as punishment, and so is the appearance of a donkey's penis on the stepsister's forehead and of a snake on her chin in the tale told by women in eastern Iran and western Afghanistan in the 1970s. The punishments ensure that these false heroines will have no chance on the marriage market, but in the latter tale, told exclusively by and for women, the "acquisition of male characteristics by a female is a grotesque punishment for disloyalty to women" (Mills in Dundes 1982, 190–91). Competition between women is not naturalized! I learned then once and for all that Cinderella cannot tell one story only about gender norms and that the tale's culturally specific performance can be just as transformative as the (god)mother's makeover of the heroine.

The volume that is in your hands now also rejects universal meanings of Cinderella, but refreshingly does not limit its inquiry to the framework of folkloristics. *Cinderella across Cultures* takes on working with the tale's multiple performances in context—one of the methodological foundations of contemporary folklore studies—and broadens our critical scope to Cinderella texts as cultural practices that, in the editors' words, are produced by and in response to "specific historical, geographical, sociocultural, discursive, literary, and mediatic *ec(h)o-system(s)*."

As such, this book exemplifies the interdisciplinary and transnational discourse of contemporary fairy-tale studies that seeks to foreground a fairy-tale text's situatedness as well as to historicize its intertextuality. Considering Cinderella as a social text means to approach its refashioning across languages, media, and cultures, as seen in the contributions that focus on translation and adaptation; to focus on how fairy-tale discourses inform our understanding of various societies and cultures, with essays on how producing and interpreting Cinderella texts are intertwined with assumptions about family, sexuality, gender, childhood, and nation; and to treat material objects in fairy tales, like glass, and fairy-tale ephemera, like posters, as cultural texts. The essays collectively provide new insights into contextualizing, retelling, and reimag(in)ing Cinderella, and, though they wisely do not aim for a global survey, they do engage cultural traditions that, while remaining rooted in a Euro-American context, decenter the Basile-Perrault-Grimms-Disney genealogy. In doing so, the editors and contributors of this volume deploy a keen awareness of the cultural work that translation, as process and trope, does in the production of and responses to Cinderella texts, thus significantly advancing a culture of translation in fairy-tale studies.

Armando Maggi in "The Creation of Cinderella from Basile to the Brothers Grimm" warns us not to assume that because the tale of Cinderella has ancient antecedents in China and Egypt it has always enjoyed the cultural prominence it has now. *Cinderella across Cultures* persuasively develops an anti-universalizing poetics by showing how variously situated Cinderella texts have intervened to make, unmake, and exploit its "all-time favorite" status today. While the magic of one Cinderella may not endure, the essays in this volume analyze the power of a range of Cinderella verbal and visual texts so as to complicate our "rags-to-riches" preconceptions in lasting ways.

Cristina Bacchilega
University of Hawai'i, Mānoa

References

Canepa, Nancy. 2007. Translation, introduction, and notes to Giambattista Basile, *The Tale of Tales or Entertainment of Little Ones*. Detroit: Wayne State University Press.

Maggi, Armando. 2015. "The Creation of Cinderella from Basile to the Brothers Grimm." In *The Cambridge Companion to Fairy Tales*, edited by Maria Tatar, 150–65. Cambridge: Cambridge University Press.

Mills, Margaret A. 1982. "A Cinderella Variant in the Context of a Muslim Women's Ritual." In *Cinderella: A Folklore Casebook*, edited by Alan Dundes, 180–92. New York: Garland.

Acknowledgments

We are grateful to Monika Woźniak for hosting the Rome conference in 2012 at La Sapienza, which gathered fairy-tale scholars from all over the world as well as an opera director, musicians, visual artists, and librarians to make the conference into a truly interdisciplinary event complete with an exhibition of rare editions and illustrated books, costumes and objects related to the Cinderella tale in its manifold guises across time and cultures. The conference encouraged us to pursue the project by publishing a selection of papers presented on this occasion and commissioning a few others to complement the volume and give readers a sense of the cultural ubiquity of the tale past and present.

We would like to thank the series editor, Donald Haase, and his very professional team at Wayne State University Press, especially Annie Martin, Kristina Stonehill, Carrie Teefey, and Dawn Hall, as well as the anonymous readers, for their useful feedback. Thanks also to designer and compositor Keata Brewer at E.T. Lowe.

We also thank the artists, copyright holders, academic presses, and institutions for giving us permission to (re)print images and revised book chapters, as well as the Commission des Publications de la Faculté des Lettres at the University of Lausanne for covering the extra costs of the color insert and indexing.

Last but not least, we'd like to thank our friends and families for their patience and good humor, especially Pascal, Alexis, and Noemi.

Introduction

Cinderella across Cultures

Cinderella in the Twenty-First Century

Popular among children and adults, Cinderella is a prototypical story of social mobility that is itself remarkably mobile and mutable; its long history and universal appeal reflect a singular ability to travel through time and space, circulate between languages and cultures, and cut across boundaries of genre, form, and medium. While its success demonstrates the force of a transcultural script that is constantly being retold and adapted for different audiences, contexts, and purposes, the tale cannot be reduced to a single narrative or its heroine to a fixed, unified image. In the twenty-first century, Cinderella has not only been disseminated internationally but also multiplied to carry radically different messages and serve competing interests and values—from a mere celebration of the "consumer romance" (Haase 1999, 354) of global capitalism, to socially critical retellings that experiment with the poetics and politics of wonder. Because "fairy tales interpellate us as consumers *and* producers of transformation" (Bacchilega 2013, 3), storytellers, writers, artists, actors, and filmmakers (among others) have offered their own personal, unique, and challenging takes on the tale that freely reinterpret, ironize, hybridize, or depart from the Perrault-Grimm-Disney stereotype that has come to represent the tale in the popular imagination.[1] Their work in turn feeds into a complex, multilayered, and intricately interwoven *web* of intertextual echoes and cross-medial connections that is itself in motion and contributes to changing our perception of the story.[2] Alongside the reified stereotype, then, a more fluid and dynamic understanding of the story captures the elusive identity of the emblematic fairy-tale heroine as bound up with endless reinvention.

The ambivalence of the figure is manifest in its manifold usages, from dream girl reproducing dominant sociocultural norms to an embodiment of female resilience and resistance. Perhaps the ultimate proof of the force of the Cinderella story in the twenty-first century lies in the fact that it has become a universal metaphor to promote an unjustly neglected subject, activity, region, or social cause whether in newspaper headlines, political cartoons, or self-help manuals. Thus, "fibromyalgia" is said to be "the Cinderella of rheumatism," and "allergy" is apparently "still a Cinderella subject"; "indium phosphide" has been branded "the Cinderella of electronics," and "micromechanics" "a Cinderella subject." Ironically, the Cinderella metaphor has even been used in academic discourse (see Coughlin 1991 and Shavit 1994, 4–5) to refer to children's literature as a Cinderella discipline.

Today, Cinderella has become a global cultural icon that keeps pace effortlessly with new social media and communication networks, producing countless new retellings and reinterpretations every year. This multiplication calls for a shift of critical focus from "basic similarities" to "differences between versions and the context which shapes them" (Warner 2014, 62). This new paradigm in fairy-tale studies is also echoed by Andrew Teverson, who observes that because the fairy tale is "a many-tongued genre, a cultural palimpsest" we need "to understand [each] story under analysis as both a unique story, the product of a specific time and place, and as a story that has circulated in numerous different contexts and taken numerous different forms" (Teverson 2013, 5). Accordingly, while most research on Cinderella so far has tended to emphasize the intrinsic value and meaning of the tale, the focus of an international conference held at the University of La Sapienza in Rome in 2012, which became the inspiration for this volume, was neither Cinderella as an item of folklore nor its alleged universal meaning, but rather its anchoring in and response to specific historical, geographical, sociocultural, political, economic, and material circumstances, as well as discursive, literary and mediatic *ec(h)o-system(s)*. The conference, which saw over sixty scholars from across the world presenting their research on one of the most well-known tales in Western culture that has now attained global reach, offered a forum to discuss new ways of analyzing the tale as a "text of culture(s)" and thus paved the way for new directions in fairy-tale studies. In her foreword to the volume, Cristina Bacchilega points out that the approach we have chosen to adopt in the present collection of essays does indeed focus on the transformative dimension of the tale through interdisciplinary readings and innovative approaches.

A Brief Historical Overview of the Tale and Its Global Dissemination

The possible source(s) and mode(s) of transmission of the tale known as Cinderella have been documented and debated by folklorists, cultural critics, literary scholars, and book historians since at least the nineteenth century. Folklorists have identified hundreds of distinct forms of Cinderella plots worldwide, drawing attention to the tale's cultural ubiquity (African, Algonquian, Brazilian, Chinese, European, Filipino, Indian, Indonesian, Japanese, Persian, Russian . . .) and speculated on its anthropological value through its possible connections with ancient customs and beliefs, such as animal totemism or ancestor worship.

It has been noted, for example, that the key motifs of the shoe and the royal marriage appear in the story of Rhodopis, a Greek courtesan who married the king of Egypt, as Strabo recorded in the first century BCE, and considered by some as the earliest known version of the tale, while Venus's trial of Psyche to sort out mixed grains found in Apuleius's *Metamorphoses* (second century BCE) reappears in the Grimms' "Aschenputtel" (*Kinder- und Hausmärchen*, 1812–57).[3] Duan Chengshi's *Ye Xian* (published in a ninth-century compilation of miscellanies) is closer to the story as we know it, as it features a motherless heroine oppressed by her stepmother, a magical fish, a beautiful dress made of kingfisher feathers, a festival, a lost shoe, and a royal wedding; the moderately happy ending, however, is followed by a sobering coda, with the accumulated wealth plundered by thieves and the magical bones of the fish washed away by the sea. As far as European versions are concerned, Jacob and Wilhelm Grimm's *Kinder- und Hausmärchen* collection of 1812 (and its subsequent editions) played a crucial role in documenting the history of the tale. In the *Anmerkungen*, the Grimms note in the entry for "Aschenputtel" that their version is based on three versions ("Erzählungen") from Hesse, and they go on to refer to related stories known under different names in various parts of Germany and Europe (Grimm and Grimm 1984, 1986). They also refer to the early sixteenth-century sermon by the famous Swiss predicator Johann Geiler von Kaysersberg (Strasbourg, ca. 1510), "Das irrig Schaf," a rare edition of which was on sale at Christie's (London) on June 15, 2015.[4] The Grimms also mention Giambattista Basile's *La gatta Cenerentola*, Charles Perrault's *Cendrillon ou la petite pantoufle de verre*, and Marie Catherine d'Aulnoy's *Finette Cendron* among others.

By the end of the nineteenth century, Marian Roalfe Cox's pioneering compendium listed 345 versions of the tale from all over the world (Cox 1893). In the same year, in response to Marian Cox and the debates around the historic-geographic method in the journal *Folklore* (1890–1912), edited by Joseph Jacobs, Andrew Lang outlined his approach in the article "Cinderella and the Diffusion of Tales" (Lang 1893). In an effort to organize the abundant material collected by the folklorists, Antti Aarne subsequently defined Cinderella as ATU 510 (*The Persecuted Heroine*) in his famous classification system of tale types. According to the revised

Aarne-Thompson-Uther's catalog, the tale exists in three main forms, the main type featuring a persecuted stepdaughter rescued from her condition by a magical animal helper (Cinderella ATU510a), a girl fleeing an incestuous father who wants to marry her (Donkey-Skin ATU510b), a kind and beautiful girl persecuted by her mother is rewarded while her ugly and nasty sisters are punished after a moral test (One-Eye, Two-Eyes, Three-Eyes ATU511), and male Cinderella stories sometimes distinguished from the main type (ATU411b). Later, Marian Cox's work was taken up and extended by Anna Birgitta Rooth in *The Cinderella Cycle* (1951), which includes versions from Eastern Europe, Indochina, and the Near East.[5] Rooth argues that the Near Eastern and Indo-Malayan versions spread to Europe and developed into the story as we know it. Neil Philip also subscribes to this theory in *The Cinderella Story: The Origins and Variations of the Story Known as Cinderella* (1989), where he dismisses August Nitschke's theory that "Cinderella originated toward the end of the Ice Age" and argues instead that "the Cinderella cycle is essentially Eur-Asian" (Philip 1989, 7).

According to the *Enzyklopädie des Märchens*, *The Greenwood Encyclopedia*, and other scholarly sources, the first literary version of the full tale is found in Giambattista Basile's "La gatta Cenerentola," collected in *Lo cunto de li cunti* (also known as *Pentamerone*, 1634–36), which Nancy Canepa presents as the first "integral collection of authored, literary fairy tales in Western Europe" (Canepa 2007, 1).[6] Basile's collection preceded (and probably influenced) the emergence of the *conte de fée* as a salon pastime in late seventeenth-century Paris, and the collection was also familiar to the Grimms (via Clemens Brentano). Marie-Jeanne L'Héritier de Villandon's "L'Adroite Princesse ou les Aventures de Finette" in *Oeuvres meslées* (1696) and Marie-Catherine d'Aulnoy's "Finette Cendron" in *Contes nouveau, ou Les Fées à la mode* (1698), both markedly longer, more elaborate and openly ironic than Charles Perrault's own "Cendrillon ou la petite pantoufle de verre" in *Histoires ou contes du temps passé, avec des moralités* (1697), all provide playful and humorous variations on the story. Eventually it was Perrault's mock-naive and compact version that would gain the most popularity and recognition with the rise of children's literature in Europe in the eighteenth century. Perrault's literary tale was later complemented by the Grimms' much darker folktale of "Aschenputtel" in *Kinder- und Hausmärchen* (1812–57).[7] Read privately or aloud in illustrated editions or chapbooks, seen on stage, and constantly adapted to new genres, forms, and media for diverse audiences in Europe and abroad, Cinderella soon became an "all-time favorite" story for children and adults alike.

Travel, emigration, colonization, and communication in oral, print, and new media forms ensured the worldwide transmission and dissemination of the tale. The popularity of Cinderella has crucially depended on the work of translators and adaptors who were often anonymous or whose role and impact was long neglected, as in the case of the first translator of Perrault's tale into English (Lathey 2010, and in this volume). Those invisible storytellers and their named successors, together with the editors and publishers of fairy-tale collections, reframed, repurposed, and altered the form, style, and meaning of the tale, with significant social and ideological implications. Even in versions that are labeled as direct or "faithful" translations, the translation process inevitably and necessarily involves a degree of transformation and domestication, revision and reinterpretation—all the more so since the fairy tale was considered as an authorless genre assimilated to children's literature and therefore invited free adaptation and retelling. Once child readers became the target audience for collections of fairy tales, or of illustrated editions of individual tales such as Cinderella, translators adapted the texts to prevailing expectations of child behavior and experience, perceived needs and competences, often with a didactic, moral, and religious intent. Sometimes encouraged by editors, publishers, or patrons, translators practiced subtle or more overt adaptations of language and content, whether by omitting the heel and toe mutilation episode in the Grimms' "Aschenputtel" in editions for children, or reclaiming the tale as part of their national and cultural heritage.

In addition to retellings and adaptations based on existing translations, relay translation has played a part in the history of the interlingual journeys of the Cinderella tale. Relay translation is an expedient means of conveying a text into a third language when a translation of the source text into a second, intermediary language is widely available, or when the language of the source text is not particularly well known in the target culture. Economic considerations also come into play in the planning of new editions of fairy tales, so that a publisher will sometimes make use of an existing translation rather than commission a new one. For example, the Grimms' tales first reached the vernacular languages of India via English sources (Roy 2014). A second phenomenon is the blending of tales from the French and German traditions. Given the overlap of material, it is not surprising that the Grimms' and Perrault's versions of a specific tale have tended to merge, particularly of Cinderella and Sleeping Beauty (Seago 2006; Dutheil de la Rochère 2013; Joosen and Lathey 2014).

The Romantic conception of the fairy tale as an "authentic" expression of folk art and national culture, together with the considerable license that early translators took with the original material, have influenced the process of assimilation and appropriation of the tale since the nineteenth century. This has also led to the creation of strongly "nationalized" and patriotic versions of the Cinderella story that illustrate the political exploitation of folktales with a more-or-less explicit ideological agenda, and more recently as part of a postcolonial cultural reclamation strategy.[8] Such was the case of the American reception of the tale (Yolen 1982 [1977]) or of the Polish identification of Cinderella with national ideals of valor and virtue (Woźniak 2013). In Japan, where Cinderella translations began to appear in the 1880s, culture-specific changes were a common practice, and the illustrations, such as those made by the famous painter Yamamoto Shōun (1896), transformed "Shinderera" into a markedly Japanese beauty (Lucci 2012). In view of these varied practices and transformations, the collective and individual contributions of translators, and indeed illustrators, to the impact and narrative development of the Cinderella tale in target cultures should not be underestimated.

Picture Books and Illustrations

Illustrated editions have played a pivotal role in the international success of the Cinderella story from the hand-colored frontispiece and vignettes of the dedication manuscript of Perrault's *Contes de ma Mère l'Oye* (1695) to mass-produced children's books. Jack Zipes even speaks of a veritable "epidemic of 'Cinderella' picture books" in the twentieth century (Zipes 2006, 116), and Heidi Ann Heiner's invaluable Surlalune website lists dozens of picture books for young readers published in recent years (see also Joosen 2008). Cinderella textbooks are currently used in schools' multicultural curricula in the United States (Hollenbeck 2003; Alexander and Morton 2007). Some bear titles indicating the national, cultural, or religious orientation and refocusing of the retellings, as in *The Golden Sandal: A Middle Eastern Cinderella Story* (1998), based on an Iraqi folktale, or rename the heroine, such as *Adelita: A Mexican Cinderella* (2004), which incorporates Spanish words and phrases and features a Mexican heroine. While modern picture books tend to capitalize on the magical scenes found in the Perrault version rather than on the protestant piety and sentimentalism of the Grimms' version, some retellings make the story conform to their own religious norms and worldviews, as in *The Way Meat Loves Salt: A Cinderella Tale from the Jewish Tradition* (1998), where the fairy godmother is the prophet Elijah, or the ancient Vietnamese story of *Tấm and Cám* (2010), where the helper is Buddha, while in *Little Gold Star:*

A Spanish American Cinderella Tale (2000), she is the Virgin Mary. In the Afro-American *The Gospel Cinderella* (2004) the action takes place in and around the church, and instead of a glass slipper, the prince, who is piano player for a choir, identifies Cinderella from an enchanted melody and a lovely voice that praises the Lord. Fawzia Gilani's *Cinderella: An Islamic Tale* (2011) upholds the model of an Islamic Cinderella who prays, reads the Koran, and is modest and humble. These illustrated adaptations reflect the continuing didactic role and ideological subtext of children's literature across the world.

Illustrations of Cinderella are, then, far more than subsidiary and "decorative" images. They orient the reception and message of the tale and constitute a visual interpretation of its significance, from the scenes chosen for illustration in early woodcuts (see Verheij in this volume) to the present day.

Stage, Opera, Ballet, and Film Versions

The Cinderella story has long been adapted for the stage as children's theater and pantomime, as well as in opera and ballet. While each production speaks to the time, place, and audience in which it is set, the scenes of magical transformation pose scenographic challenges and stimulate metatheatrical reflection on the role and nature of illusion. The tale was remolded in fashionable genres such as comic theater, melodrama, vaudeville, and burlesque, starting with the risqué humor of Louis Anseaume's *Cendrillon* (1759), which opens the morning after the ball when Cinderella hesitates to tell her godmother what she has lost during the night, and ends with the prince trying on the slipper. After the revolution, Charles-Guillaume Étienne's libretto for the Maltese composer Nicolas Isouard (known as Nicolò), where the prince follows the advice of his preceptor, is more sentimental and moralizing. Many tears are shed in this *opéra-féerie* in three acts created on May 24, 1810, at l'Opéra Comique, and it met with such success that it soon inspired several parodies. Initially very popular throughout Europe, it is almost forgotten today, even though it inspired Gioacchino Rossini's *La Cenerentola, ossia La bontà in trionfo* (an operatic *dramma giocoso* with a libretto by Jacopo Ferretti) first performed in Rome on January 25, 1817. Cinderella's mother, a poor widow, remarries with don Magnifico, who plays the wicked stepfather. He scorns Angelina/Cinderella, but the heroine is helped by a beggar philosopher and courted by a prince in disguise. The shoe becomes a bracelet to prevent the female singer from showing too much leg. Rossini's opera quickly won international acclaim and was for many years even more beloved than *Il barbiere di Siviglia*, still remaining one of the most successful of Rossini's works. In Italy, this operatic version was far better known than Perrault's and the Grimms' versions of Cinderella, which only became popular in the second half of the nineteenth century. Another spectacular and very successful production was Clairville, Monnier, and Blum's three-hour-long *Cendrillon* created at the Châtelet (Paris) in 1866, featuring twenty-six actors-singers and a hundred dancers. Also based on Perrault, Jules Massenet's *Cendrillon* (libretto by Henri Cain), celebrating the fairy electricity, was first performed at the Opéra Comique in Paris in 1899. Famed mezzo-soprano Pauline Viardot (1821–1910) wrote music and composed a chamber operetta based on *Cendrillon* (1904). More recent adaptations include Chilean composer Jorge Peña Hen's (1928–1973) *La Cenicienta*, a famed children's opera that toured Chile and Colombia before the military arrest and murder of the artist, and was later shown at the Fenice (Venice). Peter Maxwell Davies (British, b. 1934) also revisited traditional material for his pantomime opera for children (1979) (see Osborne 2004).

Prior to Prokofiev's world-famous ballet version *Cinderella/Zolushka* (composed between 1940 and 1945), the French dancer and choreographer Marius Petipa, in collaboration with Enrico Cecchetti and Lev Ivanov, created the famous ballet version of Cinderella in three acts for the Theatre Mariinsky in Saint Petersburg in 1893. Various versions followed throughout the twentieth century, the most influential being Prokofiev's ballet, first performed at the Bolshoi and subsequently shown in most European capitals, and inspiring many choreographers from Rudolf Nureyev to Frederick Ashton and David Bintley. It is not surprising that the Cinderella tale is also the basis of musicals, among them the popular version written for television by the composer Richard Rodgers and the writer Oscar Hammerstein, first aired in 1957 live on CBS with Julie Andrews in the title role and viewed by millions of people. Two new TV versions followed: first in 1965 as another CBS production with a changed script by Joseph Schrank, and later in 1997 by Walt Disney Television, featuring a multiethnic cast. Both shows were a hit among audiences and were broadcast several times. Hammerstein and Rodgers's musical also had several stage adaptations, among them a very successful, Tony nominated, Broadway remake with a new text by Douglas Carter Beane, running from 2013 to 2015.

Cinderella has of course been a traditional feature of Christmas shows throughout England since at least the nineteenth century, from upmarket ballet and opera spectacles to slapstick pantomime. Camped-up music-hall shows are still popular today, both as traditional family entertainment and more experimental or extravagant spectacles, for example Davies's comic-opera version for children with costumes by French fashion designer Christian Lacroix, or the daring musical *Into the Woods* created by Stephen Sondheim and James Lapine in 1987, transposed to the screen by Disney in *Into the Woods* (2014). Cinderella even occasionally appears as a pop music muse or rock 'n' roll antiheroine: an American rock band is named after her, and several songs evoke the story of the miserable girl turned into a princess, or turn the convention of the happy ending on its head, as in Louis Bertignac's junkie "Cendrillon" (1982).

The Cinderella story dominates films based on classic fairy tales plots, and Jack Zipes mentions over 140 Cinderella movies in his 2010 filmography of fairy tales.[9] Film adaptations, from Lotte Reiniger's silhouette *Aschenputtel* (1922) to Disney's takes on the story, have played a central part of the tale's global success in the contemporary world and have firmly embedded its emblematic visual representations in the popular imagination. Disney's animated feature from 1950 became a frequent iconographic point of reference in further visual depictions of Cinderella, for example in *Shrek* movies or in the recent *Once Upon a Time* TV series (2011–). However, some countries reacted to these US imports by producing their own, culturally inflected versions of Cinderella movies, which came to play an important part in national contexts. Such was the case of German-Czechoslovak coproduction *Tři oříšky pro Popelku* (1973) based on Božena Němcová's nineteenth-century adaptation, which turned into a holiday classic in several Eastern European countries, while in the Soviet Union the most beloved Cinderella became Shapiro's 1947 musical film *Zolushka*. Because "the morality of the Cinderella films . . . is designed to demonstrate in its narrative how a child, who has the odds stacked against her, must develop strategies for dealing with the brutal treatment by stepmothers and stepsisters, who test her" (Zipes 2010, 174), it has served as anything from coded narrative of resistance against oppression to nostalgic and sentimental mythmaking. Much of Cinderella's appeal can be ascribed to the flexible form and optimistic message of the tale, which has been transformed into a realistic story taking place in postwar Rome (Italian 2011 TV miniseries *Cenerentola*), today's Moscow (Russian comedy *Zolushka*, 2012), or Chinatown (social drama *Year of the Fish*, 2008), or indeed a typical modern-day American girl success story, as in *Working Girl* (1988) or *Pretty Woman* (1990) (see Williams 2010; also Zipes in the volume).

Disney and the Role of Cinderella in Popular Culture

A recent McDonald's "Come as You Are" advertising campaign (2014) features a teenage Cinderella sitting astride a pumpkin, her mauve dress in rags, as she stops at a drive-in for a burger. Cinderella tropes such as the glass slipper, the ball, the escape down the stairs of the palace, the clock striking midnight, the wonder-filled scenes of magical metamorphosis (including the comic potential of the splendid coach turned back into a pumpkin exploited by the McDonald's ad) have now acquired an autonomous iconic status used effectively in advertising, photography and fashion. Because of the crucial role dress and shoes play in the radical transformation of the heroine's identity, social image, and life trajectory, Cinderella has become a veritable emblem of late capitalist commodity fetishism, be it Christian Louboutin's glamorous-kitsch, crystal glittery, butterfly-embroidered heels designed for the release of Disney's *Cinderella* in a Blu-Ray Diamond Edition (2012),[10] or the buzz created by Lupita Nyong'o, Oscar winner for her best supporting actress role in Steve McQueen's *12 Years a Slave* (2014), when she came to collect her prize in a blue iridescent Prada gown and matching headband *à la Cinderella*, and was promptly dubbed "Lupitarella" by the media. It is amusing to see the obsession with fashion mocked in Perrault's late seventeenth-century *conte* being thus revived in today's celeb culture and mass media, though often without the humorous touch characteristic of the urbane and witty literary tale.[11]

Cinema has both popularized the tale in the United States and exported its commodified image abroad.[12] Cinderella mostly lives on today in the global world of the Disney franchise with *Cinderella* I, II, and III, Kenneth Branagh's latest live-action remake released in 2015, through mass family pilgrimages to Disneyland Orlando, Paris, Tokyo, Hong Kong, and Shanghai (to open in 2016 and advertised as "authentically Disney and distinctly Chinese") complete with neo-Bavarian Sleeping Beauty and Cinderella castles, as well as in countless products from dolls and toys to DVDs, video games, e-books, apps, dresses, magic wands, tiaras, trinkets, and cosmetic cases. In 2000, Disney created the "Disney Princess" franchise, which brought together all the Disney fairy-tale princesses in a line of merchandise that earns Disney over $4 billion a year (see Orenstein 2011).

The ubiquitous nature of Disney's commercialized version of Cinderella has had such a profound impact on popular culture worldwide that it has elevated the fairy-tale film to the status of a new pre-text (Stephens and McCallum 1998, 5) with which many new retellings and reinterpretations further engage. This is especially true of the American reception of the tale. As Jane Yolen observed, the Disney Cinderella set the new pattern for the tale and transformed the heroine into "a coy, helpless dreamer, a 'nice' girl who awaits her rescue with patience and a song" (1982 [1977], 297). This ideologically loaded representation of female aspirations has been an inexhaustible source of inspiration for airport novels and global best sellers, from Mary Higgins Clark and Alafair Burke's thriller *The Cinderella Murder* (2014) to sentimental formulaic romance such as Jessica Gilmore's *His Reluctant Cinderella* (2014) in Harlequin's Mills and Boon series. Even the best-selling soft porn/SM *Fifty Shades of Grey* (2011), as Alessandra Stanley argues in "Glass Slipper Fetish" (Stanley 2012), follows a Cinderella plot: "As female fantasies go," she notes, "it's a twofer: lasting love and a winning Mega Millions lottery ticket. And what is shameful about 'Fifty Shades of Grey' isn't the submissive sex, it's the Cinderella story."[13]

Subversive Cinderellas

The commercial exploitation of the wish-fulfillment fantasy at the core of the Cinderella tale has nevertheless generated ironic and thought-provoking responses that seek to break the spell of the Cinderella myth as embodying the lure of advanced capitalist logic, ruthless competition, media culture, and socially conformist aspirations, as in Banksy's recently opened Dismaland park in Weston-super-Mare featuring a crashed pumpkin-coach that alludes to Princess Diana's accidental death with her lover in Paris when she was hunted down by paparazzi. Since the 1970s, second-wave feminists have debated the representation of gender roles, behaviors, and social expectations encoded in fairy tales, raised the issue of female agency and desire, and questioned the heteronormative model of romance, marriage, and family exemplified by Sleeping Beauty, Snow White, or Cinderella.[14] Cinderella lends itself particularly well to gender-reversed narratives: transforming the female heroine into a male hero is not an unknown twist in the history of the tale and in some rewritings of other tales (Joosen 2011, 96). The Cinderella story has elicited extremely diverse critical and creative responses in visual art and literature, from a feminist, queer, socially, racially, or culturally marginalized perspective that interrogates the assumptions and values at work in the fairy-tale type, recovers silenced voices or obscured traditions, or explores the effects of hybridization.[15]

Subversive, transgressive, and parodic takes on Cinderella are often part of thematic visual cycles. Following her disturbing *Fairy-Tale* series, Cindy Sherman's 1993 *Untitled #276* is a punning, jubilant, and grotesque self-portrait as a defiant, slattern Cinderella. More recently, Dina Goldstein has revisited the Disney princesses in darkly comic scenes of ordinary life in *Fallen Princesses* (2009), including a middle-aged blond barfly in a

Disney-blue ball dress.[16] The Japanese artist Yayoi Kusama, who places fantasy at the heart of her work, evokes the Cinderella tale in several gigantic outdoor sculptures of yellow or red "magical" pumpkins in her signature polka-dotted pop style. In a more somber tone, the Egyptian artist Shayma Kamel's *Cinderella Tales* exhibition (2014) explores the condition of women and stresses contradictions between the realities of a Muslim country and children's fairy-tale fantasies. Similarly, the Kenyan-born, New-York-based painter and sculptor Wangechi Mutu revisits the story in a compelling fashion in *The Cinderella Curse* (2007) exhibition to comment on the genocide in Rwanda. Less openly political but drawing attention to intermedial creative practices, the British painter Ian Andrews combines a folktale with an image from the history of art as a starting point "from which to playfully but reverently deviate" in his paintings, including one based on Angela Carter's memorable retelling of "Ashputtle *or* The Mother's Ghost."[17]

Cinderella thus remains an inspirational figure for writers and artists who deliberately challenge and displace the dominant stereotype by revisiting or de-centering the fairy-tale canon, from Anne Sexton's ironic retelling of the Grimms' Ashputtle in *Transformations* (1971) to Carter's variations on the folk tradition in *American Ghosts and Old World Wonders* (1992), or Emma Donoghue's "The Tale of the Shoe" in *Kissing the Witch: Old Tales in New Skins* (1997), which retells the tale from a queer perspective and pays homage to a marginalized female tradition (see Warner 1995, 2014; Bacchilega 1999, 2013; Dutheil de la Rochère 2009, 2012, 2013; Joosen 2011). Intersections between postcolonial and queer strategies are further exemplified in *Sinalela*, Samoan Dan Taulapapa McMullin's film (2001).[18] Interart experimentations feature Cinderella in "mash-up" graphic novels that bring together several fairy-tale characters, as in the famed *Fables* series created by Bill Willingham, which imagines their modern-day adventures in the underworld community of Fabletown below New York City.[19] The rediscovery of the Grimms' tales in Japan leading to a veritable "Grimm Boom" (Murai 2014) has also resulted in cultural, generic, and aesthetic fusions such as Junko Mizuno's "kawai-guro" manga fairy tales mixing horror and cuteness; the blending of sugary and macabre elements in her *Cinderalla* (2000) can even be said to reflect the duality of the Cinderella tradition.

Critical Approaches to the Tale in the Twentieth Century and Beyond

In his classic *Cinderella: A Casebook* (1982), Alan Dundes reproduces the canonical texts by Perrault and Grimm alongside Russian, English, Chinese,

Greek, and French folktales, as well as significant scholarly contributions reflecting late twentieth-century methodologies and perspectives on the tale, including social-historical, psychoanalytical, and cultural approaches. Nicole Belmont and Elisabeth Lemirre's anthology *Sous la Cendre: Figures de Cendrillon* (2007) also includes two essays by the editors that raise the issue of the gendered dimension of the Cinderella tale and the sexual implications of the shoe. This reflects two important interpretative frameworks through which the story has been understood in the twentieth century, namely, psychoanalysis and feminism. Psychoanalytical theory has had a huge influence on modern understandings of the tale, starting with Freud's essay "Das Motiv der Kästchenwahl" ("The Theme of the Three Caskets," 1913). Freud examines the motif of the third daughter found in various forms in Shakespeare's *King Lear* and *The Merchant of Venice*, but also in the stories of Cupid and Psyche/Beauty and the Beast and Cinderella. Linking the figure to the three fates, he suggests that the youngest, quiet, and rejected daughter represents the inevitability of death (Atropos) that is nevertheless transformed into love so that the tale enacts "a complicated form of denial and consolation: a 'wishful reversal'" as its latent content and hidden significance (Teverson 2013, 115). Even more influential is Bruno Bettelheim's psychoanalytical interpretation of the Cinderella story in *The Uses of Enchantment* (1976) as a tale about sibling rivalry and Oedipal jealousy that allows children to move beyond the narcissistic phase of early childhood. The cultural historian Robert Darnton, in his essay "Peasants Tell Tales: the Meanings of Mother Goose" (1984), has challenged this symbolic reading by drawing attention to the significance of the tale as a sociohistorical document hinting at actual rivalries between siblings in the harsh and brutal conditions of the peasantry during the Enlightenment in Europe (Teverson 2013, 125). Sociohistorical criticism has developed under the aegis of Jack Zipes and feminist cultural historians have also explored the idea that folk and fairy tales provide access to the life experiences of disenfranchised social groups, like Marina Warner in *From the Beast to the Blonde: On Fairy Tales and Their Tellers* (1984), who is careful to analyze the versions of the tale in their original literary and cultural context of production, or postcolonial critics such as Edward Kamau Brathwaite and Patrick Chamoiseau (Teverson 2013, 126). Moreover, creative retellings are often closely intertwined with fairy-tale criticism (Joosen 2011); Anne Sexton's *Transformations*, for example, inspired Gilbert and Gubar's feminist analysis of Snow White in *The Madwoman in the Attic*, whereas Carter's rewritings in *The Bloody Chamber* fed into Zipes's and Warner's epochal studies.

From Cinderella as a Text of Culture to Cinderella across Cultures

The present collection seeks to avoid two pitfalls: ideologically and politically problematic national, cultural, and linguistic reifications of the fairy tale that seek to promote a narrow, static and essentializing identity politics on the one hand, and equally questionable universalizations of the Cinderella story erasing all differences on the other. As Sherry Simon usefully reminds us to ask ourselves: "But what do we mean by 'culture'?"

> While "culture" is recognized as one of the most difficult and overdetermined concepts in the contemporary human and social sciences, it often appears . . . as if it had an obvious and unproblematic meaning. Translators are told that in order to do their work correctly they must understand the culture of the original text, because texts are "embedded" in a culture. . . . The difficulty with such statements is that they seem to presume a unified cultural field which the term inhabits . . . (Simon 1996, 137)

This is why we prefer to adopt the new paradigm of translation that posits differences as a means to establish relationships between tales and yet capture the uniqueness of each version of Cinderella, and to engage with its specific historical, geographical, linguistic, and cultural locations and manifestations. Because texts and images, in Pauline Greenhill's words, "often engage not only with individual tales and motifs, but also with the popular conception of the genre and thus contribute to an ongoing cultural renegotiation, repetition and reconfiguration of fairy tales" (Greenhill 2014), we insist on the dynamic, transformative dimension of the tale as it is retold across genres, media, and cultures. We thus prefer to refer to *versions* or *variations* of the tale rather than the more common term *variant* found in folkloristics. The idea of an Ur-text underpinning the tale type and the sacralization of "origin" that it entails, equated with "authenticity" (a concept that in its modern sense dates back to the mid-nineteenth century), probably derives from the logo-centric mindset that informed the emergence and development of the discipline. As Francisco Vaz da Silva argued in a plenary talk presented at the 2013 ISFNR Vilnius conference (a point he develops in a forthcoming book titled *The Clockwork of Fairy Tales*), it may also reflect the philological background and methodology of early folklore scholars. The present book seeks to "de-theologize" the field and explore the possibility of an alternative paradigm alert to the palimpsestic, transformative, performative, and creative dimension of each retelling in an effort to eschew the binary, hierarchical model that prioritizes type versus variant, oral versus literary tradition, textual versus cultural manifestations—or vice versa. The Cinderella tale is therefore not considered as based on a preexisting essence or model of an unproblematic expression of "culture," but rather focuses on the transfers, appropriations, manipulations, and recreations that give it an ever-changing existence, significance, and relevance in its manifold "de-territorializations"—neither adopting a universalism that obscures the differences between languages, contexts, and media, nor endorsing the nationalist ontology that essentializes language and culture. Thus the contributions acknowledge the difference *between* but also *within* languages, literatures, and cultures, and therefore analyze individual versions as unique textual-visual-mediatic (re)productions that nevertheless reveal an inherent—even a constitutive—hybridity. Some chapters also stress the connection between different discursive or intellectual enterprises, such as the relationships between translation, scholarship, and rewriting, or between different genres and media. Thus Ralph Manheim's "anthropologizing" and archaizing retranslation of the *Kinder- und Hausmärchen* collection inspired Carter's rewriting of Ashputtle, which also responds to the work of late twentieth-century cultural historians and feminist critics (see Dutheil de la Rochère 2013).

The theoretical background to this renegotiation unites a wide-ranging set of essays. A number of different concepts of culture and cultural history are deployed in the volume, including the cultural turn that rethinks "culture" in a dynamic fashion in terms of translation, adaptation, and appropriation. The notion of *cultural translation* theorized in Homi Bhabha's *The Location of Culture* (1994) is especially pertinent inasmuch as it suggests that Cinderella becomes a cultural script when it *crosses* the boundaries of languages, cultures, and countries. In Bhabha's terms there could be no fixed or universal Cinderella figure, since the tale is inherently transcultural as it is constantly on the move, and hence endlessly transposed, reconceived, and repurposed, as the chapters in this volume testify.

The aim of the editors of and contributors to the present collection of essays is therefore to examine how Cinderella has been mobilized in specific contexts and periods and also across national frontiers and boundaries. The discussion of the many Cinderellas that have populated cultures past and present at the Rome conference offered a welcomed insight into the cultural moment in which they emerged, and as such encouraged explorations of lesser known aspects and issues raised by the tale, some of which have been further analyzed in the present volume. The articles selected for the volume thus reflect the importance of situating and interpreting the tale in context.

They also respond to Donald Haase's call in "Decolonizing Fairy-Tale Studies" (2010) for a renewal of fairy-tale studies through close reading, combined literary and cultural scholarship, transculturality, and interdisciplinarity. Accordingly, the volume deals with the presence of Cinderella in and across various cultures and media as a multilayered script, paying particular attention to its textual, editorial, and discursive dimension as well as its visual and intermedial *reformulations* (to use Angela Carter's word).

While primarily centering on the European fairy-tale tradition, mainly Italy, France, Germany, Britain, the Netherlands, Poland, and Russia, the essays also deal with Cinderella in China, Australia, and the United States. Nevertheless, the volume has no ambition to encompass the multiple incarnations of Cinderella past and present, let alone its boundless cultural variations. The aim of the book, however, is to exemplify how each version reflects a singular project that speaks to a particular moment, context, and audience, and reflects a material history, socioeconomic and political constraints, as well as new technological possibilities.

We have included essays that offer a national history and perspective on the tale, for example, in the focus on Poland in the third section of the volume, but also others that present a panorama of Cinderellas across linguistic and cultural borders (Bottigheimer, Beckett, and Zipes, chapters herein). The emphasis throughout the volume, therefore, is twofold: firstly on national developments that illustrate ideological shifts and appropriations, and secondly, in response to Cristina Bacchilega's plea in *Fairy Tales Transformed?* (2013), more culturally diverse and hybrid versions of the tale that testify to cultural and artistic exchanges. Likewise, we show that fairy tales always circulate in plural versions: this is not only in order to shift attention away from the old fairy-tale canon to focus on alternative versions, voices, values, and knowledge but also to read the classic texts against the grain of the Cinderella stereotype that has often obscured their complexities and emancipatory potential or at least their ability to inspire new creations.

The articles have been divided into three sections that cover different areas of research. Before beginning a more wide-ranging examination of the cultural and international history of the Cinderella tale, it is important to return to what might be called the classical tradition in order to establish a context for the pre-texts of many subsequent versions and adaptations. The first section, "Contextualizing Cinderella," therefore investigates the historical and cultural contexts of canonical literary versions of the tale, in particular the version by Charles Perrault that has dominated the tale's history, and their diachronic transformations in translation. It includes the framing contribution by Ruth Bottigheimer, addressing long-term cultural changes that take place in the media, and several contributions that shed light on the material context in which Perrault's version was embedded. Kathryn Hoffmann's paper examines seventeenth-century glassworks and their impact on the distribution and specific material aspects of the Cinderella tale, while Talitha Verheij analyzes the development of print techniques for the mass market in Dutch in the late nineteenth century. Contributions by Gillian Lathey, Cyrille François, and Daniel Aranda address the linguistic, textual, editorial, and translation strategies that shaped the reproduction and reception of the tale. Lathey introduces the maverick Robert Samber's first translation into English of Perrault's tales; François draws attention to significant cultural differences between the French and the German traditions, and Aranda illustrates moral adjustments to Perrault's tale in the late nineteenth century. The second section, "Regendering Cinderella," tackles innovative and progressive literary rewritings of the tale in the twentieth and twenty-first centuries, in particular feminist and/or queer takes on the classic plot whose resonances can also be felt in children's and juvenile literature. Drawing on gender and queer studies, translation studies, and word and image studies, Martine Hennard Dutheil's, Jennifer Orme's, Rona May-Ron's, Ashley Riggs's, Mark Macleod's, and Roxane Hughes's contributions testify to the role played by the tale in articulating contemporary concerns ranging from female emancipation to coming out, along with the development of innovative poetics.

Finally, the third section, "Visualizing Cinderella," concerns visual transformations of the tale, especially the interaction between text and image in children's books and the consolidation, questioning and renewal of the tale's iconographic tradition in several cultural and national contexts. Monika Woźniak's paper on the Polish iconographic tradition of the tale is followed by Agata Hołobut's contribution on Polish posters that works here as a case study, showing how a particular set of textual and extratextual factors can result in distinct and sometimes surprising strategies and transformations. Another intriguing case study is Van Coillie's diachronic overview of Cinderella depictions in Holland and Belgium across 150 years. Mitrokhina's chapter analyzes the appropriation of the Cinderella story by the Stakhanovite movement in the Soviet Union in the 1930s and 1940s, while Jack Zipes's essay, based on a chapter from *The Enchanted Screen* (2010), gives an updated general historical overview of Cinderella in film. Finally, Sandra Beckett's chapter, organized around the phenomenon of crossover audiences, offers a panorama of recent trends in picture books.

Cinderella thus appears as a multilayered and ever-changing story endlessly adapted and reinvented in different media and traditions—very much like the elusive and multifaceted heroine herself. As such, the present volume may be of interest not only for fairy-tale and children's literature scholars but will, the editors hope, also attract the interest of scholars interested in the visual arts, cultural history, translation studies, or popular culture, as well as a wider audience interested in rediscovering the favorite tale anew.

Notes

1. Armando Maggi confirms that "the vast majority of 20th century retellings of Cinderella are based on this visual-verbal narrative type, which still holds a firm grip on the contemporary imagination. Given the increasing globalization of our culture, it is fair to say that the Perrault-Grimm-Disney type has imposed itself as the 'correct' version of the Cinderella tale" (2015, 150).
2. Cristina Bacchilega has theorized the idea of the fairy-tale web in *Fairy Tales Transformed? Twenty-First-Century Adaptations and the Politics of Wonder* (2013).
3. These early sources are mentioned in the "Cinderella" entry of the *Enzyklopädie des Märchens* (3: 39–57). Rainer Wehse begins by noting that "Die Erzähltypen des C-Zyklus sind weltweit verbreitet und der vielleich beliebteste Märchenkreis überhaupt" (3: 39). In *Fairytale in the Ancient World*, Graham Anderson proposes that "the Cinderella story existed in a more or less recognisable form in antiquity" (2000, 42). He suggests that elements from stories across various genres and cultural contexts fed into the Cinderella tradition, first and foremost Rhodopis (in Herodotus and Strabo), but also the legend of Aspasia of Phocea and the Jewish-biblical story of Asenath, and perhaps even the story of the Sumerian goddess Inanna.
4. http://daten.digitale-sammlungen.de/bsb00004509/image_291. This is the first appearance of the sermon, printed in the 1510 *Das Irrig Schaf.* http://daten.digitale-sammlungen.de/bsb00009582/image_374. This is the second appearance of the sermon, printed in the 1517 *Broesamlin doct. Keiserspergs.* We are grateful to Julie Koehler for signaling these electronic versions to the editors of the volume. For an overview of medieval and early modern versions of the tale in European literature (mostly saints' legends, romances, and lays), including Jean Bonaventure des Périers's *Nouvelles Recréations et Joyeux Devis* (1558), see Cox.

5. For a good overview of the emergence of fairy-tale theory from folkloristics to psychoanalysis, feminism, cultural, and sociohistorical approaches, see Teverson (2013).
6. See Bottigheimer in this volume, as well as Nancy Canepa (1999, 2007) and Jack Zipes (2001) in particular.
7. A rediscovered collection of nineteenth-century folktales by Franz Xaver von Schönwerth features a Cinderella who is, in Maria Tatar's words, "a woodcutter's daughter who uses golden slippers to recover her beloved from beyond the moon and the sun," along with a number of "Cinderfella" stories: http://www.theguardian.com/books/2014/dec/26/fairytale-ending-forgotten-folklorist-schonwerth; http://www.newyorker.com/books/page-turner/cinderfellas-the-long-lost-fairy-tales. In *The Classic Fairy Tales*, Maria Tatar (1999) recognizes the variety of Cinderella figures and stories, observing that "Cinderella has been reinvented by so many different cultures that it is hardly surprising to find that she is sometimes cruel and vindictive, at other times compassionate and kind. Even within a single culture, she can appear genteel and self-effacing in one story, clever and enterprising in another, coy and manipulative in a third" (102). After Jane Yolen (1982 [1977]), however, she distinguishes between the resourceful folk heroines of the Catskin type and the more passive literary Cinderella figures.
8. On the exploitation of the Grimms' collection as a pedagogical tool to reinforce nationalism in Nazi Germany, see Zipes (1983, 2002). In the present volume, Mitrokhina documents the exploitation of Cinderella as a communist heroine, while examples of recent editions for children promoting a religion are listed above.
9. See "The International Fairy-Tale Filmography" hosted by the University of Winnipeg, co-created by Jack Zipes, Pauline Greenhill, and Kendra Magnus-Johnston, at http://iftf.uwinnipeg.ca.
10. Whether deliberately or not, the signature blood-red soles of Louboutin's stylish (but almost unwearable) stilettoes evoke the mutilation of the sisters' feet in the Grimms' much darker version of the tale.
11. See Martine Hennard Dutheil's chapter herein for a discussion of the social commentary hidden in Perrault's faux-naïf *conte* and Carter's reactualization of the tale's critical potential in the aftermath of the feminist movement.
12. See Jack Zipes's article in this volume for an overview of Cinderella on screen, from the early cinema (Méliès) to cartoons, but also comedies such as *Cinderfella* (1960) and *Pretty Woman* (1990), a "Cinderella for the

1990s" with a Hollywood prostitute finding love and achieving respectability (and a golden credit card).

13. Unsurprisingly, Cinderella also inspires fanfiction. https://www.fanfiction.net/s/8054719/1/Cinderally, http://archiveofourown.org/tags/Cinderella%20(Fairy%20Tales)/works), and e-fiction, as in *Cinderella Gets a Brazilian: An eShort Story* by Emma McLaughlin and Nicola Kra.
14. See Crowley and Pennington (2010) for an interesting discussion of two main strands of Cinderella retellings from a feminist perspective.
15. See Warner (1995, 2014), Bacchilega (1999, 2013), Wanning Harries (2003), Dutheil de la Rochère (2012, 2013), as well as several contributions in this volume.
16. See also Jeffrey Thomas's *Twisted Princesses* series (2009), J. Scott Campbell's eroticized *Fairy-Tale Fantasies* 2012 calendar, Thomas Czarnecki's macabre photographs in *From Enchantment to Down* (2012), and Jeff Hong's collages in *Unhappily Ever After* (2014). Female artists have produced particularly daring fairy-tale-inspired artwork, such as Marie Clayton's transgressive scenarios for Barbie dolls that reenact the mutilation of the stepsister's feet in the Grimms' "Ashputtle." http://500photographers.blogspot.ch/2011/04/photographer-275-mariel-clayton.html. The mutilation scene is also the main focus of Miwa Yanagi's take on Cinderella, in her series of enigmatic and haunting black-and-white photographs collected in *Fairy Tales* (2005).
17. http://www.richardkentonwebb.com/resources/Kenton-Webb_Andrews_PressRelease-2.pdf.
18. See Cristina Bacchilega's discussion in *Fairy Tales Transformed?* (2013).
19. See, in particular, Chris Roberson's (author) and Shawn McManus's (artist) spin-off *Cinderella: From Fabletown with Love* (2010), Chris Roberson's (and various illustrators) *Cinderella: Fables Are Forever* (2012), and Marc Andreyko (author) and Shawn McManus (artist)'s *Fairest: of Men and Mice* (2014).

References

Alexander, Linda, and Mary Lou Morton. 2007. "Multicultural Cinderella: A Collaborative Project in an Elementary School." *School Libraries Worldwide* 13 (2): 32–44.

Anderson, Graham. 2000. *Fairytale in the Ancient World*. London: Routledge.

Andreyko, Marc (writer) and Shawn McManus (artist). *Fairest: Of Mice and Men*. New York: Bill Willingham and DC Comics.

Bacchilega, Cristina. 1999. *Postmodern Fairy Tales: Gender and Narrative Strategies*. Philadelphia: University of Pennsylvania Press.

———. 2013. *Fairy Tales Transformed? Twenty-First-Century Adaptations and the Politics of Wonder*. Detroit: Wayne State University Press.

Bettelheim, Bruno. 1976. *The Uses of Enchantment: The Meaning and Importance of Fairy Tales*. New York: Random House.

Bhabha, Homi K. 1994. *The Location of Culture*. New York: Routledge.

Bottigheimer, Ruth. 2010. "*Fairy Godfather*, Fairy-Tale History, and Fairy-Tale Scholarship: A Response to Dan Ben-Amos, Jan M. Ziolkowski, and Francisco Vaz da Silva." *Journal of American Folklore* 123 (490): 447–96.

Canepa, Nancy. 1999. *From Court to Forest: Giambattista Basile's "Lo cunto de li cunti" and the Birth of the Literary Fairy Tale*. Detroit: Wayne State University Press.

———. 2007. Translation, introduction and notes to *Giambattista Basile, The Tale of Tales or Entertainment of Little Ones*. Detroit: Wayne State University Press.

Coughlin, Ellen K. 1991. "A Cinderella Story: Research on Children's Books Takes on New Life as a Field of Literary Study." *Chronicle of Higher Education*, February 13, 5–7.

Cox, Marian R. 1893. *Cinderella: Three Hundred and Forty-Five Variants of Cinderella, Catskin, and Cap O'rushes*. London.

Crowley, Karlyn, and John Pennington. 2010. "Feminist Frauds on the Fairies? Didacticism and Liberation in Recent Retellings of 'Cinderella.'" *Marvels & Tales* 24 (2): 297–313. http://people.stfx.ca/x2011/x2011bwz/Cinderella%20Remakes.pdf.

Dutheil de la Rochère, Martine Hennard. 2009. "Queering the Fairy Tale Canon: Emma Donoghue's *Kissing the Witch*." In *Fairy Tales Reimagined: Essays on New Retellings*. edited by Susan Redington Bobby, 13-30. Jefferson, NC: McFarland.

———. 2012. "Cenerentola alla moda (femminista)." In *Mille e una Cenerentola: Illustrazioni, adattamenti, oggetti consueti e desueti*, edited by Monika Woźniak, 37–40. Rome: Onyx.

———. 2013. *Reading, Translating, Rewriting: Angela Carter's Translational Poetics*. Detroit: Wayne State University Press.

Edwards Janis L. 1997. *Political Cartoons in the 1988 Presidential Campaign: Image, Metaphor, and Narrative*. Studies in American Popular History and Culture. New York: Routledge.

Greenhill, Pauline. 2014. "Fairy-Tale Cultures and Media Today." Conference, University of Winnipeg, welcome talk, August 7.

Grimm, Jacob, and Wilhelm Grimm. 1984. *Kinder- und Hausmärchen*, edited by Heinz Rölleke. 3 vols. Stuttgart (1857). See Band 3, "Aschenputtel," 34–39.

———. 1986. *Kinder- und Hausmärchen*, edited by Heinz Rölleke. 3 vols. Göttingen (1812).

Haase, Donald. 1999. "Yours, Mine, or Ours? Perrault, the Brothers Grimm, and the Ownership of Fairy Tales" (1993). Reprinted in *The Classic Fairy Tales: A Norton Critical Edition*, edited by Maria Tatar, 353–64. New York: Norton.

———. 2010. "Decolonizing Fairy-Tale Studies." *Marvels & Tales* 24 (1): 17–38.

Hollenbeck, Kathleen M. 2003. *Teaching with Cinderella Stories from around the World*. New York: Scholastic Teaching Resources.

Joosen, Vanessa. 2008. "Cinderella." In *The Greenwood Encyclopedia of Folktales and Fairy Tales*. Edited by Donald Haase. 3 vols. Westport, CT: Greenwood Press, 201-205.

———. 2011. *Critical and Creative Perspectives on Fairy Tales: An Intertextual Dialogue between Fairy-Tale Scholarship and Postmodern Retellings*. Detroit: Wayne State University Press.

Joosen, Vanessa, and Gillian Lathey, eds. 2014. *Grimms' Tales around the Globe: The Dynamics of Their International Reception*. Detroit: Wayne State University Press.

Lang, Andrew. 1893. "Cinderella and the Diffusion of Tales." *Folklore* 4 (4): 413–33.

Lathey, Gillian. 2010. *The Role of Translators in Children's Literature: Invisible Storytellers*. New York: Routledge.

Lucci, Matteo. 2012. "Cenerentola giapponese." Unpublished conference paper—in print.

Maggi, Armando. 2015. "The Creation of Cinderella from Basile to the Brothers Grimm." In *The Cambridge Companion to Fairy Tales*, edited by Maria Tatar, 150–65. Cambridge: Cambridge University Press.

Miller, Laura. 2008. "Japan's Cinderella Motif: Beauty Industry and Mass Culture Interpretations of a Popular Icon." *Asian Studies Review* 38: 393–409.

Murai, Mayako. 2014. "Before and After the 'Grimm Boom': Reinterpretations of the Grimms' Tales in Japan." In *Grimms' Tales around the Globe: The Dynamics of Their International Reception*, edited by Vanessa Joosen and Gillian Lathey, 153–78. Detroit: Wayne State University Press.

Orenstein, Peggy. 2011. *Cinderella Ate My Daughter: Dispatches from the Frontlines of the New Girlie-Girl Culture*. New York: HarperCollins.

Osborne, Charles. 2004. *The Opera Lover's Companion*. New Haven, CT: Yale University Press.

Philip, Neil. 1980. "Cinderella's Many Guises: A Look at Early Sources and Recent Versions." *Signal* 33: 130–46.

———. 1989. *The Cinderella Story: The Origins and Variations of the Story Known as Cinderella.* New York: Penguin.

Roberson, Chris (author), and Shawn McManus (artist). 2010. *Cinderella: From Fabletown with Love.* New York: Vertigo.

Roberson, Chris, and Bill Willingham (authors), and various illustrators. 2012. *Cinderella: Fables Are Forever.* New York: Vertigo.

Roy, Malini. 2014. "The Grimm Brothers' *Kahaniyan*: Hindu Resurrections of the Tales in Modern India by Harikrishna Devsare." In *Grimms' Tales around the Globe: The Dynamics of Their International Reception*, edited by Vanessa Joosen and Gillian Lathey, 135–52. Detroit: Wayne State University Press.

Schonwerth, Franz Xaver von. 2015. *The Turnip Princess and Other Newly Discovered Fairy Tales.* London and New York: Penguin Classics. Edited by Erika Eichenseer, illustrated by Suss Engelbert, and translated by Maria Tatar.

Seago, Karen. 2006. "Nursery Politics: 'Sleeping Beauty' or the Acculturation of a Tale." In *The Translation of Children's Literature: A Reader*, edited by Gillian Lathey, 175–89. Clevedon, England: Multilingual Matters, 2006.

Shavit, Zohar. 1994. "Beyond Restrictive Frameworks of the Past: Semiotics of Children's Literature." In *Kinderliteratur in Interkulturallen Prozess*, edited by Hans-Heino Evers and Emer O'Sullivan, 3–15. Stuttgart: Metzler.

Simon, Sherry. 1996. *Gender in Translation: Cultural Identity and the Poetics of Transmission.* New York: Routledge.

Stanley, Alessandra. 2012. "Glass Slipper Fetish," *New York Times*, April 2.

Stephens, John, and Robyn McCallum. 1998. *Retelling Stories, Framing Culture: Traditional Story and Metanarratives in Children's Literature.* New York: Garland.

Tatar, Maria, ed. 1999. *The Classic Fairy Tales: Texts, Criticism.* New York: Norton.

Teverson, Andrew. 2013. *Fairy Tale.* New Critical Idiom. New York: Routledge.

Wanning Harries, Elizabeth. 2003. *Twice upon a Time: Women Writers and the History of the Fairy Tale.* Princeton, NJ: Princeton University Press.

Warner, Marina. 1995. *From the Beast to the Blonde: On Fairy Tales and Their Tellers.* London: Vintage.

———. 2014. *Once Upon a Time: A Short History of Fairy Tale.* Oxford: Oxford University Press.

Wehse, Rainer. 1981. "Cinderella." In *Enzyklopädie des Märchens*, cols. 39–57. Berlin, New York.

Williams, Christy. 2010. "The Shoe Still Fits: 'Ever After' and the Pursuit of a Feminist Cinderella." In *Fairy-Tale Films: Visions of Ambiguity*, edited by Pauline Greenhill and Sidney Eve Matrix, 99–115. Logan: Utah State University Press.

Woźniak, Monika. 2013. "Where (and When) Do You Live, Cinderella? Cultural Shifts in Polish Translations and Adaptations of Charles Perrault's Fairy Tales." In *Textual Transformations in Children's Literature: Adaptations, Translations, Reconsiderations,* edited by Benjamin Lefebvre, 87–100. New York: Routledge.

Yolen, Jane. 1982 [1977]. "America's Cinderella." In *Cinderella: A Casebook*, edited by Alan Dundes, 294–308. Madison: University of Wisconsin Press.

Zipes, Jack. 1983. *Fairy Tales and the Art of Subversion*. New York: Methuen.

———. 2001. *The Great Fairy Tale Tradition: From Straparola and Basile to the Brothers Grimm*. New York: Norton Critical Editions.

———. 2002. *The Brothers Grimm: From Enchanted Forests to the Modern World*. 2nd ed. New York: Palgrave Macmillan.

———. 2006. *Why Fairy Tales Stick*. New York: Routledge.

———. 2010. *The Enchanted Screen: The Unknown History of Fairy Tales Films*. New York: Routledge.

I

~

Contextualizing Cinderella

1

Cinderella

The People's Princess

Ruth B. Bottigheimer

Nearly every reader of this volume will have grown up with Cinderella as a beloved and archetypal fairy tale, in which a deserving girl rises from misery and mistreatment to marriage to a prince. In the United States, little girls who dress up as Cinderella at Halloween literally embody this fairy-tale princess. Modern girls incarnating Cinderella do not know that their Cinderella is the product of a nearly four-century-long evolution that began with a very different heroine, one who was fully characterized and singularly complex. In this form Cinderella came to life in early seventeenth-century Naples, but subsequent Cinderella figures were envisaged in increasingly generalized terms until Walt Disney created Cinderella as an Everygirl figure, a princess of and for the people.

The earliest Cinderella figures emerged within aristocratic milieus. Basile's was prepared for academicians or their highly placed friends and acquaintances; Perrault's was written for a princess of the blood; and d'Aulnoy's was crafted for fellow *salonières*. In all three seventeenth-century tellings, Cinderella reproduced and represented aspects of aristocratic imaginaries.

Today's Cinderella figure has become a people's princess; in the course of the nineteenth century the tale was imbued with powerfully normative messages that were more appropriate for a broad audience and for society's rank and file than for its earlier aristocratic audiences. Specifically, from the nineteenth century onward, Cinderella conveyed the explicit message that personal goodness and virtue merit reward, and that goodness and virtue are, and will be rewarded. As a generality, it is fair to say that most people believe themselves both good and deserving; thus the message that goodness will be rewarded is well suited to the hopes and needs of the large part of every country's population that does not live in comfort. Furthermore, stories like Cinderella, in which magical assistance plays a prominent role, foster an existential belief in eventual assistance, whatever the presenting problem may be, and support hope for a happier and better future. For poor girls in the nineteenth century, for whom so few opportunities for social rise from the depths of misfortune to the highest imaginable joys existed, Cinderella could stand for a way out and a way up. It is no accident that dramatically increasing levels of literacy among the poor in the early 1800s meant that a brief narrative of social hope like Cinderella could be—and was—marketed to broad swaths of Europe's populations, in numbers far greater than had been the case among earlier seventeenth-century aristocratic readerships.

A second understanding of the Cinderella plot—of suffering relieved—made the story equally attractive to children of plenty in recent centuries. Although privileged youth may not have to sweep the hearth or suffer hunger, the tumultuous emotions of adolescence often foster a state of perceived misery, even among children of privilege. It is but a short step from such perceptions to considering the conditions in which they live their young lives as unjust, so that it becomes both easy and natural for middle- and upper-class children to identify with the unhappiness from which Cinderella rises, while the personal goodness necessary for attracting a fairy godmother's notice can be taken for granted. Twentieth- and twenty-first-century sociocultural conceptualizations of Cinderella tend to revolve around a heroine's grinding poverty, hardscrabble labor, and unending deprivation, which she escapes with the help of magic by marrying royalty, rising to royal status, and living happily ever after, first as a princess, and later—we are to understand—as a queen. Twentieth-century feminism has encouraged variations to this plot, so that, for example, a girl's feistiness might replace a godmother's magic as a route to narrative resolution, a narrative strand that is developed in several essays in this volume.

Different kinds of plots accommodate a *boy* Cinderella protagonist in today's world. For contemporary boys, the Cinderella tale means coming from behind and winning, like the titular hero in *Sydney Rella and the Glass Sneaker* (1996) or like the University of Utah basketball team in 1944, whose hard-won victory lies at the heart of Josh Ferrin's *Blitz Kids: The Cinderella Story of the 1944 University of Utah National Championship Basketball Team*. The western world's original male Cinderella fairy-tale figures, however, resembled today's girl Cinderellas: Giovan Francesco Straparola's (ca. 1480–ca. 1557) Costantino Fortunato and his Pietro Pazzo both rose from impoverishment with the help of magic to marriage to a royal princess and a happy life of health, wealth, and many children. That formulation for a boy Cinderella's happy ending has become a rarity in the modern world, whereas girl Cinderellas have proliferated into a thousand different iterations, as demonstrated in the exhibit curated by Monika Woźniak and Giuliana Zagra at the National Library of Rome to accompany the conference from which the following essays emerge. Of those thousand Cinderellas, it is rewarding to look closely at the Cinderellas from whom the modern people's princess has descended. These characters' evolution begins with a fully characterized, singularly complex heroine in Giambattista Basile's "Gatta Cenerentola" (1634) and in Marie-Catherine d'Aulnoy's "Finette Cendron" (1697) who were replaced by the increasingly generalized girls of Charles Perrault's "Cendrillon" (1697) and Jacob and Wilhelm Grimm's "Aschenputtel" (1812) on the way to Walt Disney's *Cinderella* (1950), an Everygirl figure who is a true people's princess. The twentieth-century development of film for mass markets exposed Disney's newly constituted Cinderella to the world's population, the people for whom she was fabricated as a people's princess. The historical changes in Cinderella characterizations that preceded filmic presentations chart a devolutionary sequence of losses of autonomy and a stripping away of individuating characteristics. These processes left the Cinderella figure a narrative vessel into which ordinary girls could pour their own identities and only began to reverse in the late twentieth and early twenty-first centuries, as feminist writers pushed for new sets of narrative models for young girl readers.

Giambattista Basile's "Gatta Cenerentola"

In the early 1600s the Neapolitan Giambattista Basile created the first Cinderella as a scheming and matricidal slip of a girl named Zezolla. To her governess she complains about

> her stepmother's ill treatment, saying, "Oh, God, couldn't you be my little mommy, you who give me so many smooches and kisses?" She chanted this so incessantly that she planted a wasp in the teacher's ear. (Basile 2007, 84, trans. Canepa)

> *li male trattamiente che la faceva la matreia, dicennole: "O dio, e non potisse essere tu la mammarella mia, che me fai tante vruoccole e cassesie?" E tanto secotaie a fare sta cantelena che, puostole no vespone a l'aurecchie.* (Basile 1987, 124, 126, ed. Rak)

It is but a short step from wishing, to hatching a plan to murder her stepmother:

> one day . . . the teacher said to her, "if you follow the advice of this madcap, I'll become your mother and you'll be as dear to me as the pupils of these eyes." She was about to go on speaking when Zezolla (for that was the girl's name) said, "Forgive me if I take the words out of your mouth. I know you love me dearly, so mum's the word, and *sufficit*; teach me the trade, for I'm new in town; you write and I'll sign." (Basile 2007, 84, trans. Canepa)

> *le disse na volta: "Se to vuoi fare a muodo de sta capo pazza, io te sarraggio manna e tu me sarrai cara comm'a le visciole de st'uocchie." Voleva secotiare a dicere quanno Zezolla (che cossì la figliola aveva nomme) disse: "Perdoname, si te spezzo parola 'n mocca. Io saccio ca me vuoi bene, perzò zitto e zuffecit: 'nmezzame l'arte, ca vengo da fore, tu scrive io firmo."* (Basile 1987, 126, ed. Rak)

Zezolla understands her governess's meaning perfectly and affirms her own complicity by taking the words out of her mouth and promising not to tell. Next, with the Latin verb *sufficit* (it is enough), she asks her teacher for precise instructions ("teach me the trade"). Naturally, Zezolla doesn't acknowledge the plot's murderous intent as the plan develops. Instead she presents herself metaphorically as inexperienced: "I'm new in town." And finally she makes a contractual commitment to whatever plan her teacher produces, saying, "you write and I'll sign." The rhetoric in this passage reveals the little heroine's eagerness to rid herself of her stepmother and her willingness to do anything to achieve that goal. For her part, the governess grasps a rare opportunity to rise from a service status to a governing role in the household, and as wife to a prince, to prominence in the larger community. She plunges ahead, cunningly promising Zezolla a rosy future:

> "All right, then," replied the teacher, "listen carefully; keep your ears open and your bread will come out as white as flowers. As soon as your father leaves, tell your stepmother you want one of those old dresses in the big chest in the storeroom so that you can save the one you're wearing. Since she likes to see you all patched up in rags, she'll open the chest and say, "Hold the lid up." And as you're holding it while she rummages around inside, let it bang shut, and she'll break her neck." (Basile 2007, 84, trans. Canepa).

> *"Ora susso," leprecaie la maiestra, "siente buono, apre l'aurecchie e te venerà lo pane ianco comm'a li shiure. Comme esce patreto, dì a matreiata ca vuoi no vestioto de chille viechhie che stanno drinto lo cascione granne de lo retretto, pe sparagnare chisto che puorte 'n cuollo. Essa, che te vo' vedere tutta pezze e peruoglie, aprerà lo cascione e dirrà: —Tiene lo copierchio. E tu, tenennolo, mentre iarrà scervecanno pe drinto, lassalo cadere de botta, ca se romparrà lo cuollo."* (Basile 1987, 126, ed. Rak)

Part one of the plan is now in place: kill the stepmother. Knowing that Zezolla's father the prince would do anything for his daughter, even break the law, the teacher presents part two of her plan.

> Once that's done, you know that your father would coin counterfeit money to make you happy, so when he caresses you, beg him to take me for his wife and lucky you, you'll become the mistress of my life. (Basile 2007, 84, trans. Canepa)

> *Fatto chesto, tu sai ca patreto farria moneta fauza pe contentarete e tu, quanno te fa carizze, pregalo a pigliareme pe mogliere, ca viata te, ca sarrai la patrona de la vita mia.* (Basile 1987, 126, ed. Rak)

Zezolla wastes no time carrying out her part of the governess's carefully constructed plot.

> After Zezolla heard this, every hour seemed like a thousand years to her. She followed her teacher's instructions to a tee, and once the mourning for the stepmother's accident was over, she began to play her father's keys to the tune of marrying the teacher. (Basile 2007, 84, trans. Canepa)

> *'Ntiso chesto Zezolla le parze ogn'ora mill'anne e, fatto compritamente lo conziglio de la maiestra, dapo' che se fece lo lutto pe laa desgrazia de la matreia, commenzaie a toccare li taste a lo patre, che se 'nzorasse co la maiestra.* (Basile 1987, 126, ed. Rak)

Zezolla, who was eager to kill her stepmother and even more eager to manipulate her father into marrying the woman who promised to improve her daily bread, soon gets an unpleasant surprise:

> in no time at all [her teacher] annulled and completely forgot about the service rendered (oh, sad is the soul housed in a wicked mistress!), and began to raise to all heights six daughters of her own whom she had kept secret up until then. And she worked her husband over so well that as his stepdaughters entered into his graces, his own daughter fell from his heart, and from one day to the next, Zezolla ended up being demoted from the royal chamber to the kitchen and from a canopied bed to the hearth, from sumptuous silks and gold to rags, from the scepter to the spit. And not only did her status change, but her name as well, for she was no longer called Zezolla but [Gatta Cenerentola] Cinderella Cat (Basile 2007, 84–85, trans. Canepa)
>
> *passato a mala pena po poco de tiempo, mannato a monte e scordato affatto de lo servizio receputo (oh, trista l'arma c'ha mala patrona!) commenzaie a mettere 'mpericuoccolo seie figlie soie, ch fi'n tanno aveva tenuto secrete; e tanto fece co lo marito, che receputo 'a grazie le figliastre le cadette da cote la figlia propia, tanto che, scapeta oie manca craie, venne a termene che se redusse da la cammara a la cocina e da lo vardacchino a lo focolare, da ali sfuorge de seta e d'oro a le mappine, da le scettre a li spite, né sulo cagnaie stato, ma nomme perzì, che da Zezolla fu chiammata Gatta Cenerentola.* (Basile 1987, 126, 128, ed. Rak)

The very first Cinderella,[1] as Basile characterized her, fits historically into a political and personal climate of casual stranglings and routine poisonings that had, a century earlier, brought about the social and political aims of families like the bloody-handed Borgias. Basile's Cinderella is a mistreated *princess*, whose once doting princely father neglects her in favor of his new wife's six indulged daughters. Basile has these "harpies of her sisters" (*le scerpie de le sore*) taunt Zezolla by telling "her of all the fine things they had seen" (*tante cose belle che avevano visto*) [at the ball] "just to make her boil" (*per darele cottura* [Basile 2007, 86, trans. Canepa; Basile 1987, 132, ed. Rak]). Even though Zezolla's appearance at the second ball as an unknown beauty "compounded the astonishment in her sisters' hearts" (*agghionze maraviglia a lo core de le sore* [ibid.]), the sisters and Zezolla have nothing further to do with each other until the tale's final paragraph, when together with all the court the sisters must curtsey to Zezolla to "show her their veneration, for she was their new queen" (*le 'facessero ncrinate e leverenzie, comme a regina loro* [Basile 2007, 89, trans. Canepa; Basile 1987, 136, ed. Rak]).

> Upon seeing this the sisters nearly died of anger, and not having the stomach to stand this heartbreak, they quietly stole away to their mother's house, confessing in spite of themselves that *those who oppose the stars are crazy*. (Basile 2007, 89, trans. Canepa)
>
> *Le sore vedenno chesto, chiene de drepantiglia, non avenno stommaco de vedere stop scuoppo de lo core lloro, se la sfilaro guatto verso la casa de la mamma, confessanno a dispietto loro ca Pazzo é chi contrasta co le stelle.*" (Basile 1987, 136, ed. Rak)

The narrative significance of this passage lies in the six stepsisters' quiet disappearance from the scene. No narrative memory remains of Zezolla's having suffered mockery, cruelty, and humiliation at her stepsisters' hands. Instead, the six antagonists leave readers with an Italian proverb: "*those who oppose the stars are crazy.*" It is as if the whole story has been told to exemplify the folk wisdom that affirms fate, that is, the stars, as the true determiner of social rewards. Certainly, as Basile tells the story, it is not *virtue* that raises Zezolla from the ashes of the hearth. Therefore, the stepsisters'—and behind their words, Basile's—assertion that the stars determined Zezolla's fate, is perfectly logical. Furthermore, the stars' very distance from communities and their moral or ethical values makes it narratively possible for Zezolla's amoral actions to coexist comfortably with the earthly reward of her fairy-tale happy ending.

The unaccustomedly large amount of text quoted from Basile's "Cat Cinderella" lets readers see for themselves how alien a persona this early seventeenth-century Cinderella is to the fairy tale canon of succeeding centuries. Glimpses of Basile's language and plot thus familiarize the unknown. In addition, the sharp contrast between the course of events in Basile's plot and later Cinderella plots throws into high relief the alterations subsequently made to the "Cinderella" plot. The same can be said of the Cinderella character itself in succeeding seventeenth-, eighteenth-, and nineteenth-century versions and to the meanings imputed to their fairy tale heroines.

Charles Perrault's "Cendrillon"

After its initial 1634 printing, Basile's "Cat Cinderella" was republished several times in Italy in the 1600s. Then sometime in the late 1680s or early 1690s, the Neapolitan publisher Antonio Bulifon (born Antoine Bulifon in France) apparently took along a copy of his recently republished *Pentamerone* on a commercial trip to Paris (Magnanini 2007, 85–89). By 1694 Perrault seems to have read Basile's collection,[2] since a close reading of the initial publication of his "Peau d'Asne" (Donkeyskin) fairy tale shows that he amalgamated Basile's "Orsa" (The She-Bear, Day 2, Story 6) with Straparola's "Tebaldo" (Night 1, Story 4) in a long versified narrative (Bottigheimer 2008, 175–89), while Perrault's "Puss in Boots" (Le Maistre chat) echoes Straparola's "Costantino Fortunato" (11, 1) paragraph by paragraph (Bottigtheimer 2002a, 126–28). This exercise demonstrates that the structure and content of Basile's *Cunto de li cunti* was familiar to Perrault as he began to write the "Cendrillon" (Cinderella) that appeared in his *Histoires; ou, Contes du temps passé* (Stories; or, Tales of Passed Times, 1697). Perrault made judicious excisions to Basile's "Cat Cinderella" to align his characterization of its heroine with then-reigning moral values and to make her into a paragon of early modern virtues, the first step toward creating a princess for the people.

Perrault's Cinderella is a girl named Cendrillon who patiently accepts her sisters' mockery. When the day of the ball arrives, she irons their ruffles and good-naturedly dresses their hair. They thank her with a taunting question, "Cinderella, wouldn't you like to go to the ball?" ("*Cendrillon, serois tu bien aise d'aller au Bal?*"; Perrault 1969, 68–69, trans. Johnson; Perrault 1980, 124, ed. Barchilon) Cinderella knows exactly what they mean and responds, "Ah, but you fine young ladies are laughing at me" ("*Helas, Mesdemoiselles, vous vous mocquez de moy*"; Perrault 1969, 69, trans. Johnson; Perrault 1980, 123–24, ed. Barchilon). In developing the heroine's virtue, Perrault distances her from Zezolla's straightforward and unbridled achievement of her goals. Similarly, unlike Basile's Zezolla, who marches up to a magical date tree to prepare for the ball, Perrault's Cinderella gives way to tears after her stepsisters set off. Immediately, however, a fairy godmother appears, comforts her, and more importantly, directs her to fetch a pumpkin, six mice, and six lizards, while Cinderella hits upon the idea of a rat to provide a coachman. And finally the fairy godmother touches her with her wand, so that immediately her clothes are changed into ball garments of gold, silver, and jewels, and her feet are shod with luxuriously extravagant glass slippers (see Hoffmann in this volume).

At the ball, Perrault's mannerly Cinderella further distinguishes herself from Basile's Zezolla by graciously sharing with her sisters (Perrault always called the stepsisters of his Cinderella her *soeurs*) the oranges that have been given to her and by her obedience in leaving the ball before midnight. Nor does she quarrel, as she might well do, but dissembles by playing word games with the elder of the two sisters while pretending to know nothing of the ballroom's splendors. At the end of the second ball, Cinderella loses her slipper and her finery as she flees, which prepares readers for the famous shoe scene, the turning point that lifts Perrault's Cinderella from her domestic misery and carries her into the palace and eventually to the highest position in the land. With sovereign grace, the nobly born Cinderella lightheartedly inquires if she might not try on the shoe. Perrault's fairy tale ends with family advancement rather than solely with an individual enhancement, as Cinderella, married a few days later to the prince, not only forgives her sisters but also "married them the very same day to two gentlemen of high rank about the Court" (*les maria dés le jour même à deux grands Seigneurs de la Cour*), demonstrating that she was "as good as she was beautiful" (*aussi bonne que belle*; Perrault 1969, 77, trans. Johnson; Perrault 1980, 146, ed. Barchilon).

Perrault concluded his tale with two versified morals. The first recognizes beauty as a rare treasure and names *bonne grace* as the fairies' true gift. But the cynical second moral acknowledges that "for your advancement" (*pour vostre avancement*) a few godfathers or godmothers (*des parrains ou des marraines*) are utterly indispensable (Perrault 1969, 78, trans. Johnson; Perrault 1980, 148, ed. Barchilon). That only the wealthy or the well connected have such godfathers and godmothers was a fact of life in late seventeenth-century France; consequently, his observation was of little use to humbly born girls in search of a prosperous, well-positioned, or royal husband. Little surprise that twentieth-century democratically minded authors later omitted Perrault's pragmatic reference to friends at court and focused instead on the socially stabilizing virtues of personal goodness and patient forbearance for their Cinderella heroines.

Marie-Catherine d'Aulnoy's "Finette Cendron"[3]

It may surprise readers that Perrault's Cinderella at first spread only slowly throughout the world. The taste of the times—the late 1600s and the early 1700s—favored complex plots and detailed descriptions of clothing, jewelry, and behavior. Consequently, it was the long wordy tales of Marie-Catherine d'Aulnoy that summed up public taste. Her Cinderella story is little known to the general public today and remains relatively unfamiliar even in the academic world.

Mme d'Aulnoy called her Cinderella heroine Finette Cendron and drew her plot from Basile's "Cat Cinderella," as had Perrault, and embellished it with elements from Basile's "Nennillo and Nennella" (Day 5, Story 8), which underlay the Grimms' "Hansel and Gretel." In terms of genre, Mme d'Aulnoy preferred lengthy fairyland fictions with restoration fairy-tale plots in which royalty that stumbles from wealth is later restored to wealth and glory. Hence, she made Cinderella's parents into a king and queen who manage their financial affairs so badly that they must sell everything they own—their furniture, their clothing, even their crowns. Burdened by three daughters, the queen advises making a fresh start on their own by abandoning them in the woods. The youngest daughter overhears the conversation, seeks advice and help from her fairy godmother, and after their mother abandons them in the woods, Finette saves herself and her sisters, returning home to paternal delight but maternal consternation. Predictably, more abandonments follow, the third of which finds the three girls starving in a distant forest. It goes perhaps without saying that Finette Cendron's two elder sisters are vain, selfish, and empty-headed, while she is both loving and astute, as suggested by her name "Finette" ("astute" in French). After much suffering, Finette finds and plants an acorn (as in a similar passage in Basile's "Cat Cinderella") that grows so fast she can soon climb it to spy "a large mansion, so beautiful, so beautiful that I wouldn't know [how to describe it] the walls of it are emeralds and rubies, the roof of diamonds, it's all covered with gold bells, the weathervanes go and come as the wind [blows]" (*une grande maison, si belle, si belle, que je ne saurais assez le dire; les murs en sont d'émeraudes et de rubis, le toit de diamants, elle est toute couverte de sonnettes d'or, les girouettes vont et viennent comme le vent* [d'Aulnoy 2004, 446, ed. Jasmin; trans. Bottigheimer]). The two older girls immediately dress up in two of Finette's dresses and set off for this promising building, and when Finette catches up with them, they allow her to accompany them, but only as their servant.

In this and many other respects, Mme d'Aulnoy invents new scenarios for a plot that had already passed through Basile's and Perrault's imaginations. (Perrault had composed "Cendrillon" and presented it to Louis XIV's niece Élisabeth-Charlotte d'Orléans in 1695, and had published it in January 1697, whereas Mme d'Aulnoy's "Finette Cendron" appeared several months later in volume 3 of *Les Contes des Fées*.) In this case, the mansion does not house a prince, as the two older sisters had hoped, but an ogress "fifteen feet tall" (*quinze pieds de haut*) and "thirty feet around" (*trente de tour* [d'Aulnoy 2004, 447, ed. Jasmin; trans. Bottigheimer]) and an ogre "six times taller" (*six fois plus haut* [d'Aulnoy 2004, 448, ed. Jasmin; trans. Bottigheimer]) than his wife. Both ogre and ogress want to eat the girls, but the ogre stumbles as he checks the oven's temperature and burns to cinders. Mme d'Aulnoy's Finette Cendron, echoing Basile's Zezolla, beheads the ogress, but with an ax instead of a heavy trunk lid.

Now rich with the ogre's and ogress's treasure, the two older girls, wearing Finette Cendron's gowns, attend a ball given by a king's son and return home crowing about their success. That night, sitting among the cinders at the hearth, Finette finds first a golden key and then a pretty little coffer that it unlocks. True to her style and interests, inside Mme d'Aulnoy's box are "clothes, diamonds, lace, linens, and ribbons worth immense amounts of money" (*des habits, des diamants, des dentelles, du linge, des rubans, pour des sommes immenses* [d'Aulnoy 2004, 451, ed. Jasmin; trans. Bottigheimer]), and keeping them secret, Finette dresses and goes to the second night's ball, where she dazzles everyone, including her sisters. Many balls later, Finette loses a red velvet slipper, at which point Mme d'Aulnoy returns to Basile's oeuvre. As in the "Cat Cinderella" the prince gazes upon the slipper, and as in another Basile tale, "The She-Bear" (Day 2, Story 6), he becomes so lovesick that his mother calls in physicians from Paris and Montpellier. Learning the cause of his illness when the prince shows her the red velvet slipper, his mother initiates a search for the shoe's owner.

Other Perrault, Basile, and Straparola tales glimmer through Mme d'Aulnoy's prose. The gown that Finette Cendron wears to the slipper test recalls Perrault's Donkeyskin tale, where gowns shine like the sun, moon, and stars, while the mud that her horse spatters on her perfidious sisters' gowns renews Straparola's imagery from "Prince Pig." As in Basile's "She-Bear," the heroine enters the room of the dying prince, who revives instantly when the slipper he cherishes fits her and when she produces its mate as proof that she is truly the prince's beloved.

Mme d'Aulnoy's concluding scenes for "Finette Cendron" echo Perrault's love of narrative reconciliation; the prince's parents, realizing that they themselves were responsible for having despoiled the realm of Finette Cendron's parents, hastily restore them to their former eminence. In a further reconciliation, the parents' restored wealth enables Finette Cendron's two unworthy sisters to marry and also become queens, a reflection of Perrault's conciliatory conclusion. In addition, her tale shows in detail how a narrative tradition grows over time and how authors draw on existing stories to craft new tellings for new audiences.

Mme d'Aulnoy's bold Finette Cendron is far closer to Basile's Zezolla than to Perrault's Cendrillon. Finette Cendron cries only once, and Mme d'Aulnoy signals her heroine's fortitude by having her remain dry-eyed as her two sisters weep when they discover that their mother has abandoned them in the woods. Like Zezolla, Finette Cendron does not accept her fate. Deceiving the ogress, she adroitly murders her with a quick swing of a sharp hatchet. Finette Cendron is *sweetly* cunning, *wisely* manipulative, and *patiently* calculating. In other words, Mme d'Aulnoy makes her sweet, wise, and patient like Perrault's Cendrillon, but cunning, manipulative, and calculating like Basile's Zezolla. Her complexity and her royal status as the daughter of a royal couple, a king and a queen, make it hard for the general population to identify with her. So too, does her amorally direct action—chopping off the ogress's head. Finette is not written as a role model for the majority, nor is she a princess for the people. But she was a publishing phenomenon in French and English. The first English translation and publication was meant for aristocratic readers; the second, about ten years later, was edited to take the experience of an urban merchant class into account, and several years later, the tales were reworked yet again for urban artisanal readers, as their shifting dedications and internal points of reference clearly show (d'Aulnoy 1707, 1716, 1721; Jones 2008, 242). Finally at midcentury, the London publisher Mary Cooper rewrote a selection of Mme d'Aulnoy's tales for child readers. Mme d'Aulnoy's tales saturated the English-speaking book market, with the result that her "Finette Cendron" became known within three different market segments well before Robert Samber's 1729 translation of Perrault's tales into English. The greater market success of Mme d'Aulnoy's tales becomes even clearer from the fact that Perrault's tales first achieved acceptance not as a tale collection but as a dual-language French-English textbook for schoolboys learning French (Bottigheimer 2002b, 7–9). In France, Mme d'Aulnoy's "Finette Cendron" was also published as a stand-alone story in eighteenth-century *Bibliothèque bleue* chapbooks. Translated into German, "Finette Cendron" furnished motifs and themes for several tales collected by Wilhelm and Jacob Grimm, including the oven temperature-testing scene in their "Hansel and Gretel."

Jacob and Wilhelm Grimm's "Aschenputtel"

We might ask ourselves about Jacob (1785–1863) and Wilhelm (1786–1859) Grimm's purpose in collecting and publishing fairy and other kinds of tales. For the brothers, chafing under Napoleon's military occupation of their beloved Kassel, fostering national pride was a principal motivation for their tale collecting. They also hoped to earn a bit of income. But above all, their tale collection *Kinder- und Hausmärchen* (Children's and Household Tales) was to be, in their words, an educational manual for the folk, with tales whose morality would educate Germans in German-ness. The Grimms edited their collection's tales over a fifty-year period, during which they crafted a literarily consistent folk style and an internally coherent moral system. Both affected their creation of a Cinderella figure as a begrimed girl named Aschenputtel in a version that was decisive in making her a people's princess.

The Grimms' Aschenputtel begins her life as the beloved daughter not of a prince, but of a rich man and his pious wife. Adjured to be good and pious herself, she remains so throughout the trials imposed on her by a cruel stepmother and her two beautiful but black-hearted daughters. They belittle their stepsister, take her beautiful clothes, force her into the scullery, mock her, work her to exhaustion, and leave her to sleep among the ashes—hence her name Aschenputtel. When her stepsisters ask their father to bring them jewels and clothing from a trip abroad, Aschenputtel, in humble contrast, asks only for the first twig that brushes against his hat. The plots of Basile's and d'Aulnoy's earlier Cinderella tales tell readers that this twig will help the suffering heroine, and indeed it does: the hazel twig, planted on her mother's grave, grows and becomes home to a little bird that grants Aschenputtel's wishes.

When a king organizes a great party, so that his son might choose a bride, Aschenputtel's stepsisters exploit her energy, her compliance, and her good taste, while cruelly mocking her wish to go to the festivities. Aschenputtel reacts with tears, but with the bird's magical assistance, she is eventually clothed in a gown of silver and gold and shod with silken slippers embroidered with silver thread and goes to the ball.

In the Grimm version, from the 1819 edition onward, the playful badinage in conversations between Perrault's Cinderella and her fairy godmother begins to disappear. Similarly absent is the Basile and d'Aulnoy heroines' physical determination, exemplified in their use of the trunk lid and hatchet to gain their ends. Instead, the Grimm heroine's quiet and mostly wordless demeanor (Bottigheimer 1987, 57–70) is consistent with Wilhelm Grimm's overall vision of good girls and women as silent. (In their collection, females' speech typically signals wickedness [Bottigheimer 1987, 167–72].) Aschenputtel also differs from earlier Cinderellas in being the prince's possession from an early point: he repeatedly announces his interest in her by stating, "That is my dancer."

The Grimms' Cinderella takes a grisly turn when the stepsisters hack off their heels and toes and when birds peck out their eyes, as part of the tale's triumphal conclusion. But bloody heels and toes and eyes pecked out are of less concern here than the Aschenputtel character created by the Grimms. Does she playfully tease the officer sent to try the fateful shoe on the country's girls and women, as did Perrault's Cendrillon and Mme d'Aulnoy's Finette Cendron? Not at all. Instead, her father denies her existential significance by announcing that there is no other daughter in the house, only his dead wife's stunted little Aschenputtel, who couldn't possibly become the prince's bride. From this point forward Aschenputtel remains silent, speaking not a single word to her father, to the prince's officer, to her stepmother, to the stepsisters, or even to the prince who comes to marry her.

In the German-speaking world, it was the Grimms' suffering Aschenputtel that dominated the nineteenth-century imagination. In France Perrault's beautiful, seemly, and gracious Cendrillon carried the day, easily winning out over Basile's trunk-lid-slamming or Mme d'Aulnoy's hatchet-wielding girl as behavioral models. In England's book market, the Grimms' Aschenputtel existed alongside Perrault's Cendrillon, largely because of the Grimms' enormously influential reputations for scholarship as well as for their championing ideas of folk creation and oral transmission. Ideas that animated England's intellectuals in the course of the 1800s also drove England's authors and publishers. And for as long as authors and publishers controlled public story production, Cinderella was either a princess (Basile and d'Aulnoy) or the daughter of a nobly born *gentilhomme* (Perrault) or of a rich merchant (Grimm). She had not yet become the people's princess.

Schooling and Storytelling

Two creative processes, each very different from the other, made Cinderella the people's princess. The first creative process developed from the folk, because of widespread schooling newly instituted in most of western Europe. In the early 1800s, country after country introduced government-supported schooling for the poor. Elementary school curriculums fostered basic literacy, religious orthodoxy, and public morality. Simplified Bible stories introduced children to religious education, and moral tales provided the raw material for basic literacy. By the 1830s in Central Europe the Grimms' tales entered the elementary school curriculum, where they remained decade after decade (Bastian 1981; Jäger 1981, 100–102, 108, 118; Gerstl 1963, 38–50; Bottigheimer 1993, 83–89), eventually taking over the slot for moral education. The sheer number of Grimm tales, over two hundred in all, allowed educators to divide them into groups according to their suitability for different age groups, using the tales' ethical or moral complexity as a guide. Hence the littlest pupils read the simplest stories, like "The Star Dollars" (Die Sterntaler), while older children studied more complex tales like "Aschenputtel" (Dahrendorf 1970; Bastian 1981, 69).

If we were magically transported into a nineteenth-century Central European public school classroom, we would encounter pedagogical practices of a different nature from those of today. In a school where only the teacher had a textbook (and many elementary schools fit this pattern), a text would be presented orally, and pupils would memorize it, subsequently responding to set questions with correct answers. As this methodology was advocated and implemented in Germany, a story like "The Star Dollars" or "Aschenputtel" would be memorized by each child, sentence by sentence (Troll 1911, 18–21). Questions asked by teachers, one question per sentence, aided memorization. Since it so closely resembled the catechism sessions that inculcated the rudiments of religious education (Reents and Melchior 2011, 91–96), the schooling process of set answers for set questions would have been familiar to children reading fairy tales. Using fairy tales and moral stories to teach reading comprehension effectively brought fairy tales like Cinderella to the Continent's public school children in nineteenth-century Europe. Those children, growing up to become the nation's *people* in the following decades, knew stories their parents had not known, because they had either learned or had memorized them in school.

Although some of the parents of the nineteenth century's newly literate children were themselves literate, the large majority were not. But enjoying a well-told story does not require literacy. Reading aloud to nonliterate listeners, which the scholar of historical folk narrative Rudolf Schenda (2007) called a "semi-literate" process, had familiarized earlier generations of nonreading listeners with a variety of stories. But those earlier generations had neither memorized word for word the stories they heard, nor had they responded to questions about them with word-perfect answers to fix it in their memories. They had simply listened and enjoyed.

Let us now return to the nineteenth-century school-attending children and consider how their new literacy might have affected their ability to tell stories as adults. Once they had become literate, as many of their parents had not been, they could read for themselves stories they had heard or learned in school, as well as other stories, and they could also *tell* or *read* them to their own children. The nineteenth century was above all an era in which printed stories flooded populations all over the world. Nineteenth-century literacy brought stories to people at an unprecedented rate and dramatically increased the rate and extent of story dissemination. This process in turn prepared the way for an explosion of *tellings* of remembered stories. Stories like Cinderella now belonged to the people, with the result that they were able to retell Cinderella stories in ways that made sense to their tellers and to the stories' hearers. In village societies, where churches provided weekly gatherings for local populations, Cinderella stories had a prince catch a glimpse of a poor but beautiful (or generous) heroine in a church, rather than in a royal palace, the location where Basile, Perrault, d'Aulnoy, and Grimm had arranged their meetings. And so it is natural that one Greek Cinderella encounters a prince in church three Sundays in a row (Manna and Metakidou 2011). The mother's bones of another Greek Cinderella turn into liras and gold florins that the Cinderella heroine throws among the congregation at the end of an Easter Day service, an act of rich generosity that attracts a prince's attention. Going to the church, he spreads honey on the steps to slow the mysterious heroine's flight, but catches only her slipper (Kaliambou 2012).

The Greek tellings above demonstrate the people's ownership of the Cinderella figure and of the Cinderella tale itself. Plot and content analysis suggest that the tales that two Greek tellers told originated in earlier translations and transformations of Perrault's fairy tale, of which hundreds, if not thousands, were sold in Greece in the late 1800s and early 1900s in the form of chapbooks and tales in tale collections.[4] Much the same process was enacted all over Europe and indeed all over the world, as cheap print brought stories like Cinderella to newly literate readers, some of whom read for themselves, while others read to their children and to their friends, or even to listeners in marketplaces. These were the routes by which Cinderella became the people's princess. Individuals from all over the world could and did reshape the Cinderella figure in images familiar from their own daily life.

Film and the People's Princess: Walt Disney's *Cinderella*

Film, a storytelling instrument even more powerful than the written word, emerged at the turn of the twentieth century. With the development of television, tapes, DVDs, and national and international cinema chains by the end of the twentieth century, the filmic medium could tell the same story at more or less the same time to thousands or even millions of people all over the world. It was in this pictorial medium that Walt Disney brought his Cinderella character to the world's watching eyes, and who, more than anyone else, made Cinderella the people's princess.

Walt Disney's Cinderella, the people's princess par excellence, is essentially an empty mold into which every girl can pour her identity, her life, her desires, and her emotions. Disney achieved this ready-made universalization by creating a character who epitomizes smiling good nature and who sings happy songs, but who herself expresses little or nothing that defines her individually. The wordlessness of Disney's heroine parallels the silence that Wilhelm Grimm increasingly built into his telling of "Aschenputtel" in one edition after another of the *Children's and Household Tales* (Bottigheimer 1987, 57–70).

In Disney's films, Cinderella is good, but it is the mice who carry the action forward and who provide both the film's humor and drama. Disney's Cinderella gets to the ball, dances the entire evening with the first man she encounters, and falls in love with him knowing neither his name nor his identity, an ignorance that Disney's script emphasizes by having Cinderella cry out, "But I never met the prince," when she flees the ball at midnight.

Disney's narrative devices ensure that his audiences understand that the filmic Cinderella follows her heart rather than her ambition. As different from Basile's determinedly active Zezolla as it is possible to be, Disney's Cinderella makes no plans. It is solely her innate goodness that precipitates animal assistance and a fairy godmother's magic intervention. In this way Disney's Cinderella avoids individualizing characterization, defining intentions, and distinguishing actions and becomes an Everygirl exemplar and template, the quintessential people's princess. Disney's Cinderella figure invites every girl viewer into her persona and provides a pattern for behavior.

Cinderella for Young Contemporary English Speakers

Let us briefly summarize the history of the Cinderella tale. Having begun as Basile's early seventeenth-century clever and wily princess, the Cinderella figure developed into two contrasting figures in the late seventeenth century: Perrault's sweet but witty and nobly born girl and d'Aulnoy's quick-thinking and quick-acting youngest royal sister. In the early nineteenth century the Grimms transformed Cinderella into a downtrodden stepsister. In the twentieth century, no trace of Basile's and d'Aulnoy's quick-witted Cinderella figures remained in the imaginary of commercially produced single-story picture books for young readers. At the end of the twentieth and beginning of the twenty-first centuries the Grimms' model retains a foothold in single-story popular publications for children, but it is the plot of Perrault's Cinderella that dominates retellings.

Social class plays a prominent role in the evolution of Cinderella stories. Basile's woefully neglectful father had been a prince, but in contemporary Cinderella rewritings, authors routinely ignore Basile's princely social position and the wealth with which Perrault and the Grimms endowed the men who are Cinderella's father. This slow move from royalty to commoner continued into the twentieth century, as authors have Cinderella born into ever lower social circumstances. What had been a restoration fairy tale for Basile, Perrault, and d'Aulnoy was restructured as a rags-to-riches plot that might begin in a "little cottage" (Karlin 2001 [1989]).

From the early nineteenth century onward, Cinderella figures are isolated within the human world but gain assistance from the animal world to relieve their woes. Birds first help Cinderella rise from suffering to happiness in the Grimms' version. Into the twenty-first century birds have proved to be enduring animal helpers, whether they were doves in Ruth Sanderson's 2002 *Cinderella*, bluebirds in Disney's films, or Susan Jeffers's (in Ehrlich 2004 [1985]) red bird who cheers the heroine in her loneliness. Additional animals have been added to accompany Cinderella through her travails, such as a small gray cat that Barbara McClintock (2005) puts into the otherwise harsh household, or James Marshall's feline commentator on the plot (in Karlin 2001 [1989]), or even a pink-frocked mouse in Niamh Sharkey's cartoon-like illustrations (in Eilenberg 2008).

In narrative terms each of the animal familiars amplifies Cinderella's personality or extends her reach. Whether the result is intended or not, the process of externalizing agency away from Cinderella by introducing animals to solve her problems also effectively strips the heroine of individualizing characteristics. To put this another way, each new animal familiar in contemporary rewritings contributes to universalizing the Cinderella figure by denaturing personal individuality.

Despite the presence of animal helpers, most contemporary Cinderellas still have a fairy godmother, and the words that accompany her magical transformations position her actions within small children's speech patterns. "Let's get going," she says encouragingly (McClintock 2005). Max Eilenberg has the fairy godmother transform Cinderella to the accompaniment of words like "Tap tap WHOOOSH," "Tap tap WHISH!," and "KAPOUFF! KAPAFFF!" (2008, 19–23), all phrases that a young American Everygirl might herself imagine or actually produce. Whatever could appear as alien, like parquet floors and the details of the lace and velvet of the two stepsisters' gowns in Perrault's telling, disappears completely.

Who then, is a Cinderella stripped of so many of the qualities of her prior incarnations in Basile's, Perrault's, d'Aulnoy's, and the Grimms' tales? In the decades between the mid-1980s and 2010 Cinderella is rarely a "daughter": once in Ehrlich (2004 [1985]), Piumini (2010 [2006]), McClintock (2005), and Eilenberg (2008); and three times in Karlin (2001 [1989]), with Sanderson's five instances of "daughter" a notable exception (2002). She is more often a "girl": once in Karlin (2001 [1989]), and McClintock (2005); twice in Bell (1999); three times in Piumini (2010 [2006]); four times in

Sanderson (2002); and five times in Ehrlich (2004 [1985]) and Eilenberg (2008). She is designated a "princess" by those who guess at her identity at the ball, but rarely is she called a "princess" with reference to her wedding to a prince, an avoidance that vitiates the story's culmination in a royal marriage. The decided preference for "girl" is integral to the ease with which Cinderella's girl-ness overlaps with ordinary girls' self-identity, as does the fact that modern rewritings' moniker for the heroine is overwhelmingly the name Cinderella, the name that bears within itself the iconic details of the modern Cinderella plot. In sharp contrast, the Greek folk Cinderella figure who participates in none of the familiar moments of the Perrault plot is called "the orphan," with the addition of "the girl" and "the maiden" only toward the end of the story (Kaliambou 2012).

Cinderella as a universalized people's princess appears most dramatically in rewritings of the tale by contemporary children themselves. At the website multiculturalcinderella.blogspot.com, the Cinderella who begins her life as the daughter of a prince, of a prominent public figure, or of a rich merchant is a rarity. Equally absent is Cinderella as a quick-witted maiden. Nonetheless, every blogspot Cinderella marries a prince. An ordinary girl's marrying up the social scale is fundamental to the modern Cinderella plot. She becomes whatever her evolving future requires, a goal more easily achieved if her persona remains inchoate, unspecified, generalized, universally and undifferentiatedly female. A wedding to a royal prince, the single constant in the blogspot's tellings of the Cinderella tale, illuminates the historical process of universalization that Cinderella has undergone from the nineteenth century onward.

Notes

1. The Cinderella canon is held to embrace an "Egyptian" Cinderella figure, Rhodopis, from the Ptolomaic period, and a ninth-century Chinese figure named Yeh-Hsien. Because of my scholarly reservations about these attributions (see Bottigheimer 2010, 453), I do not incorporate a discussion of Rhodopis here. I am still in the process of exploring the problematics of considering the Yeh-Hsien story as a ninth-century narrative.
2. Straparola's *Piacevoli notte* (in their French translation *Les Facecieuses Nuictz*) and Basile's *Cunto de li cunti* were both known in 1690s Paris: Perrault's "Puss in Boots" was reworked from Straparola's "Costantino Fortunato" (Night 11, Story 1). Mlle Lhéritier and Mlle de La Force reworked tales from Basile's *Cunto de li cunti*, or *Pentamerone*, as it was also titled. Mme d'Aulnoy clearly had access to a copy of Basile's collection, drawing on it for

motifs and themes. I haven't yet investigated Mme de Murat's awareness of Basile's tales.

3. Told by Doña Juana as "a simple romance" (Raynard 2012, 174), "Finette Cendron" is a framed tale within "Don Gabriel Ponce de Leon: A Spanish Novella," itself a component of d'Aulnoy's four-volume *Tales of the Fairies* (1697).
4. Maria Kaliambou has provided me with six examples, whose particulars follow: *I Stachtopouta: Paramithi dia ta kala paidia* [Cinderella: Folktale for the Good Children] (Athens: Printing G. Fexi, 1887); "Ai treis adelfai pou efagan tin mitera ton kai i Staktokilismeni" [The three sisters who ate their mother and Cinderella]. In *Ta nea 44 Paramithia tou laou. Anekdota, sillegenta kai grafenta ipo Antoniou Georgiou. Astiotata. Diavaste kai gelaste!* [The new 44 folktales of the people. Unpublished, collected and written by Antonios Georgiou. Very funny. Read them and laugh!] (Athens: Antonios Georgiou, 1892); "Ai treis adelfai pou efagan tin mitera ton kai i Staktokilismeni" [The three sisters who ate their mother and Cinderella]. In *Ta nea peninta paramithia tou laou.* [The new fifty folktales of the people] (Athens: Saliveros, 1914); "I Stachtopouta" [Cinderella]. In *Ta penintadio paramithia tou laou* [The fifty-two folktales of the people]: (Athens: Saliveros, 1914); "I stachtopouta" [Cinderella]. In *Ta saranta laika paramithia. Sillogi eidikou* [The forty popular folktales. Special Collection] (Athens: M. und G. Gelantalis und G. Chrisogelos, 1924 (= Laiki vivliothiki) [= Folks Library]); *I Stachtopouta* [Cinderella] (Athens: Astir, n.d. [ca. 1950s]).

References

CANONICAL FAIRY TALE EDITIONS

Aulnoy, Madame (Marie-Catherine) d'. 1697. *Les Contes des Fées.* 4 vols. Paris: Claude Barbin.

Critical Edition

Aulnoy, Madame (Marie-Catherine) d'. 2004. *Contes des fées suivis des Contes nouveaux ou Les Fées à la Mode.* Edited by Nadine Jasmin. Paris: Honoré Champion.

Early English Translations

Aulnoy, Madame (Marie-Catherine) d'. 1707. *The Diverting Works of the Countess d'Anois.* London: Nicolson, Sprint, Bell, and Burows. (Oxford: New Bodley Opie.)

———. 1716. *The History of the Tales of the Fairies. Newly done from the French. Containing I. Graciosa and Percinet. II. The Blew-Bird and Florina. III. Prince Avenant. IV. King of the Peacocks and Princess Rosetta. V. Prince Nonpariel* [sic]*) and Princess Brilliant. VII.* [sic] *The Orange-Tree and Its Beloved Bee: Dedicated to the Ladies of Great Britain.* London: Ebenezer Tracy, 1716.

———. 1721. *A Collection of Novels and Tales, Written by that Celebrated WIT of France, the Countess d'Anois* [sic]*. In Two Volumes*. London: William Chetwood.

Modern English

Aulnoy, Madame (Marie-Catherine) d'. 1989. "Finette Cendron." In *Beauties, Beasts, and Enchantment: Classic French Fairy Tales*, edited by Jack David Zipes. New York: New American Library.

Modern German

Finette Cendron seems not to have been translated into German. —RBB

Modern Italian

Aulnoy, Madame (Marie-Catherine) d'. 2000. "Finette Cendron." In *La Bella dai Capellli d'oro et Altre Fiabe*, edited by Anna Maria Rubino Campini. Palermo: Sellerio.

Basile, Giambattista. 1634–36. *Cunto de li Cunti.* Naples: Ottavio Beltrano (Days 1, 2, 5) and Lazzaro Scoriggio (Days 3, 4).

Critical Edition

Basile, Giambattista. 1987. *Lo cunto de li cunti.* Edited by Michele Rak. Milan: Garzanti.

English

Basile, Giambattista. 2007. *Giambattista Basile's The Tale of Tales, or Entertainments for Little Ones.* Translated by Nancy Canepa. Detroit: Wayne State University Press.

French

Basile, Giambattista. 1995. *Le Conte des contes.* Translated by Françoise Decroisette. Paris: Circé.

German

Basile, Giambattista. 2000. *Das Märchen der Märchen: Das Pentamerone.* Edited by Rudolf Schenda. Munich: C. H. Beck.

Grimm, Jacob and Wilhelm. 1857. *Kinder- und Hausmärchen*. Göttingen: Dieterische Buchhandlung.

Critical Edition

Grimm, Jacob and Wilhelm. 1980. *Kinder- und Hausmärchen*. Edited by Heinz Rölleke. Stuttgart: Philipp Reclam.

English

Grimm, Jacob and Wilhelm. 1977. *Grimms' Tales for Young and Old: The Complete Stories*. Translated by Ralph Manheim. Garden City, NY: Doubleday.

French

Grimm, Jacob and Wilhelm. 2009. *Contes pour les enfants et la maison*. Translated by Natacha Rimasson-Fertin. 2 vols. Paris: J. Corti.

Italian

Grimm, Jacob and Wilhelm. 2015 [1951]. *Le fiabe del focolare*. Translated by Clara Bovero. Torino: Einaudi.

Perrault, Charles. 1697. *Histoires; ou, Contes du temps passé: Avec des Moralitez*. Paris: Claude Barbin.

Facsimile of 1697 Publication

Perrault, Charles. 1980. Edited by Jacques Barchilon. Geneva: Droz.

Critical Edition

Gheeraert, Tony, ed. 2005. *Perrault, Fénelon, Mailly, Préchac, Choisy, et anonymes: Contes merveilleux*. Paris: Honoré Champion.

English

Perrault, Charles. 1969. *Perrault's Fairy Tales*. Translated by A. E. Johnson. New York: Dover.

German

Perrault, Charles. 1986. *Sämtlich Märchen*. Translated by Doris Distrelmaier-Haas. Stuttgart: Reclam.

Italian

Perrault, Charles. 2002. *Fiabe*. Translated by Antonio Faeti and Myriam Cristallo. Milan: Fabbri.

Straparola, Giovanni Francesco. 1551, 1553. *Le piacevoli notti*. Venice: Comin da Trino.

Critical Edition

Straparola, Giovanni Francesco. 2000. *Le piacevoli notti.* 2 vols. Edited by Donato Pirovano. Rome: Salerno, 2000.

English

Straparola, Giovanni Francesco. 1898. *The Facetious Nights of Straparola.* 4 vols. Translated by W. G. Waters. London: Society of Bibliophiles.

Straparola, Giovanni Francesco. 2012. *The Pleasant Nights.* Edited by Donald Beecher. Toronto: University of Toronto Press.

French

Straparola, Giovanni Francesco. 1999. *Les nuits facétieuses.* Edited by Joël Gayraud. Paris: José Corti.

German

Straparola, Giovanni Francesco. 1947. *Die ergötzliche Nächte.* Translatd by Hanns Floerke. Munich: K. Desch.

CITED VERSIONS OF CINDERELLA

Bell, Anthea, trans. 1999. *Cinderella: A Fairy Tale by Charles Perrault.* Illustrated by Loek Koopmans. New York: North-South Books.

Disney, Walt. 1950. *Cinderella.*

Ehrlich, Amy. 2004 [1985]. *Cinderella.* Illustrated by Susan Jeffers. New York: Dutton Children's Books.

Eilenberg, Max. 2008. *Cinderella.* Illustrated by Niamh Sharkey. Cambridge, MA: Candlewick Press.

Ferrin, Josh, and Tres Ferrin. 2012 [1985]. *Blitz Kids: The Cinderella Story of the 1944 University of Utah National Championship Basketball Team.* Layton, UT: Gibbs Smith.

Jeffers, Susan. See Ehrlich.

Kaliambou, Maria, ed. 2012. *Cinderella: The Light of God.* New Haven, CT: Yale Printing and Publishing.

Karlin, Barbara. 2001 [1989]. *James Marshall's Cinderella.* Illustrated by James Marshall. New York: Puffin/Dial.

Koopmans, Loek. See Bell.

Manna, Anthony L., and Soula Metakidou. 2011. *The Orphan: A Cinderella Story from Greece.* Illustrated by Giselle Potter. New York: Random House.

Marshall, James. See Karlin.

McClintock, Barbara. 2005. *Cinderella.* New York: Scholastic Press.

Myers, Bernice. 1996. *Sydney Rella and the Glass Sneaker.* Boston: Houghton Mifflin. multiculturalcinderella.blogspot.com.

Piumini, Roberto. 2010 [2006]. *Cinderella*. Illustrated by Raffaella Ligi. Mankato, MN: Picture Window Books.

Rousseau, Jean-Jacques. 1979 [1762]. *Emile; or, On Education*. Translation, introduction, and notes by Allan Bloom. New York: Basic Books.

Rylant, Cynthia. 2002. *Walt Disney's Cinderella*. Illustrated by Mary Blair. New York: Disney Press.

Sanderson, Ruth. 2002. *Cinderella*. Illustrated by Ruth Sanderson. Boston: Little, Brown.

Sharkey, Niamh. *See* Eilenberg.

FURTHER REFERENCES

Bastian, Ulrike. 1981. *Die "Kinder- und Hausmärchen" der Brüder Grimm in der literaturpädagogischen Diskussion des 19. und 20. Jahrhunderts*. Frankfurt am Main: Haag and Herchen.

Bottigheimer, Ruth. 1987. *Grimms' Bad Girls and Bold Boys: The Moral and Social Vision of the Tales*. New Haven, CT: Yale University Press.

———. 1993. "The Publishing History of Grimms' Fairy Tales: Reception at the Cash Register." In *The Reception of Grimms' Fairy Tales: Responses, Reactions, Revisions*, edited by Donald Haase, 78–101. Detroit: Wayne State University Press.

———. 2002a. *Fairy Godfather: Straparola, Venice, and the Fairy Tale Tradition*. Philadelphia: University of Pennsylvania Press.

———. 2002b. "Misperceived Perceptions about Perrault's Fairy Tales and the History of English Children's Literature." *Children's Literature* 30: 1–19.

———. 2008. "Before *Contes du temps passé* (1697): Charles Perrault's 'Grisélidis' (1693), 'Souhaits ridicules' (1693), and 'Peau d'Asne' (1694)." *Romanic Review* 99 (3–4): 175–89.

———. 2010. "*Fairy Godfather*, Fairy-Tale History, and Fairy-Tale Scholarship: A Response to Dan Ben-Amos, Jan M. Ziolkowski, and Francisco Vaz da Silva." *Journal of American Folklore* 123 (490): 447–96.

Dahrendorf, Malte. 1970. *Das Mädchenbuch und seine Leserin: Jugendlektüre als Instrument der Sozialisation*. Weinheim: Beltz.

Gerstl, Quirin. 1963. "Die erzieherische Gehalt der Grimmschen *Kinder- und Hausmärchen*." PhD diss., University of Munich.

Hoffmann, Kathryn. 2012. "Perrault's 'Cendrillon' among the Glass Tales: Crystal Fantasies and Glassworks in Seventeenth-Century France and Italy." Paper presented at the "Cinderella as a Text of Culture" conference. Rome: Sapienza University, November 8–10.

Jäger, Georg. 1981. *Schule und literarische Kultur: Sozialgeschichte des eutschen Unterrichts an höheren Schulen von der Spätaufklärung bis zum Vormärz*. Stuttgart: Metzler.

Jones, Christine. 2008. "Madame d'Aulnoy Charms the British." *Romanic Review* 99 (3–4): 239–56.

Magnanini, Suzanne. 2007. "Postulated Routes from Naples to Paris: Antonio Bulifon and the Italian Literary Fairy Tale in France." *Marvels & Tales* 21 (2): 78–92.

Raynard, Sophie. 2012. "Marie-Catherine d'Aulnoy, *Tales of the Fairies* (1697) and *New Tales, or, The Fashionable Fairies* (1698)." In *Fairy Tales Framed: Early Forewords, Afterwords, and Critical Words*, edited by Ruth B. Bottigheimer, 167–93. Albany: State University of New York Press.

Reents, Christine, and Christoph Melchior. 2011. *Die Geschichte der Kinder- und Schulbibel: Evangelisch—katholisch—Jüdisch*. Göttingen: Vandenhoeck and Ruptrecht UniPress.

Schenda, Rudolf. 2007. "Semi-Literate and Semi-Oral Processes." Translated by Ruth B. Bottigheimer. *Marvels & Tales* 21 (1): 127–40.

Tomkowiak, Ingrid. 1989. "Traditionelle Erzählstoffe im Lesebuch: Ein Projekt zur schulischen Geschichtspädagogik zwischen 1770 und 1920." *Fabula* 30: 96–110.

———. 1993. *Lesebuchgeschichten: Traditionelle Erzaehlstoffe in Deutschsprachigen Schullesebuechern 1770–1920*. Berlin: de Gruyter.

Troll, Max. 1911. *Das Märchenunterricht in der Elementarklasse*. Langensalze: Beyer.

2

Perrault's "Cendrillon" among the Glass Tales

Crystal Fantasies and Glassworks in Seventeenth-Century France and Italy

Kathryn A. Hoffmann

Glass slippers on the feet of one fairy-tale girl and glass caskets that encase another for long years, growing along with her. Mythological figures cavorting among millefiori on a glass table made for Louis XIV. Lost recipes for ruby glass created by an alchemist, and tales of glass workers murdered by spies or accidentally poisoned. Real girls in glass caskets, objects of religious fervor. Endless reflections of courtiers in the hall of mirrors at Versailles.... The glass slippers of Charles Perrault's 1697 tale "Cendrillon ou la petite pantoufle de verre" ["Cendrillon or the Little Glass Slipper"] need to be reset, in part, within seventeenth-century literary fairy tales in Italy and France with glass elements that include shoes, caskets, fairy palaces, grottoes, and tunnels. They need to find their place as well within the stories of objects of art, power, and reverence, among forgotten alchemical recipes, fanciful objects made for collectors, and tales of commercial espionage. The glass slippers in "Cendrillon" are crisscrossed with stories still only partially told of eroticism, consumption, death, magic, and desire.

To read glass in the version of the tale written by Perrault, the methodologies here are mixed, combining reading strategies developed for literature and folklore with theoretical approaches developed for museum studies, and for the broader category of what might be called "object studies" or "thing studies."[1] Perrault's version of Cinderella can be read not simply among the tales that fit Aarne-Thompson-Uther type 510A (see Thompson 1955–58; Ranke et al. 1977–; and Ashliman 1998–2012), but among other seventeenth-century tales from Italy and France with glass objects. Shifting, even momentarily, the grouping of the tale from character types and episodes to objects alters the way in which the tale makes meaning. I don't find the marvelous objects of fairy tales to be merely decorative intrusions, or a baroque proliferation of decor at the expense of structure ("prolifération du décor aux dépens de la structure," Rousset 1954, 181–82), or digressions from the roles of *actants*, or always interchangeable, certainly not without altering the tale itself. Glass slippers are certainly part of what Malarte-Feldman calls "baroque ostentation" in the tales, and yet they exceed the particular excesses of the baroque (Malarte-Feldman 1997, 115). Elements such as glass slippers for Cinderella or glass coffins for legions of Sleeping Beauties can become so intimately associated with the tale type that they become part of its logic; no longer accident, periphery, or intrusion into a world dominated by actants and their actions, but pleasant object-actants themselves. Other elements, like the barrettes, parquet floors, and lemons of Perrault's version slip quietly away from the tale barely noticed and quickly forgotten. Slippers are among the fairy objects that retain a special kind of thingness infused with a marvel so strong that the tale type shifts and settles about them, its meanings flowing around and through them for centuries to come.[2]

That significant kind of thingness, however, seems to develop at particular moments, where it is fed by multiple areas of the literary and the social imaginary. I will read some fragments of the history of real glass as well in the seventeenth century: in reliquaries, decorative items, tableware, and furniture, including a fantastic glass table offered to Louis XIV, and in a lost recipe for ruby glass. Glass is unquestionably a "thing that talks," to borrow the title of a book edited by Lorraine Daston (2004). Glass is not a simple tale accessory, a kind of accident of historical decoration. Glass, when it appeared in Perrault's tale, was shot through with tales of collection, international competition, power, desire, intrigue, and death. In Claude Lévi-Strauss's terminology, what follows below might be described as "bundles of relations" (Lévi-Strauss 1955, 431). But they are bundles of relations that cross the boundaries of the disciplines. They involve literature, objects, once-living bodies, industrial development, politics, and practices of consumption. The relations themselves suggest the need for reading strategies that function in cross-disciplinary ways.

The shoe is a frequent but not universal element of the tales grouped under 510A or often read as variants. It is just a beautifully shaped sandal in the tale of Rhodopis told by Strabo,[3] a gold shoe lost at a cave festival in the Chinese tale (Waley 1947), a bejeweled gold slipper in the Indian tale of Sodeva Bâî (Cosquin 1922, 31, cited in Saintyves 1987, 113),[4] a red velour mule with pearls in d'Aulnoy's "Finette Cendron" (Aulnoy 1994). One could summarize Pierre Saintyves's early twentieth-century study *Les contes de Perrault et les récits parallèles* and retell every tale Saintyves had ever read or heard in the myth and folklore of the world, or local French wedding practices about feet and shoes. But it will not help to understand glass.

A parenthesis is needed at this point. Scholars of Perrault are well aware that the title of the tale Perrault published was "Cendrillon ou la petite pantoufle de verre" and that the slipper in the story published in 1697 was indeed of "verre" "glass." Yet for the mass public, the suspicion lingers that there might be a different story, one involving *vair* [fur] not *verre* [glass]. The story of a fur slipper seems to have made its debut on November 4, 1839, no more than a parenthetical remark in Théophile Gautier's review of a production of Rossini's *Cenerentola* at the Théâtre Italien. Gautier said simply: "the slipper of *vair* (and not glass, a matter hardly suited to slippers), seems to us to be a dramatic device not inferior to that of Othello's handkerchief."[5] A little over a year later, on March 23, 1841, it appeared again, slightly embellished, in *Le Siècle,* in the first episode of Honoré de Balzac's serialized fiction "Les Lecamus." Balzac's narrator praised Gautier's erudition, declaring that an "infinite number" of editions of Perrault's tales had been wrong and the slippers had "doubtless" been of *menu vair*—a blue-gray and white squirrel fur—not glass. The story clearly fit Balzac's own preoccupations with fur and skins. Balzac had already written his own fantastic tale about a magically shrinking animal skin, *La Peau de Chagrin,* in 1831. In the popular press, in a work of fiction set in "a house which no longer exists, on a corner which no longer exists of the Street of the Old Fur Trade which no longer exists, in a Paris which no longer exists" the story of a fur slipper that never existed, took on a life of its own.[6]

The tale of fur took routes through lexicography and psychoanalysis that, as they intertwined, shaped public conceptions. In 1867 Pierre Larousse embellished the story in a lengthy and imaginative entry in his *Grand dictionnaire unversel du XIXe siècle*. Larousse declared with conviction that it was "historical truth" ("la vérité historique") that Perrault had intended the slippers to be of *vair* and not *verre*. He supposed that *verre* might have been the result of a change introduced by an editor (either out of ignorance or a desire to heighten the marvel of the tale) or by a printer who did not know the by-then-outdated word. He made light of the idea that a girl could walk or dance in shoes of glass and included his own rather odd reverie on a shoe that could reveal a charming little foot as if it were naked. In 1873, Émile Littré, in the *Dictionnaire de la langue française*, opined in a somewhat less elaborate passage under the entry "vair," that glass slippers were "absurd" and that it had been *souliers de vair*, which Littré interpreted as *fur-lined* shoes. The 1867 and 1873 entries by Larousse and Littré are included in full in the appendix to this piece. In the appendix too are several other "Cendrillon" entries in the Larousse dictionaries from the nineteenth through the late twentieth centuries, showing several of the stages by which the Larousse writers and editors slowly and bit by bit, divested their dictionary of the tale. By the mid-twentieth century, Pierre Larousse's original volubility on fur, printers' errors, and charming naked feet now gone, the Larousse editors were explicit that the slipper was "not of fur" attributing the "hypothesis" of fur to the ambiguous French "on," which means "someone" but clearly not Pierre Larousse in particular. A *pantoufle de vair* retains a lexicographical life in several French dictionaries today (see the appendix).

The story of fur was introduced to English-speaking readers through sixty-three years of *Encyclopaedia Britannica* entries for "Cinderella." From 1910 through 1973 the *Encyclopaedia Britannica* declared that *glass* in English versions had been the result of a mistranslation of *vair*. The double error (fur plus a mistranslation) was not corrected until 1974, in the fifteenth edition that remains online today. Yet even today, the tale of fur seems barely hidden behind quotation marks that all too clearly imply that *glass* might be something else: "The prince's recognition of the cinder maiden by the token of a 'glass' slipper is unique in Perrault." In the latter half of the 20th century, the story of fur was in an oddly belated fashion, introduced into the *Encyclopedia Americana*, replacing a previous entry that was in fact correct.

Psychoanalytic approaches to sex and folklore perpetuated the tales of fur. In his *Drei Abhandlungen zur Sexualtheorie* (*Three Contributions to the Theory of Sex*), Freud, without specifically mentioning Cinderella, drew connections among slippers, genitalia, and fur.[7] Bruno Bettelheim's *Uses of Enchantment* helped make the tale of fur stick in the popular imagination (Bettelheim 1976, 251). Bettelheim believed that Perrault had intended to write *verre/glass*, and Bettelheim built his own elaborate interpretation of Cinderella involving a glass hymen, a girl with a penchant for consorting with phallic mice, and a prince and Cinderella with competing castration complexes. Yet Bettelheim followed Balzac, suggesting that Perrault had readapted the story for the court, and had eliminated the vulgar content of a missing earlier version. The notion that the slipper was really of "fur" became the popular dirty little secret of Cinderella. And being the insider with the knowledge of dirty little secrets is very popular indeed.

Scholars have struggled to dispel the charm of the tale of fur. As early as 1896, D. B. suggested in *Notes and Queries* that Pierre Larousse might have been convicted of "gross carelessness" in researching his "Cendrillon" entry (B. 1896, 332). Latham described the error bluntly in the same journal a half a century later: "La bévue est on ne peut plus stupide" ["The blunder could not be more stupid"] (Latham 1946, 234).[8] Scholarly notes in *Notes and Queries,* however, were hardly positioned to unseat the Larousse and Littré dictionaries for the general public. In 1951, after a new piece on *verre/vair* had appeared in *Le Monde*, Paul Delarue tried to reach the French public in a response article (reprinted in Delarue 1982). By the mid-twentieth century, editors of French editions of Perrault's tales were taking increasing care in their introductions to note that the slippers were indeed of *verre* in Perrault's original edition, and scholars addressed the issue.[9] In 1982 however, Dundes could still bemoan the fact that the tale of fur kept coming back to life, no matter how many times scholars thought they had dispatched it: "For decades, folklorists have been kept busy refuting the unfounded verre/vair hypothesis but to no avail. No sooner was one ignorant writer corrected than another sprang up to take his place" (Dundes 1982, 111). The discussion remains a popular one on fairy tale and trivia sites today. It can even be found on a shoe blog.[10]

Yet there are things and tales that Balzac, Larousse, and Bettelheim did not know.

Tales of Glass

In Perrault, the glass slippers are a fairy gift, the last in a series of transformation-gifts: the pumpkin-carriage, the mouse-horses, the lizard-servants, the rat-coachman, and the poor clothes turned into a dress of gold and silver fabric covered in jewels. The slippers "les plus jolies du monde" ["the prettiest in the world"] are not a transformation of an existing creature/object but a pure gift (presumably Cendrillon had none). The shoes of glass are not the only pretty objects in the tale. Under Perrault's pen, the tale filled with precious objects reflecting the tastes of the day in luxury items. The stepsisters spend their days in rooms with parquet floors looking at themselves from head to toe in mirrors. They go to the ball, one in her red velour dress with English lace, the other in a coat with gold flowers and a diamond barrette in her hair. They send their servants to the best address to buy "mouches" (the popular false beauty marks of the day). At the ball, Cendrillon receives gifts of oranges and lemons, the luxury fruits of the day popular at Versailles. However, mirrors, a velour dress, and oranges seem to be no more than brief tale accessories, accidental in the encounter of the tale with the consuming contexts of the seventeenth century, to be forgotten or ignored in later retellings. The glass slippers are the memorable objects that will be retained throughout many of the retellings of the tale after Perrault. While the Grimms opted for one pair of slippers embroidered in silk and silver and another of gold, Disney returned to the glass slippers in the popular animated film version of the tale.[11] Glass slippers seem to have had more narrative weight than a parquet floor or a diamond barrette.

Perrault was not the first writer to use glass and crystal objects, and it is worth placing "Cendrillon" back among the other tales with significant glass elements. Tales of glass caskets go back at least as far as the first century CE and Strabo's report that Alexander's corpse had been transferred into a sarcophagus of glass.[12] Closer to Perrault were the crystal caskets in Giambattista Basile's tale "The Young Slave," published in the *Pentamerone* in 1634 (Basile 1932, day 2, tale 8). The caskets are the result of a series of maternal misadventures. To make a long story as short as possible, Lisa's mother had cheated at a game of jumping over rose bushes, ate the leaf she had knocked off, found out the leaf was enchanted and had made her pregnant. She then invited the fairies to give her baby gifts. A fairy fell in her haste, twisted her ankle, and cursed the newborn to die at the age of seven, when her mother would leave a comb in her hair. When the disaster occurred, the mother put Lisa's body in seven caskets of crystal, one inside the other in a locked room. The mother died, leaving the caskets in the care of her brother the baron who was directed never to enter the room. However, he departed, and his curious wife opened the room to find the glass caskets. Inside, Lisa was not dead but "had grown like any other woman," and the glass caskets "had lengthened with her, keeping pace as she grew." The association of glass caskets and the themes of sleep and death or pseudo-death for young girls would of course remain a durable element of Snow White tales.

The association of rock crystal with purity, especially female purity, and with marvelous states between life and death, was centuries old. Since the Middle Ages, rock crystal had been the material of reliquaries, indicative of the purity of the saint. As Basile wrote his tales in seventeenth-century Italy, the remains of saints were being translated out of marble tombs and into increasingly elaborate caskets of glass, gold, and silver throughout Italy. While some were males, there would be a long-lived fascination in both Italy and France with the young women believed to be "incorruptibles," saints incapable of putrefaction. Displays of the preserved remains of pretty girls lying on silken sheets in glass caskets bordered in gold and silver were long-lived.[13] Some still seem to dream today, wax-covered hands crossed on their breasts. In the absence of a letter from Basile indicating he had seen a reliquary, or the diary of a priest or nun admitting they were reading literature, we will never be sure who inspired whom in the displays of young girls in glass in the seventeenth century. What is certain is that purity, slumber, and death, and themes of seeming and being, are part of a narrative cycle that crossed religious display and fairy tales and constructed narrations—in word and image—of states of incomplete death.

In Basile's "Verdeprato" ("Green Meadow"), glass was associated with enchantment and with sexuality. The binary combination of purity and its opposites (sexuality, danger, and death) is not unexpected.[14] In "Verdeprato" an enchanted prince constructs a crystal road in an underground crystal tunnel to travel to his lover. From Basile's tale in Nancy L. Canepa's English translation, followed by Ruggero Guarini's Italian translation:

> In that land there was an enchanted prince who sailed on the sea of her beauty, and he threw the hook of amorous servitude to that bream so many times that he finally stuck her in the gills of her affection and made her his. And in order to take their pleasure without causing any suspicion on the part of her mother, who was a wicked little demon, the prince gave her a special powder, and he constructed a crystal tunnel that ran from the royal palace to right up under Nella's bed, even though it was eight miles away. And he said to her, "Whenever you want to feed me like a sparrow on your lovely grace put a little bit of this powder in the fire, and I'll immediately come through the tunnel and respond to your call, running down a road of crystal so that I can enjoy that face of silver." (Basile 2007, Second Entertainment of the Second Day, 153)

> Ora c'era in quella terra un principe fatato, il quale andava per mare in cerca della bellezza sua, e tanto gettò l'amo della servitù amorosa a questa bella aurata finché non l'agganciò per le branchie dell'affetto e la fece sua; e affinché senza sospetto della mamma, che era una diavolessa, potessero godersela insieme, il principe le diede una certa polvere, et fece un canale de cristallo che rispondeva dal palazzo reale fin sotto il letto di Nella, ancorché stesso otto miglia lontano, dicendole: "Ogni volta che tu mi vuoi cibare come passero co 'sta bella grazia, metti un po' di 'sta polvere sul fuoco, ché io subito per entro il canale me ne vengo al fischio, correndo per una strada di cristallo a godere 'sta faccia d'argento." (Basile 1994, 190)

One day as the prince runs naked down the crystal tunnel to visit his lover, her jealous sisters break the tunnel. The shards of crystal that cut him are enchanted, and no human remedies can cure him.[15]

Among the *conteuses*, the female authors of fairy tales in the seventeenth century, crystal and glass became not only enchanted but also the very home of enchantment—the building material of fairy grottoes and palaces. The examples are too numerous to cite here; a few will need to suffice. In Madame D'Aulnoy's "La Grenouille bienfaisante" ["The Beneficent Frog"], a queen and her daughter are imprisoned in an enchanted crystal palace set in the center of a lake of mercury.[16] The kidnapping fairy engages monsters who "promised to neglect nothing in protecting it; they surrounded the palace of crystal; the lightest placed themselves on the roof and the walls; the others at the doors, and the remainder in the lake" ["Les monstres promirent de ne rien négliger de ce qu'ils pouvaient faire; ils entourèrent le palais de cristal; les plus légers se placèrent sur le toit et sur les murs; les autres aux portes, et le reste dans le lac"] (Aulnoy 1785, 333). In her "L'oiseau Bleu" ["Blue Bird"] the walls of the palace are of clear diamonds (Aulnoy 1994, 123). In "La chatte blanche" ["White Cat"], the transparent palace of porcelain is the home of the fairies and the site where fairy tales are magically recorded:

> Thus guided by the light he saw, he arrived at the door of a palace, the most superb imaginable. This door was of gold, covered with carbuncles whose bright and pure light illuminated all that was around. It was this door that the prince had seen from afar; the walls were of transparent porcelain, mixed with several colors, which depicted the history of all the fairies, from the creation of the world until then; the famous adventures of Donkeyskin, of Finette, of the Orange Tree, of Gracieuse, of Sleeping Beauty, of Green Snake, and a hundred others were not forgotten there.

> Ainsi guidé par la lumière qu'il voyait, il arriva à la porte d'un château, le plus superbe qui se soit jamais imaginé. Cette porte était d'or, couverte d'escarboucles dont la lumière vive et pure éclairait tous les environs. C'était elle que le prince avait vue de fort loin; les murs étaient d'une porcelaine transparente, mêlée de plusieurs couleurs, qui représentaient l'histoire de toutes les Fées, depuis la création du monde jusqu'alors; les fameuses aventures de Peau d'Âne, de Finette, de l'Oranger, de Gracieuse, de la Belle au bois dormant, de Serpentin Vert, et de cent autres n'y étaient pas oubliées. (Aulnoy 1994, 23)

Later in the tale, the cat/princess hides in a rock crystal star for her presentation to the king. In the Comtesse de Murat's "Le Palais de la vengeance," lovers are imprisoned in a crystal palace peopled with nymphs and dwarves, the crystal inscribed with their spell of unending visibility to each other (Murat 1710 [1698]).[17]

In Marguerite de Lubert's *La Princesse Camion*, first published in 1743, a prince traveling in a boat of mother-of-pearl encounters a fairy palace of rock crystal on piles, with "admirably engraved" walls that create the loveliest effect in the world ("le plus bel effet du monde," Lubert 2005, 146). In "Le Prince Glacé et la Princesse Etincelante" the prince is drawn for three hours down a path through dark caverns to arrive in an enchanted grotto, its vault and walls covered in pure crystal, lit with thousands and thousands of crystal chandeliers (Lubert 2005, 294). As time went on crystal and glass caskets multiplied in the Snow White tales.[18] Read among the glass tales, the slippers in Perrault's "Cendrillon" fit, not only the foot but also the tale type. It simply entails constructing "types" differently, through content-rich material elements such as glass, rather than through plot and characters as in the Aarne-Thompson-Uther index. Glass fits thematic patterns of death/abandonment (the forgotten girl among the cinders or encased in glass caskets, the prince wounded by the shards of his tunnel) and magical sexuality in a number of tales.

The glass slippers in Perrault's tale are the prince's connection to Cendrillon as the glass tunnel was for the girl and the prince in "Green Meadow." The glass slipper does not need to be a fragile object, proof of Cinderella's "fettered mobility" as Patricia Hannon (1988) interprets it in *Fabulous Identities*. She suggested that Cinderella's breakable glass slippers "should keep the heroine well within the bounds prescribed for her by the century's theorists on the nature of women" (Hannon 1988, 71).[19] On the contrary, Cendrillon's slippers seem to be agents of mobility, taking her back and forth and in and out of garden, carriage, and palace. She dances in them "so gracefully that she was even more admired" ["avec tant de grace qu'on l'admira d'avantage"]. When she flees from the prince in her slippers it is "as lightly as a doe" ["aussi légèrement qu'aurait fait une biche"], and she will keep the second slipper in her pocket to prove her identity (Perrault 1981, 176). In *Things That Talk*, Daston (2004) describes the imaginary of a world in which there are no things against which to struggle, with which to argue, or against which to stub a toe. Glass slippers are objects that thwart the feet of proud sisters and fix the gaze of the prince.[20] The slipper, like other glass objects in seventeenth-century tales, is the magical and visible/invisible connector, the object-proof of fairy power and of the ability of the fairies to write the stories they please. It is a narrated object on which a reader might usefully stub a metaphorical toe.

In both Basile and Perrault, crystal and glass have a potentially malleable form. In Basile it grows, in Perrault it fits "like wax" ["elle y était juste comme de cire"]. This may well be more than a metaphorical expression, the equivalent of "it fits like a glove" in English.[21] The fact that Antoine Furetière felt compelled to emphasize in his *Dictionnaire Universel* (1680) that glass was not malleable means that at least some of his contemporaries thought it was: "C'est une imagination de croire qu'on ait jamais eu l'invention du verre malleable" ["The notion that malleable glass has ever been invented is a fantasy"]. Furetière was not entirely sure himself, reporting in the next sentence that glass could have some flexibility and describing German glass bottles with such thin bottoms that one could make the bottles concave or convex by blowing into them or gently sucking the air out (Furetière 1978 [1690]). Not that it needs to be rationalized, but even for those who insist on rationalizing fairy marvel, a glass slipper that fits like wax makes sense within the imaginaries of glass in seventeenth-century Europe. I have never been sure what the rationalists do with frog fairies, butterfly men, or flying moles with rose leaf wings.[22]

The fairy tales by Basile, Perrault, d'Aulnoy, Murat, and others can easily be read among the reliquaries and the rock crystal and glass collections of the sixteenth and seventeenth centuries. It is pleasant to read them in the Museo degli Argenti in the Pitti Palace in Florence today, among the rock crystal animals: the winged crystal dragons and birds, and the fantastic crystal fish with swirling images etched on its sides.[23] The glass tales slip easily among the bowls and vases with gold and jeweled monsters that seem to be telling tales themselves, hybrids wrapping themselves into handles, hanging like the monsters sitting on d'Aulnoy's crystal palace. Luxury crystal objects played at the boundary between animal and mineral. One can easily imagine elaborate ships of rock crystal sailing off with the Italian court dwarf Morgante and tiny fairies on board.[24]

By the time Basile and then Perrault, D'Aulnoy, Murat, Lubert, and others wrote their tales of glass, luxury consumers and collectors purchased, used, and displayed an astounding array of glass objects as fanciful as any in a fairy tale, in styles that shifted with the technologies and the tastes of the day. Delicate glass birds perched on bowls and winged dragons coiled around the fragile stems of goblets. Wine was poured from ewers in the shape of blue or gilded leaping lions. Serving dishes for candy took the form of dolphins or putti. Scent bottles with elaborate glasswork on their round bellies sported exotic human heads as stoppers. In the Netherlands, an elegant glass beaker was mounted into a mechanical silver windmill,

Fratelli Saracchi, Vessel in the shape of a boat, 1587. Rock crystal, gold, enamels, cameos, emeralds. Museo degli Argenti, Polo Museale della città di Firenze, inv. Bg 1917 (III), no. 1.

probably for a drinking game. The notion of a glass shoe was hardly shocking or even particularly novel; drinking glasses in the form of gilded riding boots, or the footwear of a Roman soldier (see color insert, plate 1), had been part of the repertoire of Venetian glassmakers since the late sixteenth century. A seventeenth-century reader of Perrault who happened to have a copy of "Cendrillon" along with her/him during a visit to the *Kunstkammer* developed by Archduke Ferdinand II (r. 1563–95) and then by Archduke Leopold V (r. 1619–33) at Castle Ambras would have seen both the glass boot and the glass musical instrument that was displayed not with the glass collection, but among the musical instruments, as if it might itself produce music. Glass, in its construction and display throughout the Renaissance and the seventeenth century, was a substance of playful liminalities.[25]

It is not illogical to seek some meaning of tale elements in the places in which they grew. The Chinese version of the tale, with gold shoes, came from a gold-mining center, as Arthur Waley (1947) told us. Perrault's glass slipper appeared in a line of fairy tales with glass elements and at the time of what can only be described as a French mania for glass. Raymonde Robert, in *Le conte de fées littéraire en France*, tells some of the history of mirror and porcelain in society and in tales, reading them within the Rococo temptation of the vertigo of excess (Robert 1982, esp. 357–61). One can tell mercantile and political mirror tales of Versailles with workers brought in from Venice, spies sent to intercept them, bribes and incentives on both ends, laws about mirror imports, boatloads of mirrors confiscated, contraband circulating around France, inquisitors in Venice, murders in France during fights between workers, and a few suspicious deaths ascribed to poisoning (murder or accident we'll never know). Sabine Melchior-Bonnet, in *Histoire du Miroir* (1994), tells historical tales worthy of the fairies, or a spy novel.

Perrault's readers were consumers of crystal and glass. As Melchior-Bonnet reminds us, while a Venetian mirror framed in glass cost 8,000 livres, more than twice a painting by Raphael, there were also mirrors for all prices (Melchior-Bonnet 1994, 39). In 1686 Parisians watched the king ride across the Pont Notre-Dame lined with mirrors. They consulted Abraham du Pradel's *Livre commode des adresses* to learn where to buy microscope lenses (quai de l'Horloge) or to rent crystal chandeliers for their balls (a shop on rue St. Denis) (Blegny 1878, 2: 44; and Melchior-Bonnet 1994, 88). They bought so much Venetian glass that the French coffers hemorrhaged.[26] They were consumers and producers as well of the narratives of glass. They wrote letters about the latest discoveries and diplomatic skirmishes between Versailles and Venice; they read the news in the *Mercure Galant* of the ambassador of Siam's visit to the royal glassworks in Orléans. Some attended talks at the Académie des Sciences, others experimented with techniques in their own academies or gossiped about the alchemists who created the colors and the latest episode of false letters, intrigue, and dead glassworkers.

Unfortunately, in its transformation from a visual presentation to a written one, this article has had to shed most of its images, and the reader will have to look in books for the photographs that in Rome paraded behind these words. My reading of glass in "Cendrillon" has been done in the context of new historical work on one of the master glassmakers of the seventeenth century, Bernardo Perrotto, who became Bernard Perrot in France. He was an Italian glassmaker from Liguria who established himself in France. His inventions of glass and enamel that counterfeited agate and porcelain,[27] of a ruby red seen nowhere else, and of pouring large plate glass earned him a royal privilege, and he founded the royal glassworks at Orléans. The ruby glass has only recently been analyzed to reveal its secret recipe created by an alchemist in Torino (a recipe that apparently Perrot himself did not know): arsenic and gold.[28] Items made by Perrot or attributed with some degree of certainty to him include several glass portraits of Louis XIV, cups, glasses, bowls, serving dishes and decorative items with bits of his famous red, a suitor and a dolphin that look like they could be transformed objects from a fairy tale, marvelous bottles and flasks with fanciful human glass heads.[29] While I cannot include more than a few here, they can be seen in the richly illustrated catalog made on the occasion of a 2010 exhibition of Perrot's works: *Bernard Perrot (1640–1709): Secrets et Chefs-d'oeuvre des verreries royales d'Orléans.*

The exhibition catalog includes photographs of a table made for Louis XIV between 1668 and 1681 and attributed to Perrot (see color insert, plates 2 and 3). The table is mentioned in the inventory of the royal furniture in 1681, described as a table covered in various pieces of molten glass in several colors decorated with gilded incised copper dividers. It is 117 by 81 centimeters. How it traveled from Versailles to the collection of Sir Adrian Beecham in Stratford-upon-Avon is uncertain. It might have been in the collection of the painter François Boucher in 1752. It surfaced in London at an auction at Christie's in 1975 and then passed into private hands again in November 1988 in a sale at Sotheby's. The central scene is the judgment of Paris. Paris is surrounded by his dog, sheep, a bird, a butterfly, and a snail. Around him are ovals with Mercury and the three goddesses. At the corners are hunting scenes with forests, flowers, characters, and animals. Erwin Baumgartner and Jeannine Geyssant write that nothing like it has ever been known in the history of glass ("On peut conclure avec Hollister que cette table représente un tour de force et, aussi loin qu'on puisse remonter dans l'histoire du verre, que rien de semblable n'a été réalisé"; Baumgartner and Geyssant 2010, 66). It is at this table that I imagine Charles Perrault's book lying open as a courtier reads of Cendrillon and her shoe, perhaps an elegant glass by Bernard Perrot in hand.[30] Both works of glass—the literary work and the artistic table—belong to the world of the French court, and deciding which one is more fanciful would be almost impossible.

Michel Butor defined a fairy as what connected pumpkins to carriages, and his construction of a fairy as a space of connection has shaped my own work on fairy tales from the beginning (Butor 1960, 64). Fairy spaces are those of linkages among objects and within objects caught in moments of transformation, when a pumpkin shifts into a carriage, a slipper appears on a foot, and a prince finally learns through glass to recognize the body of his

Bernard Perrot. Element from a table centerpiece, late seventeenth century–early eighteenth century. Glass. Paris, Musée des Arts Décoratifs, inv. 23438. Photo les Arts décoratifs, Paris/Jean Tholance.

Bernard Perrot, Element from a table centerpiece (Dolphin), late seventeenth century. Glass. 24.5 x 11 x 8 cm. Paris, Musée des Arts Décoratifs, inv. LOUVRE OAP 788.35. Photo les Arts décoratifs, Paris/Jean Tholance.

princess-to-be. Charles Perrault was not terribly voluble on fairy details, so I will need to leave it to the reader to imagine what Cinderella's glass slippers might have looked like in the mind's eye of Perrault's seventeenth-century readers: etched rock crystal or the sparkling new glass that vied with it; a Venetian affair decorated with millefiori; or perhaps like Louis XIV's table, bearing nude gods and fanciful hunting scenes. For Cendrillon, Bernard Perrot's ruby red glass made with deadly arsenic and precious gold would work particularly well. It would remind the prince and the princess of the dangers that may be lurking in enchanted glass things—tunnels or shoes—even when they bring fairy-tale lovers together.

Appendix

Cinderella's Shoes: The *Glass/Fur, Verre/Vair* Controversy in Dictionaries and Encyclopedias

A Brief Overview

Although I originally intended to include the enduring popular notion that Cinderella's slippers had once been of *fur*, and not *glass*, as nothing more than a parenthesis in the history of perceptions of the Cinderella tale by the general public, the construction of an enduring fantasy of fur in the nineteenth-century French press and dictionaries is interesting enough to merit one more look. In the case of significant works that created or shaped the *verrre/vair, glass/fur* controversy I have located exact years when dictionary entries began, changed, or ended. In the case of twentieth-century dictionaries and encyclopedias, rather than check dozens of editions of dictionaries, I have occasionally isolated entry changes within approximately twenty-year periods. For previous discussions of the history of the slipper in dictionaries and encyclopedias, see B. (1896), Latham (1934, 1946), Delarue (1951, 1982), and Dundes (1982).

Works in French

Press, Nineteenth Century

1839. Théophile Gautier. "Feuilleton de la Presse. Théâtre Italien. *La Cenerentola.*" *La Presse*, November 4, 1839, 1–3.

1841. Honoré de Balazc. "Les Lecamus: Etude Philosophique." *Le Siècle*, March 23, 1841, 1–3 (episode 1).

Larousse

1867. Pierre Larousse, *Grand dictionnaire universel du XIXe siècle.* The third volume of the *Grand dictionnaire universel* [1866–76] appeared in 1867, with an entry for "Cendrillon":

> Beaucoup de ceux qui n'ont lu le joli conte de *Cendrillon* que dans les livres qu'on mettait entre leurs mains pour les amuser quand ils étaient

enfants seront surpris sans doute de ne plus retrouver ici cette pantoufle de *verre* qui avait frappé, plus que tout le reste peut-être, leur imagination naissante. Quoi de plus joli qu'une pantoufle transparente qui laissait voir, comme s'il eût été nu, ce charmant petit pied dont le fils du roi se montre si amoureux! Et quelle devait être la légèreté de cette jeune fille, qui pouvait marcher et danser avec des pantoufles si fragiles sans qu'elles se brisassent! Il semble que le conte de Perrault perd beaucoup de son prix dès que la pantoufle de Cendrillon n'est plus qu'une pantoufle de *vair*, c'est-à-dire une pantoufle ornée d'un peu de fourrure. Les éditeurs de contes de fée ont-ils mis *verre* à la place de *vair* par ignorance, ou pour augmenter le merveilleux du récit? Nous ne savons. Mais ce qu'il y a de certain, c'est qu'au temps de Perrault le *vair* était bien connu comme une des fourrures du blason, et que, malgré son goût pour le merveilleux, il n'a point eu la pensée de chausser sa petite Cendrillon avec du *verre*. On peut supposer que, plus tard, la science du blason étant tombée dans l'oubli, un imprimeur aura cru corriger une véritable faute en remplaçant *vair*, mot qui lui était inconnu, par *verre*; et c'est ainsi que le nom de Cendrillon se sera trouvé associé avec l'idée d'une chaussure fantastique que la vérité historique est forcée de reléguer parmi les simples coquilles typographiques.

Many who have read the pretty tale of Cendrillon only in books that were given them as children to amuse them, will doubtless be surprised to no longer find here that *glass* slipper that, perhaps more than anything else, had struck their budding imagination. What could be prettier than a transparent slipper which showed, as if it were naked, that charming little foot of which the prince becomes so enamored. And how light the young girl must have been, who could walk and dance in such fragile slippers without them breaking! The tale by Perrault seems to lose a good deal of its impressiveness when Cendrillon's slipper is no longer anything but a slipper of *vair*, that is to say, a slipper decorated with a bit of fur. Did the editors of fairy tales replace *vair* by *glass* out of ignorance, or to heighten the marvel of the tale? We do not know. But what is certain is that in Perrault's time, *vair* was well known as one of the furs of heraldry, and that, despite his taste for marvel, he had no intention at all of giving little Cendrillon shoes of glass. We can surmise that, later, the science of heraldry having been forgotten, a printer might have thought he was correcting an actual error, when he replaced *vair*, a word unknown to him, with *glass*; and it is in this way that the name of Cendrillon became associated with the idea of a

> fantastic shoe which historical truth is obliged to relegate to the realm of simple typographical misprints.

The entry included several quotations from nineteenth-century texts with Cendrillon references, including the comparison of a pair of gloves to Cendrillon's slipper in Henry Murger's *Les Vacances de Camille*, from 1857.

[1898–1904] *Nouveau Larousse illustré*

The editors/writers of the *Nouveau Larousse illustré* were still on the fence in the *verre/vair* controversy, with the entry heading now reading "Cendrillon ou *la Petite Pantoufle de verre (*ou *de vair)*" ["Cendrillon or *the Little Slipper of Glass* (or *of Fur*)"]. However, the entry now leaned clearly, if not entirely decidedly, toward "glass":

> En ce qui concerne les pantoufles de Cendrillon, on écrit tantôt de *vair* (fourrure), tantôt de *verre*. Cette dernière version paraît être la bonne, malgré son invraisemblance, parce que les ouvrages en verre filé de Venise jouirent d'une très grande vogue sous Louis XIV.

> Concerning Cendrillon's slippers, sometimes it is written [they are] of *vair* (fur), sometimes of *glass*. The latter version seems to be the right one, despite its implausibility, because works in spun glass from Venice were greatly in vogue during the reign of Louis XIV.

1960, *Grand Larousse encyclopédique*

By 1960, the Larousse had explicitly corrected the entry line, which now read: "Cendrillon ou *la Petite Pantoufle de verre* (et non *de vair*)" ["Cendrillon or *the Little Slipper of Glass* (not *of Fur*)"]. The entry attributed the "hypothesis" that had appeared in Larousse since 1867 to the ambiguous French "on," which can be translated as "they," "someone," or, as I will do below, by the guiltless passive voice:

> A propos des pantoufles de Cendrillon, on a émis l'hypothèse qu'elles étaient de *vair* (fourrure) et non de *verre*, comme l'a écrit Perrault; mais dans un conte de fées une telle recherche de la vraisemblance parait inutile.

On the subject of Cendrillon's slippers, the hypothesis was advanced that they were of *vair* (fur) and not of *glass* [*verre*], as Perrault wrote it; however in a fairy tale, such a search for plausibility seems pointless.

1982, *Grand Dictionnaire Encyclopédique Larousse*

By 1982 all mention of fur was gone, the history of the error eliminated, and the entry heading was simply "Cendrillon ou *la Petite Pantoufle de verre*" ["Cendrillon or the Little Slipper of Glass"].

Littré
1873. Émile Littré, *Dictionnaire de la langue française.*

In Littré's dictionary, the tale appeared under the entry for *vair*:

> C'est parce qu'on n'a pas compris ce mot maintenant peu usité qu'on a imprimé dans plusieurs éditions du conte de Cendrillon souliers de verre (ce qui est absurde), au lieu de souliers de vair, c'est-à-dire souliers fourrés de vair.
>
> It is because this now rarely used word was misunderstood that several editions of the tale of Cendrillon were published with the words glass shoes (which is absurd), instead of fur shoes, that is to say fur-lined shoes.

Today's online version takes care to note that certain passages bear the mark of their time, and must be read in their historic context.

Grand Robert
1985. Paul Robert. *Le Grand Robert de la Langue Française.*

While the text acknowledges that Perrault's title was "pantoufle de verre," a *pantoufle de vair* remains a lexicographical entity in this twentieth-century dictionary:

> Vx. Fourrure d'une espèce d'écureuil (le petit-gris). Menu-vair. *La pantoufle de vair de Cendrillon.* —Rem. Le texte orginal du conte de Perrault est "*la Petite Pantoufle de verre.*"

Old. Fur of a type of squirrel (common gray). Lesser Vair. *Cendrillon's slipper of vair.* —Rem. The original text of the story by Perrault is "the Little Slipper of Glass."

Tresor de la langue française
[1994–2014]. *Trésor de la langue française informatisé.*

> —Pantoufle de vair. [P. allus. au conte de Ch. Perrault, *Cendrillon*, où le mot était orthographié *verre*] Certaines fourrures rares, comme le vair [. . .] ne pouvaient être portées que par les rois, par les ducs, et par les seigneurs (. . .). Ce mot, depuis, cent ans, est si bien tombé en désuétude que, dans un nombre infini d'éditions de contes de Perrault, la célèbre pantoufle de Cendrillon, sans doute de menu vair, est présentée comme étant de verre (BALZAC, *Martyr calv.*, 1841, p. 53). C'est par erreur (. . .) qu'on a dit que les pantoufles de Cendrillon étaient de verre? (. . .) Des chaussures de vair, c'est-à-dire des chaussures fourrées ce conçoivent mieux (FRANCE, *Livre ami*, 1885, p. 321).

> —Fur slipper [Allusion to the tale by Ch[arles] Perrault, *Cendrillon*, where the word was spelled *glass*]. Certain rare furs, like vair [. . .] could be worn only by kings, dukes, and lords (. . .). This word, after a hundred years, has fallen into disuse to such an extent that in an infinite number of editions of the tales of Perrault, Cendrillon's famous slipper, doubtless of lesser *vair*, is presented as being of *glass* (BALZAC, *Martyr calv.*, 1941, p. 53). Was it by error (. . .) that it has been said that Cendrillon's slippers were of glass? (. . .) Fur shoes, that is to say shoes lines with fur are more believable (FRANCE, *Livre ami*, 1885, p. 321).

The excerpted quote in the entry is from Anatole France's 1885 "Dialogue sur les contes de fées" in *Le Livre de mon ami*. In the dialogue the character Laure's remarks on fur-lined slippers concluded comically that it had been a bad idea to give a girl going to a ball fur-lined shoes, for Cendrillon must have had feet "pattus comme un pigeon" ["like those of a feather-footed pigeon"]. It provokes a rebuke from Raymond, one of her two interlocutors: "Cousine, je vous avais pourtant bien avertie de vous défier du bon sens. Cendrillon avait des pantoufles, non de fourrure, mais de verre, d'un verre transparent comme une glace de Saint-Gobain, comme l'eau de source et le cristal de roche. Ces pantoufles étaient fées; on vous l'a dit, et cela seul lève toute difficulté" ["Cousin, I had already warned you however to beware of common sense. Cendrillon had slippers not of fur, but of glass, a glass that was transparent like a Saint-Gobain mirror, like spring water and rock crystal. Those slippers were enchanted, you were told, and that in itself gets rid of the entire problem] (France 1892, 322). The dialogue was a playful overview of a variety of nineteenth-century approaches to fairy tales.

Works in English

Encyclopaedia Britannica
1910–11 through 1973

An entry "Cinderella" was added to the eleventh edition of the *Encyclopaedia Britannica* in 1910–11. There was no entry on Cinderella in either the first or in the ninth editions (and it was presumably not in any of the intervening ones as well, although I did not check them). The claim that *glass* in English was the result of a mistranslation in some unspecified English translation, added a new dimension to the argument:

> In the English version, a translation of Perrault's Cendrillon the glass slipper which she drops on the palace stairs is due to a mistranslation of *pantoufle en vair* ("a fur slipper"), mistaken for *en verre.*

1974

The entry was changed in the fifteenth edition, first published in 1974, and still available online today, to:

> The prince's recognition of the cinder maiden by the token of a "glass" slipper is unique in Perrault. In other versions of the story the test of recognition is often a golden or silver slipper or ring.

The quotation marks around *glass* but not around *golden* or *silver* clearly imply that *glass* might be something other than *glass*. This case of an implied questioning of one a word in an entry—the logic of which is not clarified for readers—is worth a study in itself.

Encyclopedia Americana
[post 1965]

The *Encyclopedia Americana*, first published in 1829, contains a late addition of the error. While I have not checked all earlier editions, the 1918 edition had no entry for Cinderella, and the entry in the 1965 edition was correct in its description of the slipper: "In her flight she loses one glass slipper. . . . The midnight hour is Perrault's and so is the glass slipper." At some point after 1965 a new entry appeared over the byline for James Reeves [1909–1978] "author of *English Fables and Fairy Stories*": "The tradition of her 'glass' slipper is probably the result of misreading the French *vair*, which is a kind of fur, for *verre*, meaning 'glass'" (1984 edition). Ironically, Reeves introduced the *Encyclopedia Britannica*'s tale of mistranslation into the *Encyclopedia Americana* around the same time that the *Britannica* was divesting itself of it.

Acknowledgments

I thank the following individuals and institutions for their kind permission to reproduce photographs and for assistance in obtaining images and permissions: Graziano Raveggi of the Polo Museale della citta di Firenze (fig. 2.1); Florian Kugler and Ilse Jung of the Kunsthistorisches Museum, Vienna (fig. 2.2); Rachel Brishoual of the Photothèque des Musées des Arts Décoratifs, Paris and Jean Tholance, photographer (figs. 2.3 and 2.4); Joanna Ling of Sotheby's London for permission, Jeannine Geyssant for images, and Erwin Baumgartner and Jeannine Geyssant for the history of Louis XIV's table (figs. 2.5 and 2.6). Martine Hennard Dutheil, Gillian Lathey, and Monika Woźniak are thanked for their support throughout.

Notes

1. A note on works relating to museum studies or "thing studies" could easily be longer than the present article. The approaches that underlie my own work include those of Asma (2004), Bal (2004), and Daston (2004). For an overview of my own approach to object studies, see Hoffmann (2010).
2. I am playing off Claude-Gilbert Dubois's watery imagery of the baroque: "Il s'éparpille comme l'eau, il se multiplie, s'élance, rebondit, se déverse en cascades, se divise en ruisselets," ["It flows like water, it multiplies, leaps forward, splashes back, spills forth in cascades, divides itself into rivulets"] (Dubois 1995, 82, cited in Malarte-Feldman, 101–2). Translation mine, based on Malarte-Feldman's. Unless otherwise indicated, all translations are mine throughout.
3. "They tell the fabulous story that, when she was bathing, an eagle snatched one of her sandals from her maid and carried it to Memphis; and while the king was administering justice in the open air, the eagle, when it arrived

above his head, flung the sandal into his lap; and the king, stirred both by the beautiful shape of the sandal and by the strangeness of the occurrence, sent men in all directions into the country in quest of the woman who wore the sandal; and when she was found in the city of Naucratis, she was brought up to Memphis, became the wife of the king, and when she died was honoured with the above-mentioned tomb" (Strabo 1932, Book XVII, Chap. 1: 33, p. 94).

4. Saintyves's bibliography incorrectly gives the first name of Emmanuel Cosquin as "Emile."
5. "la pantoufle de *vair* (et non de verre, matière peu propice aux pantoufles), ne nous semble pas un moyen dramatique inférieur au mouchoir l'Otello" (Gautier 1839, 1).
6. From Balzac's serialized "Les Lecamus" the first episode of which appeared in *Le Siècle*, on March 23, 1841: "On distinguait le grand et le menu vair. Ce mot, depuis cent ans, est si bien tombé en désuétude que, dans un nombre infini d'éditions des contes de Perrault, la célèbre pantoufle de Cendrillon, sans doute de *menu vair*, est présentée comme étant de *verre*. Dernièrement, Théophile Gautier, un de nos poètes les plus distingués dont la prose vaut la poésie et dont l'instruction doit être remarquée par un temps où la plupart des écrivains ne savent rien était obligé de rétablir la véritable orthographe de ce mot pour l'instruction de ses confrères les feuilletonistes en rendant compte de la Cenerentola, où la pantoufle symbolique est remplacée par un anneau qui signifie peu de chose." ["In the past, the distinction was made between greater and lesser *vair*. This word, after a hundred years, has fallen into disuse to such an extent that in an infinite number of editions of the Tales of Perrault, Cendrillon's famous slipper, doubtless of *lesser vair*, is presented as being of *glass*. Recently, Théophile Gautier, one of our most distinguished poets whose prose is like poetry and whose education is notable in a time when writers know nothing, was obliged to reestablish the true spelling of the word for the edification of his serial writer colleagues in his review of Cenerentola, where the symbolic slipper is replaced by a ring that signifies little."] When the story was included as "Le Martyr Calviniste" in the *Etude Philosophique Sur Catherine de Médicis* in the *Comédie Humaine*, Gautier's name no longer appeared (Balzac 1951, 51). "Les Lecamus" was set in: "Une maison qui n'existe plus, au coin qui n'existe plus de la rue de la Vieille-Pelleterie qui n'existe plus, dans un Paris qui n'existe plus." Spoelberch de Lovenjoul recounted the history of the remarks by Balzac and Gautier on *vair* (Spoelberch Lovenjoul 1897, 68), with an error in the date of "Les Lecamus," which he gave as May 23 (23 mai). The correct date is March 23 (23 mars), 1841.

7. Freud wrote: "The foot is a very primitive sexual symbol already found in myths. Fur is used as a fetich probably on account of its association with the hairiness of the *mons veneris*." He expanded in the footnote: "The shoe or slipper is accordingly a symbol for the female genitalia" (Freud 1938, 567 and 567n2).
8. Latham hoped then the discussion was over: "Espérons donc qu'à l'avenir le mot *vair*, en ce qui concerne la pantoufle de Cendrillon, n'existera plus." ["Let us hope in the future that the word *vair* in the context of Cinderella's slipper, will no longer exist."]
9. Rougier cited both Delarue and Latham in his preface to the tale in the Garnier Frères edition (Perrault 1967, 155). See also Soriano (1968, 141–45).
10. Web pages include question and triva sites, a Disneycentral board, a shoe blog, and other blogs, and even an engineer's proposal for a workable design for glass slipper. A selection: http://disneycentralplaza.englishboard.net/t13272-cendrillon-pantoufle-de-verre-ou-vair; http://www.trivia-library.com/b/cinderella-did-not-lose-a-glass-slipper.htm; http://www.shoeblog.com/blog/friday-shoe-history-corner-fairy-tale-edition-cinderella-shoes/; http://www.eetimes.com/electronics-blogs/pop-blog/4398472/Engineer-solves-Cinderella-glass-slipper-dilemma, all last accessed April 21, 2013.
11. The Disney store today sells a presonalizable glass slipper: http://www.disneystore.com/figurines-keepsakes-collectibles-personalizable-large-cinderella-glass-slipper-by-arribas/mp/1311211/1000276/.
12. "and the body of Alexander was carried off by Ptolemy and given sepulture in Alexandria, where it still now lies—not, however, in the same sarcophagus as before, for the present one is made of glass" (Strabo, 1932, Book XVII, Chap. 1: 8, p. 37).
13. Saint Bernadette in Lourdes is one of the later girls in glass. Academic scholarship on the history of the "incorruptibles" remains sparse. Cruz (1977) is written from the perspective of a believer. It includes sites displaying "incorruptibles," dates, and a few photos, but is of limited academic use.
14. Claude Lévi-Strauss developed notions of binary oppositions and binary operators in myth. See Lévi-Strauss (1955) and (1990) (chapter "Binary Operators," 537–60).
15. "quello, che soleva venire nudo correndo di furia, si conciò in maniera tale fra quelle schegge di cristallo che vederlo faceva compassione [. . .] le ferite furono così mortali che non ci giovava alcun rimedio umano" (Basile 1994, 191).
16. "Elle bâtit au milieu du lac de vif-argent un palais de cristal, qui voguait comme l'onde; elle y renferma la pauvre reine et sa fille ["In the middle of

the lake of mercury, she built a palace of crystal that floated with the waves; she shut the poor queen and her daughter in it"] (Aulnoy 1785, 333).

17. With thanks to Tatiana Korneeva for the reference to Murat's tale.
18. The history of beliefs in the powers of crystal from the ancient world to today in alchemy, magic, astronomy, medicine, and funerary practices is too vast and complicated for this essay. In Perrault's time, the entries related to "cristal" in Antoine Furetière's *Dictionnaire Universel* include rock crystal and its use in treating diarrrhea and dysentery, clear glass manufactured at Murano as a luxury item, glass eyes, and Ptolemy's crystal spheres. Talairach-Veilmas (2013) traces the later history of crystal in Victorian fairy tales and glass archicture in *Moulding the Female Body*. Crystal maintains a lively presence in contemporary fairy tales and fantasy literature today, including, to mention just two, the crystal balls of the Harry Potter series (Rowling 1999) and the crystal Lacrima of the *Fairy Tail* manga (which confer a range of powers from communication to explosion and even tanning). Thousands of books on "crystal healing" and innumerable websites and boutiques attest to the continuing fascination with crystal and beliefs in its magical powers.
19. Hannon's symbolic interpretation of the fragility of glass is shared by other critics, including Dundes, who wrote: "Glass is a standard symbol of virginity. It is fragile and can be broken only once. In Jewish wedding ritual, the groom crushes a glass under his foot—for good luck" (Dundes 1982, 111).
20. "Imagine a world without things. It would not be so much an empty world as a blurry, frictionless one: no sharp outlines would separate one part of the uniform plenum from another; there would be no resistance against which to stub a toe or test a theory or struggle stalwartly. Nor would there be anything to describe, or explain, remark upon, interpret, or complain about—just a kind of porridgy oneness. Without things, we would stop talking" (Daston 2004, 9).
21. "On dit aussi, d'un habit qui est fort juste à celuy qui le porte, qu'il luy est fait comme de cire" (*Dictionaire de l'Académie française* 1694).
22. The butterfly men are in the Comtesse de Murat's "Le Prince des Feuilles" (Murat 1994, 73), the flying moles with rose-leaf wings are from La Force's "Plus Belle que Fee" (La Force 1994, 9).
23. Coppa a forma di uccello. Bottega dei Fratelli Saracchi. Seconda metà del secolo XVI. Inv. Gemme 1921 n. 721; Tazza con copercio a forma di drago. Botttega dei Fratelli Saracchi. Seconda metà del secolo XVI, Inv. Bg. 1917 (III) n. 14; Vaso a forma di pesce su piede. Botteghe Granducali, 1570 ca. Pezzi di cristallo de rocca legati da bane in oro smalto. Altezza cm 18; lunghezza cm 30. Inv. Bg. 1917 (III) Cristalli n. 18 (Mosco and Casazza 2004, 68, 69, 70).

24. Fonte da tavola a forma di antica galera. Fratelli Saracchi, 1587. Cristallo di rocca con intagli. Inv. Bg 1917 (III) n. 1. (Mosco and Casazza 2004, 74).
25. Some of the examples in this paragraph are taken from the richly illustrated *Beyond Venice*, by Page, Doménech, et al. (2004), with essays on the production and consumption of Venetian and Venetian-style glassware in Austria, Spain, France, the Low Countries, and England between the sixteenth and mid-eighteenth centuries.
26. The term *hemorrhaged* is Melchior-Bonnet's, see especially pages 39–42.
27. "M. Perrot Maître de la Verrerie d'Orléans, a trouvé le secret de contrefaire l'Agathe et la Porcelaine avec le Verre et les Emaux. Il a pareillement trouvé le secret du Rouge des Anciens, et celuy de jetter le Verre en moulle pour faire des bas reliefs et autres ornemens. Il a son Bureau à Paris sur le quay de l'Orloge à la Couronne d'or" ["Mr. Perrot, Master Glassmaker of Orléans, has found the secret of using glass and enamel to counterfeit agate and porcelain. He similarly found the secrets of the Ancients' Red, and of pouring glass to make bas reliefs and other ornaments. He has his office in Paris on the Quai de l'Orloge at the Golden Crown"] (Blegny 1878, 44).
28. All the information on Perrot is taken from Geyssant 2014 and the essays in *Bernard Perrot (1640–1709): Secrets et Chefs-d'oeuvre des verreries royales d'Orléans.* See particularly: Corine Maitte "Bernardo Perrotto, un verrier migrant d'Altare au XVIIe siècle" (29–34), Christian de Valence "Bernard Perrot, maître de la verrerie d'Orléans. Biographie" (35–42), Jeannine Geyssant "Secret du verre rouge transparent de Bernard Perrot" (51–54), and Jeannine Geyssant, Isabelle Biron, and Mark T. Wypyski, "Flacons travaillés à la lampe" (979–86).
29. In addition to the pieces shown here, see; "Pièce de surtout en forme de berger de fantaisie agenouillé," attribué à Perrot, dernier tiers XVIIe–début XVIIIe siècle. Pièce de surtout. Paris: musée du Louvre, département des Objets d'art inv. OA 12173 (*Bernard Perrot*, fig. 49, 126–27); putto assis sur un socle . . . porte dans ses mains posées sur ses genoux un gobichon en verre incolore, contenant une confiserie surmontée d'un fruit rouge groseille. Verre soufflé-moulé, porcelané blanc . . . Collection particulière, fig. 51, p. 128. Flacon Lehman, New York: Metropolitan Museum of Art, inv. 1975.1.1561a, b. and Flacon en forme de gourde miniature à deux renflements, private collection J. Geyssant (*Bernard Perrot*, 78–86, 151).
30. Images in *Bernard Perrot*, 56–63.

References

Ashliman, D. L. 1998–2012. Cinderella. Aarne-Thompson-Uther folktale type 510A and related stories of persecuted heroines translated and/or edited. Available at http://www.pitt.edu/~dash/type0510a.html, last accessed May 12, 2013.

Asma, Stephen T. 2001. *Stuffed Animals and Pickled Heads: The Culture and Evolution of Natural History Museums*. Oxford: Oxford University Press.

Aulnoy, Madame (Marie-Catherine) d'. 1698. *Suite des Contes nouveaux ou des Fées à la mode*. 2 vols. Paris: Veuve de Théodore Girard.

———. 1785. *Nouveau Cabinet des Fées. 4, La Suite des "Contes des fees."* Geneva: Slatkine.

———. 1994. *Cabinet des Fées. Tome 1: Contes de Madame D'Aulnoy*. Edited by Elisabeth Lemirre. Paris: Piquier Poche, 63–83.

B., D. 1896. "Cinderella's Slipper: Glass or Fur." *Notes and Queries*, 8th series, vol. 10, 331–32.

Bal, Mieke. 2004. "Telling Objects: A Narrative Perspective on Collecting." In *Grasping the World: The Idea of the Museum*, edited by Donald Preziosi and Claire Farago, 84–102. Aldershot, England: Ashgate, 2004. Originally published in *The Cultures of Collecting*, edited by John Elsner and Roger Cardinal, 97–115 (London: Reaktion Books, 1994).

Balzac, Honoré de. 1839 [1831]. *La Peau de Chagrin*. Paris: Chaptentier.

———. 1841. "Les Lecamus: Etude Philosophique." *Le Siècle*, March 23: 1–3 (episode 1).

———. 1951. "Le Martyr Calviniste," part 1 of *Sur Catherine de Médicis, Etudes Philosophiques II, La Comédie Humaine*, 49–71. Paris: Gallimard, La Pléaide.

Basile, Giambattista. 1932. *The Pentamerone*. Translated from the Italian of Benedetto Croce by N. M. Penzer. New York: Dutton, Day 2, Tale 8. http://www.pitt.edu/~dash/type0709.html#youngslave, last accessed April 21, 2013.

———. 1994. "Verdeprato." In *Il racconto dei racconti overro Il trattenimento dei piccoli*. Translated by Ruggero Guarini. Milan: Alelphi Edizioni, 188–95. Original title: "Verde prato," in *Lo cunto de li cunti overo lo trattenemiento de' peccerille*.

———. 2007. *The Tale of Tales or Entertainment for the Little Ones*. Translated by Nancy Canepa. Detroit: Wayne State University Press.

Baumgartner, Erwin, and Jeannine Geyssant. 2010. "La table de Louis XIV." In *Bernard Perrot (1640–1709): Secrets et Chefs-d'oeuvre des verreries royales d'Orléans*, 55–66. Orléans: Musée des Beaux-Arts d'Orléans.

Bernard Perrot (1640–1709): Secrets et Chefs-d'oeuvre des verreries royales d'Orléans. 2010. Exhibition. Orléans: Musée des Beaux-Arts d'Orléans.

Bettelheim, Bruno. 1976. *Uses of Enchantment: The Meaning and Importance of Fairy Tales.* New York: Knopf.

Blegny, Nicolas de. 1878. *Livre commode des addresses de Paris pour 1692 par Abraham du Pradel.* Vol. 2, p. 44, précédé d'une introduction et annoté par Edouard Fournier. Paris: P. Daffis.

Butor, Michel. 1960. "La Balance des Fées." *Répertoire.* Paris: Minuit, 64.

Cosquin, Emmanuel. 1922. *Les Contes Indiens et l'Occident: Petites monographies folkloriques à propos de contes Maures.* Paris: Champion.

Cruz, Joan Carroll. 1977. *The Incorruptibles: A Study of the Incorruption of the Bodies of Various Saints and Beati.* Rockford, IL: Tan Books and Publishers.

Daston, Lorraine. 2004. *Things That Talk: Object Lessons from Art and Science.* New York: Zone Books.

Delarue, Paul. 1982. "From Perrault to Walt Disney: The Slipper of Cinderella." In *Cinderella: A Casebook*, edited by Alan Dundes, 112–14. New York: Wildman Press. Originally published in *Le Monde*, February 7, 1951, 7.

Dictionaire de l'Académie française. 1694. Dictionnaires d'autrefois. artflx.uchicago.edu, last accessed May 14, 2013.

Dictionnaire de la langue française. 1994. Edition nouvelle. Versailles: Encyclopedia Britannica France.

Dundes, Alan, ed. 1982. *Cinderella: A Casebook.* New York: Wildman Press.

Encyclopaedia Britannica; or, a dictionary of arts and sciences. 1768–71. 3 vols. Edinburgh: Society of Gentlemen in Scotland.

Encyclopaedia Britannica; or, a dictionary of arts, sciences, and general literature. 1878–89. 9th ed. 25 vols. New York: C. Scribner's Sons.

Encyclopaedia Britannica. 1910–11. 11th ed. Cambridge: Cambridge University Press.

Encyclopaedia Britannica. 1929. 14th ed. Cambridge: Cambridge University Press.

Encyclopedia Americana: A Library of Universal Knowledge. 1918–20. 30 vols. New York: Encyclopedia Americana Corporation.

Encyclopedia Americana. International Edition. 1984 [1965]. 30 vols. Americana Corporation. Danbury, CT: Grolier.

France, Anatole. 1892. *Le Livre de mon ami.* Paris: Calmann Lévy.

Freud, Sigmund. 1938. *Three Contributions to the Theory of Sex.* In *The Basic Writings of Sigmund Freud*, translated and edited by A. A Brill. New York: Modern Library.

Furetière, Antoine. 1978 [1690]. *Dictionnaire universel.* 3 vols. La Haye et Rotterdam. Paris: SNL-Le Robert.

Gautier, Théophile. 1839. "Feuilleton de la Presse, Théâtre Italien, *La Cenerentola.*" *La Presse*, November 4, 1–3.

Geyssant, Jeannine. 2014. "Bernard Perrot (1640–1709), maître de la verrerie d'Orléans: Ses innovations dans le context verrier européen du XVIIe siècle." *Sevres: Revue de la Société des Amis du Musée National du Céramique* 23: 30–43.

Grand Dictionnaire Encyclopédique Larousse. 1982. GDEL: Librairie Larousse.

Grand Larousse encyclopédique. 1960. 10 vols. Paris: Librairie Larousse.

Hannon, Patricia. 1988. *Fabulous Identities: Women's Fairy Tales in Seventeenth-Century France*. Amsterdam: Rodopi.

Hoffmann, Kathryn A. 2010. "Vertebrae on Which a Seraph Might Make Music." *PMLA* 125 (1): 152–60.

La Force, Charlotte-Rose de Caumont de. 1994. "Plus Belle que Fee." In *Le Cabinet des Fées*, vol. 2, edited by Elisabeth Lemirre, 7–31. Paris: Piquier Poche.

Larousse, Pierre. 1867. *Grand dictionnaire universel du XIXe siècle*. 15 vols. Paris: Librarie Classique Larousse et Boyer.

———. [1898–1904]. *Nouveau Larousse illustré, dictionnaire universel encyclopédique*. Paris: Librairie Larousse.

Latham, Edward. 1934. "A propos d'une erreur littéraire." *Mercure de France* 243: 176–79.

———. 1946. "La petite pantoufle de verre." *Notes and Queries* 191: 233–34.

Lévi-Strauss, Claude. 1955. "The Structural Study of Myth." *Journal of American Folklore* 68 (270); *Myth: A Symposium* (October–December): 428–44.

———. 1990. *The Naked Man: Mythologiques*, vol. 4. Chicago: University of Chicago Press.

Littré, Émile. 1873–74. *Dictionnaire de la langue française*, vol. 4. Paris: Hachette.

Lubert, Marguerite de. 2005. *Contes*. Edited by Aurélie Zygel-Basso. Paris: Champion.

Malarte-Feldman, Claire-Lise. 1997. "Perrault's Contes: An Irregular Pearl of Classical Literature." In *Out of the Woods: The Origins of the Literary Fairy Tale in Italy and France*, edited by Nancy L. Canepa, 99–128. Detroit: Wayne State University Press.

Melchior-Bonnet, Sabine. 1994. *Histoire du Miroir*. Paris: Hachette.

Mosco, Marilena, and Ornella Casazza. 2004. *Il Museo degli Argenti: Collezioni e collezionisti*. Florence: Giunti.

Murat, Henriette-Juliette de Castelnau (Comtesse de). 1710 [1698]. "Le Palais de la Vengeance." *Le Nouveau Cabinet des Fées. Par Madame de M****. Paris: Veuve Ricoeur, 19–28.

———. 1994 [1698]. "Le Prince des Feuilles." In *Le Cabinet des Fées*, vol. 2, 61–82. Edited by Elisabeth Lemirre. Paris: Piquier Poche.

New Encyclopaedia Britannica. 1974. 15th ed. 30 vols. *Micropedia*. Vol. 2. Chicago: Encyclopaedia Britannica. Also available at http://www.britannica.com/.

Page, Jutta-Annette, Ignasi Doménech, et al. 2004. *Beyond Venice: Glass in Venetian Style, 1500–1750*. Corning, NY: Corning Museum of Glass.

Perrault, Charles. 1697. "Cendrillon ou la petite pantoufle de verre." *Histoires ou contes du temps passé, avec dez Moralitez*. Paris: C. Barbin.

———. 1967. *Contes*, textes établis avec introduction . . . par Gilbert Rouger. Paris: Garnier Frères.

———. 1981. *Contes*. Edited by Jean-Pierre Collinet. Paris: Gallimard.

Ranke, Kurt, Hermann Bausinger, Rolf Wilhelm Brednich, et al. 1977–. Enzyklopädie des Märchens*: Handwörterbuch zur historischen und vergleichenden Erzählforschung*. Berlin: Walter de Gruyter.

Robert, Paul. 1985. *Le Grand Robert de la Langue Française*. Paris: Le Robert.

Robert, Raymonde. 1982. *Le conte de fées littéraire en France de la fin du XVIIe à la fin du XVIIIe siècle*. Nancy: Presses Universitaires de Nancy.

Rousset, Jean. 1954. *La Littérature de l'âge baroque en France: Circé et le paon*, 181–82. Paris: José Corti.

Rowling, J. K. 1999. *Harry Potter and the Prisoner of Azkaban*. New York: Scholastic Press.

Saintyves, Pierre [Emile Nourry, pseud]. 1987. *Les Contes de Perraut et les récits parallèles*. Paris: Editions Robert Laffont.

Soriano, Marc. 1968. *Les Contes de Perrault: Culture savante et traditions populaires*. Paris: Gallimard.

Spoelberch de Lovenjoul, Charles de. 1897. *Etudes balazciennes: Autour de Honoré de Balzac*. Paris: Calmann Lévy.

Strabo. 1932. *Geography*. Translated by H. L. Jones. London: Loeb Classical Library. Vol. 3. Book XVII available at http://penelope.uchicago.edu/Thayer/E/Roman/Texts/Strabo/17A3*.html, and http://penelope.uchicago.edu/Thayer/E/Roman/Texts/Strabo/17A1*.html, last accessed May 15, 2103.

Talairach-Vielmas, Laurence. 2013. *Moulding the Female Body in Victorian Fairy Tales and Sensation Novels*. London: Ashgate.

Thompson, Stith. 1955–58. *Motif-Index of Folk-Literature: A Classification of Narrative Elements in Folktales, Ballads, Myths, Fables, Mediaeval Romances, Exempla, Fabliaux, Jest-Books, and Local Legends*. Bloomington: Indiana University Press.

Trésor de la langue française informatisé. Available at http://www.atil.fr, last accessed February 9, 2014.

Waley, Arthur. 1947. "The Chinese Cinderella Story." *Folklore* 58 (1): 226–38.

3

The Translator as Agent of Change

Robert Samber, Translator of Pornography, Medical Texts, and the First English Version of Perrault's "Cendrillon" (1729)

Gillian Lathey

An international conference with the travels of one tale as its sole focus, such as the one held at Sapienza University in Rome in November 2012, depends almost entirely on the work of translators and adaptors. Cinderella texts have global currency thanks to individuals who are largely anonymous, forgotten, or ignored because, as George Steiner lamented in his book *After Babel*: "the great mass of translation has left no records" (Steiner 1975, 274). Moreover, biographical research in literary studies became deeply unfashionable in the late twentieth century, while in the same period the cultural turn in translation studies also largely left the life, if not the times, of the translator out of the picture. Yet a translator's choices and legacy depend not only on the sociocultural context within which he or she works but also on personal interest and idiosyncrasies of style. Andrew Chesterman has pursued this neglected aspect of translation studies by adopting a hypothetical translator's voice to emphasize his or her investment in a translation: "My personal beliefs and opinions, and to some extent even perhaps my personality, affect the kinds of solutions I tend to prefer, the decisions I make" (Chesterman 1998, 216). Anthony Pym has also argued in favor of the human translator as the starting point for historical research on translation: "Only through translators and their social entourage (clients, patrons, readers) can we try to understand why translations were produced in a particular historical time and place" (Pym 1998, ix). Although translators sit at the center of a nexus of publishers, economic conditions, and audience demands, they are nevertheless, as Chesterman argues, "agents of change, not just passive recipients of causal impulses" (1998, 219).

Against the background of this new interest in the translator's agency, I intend to devote the rest of this paper to the translations of one Robert Samber, who was the first to render Cinderella—or Cinderilla as he named her—into English in a translation of Perrault's Mother Goose tales in 1729. His is a translation that not only became a popular and frequently reprinted version from the late eighteenth century onward but also continues to be highly regarded. Brian Alderson, children's literature historian and critic, evaluates the English translations of Perrault thus: "It's my view that not many have equalled Robert Samber at the very start of things" (Alderson 1998, 15). So who was Robert Samber, and what does archival material tell us about his translation activity? What kind of personal touches did he add to the tales, including "Cinderilla," and in what ways did he act as an agent of change? This article addresses the context of the English version of Perrault's tales within Samber's life and work, provides evidence both of his voice in peritextual material and of the young implied reader inscribed within the translated text, and concludes with a brief overview of the literary-historical impact of Samber's translation of Perrault.

Robert Samber and Translation in Eighteenth-Century England

At a time when—according to *The Oxford History of Literary Translation in English*—there were "freer dealings with the continental publishing industry" and jobbing translators multiplied (Hopkins and Rogers 2005, 86), translators of children's books into English in the eighteenth century were a motley crew with translation as a sideline to work as journalist, cleric, author, or even stable boy and shoemaker (Lathey 2010). Anonymity was common, and to add insult to injury in Samber's case, it was thought until very recently that Samber purloined an existing translation of Perrault's tales when in fact the opposite is the case. To cut short a long story, thanks to the detective work of those great children's literature collectors and scholars Iona and Peter Opie, we now know that a translation by one G. M., assumed at one stage to be Guy Miège, did not in fact predate Samber's.[1] But, unfortunately for Samber, editions of his translation attributed to "G. M." soon outnumbered those that bore Samber's name. This was not, as we shall see, the only time that Samber's work suffered such a fate. In piecing together Samber's history I am indebted to J. M. Blom's work in rescuing him from obscurity in a substantial article with a comprehensive bibliography of Samber's publications (Blom 1989), and to the Bodleian

Library at Oxford University where I had access to copies of Samber's handwritten papers.

Samber lived from about 1682 to 1745; he was born into a wealthy professional family and was sent abroad for an education to France and Rome, where he no doubt acquired or improved his knowledge of French and Italian. On returning to England, however, Samber—as a younger son—had to earn a living. He began to do so as a writer, tackling a wide range of subject matter and issuing occasional verse such as an *Ode on Christmas-day* in 1716 and, after establishing the patronage of John Duke of Montagu, an epithalamium on the marriage of the Duke's daughter in 1730. Samber continued to work in this vein, celebrating births, marriages, and deaths in the family, while following his own mystical interests in writings on magic, necromancy, and freemasonry and drafting fiction and drama[2] that was never published.

Eclectic is the only word to use for Samber's output as translator; this was clearly not an era of specialized translation. Publications range from a travel guide to the art and architecture of Rome, to a description of Dutch trading practices, and from medical texts such as *The Art of Midwifery Improv'd* translated from the Latin of Hendrik van Deventer in 1716, to titles that seem downright bizarre. These include translations of *Long Livers: A Curious History of such Persons of both Sexes who have liv'd several Ages, and grown Young again* by Harcouet de Longeville published in 1722, with a sixty page dedication by Samber addressed to the freemasons; and *Ebrietatis encomium; or, the Praise of Drunkenness. Wherein Is Authentically, and most evidently prov'd, The Necessity of frequently getting Drunk* from the French of Albert Hendrik de Sallengre, published in 1723, in which Samber's preface disloyally mocks the freemasons' gluttony. Perhaps even more intriguing is *Eunuchism Display'd* from the French of Charles Ancillon of 1718, a text debating whether eunuchs are capable of marriage. The translation was "occasion'd," as the title page has it, by a young lady falling in love with a castrato at the opera house in the Haymarket, London, and wishing to become his wife. Last but not least, there is Samber's venture into pornography: his translation—one of many—from the French of Jean Barrin's *Venus in the Cloister; or, a Nun in Her Smock,* published in 1725. It is, indeed, one of the ironies of literary history that a translator of some of the best known children's stories—including Cinderella—was also responsible for a book seized by the authorities and cited in evidence against its publisher Edmund Curll in his trial for Obscene Libel in 1728.[3]

So, what do we glean from this list of publications that is of relevance to Samber's translation of Perrault's tales? First of all it is clear that Samber

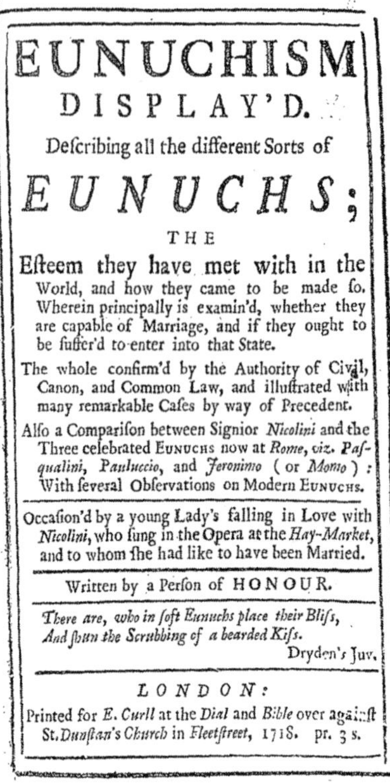

EUNUCHISM DISPLAY'D.

Describing all the different Sorts of

EUNUCHS;

THE

Esteem they have met with in the World, and how they came to be made so. Wherein principally is examin'd, whether they are capable of Marriage, and if they ought to be suffer'd to enter into that State.

The whole confirm'd by the Authority of Civil, Canon, and Common Law, and illustrated with many remarkable Cases by way of Precedent.

Also a Comparison between Signior *Nicolini* and the Three celebrated EUNUCHS now at *Rome*, *viz.* *Pasqualini*, *Pauluccio*, and *Jeronimo* (or *Momo*): With several Observations on Modern EUNUCHS.

Occasion'd by a young Lady's falling in Love with *Nicolini*, who sung in the Opera at the *Hay-Market*, and to whom she had like to have been Married.

Written by a Person of HONOUR.

There are, who in soft Eunuchs place their Bliss,
And shun the Scrubbing of a bearded Kiss.
Dryden's Juv.

LONDON:

Printed for *E. Curll* at the *Dial* and *Bible* over against St. *Dunstan's Church* in *Fleetstreet*, 1718. pr. 3 s.

Frontispiece to Samber's translation of *Eunuchism Display'd* by Charles Ancillon, 1718, London: E. Curll. British Library Board.

could turn his hand to translating almost any kind of text in the interests of earning a living from publishers and patrons. Second, proposals among the Bodleian papers for translations of the homilies and orations of the late Pope Clement XI, which exists as an unpublished handwritten manuscript, and of Ovid's *Metamorphoses* with a list of potential subscribers, support the view that Samber exercised some autonomy in deciding what to translate and was not just responding to commissions. Third, Samber appears to have exercised considerable professional acumen in his approach to the task of translation, criticizing in the preface to his translation of Castiglione's *The Courtier* of 1724 an earlier Elizabethan version and insisting that he would never translate from a translation (see Blom 1989, 518). Amendments to the draft of the Pope Clement XI text also trace Samber's thought processes as he worked.

Finally, in considering why Samber chose Perrault, the existence among his papers of drafts and unpublished fragments of stories featuring animals, princes and princesses, and plays set in various parts of the world testify to

CHINESE
TALES:
Or, The WONDERFUL
ADVENTURES
OF THE
Mandarine Fum-Hoam.

In TWO VOLUMES.

Adorned with CUTS.

Tranflated from the FRENCH.

To which is added,
An INTRODUCTION on the
Doctrine of TRANSMIGRATION.

VOL. I.

LONDON:
Printed for J. BROTHERTON at the *Bible*, and
W. MEADOWS at the *Angel* in *Cornhil*.
MDCCXXV.

Frontispiece to Samber's translation of *Chinese Tales* by Thomas-Simon Gueullette, 1725, London: E. Curll and T. Edlin. British Library Board.

a particular interest in composing fantastical tales and romances. Pursuing a hint on a freemason's website, I have also tracked down a translation by Samber of Thomas-Simon Gueullette's "Chinese Tales" ("Les Aventures merveilleuses du mandarin Fum Hoam: Contes chinois") published in 1725 by Brotherton and Meadows. Although there is no acknowledgment of the translator in this edition, *Parker's Penny Post* of Friday, December 3, 1725 (issue no. 93) identifies its serialized translation of the *Chinese Tales* as that "translated from the French by the ingenious Mr. Samber" and already on sale "by Mr. Brotherton at the Bible, and Mr. Meadows at the Angel."

In translating the *Chinese Tales* Samber no doubt wished to capitalize on the vogue for oriental tales in the wake of the *Arabian Nights*, first published in English in 1706, since—in a pattern similar to that of the "Nights"—the Chinese tales are told over a number of evenings. Moreover, English versions of Madame d'Aulnoy's *The History of Adolphus, Prince of Russia* (1691) and a further set of tales published in 1699[4] had given rise to an interest in fairy tales. But once again Samber's star was against him, for a pirated version of his translation by the Reverend Thomas Stackhouse was published in the following year, 1726, by Edmund Curll, and became far more successful than Samber's. Stackhouse has been careful to make alterations, but even explanatory footnotes are, with minor rewording,[5] copied from Samber.

Samber's Translation of Perrault's Tales

So—despite the wiles of his unscrupulous colleague—we can surmise from this translation of the Chinese tales and his own narrative fragments that Samber was predisposed toward tales of wonder and, as Blom suggests, "picked a winner" (Blom 1989, 520) when he decided to translate the Mother Goose tales. Sadly, however, there exists no evidence as to how the translation came about or a draft copy among the Bodleian papers. All that is known for certain is that Samber translated from a Dutch reprint of the French text of the 1721 edition of Perrault's tales, where the tales appear in a different sequence from that of the original 1697 edition (Barchilon and Pettit 1960). What does rapidly become clear, however, is that whereas Perrault had produced a collection of polished versions of nursery stories to serve as entertainment for the French aristocracy, Samber definitely had the child reader in mind. Samber's dedication of his translation to the Right Honourable Countess of Granville commends Perrault's morally instructive tales to her "Infant Relatives."

Moreover, in the course of the dedication Samber praises what he calls "fables" as conveyors of wisdom to the young, and responds robustly to previous criticism of some of the tales as "low and childish," asserting that "therein consists their Excellency. They therefore who made this as an Objection, did not seem very well to understand what they said; they should have reflected that they are designed for Children" (A4 verso). He also adds a few decided opinions on appropriate reading matter for the young. Samber claims, despite the inclusion of "Puss in Boots" in the collection, that animal stories are not appropriate for the young since children cannot be expected to understand "irrational" behavior and are only moved by human tales, preferably of other children. This comment ignores the anthropomorphism of Puss and countless other fictional animals, but does at least indicate the devotion of some thought to the needs of a child readership. In Samber's eyes, the stories in Perrault's collection were essentially children's tales, albeit dressed up for the French court, and he intended to return them to their rightful readers. In an instance of the shift from adult to child audience between source and target texts that Zohar Shavit has described in her *Poetics*

Frontispiece to Samber's translation of *Histories or Tales of Past Times* by Charles Perrault, 1729, London: Pote and Montagu. British Library Board.

of Children's Literature (1986), Samber places the tales firmly in the realm of childhood, and that is where they were to remain in subsequent English-language editions.

Samber's translation comprises nine tales with relevant morals in verse, including several that now dominate the English-language fairy-tale canon, such as "The Little Red Riding Hood," "The Sleeping Beauty in the Wood," "The Master Cat or Puss in Boots," and "Cinderilla, or the Little Glass Slipper." He also includes the lengthy "The Discreet Princess or the Adventures of Finetta, a Novel," written by Mlle l'Héritier, Charles Perrault's niece, a less child-friendly work that soon disappeared from English collections of the tales. As well as placing the child reader in the foreground in his dedication, Samber adds occasional footnotes and comments for his young audience that are not part of Perrault's text. In "The Sleeping Beauty" local villagers tell the prince who finds the moribund castle hidden in thick woods a story that an ogre had lived there. Samber inserts into the tale a definition of "ogre" that conveys a tongue-in-cheek admonition typical of the storyteller accustomed to speaking to children: "Now an Ogre is a giant that has long teeth and claws, with a raw head and bloody bones, that runs away with naughty little boys and girls, and eats them up" (Perrault 1729, 43). Nor does Samber hesitate to offer a wry footnote to the same story that the "Sauce Robert," which the prince's cannibalistic mother intends to use as a garnish to her roasted granddaughter, is "a French sauce, made with onions shred, and boiled tender in butter, to which is added, vinegar, mustard, salt, pepper and a little wine" (51). Elsewhere he uses domesticating strategies in the interests of his young readers: "custards" replace "galettes" in Little Red Riding Hood's basket of goodies for grandma, and the child is named "Biddy," a common form of the girl's name Bridget. In other tales Samber offers readers explanations of the meaning of the untranslated, eponymous heroes of "Riquet à la Houpe" and "Little Poucet," indicating that "*Houpe* signifies a Tuft" in the first instance and that the child's name "signifies little Thumb" in the second.[6]

"Cinderilla, or the Little Glass Slipper"

As he does in all the tales, Samber produces in "Cinderilla" a narrative that reads aloud well, is elegant in style, and corresponds very closely to Perrault's text. Samber makes fewer amendments than in other tales, but here, too, he occasionally makes tiny additions to clarify events, for example, the information that Cinderilla's stepmother had been a widow—just in case child readers had missed that point or, as the sisters depart for the ball, expanding "on partit" (Perrault 1698, 97) to "they went to court" (Perrault 1729, 77) as a reminder of their destination. In other instances Samber elaborates existing description: the coach "tout doré" (Perrault 1698, 98) is rendered as the tautologous "gilt all over with gold" (Perrault 1729, 78) to drive the point home; similarly, he exaggerates the prince's gasp of astonishment on first seeing Cinderella by repeating it: "ha! how handsome she is, ha! how handsome she is" (Perrault 1729, 82). Embellishments of this kind add to the rhythm of the prose or to the intensity of the imagined scene. There are, too, a few touches of early eighteenth-century colloquial English, as when Cinderella dare not tell her father of her treatment because he "would have rattled her off" (Perrault 1729, 75). No doubt many a child hearing or reading the tale had been "rattled off" in a similar manner. The niceties of late seventeenth-century French women's fashion present Samber with his greatest challenge, one to which he rises magnificently with a "tirewoman" to dress the sisters' heads and adjust their "double pinners" and a "diamond stomacher" (Perrault 1729, 76).

The playful wit manifested in the ogre definition and the Sauce Robert recipe in Sleeping Beauty is evident here too when Samber renders the decoration on the elder sister's red velvet outfit, in French a "garniture d'Angleterre" (Perrault 1698, 95) as "French trimming" (Perrault 1729, 76). Linguistic jokes for adult amusement offers a glimpse of Samber's personality, as well as demonstrating the double address so characteristic of later children's literature. While he clearly writes for a child audience, Samber nevertheless occasionally maintains the role of Perrault's text as adult entertainment, and does so particularly in the translation of the two morals attached to the tale. Samber's preface *appears* to take the morals seriously; he praises them for encouraging virtue and "depressing" vice, comparing them favorably to the "useless Reflection" attached to the "trifling tales" of English authors. However, Samber's loyalty to the ironic spirit of the source text, to its rhyming format and witty expression of sentiments that were never intended to be soberly didactic, indicates that these words may be mere rhetoric. In his rendering of the second moral, with its message that a child's natural accomplishments will come to naught if godparents are tardy in promoting them, Samber adroitly manipulates syntax to fit the rhyme scheme in a manner only adults are likely to appreciate:

> But none of these rich graces from above,
> In your advancement in the world will prove
> Of any use, if Godfires make delay,
> Or Godmothers your merit to display. (Perrault 1729, 91)

Samber's translation of morals originally intended for the "préciosité" of the French court sits uneasily within tales to be read to children, so it is no surprise that the morals quickly disappeared from English-language versions of the tales.

Impact

To sum up: Samber's "Cinderella" has style, wit, and all the strategies of an accomplished storyteller that have ensured the longevity of his version in editions enjoyed by generations of child readers. How, then, did Samber's words gradually permeate English children's and fairy-tale culture? A few insights into this history will have to suffice. Cinderella's name is an obvious legacy, as is the decision—possibly made by Samber's publishers Pote and Montagu—to translate the placard in the frontispiece illustration to "Mother Goose's Tales," a decision that, as the Opies assert, "was the starting-point of the Mother Goose legend in English-speaking homes" (Opie and Opie 1974, 23). By using the tools of book history, Ruth Bottigheimer has established that "Perrault's tales became popular" in London's print trade "from the 1760s" (Bottigheimer 2002, 15).[7] From that point onward editions based on the Samber translation proliferated; *The Celebrated Fairy Tales of Mother Goose* published by J. Harris in 1817, for example, is clearly indebted to Samber's translation, as is an edition of *The Entertaining Tales of Mother Goose* published in Glasgow circa 1817, where Samber's translation is reproduced and the illustrated frontispiece from the Pote and Montagu edition copied.

Individual tales from Samber's translation, too, soon found a place in anthologies for the developing children's book market, with Cinderella and Little Red Riding Hood starting out as favorites. Both were included in a reading primer, *A Pretty Book for Children; or, an Easy Guide to the English Tongue*, first issued in about 1744,[8] and the same two tales appear in *The Top Book of All, for Little Masters and Misses,* first published in about 1760; these texts are definitely Samber's. Later editions include Andrew Lang's influential use of Samber's translations as the basis for the translations of Perrault's tales in *The Blue Fairy Book* of 1889[9] and one by the publisher Harrap, titled *The Fairy Tales of Charles Perrault* of 1922, that actually credits Robert Samber with the translation, albeit "revised and corrected by J. E. Mansion." Finally, a well-loved picture-book version illustrated by Errol Le Cain of 1972 delighted many young readers and continues to do so, and many scholars continue to refer to Samber's translations in the Opies' *The Classic Fairy Tales* of 1974. Despite the omission of Cinderella's second visit to the ball, Le Cain's is a modernized version of Samber's translation in which the prose retains Samber's, and therefore largely Perrault's, syntax. And, as Martine Hennard Dutheil de la Rochère (2011) has indicated, Angela Carter's retranslation of "Cinderella," published in 1977, deliberately takes Samber's translation as the starting point for a feminist revision of the tale.

Conclusion

There have, of course, been many translations of Perrault's "Cendrillon" into English since Samber's, yet his remains not only the first but also one of the most notable and enduring. Samber's primary position within the history of the translation of Perrault's tales, and the development of the fairy tale in English, is therefore assured. Andrew Chesterman has speculated on the potential impact of translations on existing literary traditions:

"target-language norms (and the target language itself) might be affected, under the influence of incoming translations. Literary genres might shift" (Chesterman 1998, 220). Credit is therefore due to mystic and jobbing translator Robert Samber for producing an English narrative of literary quality that replicated Perrault's written style, nudged the tales toward a child audience, and gave an invaluable impetus to the gradual and multifaceted development of the children's fairy tale. A hundred years later, solicitor and amateur scholar Edgar Taylor translated a selection of the Grimms' tales—including their version of the Cinderella story—into English, thus inspiring the Grimm Brothers' own "kleine Ausgabe" or "small edition" and setting in motion what Jennifer Schacker (2003) has called the worldwide "bourgeois commodification" of the collection. Both Samber and Taylor had an inestimable impact on the trajectory of the fairy tale and the fate of the Cinderella story in English and, as a result of relay translation, in other languages too. Since Antoine Berman first characterized translators as the "great forgotten" in all discussion on translation ("le grand oublié de tous les discours sur la traduction"; Berman 1993, 46), there has been a growing recognition that translators have acted as agents of change across literary history, and that many were indeed far more influential than the standard perception of them as faceless conduits or even willful bowdlerizers allows.

Notes

1. Iona and Peter Opie offer pretty conclusive evidence that Samber's was indeed the first translation in their introduction to *The Oxford Dictionary of Nursery Rhymes* (1951, 39–40), and that the mistaken attribution of the first translation to "G. M." arose because of a misprint of the Roman numerals in copies of the eleventh edition of *Histories or Tales of Past Times, told by Mother Goose, with Morals. Written in French by M. Perrault, and Englished by G. M. Gent,* so that its date read 1719 instead of 1799 (M.DCC.XIX instead of M.DCC.XCIX). This edition is now accessible for verification in the Opie Collection in the Bodleian Library at Oxford University. If the numerals had been correct, G. M.'s translation would have appeared ten years earlier than Samber's 1729 version.
2. Drafts include a tale in verse, "The Old Mouse and Her Little One," a fictional account of the adventures of a merchant of Bengal, and "Orosmanus: A Tragedy."
3. As far as I can establish, there exists only one rather faint copy of this text in the British Library. The frontispiece has an engraving of a nun wearing

a smock with a deep décolletée and engaged in the act of lifting it above her knees.

4. Palmer and Palmer (1973) discovered that in his *List of English Tales and Prose Romances Printed before 1740*, Arundel Esdale lists the first translation of an edition of d'Aulnoy's *Contes, Tales of the Fairies* by T. Cockerill as early as 1699.
5. A giveaway mistake occurs in Stackhouse's version in the copying of one of Samber's footnotes. Samber defines "Fiquaa," a beverage that Fum-Hoam's mother sells in her shop, as a kind of "beer" (Gueullette 1725, 1: 146)—whereas Stackhouse has her selling a kind of "bear" (Gueullette 1726, 138).
6. For further examples of Samber's translation strategies, alterations to the French text, and occasional errors, see Barchilon and Flinders (1981) and Malarte-Feldman (1999).
7. This was particularly the case once Benjamin Collins of Salisbury teamed up with the Newbery and Carnan children's booksellers in St. Paul's churchyard, to produce an edition without "The discreet Princess" in about 1769 (Bottigheimer 2002, 13). Blom's bibliography refers to subsequent editions of this volume in 1772, 1777, and 1780.
8. Both tales have the same illustrations as in the 1729 edition, although there are minor alterations to the texts.
9. I am grateful to Carole Henguely (master's thesis, "Invisible Translators of Fairy Tales: From Perrault's *Histoires ou Contes du temps passé* [1697] to Lang's *Blue Fairy Book* [1889]"), University of Lausanne, for documentation of this link.

Primary Texts

Ancillon, Charles. 1718. *Eunuchism display'd.* London: E. Curll.

The Celebrated Fairy Tales of Mother Goose. 1817. London: J. Harris.

The Child's New Spelling Primer; or, First Book for Children To which is added The Stories of Cinderilla and the Little Red Riding Hood. 1799. Dublin: Printed by T. Wilkinson, No. 40, Winetavern-Street (Price Two Pence).

The Entertaining Tales of Mother Goose. ca. 1817. Glasgow: Lumsden.

Gueullette, Thomas-Simon. 1725. *Chinese Tales; or, the Wonderful Adventures of the Mandarine Fum-Hoam. In two volumes. Adorned with Cuts. Translated from the French.* London: J. Brotherton and W. Meadows.

———. 1726. *Chinese Tales; or, the Wonderful Adventures of the Mandarin Fum-Hoam. Related by Himself To divert the Sultanta, upon the Celebration of her Nuptials. Written in French by M. Gueullette. Translated by the Revd.*

Mr. Stackhouse. With some thoughts concerning transmigration by the late Mr. Secretary Addison. London: E. Curll and T. Edlin.

Perrault, Charles. 1698. *Histoires ou contes du temps passé: Avec des moralitez*. Amsterdam: Jaques Desbordes.

Perrault, Charles. 1729. *Histories or Tales of past times with Morals*. Translated by Robert Samber. London: Pote and Montagu. Facsimile of the copy in Harvard University Library.

———. 1888. *Perrault's Popular Tales. Edited from the original editions with an introduction by Andrew Lang*. Oxford: Clarendon Press.

———. 1922. *The Fairy Tales of Charles Perrault*. Illustrated by Harry Clarke with an introduction by Thomas Bodkin. Translated by Robert Samber. Translation revised and corrected by J. E. Mansion. London: George G. Harrap.

———. 1972. *Cinderella or the Little Glass Slipper*. Illustrated by Errol Le Cain. London: Faber and Faber.

A Pretty Book for Children; or, an Easy Guide to the English Tongue. 1761. Vol. 1. 5th ed. London: J. Newbery, J. Hodges and B. Collins of Salisbury.

References

Alderson, Brian. 1998. "Little Red Riding Hood: A Chronology of Perrault's Tales, Primarily of English Translations, 1691–1800." *Children's Book History Society Newsletter* 60: 15–17.

Armitage, Edward. 1898. *Robert Samber*. Margate.

Barchilon, Jacques, and Peter Flinders. 1981. *Charles Perrault*. Boston: Twayne.

Barchilon, Jacques, and Henry Pettit. 1960. *The Authentic Mother Goose Fairy Tales and Nursery Rhymes*. Denver: Alan Swallow.

Berman, Antoine. 1993. "La traduction et ses discours." In *La Traduction dans le développement des littératures*, edited by J. Lambert and A. Lefevere, 39–48. Bern: Peter Lang.

———. 1995. *Pour une critique des traductions: John Donne*. Paris: Gallimard.

Blom, J. M. 1989. "The Life and Works of Robert Samber." *English Studies* 6: 507–50.

Bottigheimer, Ruth. 2002. "Misperceived Perceptions: Perrault's Fairy Tales and English Children's Literature." *Children's Literature* 30: 1–18.

———. 2005. "The Book on the Bookseller's Shelf and the Book in the English Child's Hand." In *Culturing the Child, 1690–1914: Essays in Memory of Mitzi Myers*, edited by D. Ruwe, 3–28. Lanham, MD: Children's Literature Association and Scarecrow Press.

Chesterman, Andrew. 1998. "Causes, Translations, Effects." *Target* 10 (2): 201–30.

Dutheil de la Rochère, Martine Hennard. 2011. "Les métamorphoses de Cendrillon: Étude comparative de deux traductions anglaises du conte de Perrault." In *Autour de la Retraduction*, edited by E. Monti and P. Schnyder, 157–79. Paris, Orizons.

Hopkins, David, and Pat Rogers. 2005. "The Translator's Trade." In *The Oxford History of Literary Translation in English*. Vol. 3, *1660–1790*, edited by S. Gillespie and D. Hopkins, 81–95. Oxford: Oxford University Press.

Lathey, Gillian. 2010. *The Role of Translators in Children's Literature: Invisible Storytellers*. London: Routledge.

Malarte-Feldman, Claire-Lise. 1999. "The Challenges of Translating Perrault's *Contes* into English." *Marvels & Tales* 13 (2): 184–97.

Opie, Iona, and Peter Opie. 1951. *The Oxford Dictionary of Nursery Rhymes* (Oxford: Clarendon Press.

———. 1974. *The Classic Fairy Tales*. Oxford: Oxford University Press.

O'Sullivan, Emer. 2005. *Comparative Children's Literature*. Translated by Anthea Bell. London: Routledge.

Palmer, Nancy B., and Melvin D. Palmer. 1973. "English Editions of French *Contes de Fees* Attributed to Mme d'Aulnoy." *Studies in Bibliography* 27: 227–32.

Pym, Anthony. 1998. *Method in Translation History*. Manchester: St. Jerome Publishing.

Schacker, Jennifer. 2003. *National Dreams: The Remaking of Fairy Tales in Nineteenth-Century England*. Philadelphia: University of Pennsylvania Press.

Shavit, Zohar. 1986. *The Poetics of Children's Literature*. Athens: University of Georgia Press.

Steiner, George. 1975. *After Babel*. Oxford: Oxford University Press.

4

"Cendrillon" and "Aschenputtel"

Different Voices, Different Projects, Different Cultures

Cyrille François

Perrault's "Cendrillon, ou la petite pantoufle de verre" (hereinafter "Cendrillon") and the Brothers Grimm's "Aschenputtel" may tell similar stories, but there are significant differences between them, which can be interpreted as resulting from cultural differences. A nineteenth-century French translation of the *Kinder- und Hausmärchen* (hereinafter *KHM*), for example, specifies in a footnote:

> The German tale differs in almost every detail from that of Perrault; it is the reason why we have chosen it, to illustrate these curious differences on a same subject, reflecting the country's essence. (Grimm and Grimm 1869, 90; my translation)

The problem with such an interpretation, however, is that it is based on preconstructed visions of the German and French cultures, which are prone to lead to the reification of cultures, rather than to a cultural analysis.

There are different ways in which to study culture in fairy tales. In the field of art history, for example, one can search the texts for culturally related items, such as clothes or furniture (see, for example, Perrault 1967, 305–6; Morgan 1985, 93–94). As concerns literary analysis, the temptation has been to interpret elements of the tales––the actions of the characters, the moral message, and so on––in terms of cultural differences. Maria Tatar shows that one can be inclined to explain the end of "Cendrillon" and "Aschenputtel" by referring to "French charity and German cruelty" (Tatar 1987, 189). To counter this position, she reminds us that "Einäuglein, Zweiäuglein, und Dreiäuglein" ("One-eye, Two-eyes, and Three-eyes",

KHM 130) stages a heroine who is as compassionate toward her sisters as Cendrillon. In support of Tatar's point, it can also be stressed that cruelty can be identified in d'Aulnoy's French tale "Finette Cendron," where girls also cut off parts of their feet to fit the shoe (Aulnoy 2004, 454).

Tatar thus warns us that it would be a "hazardous business" to generalize about cultural differences based on comparisons between episodes in different versions of a tale:

> But is it really possible to compare a tale from Perrault's seventeenth-century collection of stories dedicated to the twenty-one-year-old Elisabeth Charlotte d'Orléans and a tale from the Grimms' nineteenth-century collection of stories designed for the folk? Perrault strained to please an aristocratic audience; the Grimms sought to capture the authentic voice of the common people. The manner inevitably affected the matter. (Tatar 1987, 188)

Highlighting how manner indeed affects matter, this study will demonstrate that "Cendrillon" and "Aschenputtel" are literary works that speak to their own particular context. This will be done through a textual analysis postulating, in the framework of discourse analysis, the interconnectedness and interdependence of text and context. As Maingueneau puts it:

> The "content" of a work is in fact pervaded by the reference to its conditions of enunciation. The context is not set outside the work, in a succession of layers, but the text is the actual management of its context. Works do indeed speak of the world, but their enunciation is a stakeholder in the world that they are meant to represent. (Maingueneau 2004, 34–35; my translation)

In this light, to consider a text as a "discourse" means to emphasize that textual characteristics are linked directly to the context in which a work emerges. The concept of "genre" is particularly helpful when it comes to articulating text and context. Perrault and the Grimms had different conceptions of the fairy-tale genre, and the tale-writing projects they embarked upon were influenced by their separate cultural settings and historical as well as personal circumstances: the authors belonged to a social milieu and were informed by and positioned themselves within a distinct literary and intellectual context. Now, textual differences between "Cendrillon" and "Aschenputtel" are related to Perrault's and the Grimms' understanding of the fairy-tale genre, which influenced their own literary practice; for example, is the narrator supposed to explain what happens and rationalize magic; does he use coordination or subordination; does he resort to humor, and if so, of what kind? All this is connected to the way the authors apprehended the genre, and hence the way they related to other texts, other authors, and, more generally, to their specific cultural context.

In an extensive foreword, the Grimms presented their project as an attempt to prevent German folktales from disappearing. They did in fact not do what they purported to be doing, as it is generally acknowledged that their sources were not the peasants they claimed to be their main informants, but principally young women from the local bourgeoisie, some of whom were of French descent (see for example Rölleke's afterword in Grimm and Grimm 1997 [1980] [1857], vol. 3). Furthermore, they made important changes and combinations, hence assuming an authorial role. Nonetheless, their project to collect German folktales can still be seen to have shaped the *KHM*. As regards Perrault, the frontispiece and the foreword of his *Histoires ou contes du temps passé* (*Stories or Tales of Past Times*) depict the texts as folktales of interest for France's rulers. This apparent simplicity hides the complexity of a double voice. The tales seem to tell simple stories for children, but throughout the book one hears an intrusive narrator who addresses the readers in a way that is typical of the burlesque tradition (see Escola 2005, and Sermain 1987). Perrault's project thus participates in a literary fashion of salon entertainment, while also playing an important role in the Quarrel of the Ancients and Moderns (see Morgan 1985, and Adam and Heidmann 2010).

This article explores the links between the narrative strategies and the particular cultural and historical contexts in which the tales of "Cendrillon" and "Aschenputtel" were written. First, an analysis of the moral message, the use of magic, and the characters will delineate the world in which the tales are set, linking this to the individual projects of the two authors. This part will also examine the transformations that the Grimms made between the first and the last editions of "Aschenputtel" in order to make the tale conform to the genre of the *Märchen* they were inventing and formalizing, and which came to distance their version of the story even further from Perrault's "Cendrillon." The analysis will then distinguish between Perrault's and the Grimms' narrators through a study of the type and length of the sentences as well as of causality. The way the tales are told will also be linked to the cultural specificity of the authors' differing projects.

The World of the Tales

“Cendrillon” and “Aschenputtel” are arguably set in different worlds, but rather than linking these worlds directly back to seventeenth-century France and nineteenth-century Germany, we will see how they can be identified in relation to specific tale-writing projects.

Beginnings, Endings, and the Moral

Both Perrault’s and the Brothers Grimm’s tales portray a heroine who is mistreated after her father marries an evil woman. In both cases, the heroine pulls through and marries a prince, but the two tales do not tell their stories in the same way, and they focus on different elements.

In “Cendrillon,” the narrator starts by describing a reconstituted family, composed of a widower and his daughter of “unparalleled goodness and sweetness of temper” as well as his second wife and her daughters, the “proudest and haughtiest” women ever seen (Perrault 1980 [1697], 117–18). From the outset, the text thus makes a clear parallel between Cendrillon and her sisters.

“Aschenputtel” does not start with a description of a recreated family, but with the dramatic episode of the death of the mother and the second wedding of the father. It emphasizes the special bond between the heroine and her dying mother, and the recommendation by the latter to remain good and pious (*fromm und gut*; Grimm and Grimm 1997 [1980] [1857], 119). As in many other tales of the *KHM*, family plays an important role, and the destabilizing influence of the stepmother is emphasized (see also *KHM* 13, *KHM* 15, *KHM* 49, or *KHM* 53, for example). As Tatar puts it, stepmothers are “alien intruders” that “disturb the harmony among blood relations” (Tatar 1987, 142).

The beginnings of “Cendrillon” and “Aschenputtel” both highlight the opposition between the heroine and her stepsisters, but differences emerge here as well, leading to two very different endings. Perrault’s text emphasizes the good attitude of the heroine that in the end even brings her to forgive her stepsisters “with all her heart” and to find them great lords for husbands (Perrault 1980 [1697], 145–46). The Grimms on the other hand highlight how the sisters are punished for their “wickedness” (*Bosheit*) and their “malice” (or “falseness”; *Falschheit*): two doves peck out their eyes as they walk with Aschenputtel to church for her wedding and then again as they leave (Grimm and Grimm 1997 [1980] [1857], 126). In their 1812 edition, the Grimms did not insist on the sisters’ punishment (their mutilation would seem punishment enough), and the tale ended on the birdsong that confirmed that Aschenputtel was the right bride. The Grimms introduced numerous changes between the 1812 and the 1857 editions of the *KHM*, mainly in the 1819 one, as they combined various similar stories in an attempt to reconstruct what they thought was the authentic folktale. These transformations were the result of choices that developed certain aspects found in other tales as well, and that contributed toward the creation of a *KHM*-type. The second ending of "Aschenputtel" thus corresponds better to their vision of the tale, where the punishment would have to be exemplary (see Grimm and Grimm 1986 [1812], XI).[1]

In terms of the morality of the tales, Aschenputtel consequently appears always to overcome adversity, because she follows her mother's advice: she remains good and pious ("fromm und gut"; about these adjectives, see Robinson 2010, 129–30 and 133–36) in spite of all the humiliations she suffers.[2] These qualities make her a "prototype of a bourgeois education," as noted by Uther (2008, 52). Like many other tales in the *KHM*, the educational dimension of "Aschenputtel" was further developed between the 1812 and 1857 editions.

In Perrault's *conte*, the heroine also demonstrates her "goodness," which is associated with her "sweetness of temper." In the moral attached to the French tale, the notion of "good grace" is used to complete her portrait. Sweetness, goodness, and good grace all forge a certain image of humanity, which can be associated with Christian morality, as suggested by Furetière in the entry on "bonté" (goodness) in his dictionary:

> in Christian morality, is used for virtue and especially charity, gentleness, morality, the inclination to help one's neighbor, patience to suffer afflictions, [and] insults. (Furetière 1690; my translation)

The definition suits Cendrillon well, since she suffers her sisters' taunts with patience.

At this point, it should be stressed that the moral message is given in a straightforward manner in "Aschenputtel," as the mother herself preaches to the heroine, reflecting the way morality is usually transmitted from an adult to a child. In "Cendrillon," the morality is only provided in the "morals," where the narrator directly addresses his adult contemporaries. We will see that Perrault's expression of a moral message leads to more ambiguity.

Both tales convey a morality based on cultural, and more precisely Christian, values, but there is a difference that may hint at a religious divergence. Perrault's tale takes place in a catholic society in which goodness and forgiveness are fundamental; as sins can receive absolution through confession, the sisters make an act of contrition (or at least seem to) and are forgiven by Cendrillon. The Grimms' tale, on the other hand, reflects a protestant society in which only God has the power to punish or to absolve. Aschenputtel neither forgives nor punishes her sisters, but acceptingly continues to live her life, while it is the doves that punish the sisters. Ever since the gospels, doves have been linked to the Holy Spirit (see Van der Toorn, Becking, and Van der Horst 1999, 263–64), which Ronald G. Murphy has shown to be of particular theological importance to Wilhelm Grimm. In his study of the personal bibles of the Grimms, Murphy noticed that most of the annotations made by Wilhelm in his copy of the new testament concerned the Holy Spirit, something that explains "the very prominent guiding presence" of doves in the *KHM*, "as [Wilhelm] rewrote them" (Murphy 2000, 39).

As tempting as this conclusion may be, it would be—as Tatar reminds us—hazardous to generalize cultural differences from a comparison of episodes. Considering "the manner that affects the matter," one should note that the Grimms considered the *KHM* as an *Erziehungsbuch* (educational book) in their foreword.[3] As seen earlier, according to their conception of the genre, villains have to be punished. The blinding of the sisters by the doves may thus reflect the values of a protestant society, but what we can ascertain from a textual approach is that it responds to a logic built into the book itself. While it could be argued that this logic is in turn based on protestant values, reducing the different endings of the tales to a mere religious difference is another matter.

This also applies to Perrault's tale. Perrault highlights virtues that are expected from ladies at court (like Mademoiselle, the king's niece to whom Perrault's collection of tales is dedicated). In his foreword to the *Histoires ou contes du temps passé*, Perrault expresses a wish to educate princes and princesses. This is in line with the 1695 foreword of the earlier collection known as *Contes en vers* (tales in verse), which claims that "everywhere virtue is rewarded, and everywhere vice is punished" (Perrault 1967, fifth page of the not paginated preface; my translation). Thus Cendrillon could be seen as an example of a good girl rewarded for being virtuous, and good people also forgive, so the tale is consistent with the alleged aim of the volume. But taking the forewords at face value means ignoring an important dimension of the tales. Indeed, Perrault writes not only to educate, and the cynicism of the second moral in "Cendrillon" serves as a reminder of the dimension of social critique also to be found in his tale: it is well and good to tell girls how to behave, but if they have no godmother or godfather, it will be to no avail. In such a society, the end of "Cendrillon" may underline not only the heroine's goodness but also her sense for strategy: she can manage alliances and keep her enemies close. In this light, d'Aulnoy's moral to "Finette Cendron" helps us to understand "Cendrillon" better. Finette's forgiveness is indeed all about vengeance:

> Pour tirer d'un ingrat une noble vengeance,
> De la jeune Finette imite la prudence,
> Ne cesse point sur lui de verser des bienfaits;
> Tous tes présents et tes services
> Sont autant de vengeurs secrets,
> Qui de son cœur troublé préparent des supplices. (d'Aulnoy 2004, 457)

> If it's revenge on the ungrateful you want to see,
> Then follow Finette's wise policy.
> Do favors of the undeserving until they weep.
> Each benefit inflicts a wound most deep,
> Cutting the haughty bosom to the core. (Zipes 1989, 416)

Magic

Generally speaking, Perrault's tale does not contain much magic. Moreover, it explains (humoristically) and rationalizes supernatural events, especially the fairy godmother's actions. Sainte-Beuve comments on this in his analysis of "Cendrillon":

> He has those tiny details which all of a sudden make an impossible thing probable. Thence, the mice that are changed into horses in *Cendrillon*, keep their coats in their new form, "a beautiful mouse-coloured dapple grey." The coachman, who was previously a big rat, keeps his moustache, "the finest whiskers as ever were seen." Common sense remains in all this. For a German, the fairy tale would be more marvellous, more fairylike in all aspects, uncorrected by reason. . . . But Perrault, while addressing children, knows well that these children will be rationalists tomorrow or the next day; he is from the same country and century as Descartes. . . . Perrault's soberness is French all right. His tales are not aimed at unbridled imaginations. (Sainte-Beuve 1884, 307–8; my translation, except the Perrault quote from Perrault 1729)

I would not be as categorical as Sainte-Beuve as regards the national character of these differences. Rather, they bear a similarity to those between the Grimms and Bechstein, as identified by Ruth Bottigheimer:

> Max Lüthi postulates an immediacy and directness about magic in fairy tales (Volksmärchen) which is true enough of the *KHM* but which does not characterize Bechstein's tales at all, and for good reason. Bechstein was clearly addressing a bourgeois child readership in its own language and through its own worldview. The grandchildren and great-grandchildren of the Enlightenment weren't supposed to believe in magic, and so it had to be explained. (Bottigheimer 1990, 64)

Both in Bechstein and in Perrault's tales, magic is explained. In "Cendrillon," Perrault even gives a logic to magical events (see Zuber 1997). The fairy's actions do not obey the laws of nature, but they are accomplished in a thought-through manner, following a logic that would be familiar to seventeenth-century readers. One could even speak of a parody of magic (see Sermain 1987, 543, and Barchilon 1967, 264–65), something that corresponds to Perrault's project to use fairy tales as literary entertainment.

In "Aschenputtel," however, magic is not rationalized, and its elements remain unexplained (see François 2011). This becomes even more obvious in the 1857 edition, in which Aschenputtel masters magic without the reader knowing how, as compared to the 1812 edition were she is being told what to do (see the table below). This also makes Aschenputtel into a much more active character, who does not wait for supernatural help, but who goes forward on her own.

1812	**1857**
The mother tells Aschenputtel to plant the tree	Aschenputtel has the idea herself
The birds come to help by themselves	Aschenputtel calls them
The birds tell her to ask for the dress	Aschenputtel asks the tree for what she wants
Midnight curfew, coach and clothes vanish	Aschenputtel decides to go home by herself

Unlike in "Cendrillon," magic is not rationalized in accordance with the reader's logical understanding. This sets the story in a timeless, fairy-tale world, where laws of nature do not apply in the same way as in our world. The Grimms' project aims for a collection of (allegedly) authentic folktales, hence the wish to render the story in a more neutral and universal form, close to what they thought the tale originally looked like. This wish for fidelity would be incompatible with a satiric rendering.

Characters

The relationship between the heroine and her family is also very different in Perrault's and in the Grimms' tales. In "Cendrillon," the father is absent, and, though the mother-in-law is cruel, the emphasis is put on the sisters. In "Aschenputtel," the father is present at key moments, especially at the beginning and at the end, and the mother-in-law is the main evil character. A comparison of the 1812 and the 1857 editions nevertheless shows that the first was closer to Perrault, with an absent father and sisters playing an important role. The exchange over Aschenputtel going to the ball is a good example. In the 1857 edition, she asks her stepmother if she can go to the ball. To prevent her from going, the latter responds by asking her to pick out lentils from the ashes. In the 1812 edition, Aschenputtel does not take the initiative; it is the stepsisters who ask mockingly if she wants to come along, as in Perrault's tale, and they are the ones who come up with the idea of the lentils chore. Similarly, the 1812 edition is closer to Perrault's tale in two other instances: Aschenputtel speaks to her sisters when they come back from the ball, telling her about it, and the younger sister is said to be kinder to the heroine.[4]

The changes from the 1812 to the 1857 edition therefore show that the stepsisters come to play a less important role and that the stepmother inversely gains in status. The differences with Perrault's tale are thus more clearly discernable, and "Aschenputtel" becomes more consistent with the rest of the volume, where stepmothers, as mentioned above, play an important role as villains. The shift from the stepsisters to the stepmother also affects the personality of the heroine.[5] In the 1857 edition, Aschenputtel is on the one hand more active, as seen above, in mastering magic and taking initiative, and she is mainly depicted through her actions. On the other hand, she appears as a submissive girl who obeys an abusive authority without complaint. In the 1812 edition, she was a livelier girl who denounced injustice, saying to herself, "wenn das meine Mutter wüßte!" (If my mother knew this!; Grimm and Grimm 1986 [1812], 90; my translation). She also showed her superiority to the stepsisters and manipulated them: she pretended to have been asleep when they came back from the ball (Grimm and Grimm 1986 [1812], 98), and she told them that they should have had fun at the ball when she knew that they were dying of envy (Grimm and Grimm 1986 [1812], 95). Aschenputtel's personality is thus more explicitly developed in the first edition, but while showing more temper, she is at the same time less active than in the 1857 edition. There is thus a shift from a wittier Aschenputtel who waits for good things to happen in the first edition to a submissive yet more active heroine.

In the French text, Cendrillon's wittiness is arguably one of her stronger merits. She may not be as active as Aschenputtel––although she proves resourceful when helping her fairy godmother––but remains superior to her stepsisters thanks to her spirit, as shown at the return from the ball. Perrault's use of double meaning is essential to entertain his readers, and his complex work follows a burlesque tradition. In such an endeavor, wit plays a central role, just as Cendrillon's wit appears to her advantage in the tale. For the Grimms, the tales contain an educational message in themselves. Aschenputtel is the role model of a good and pious person who is rewarded for being so. She does not need any extra features to illustrate this morality.

This goes to show that Perrault and the Grimms set their stories in very different worlds. While these worlds are anchored in seventeenth-century France and nineteenth-century Germany, they primarily reflect the projects developed by their authors, as expressed in their forewords. We will now see how a similar argument can be made with regard to the ways in which the tales are narrated.

Narration

The Grimms' tale opens with a sequence of actions: the sick mother calls her daughter, speaks, closes her eyes, and dies; the daughter goes to visit her grave, weeps, lives up to her mother's recommendations; the father takes a second wife. One can feel from the beginning the action-oriented narration, which gives the tale a quick rhythm:

> Einem reichen Manne dem wurde seine Frau krank, und als sie fühlte daß ihr Ende heran kam, rief sie ihr einziges Töchterlein zu sich ans Bett und sprach "liebes Kind, bleib fromm und gut, so wird dir der liebe Gott immer beistehen, und ich will vom Himmel auf dich herabblicken, und will um dich sein." Darauf that sie die Augen zu und verschied.
>
> Das Mädchen gieng jeden Tag hinaus zu dem Grabe der Mutter und weinte, und blieb fromm und gut. Als der Winter kam, deckte der Schnee ein weißes Tüchlein auf das Grab, und als die Sonne im Frühjahr es wieder herabgezogen hatte, nahm sich der Mann eine andere Frau. (Grimm and Grimm 1997 [1980] [1857], 119)

> The wife of a rich man fell ill, and as she felt her end approaching, she called her only daughter to her bedside and said, "Dear child, be good and pious. Then the dear Lord shall always assist you, and I shall look

> down from heaven and take care of you." She then closed her eyes and departed.
>
> After her mother's death the maiden went every day to visit her grave and weep, and she remained good and pious. When winter came, snow covered the grave like a little blanket, and by the time the sun had taken it off again in the spring, the rich man had a second wife. (Grimm and Grimm 2003, 79)

The beginning of Perrault's text contains fewer actions and more descriptions (here in bold):

> Il estoit une fois un Gentil-homme qui épousa en secondes nopces une femme, **la plus haütaine & la plus fiere qu'on eut jamais vuë.** Elle avoit deux filles **de son humeur, & qui luy ressembloient en toutes choses.** Le Mari avoit de son costé une jeune fille, **mais d'une douceur & d'une bonté sans exemple,** <u>elle tenoit cela de sa Mere, qui estoit la meilleure personne du monde.</u>
>
> Les nopces ne furent pas plûtost faites, que la Belle-mere fit éclater sa mauvaise humeur, <u>elle ne pût souffrir les bonnes qualitez de cette jeune enfant, qui rendoient ses filles encore plus haissables.</u> (Perrault 1980 [1697], 117–19)

> There was once upon a time, a gentleman who married for his second wife the proudest and most haughty woman that ever was known. She had been a widow, and had by her former husband two daughters of her own humour, who were exactly like her in all things. He had also by a former wife a young daughter, but of unparalleled goodness and sweetness of temper, which she took from her mother, who was the best creature in the world.
>
> No sooner were the ceremonies of the wedding over, but the mother-in-law began to display her ill humour; she could not bear the good qualities of this pretty girl; and the less, because they made her own daughters so much more hated and despised. (Perrault 1729, 73–74)

These descriptions are particularly important, as they are hyperbolic, that is, they place the events in a type of world where everything is exemplary, good or evil. The action-chain is also interrupted by explanations (underlined in the quote): the narrator says something and then pauses to explain.

Comparing the two beginnings, one notices that "Cendrillon" is told by a narrator with a strong presence, who organizes the various elements of the story into a narrative. The chain of events is interrupted to add details that explain and justify these events. In "Aschenputtel," the events "seem to tell themselves" (Benveniste 1966, 41); they follow chronologically without any need for added explanations.

On the level of syntax, this results in a very characteristic type of writing. The Grimms make use of short sentences, often with one subject to which several verbs are attached:

> Das Mädchen hieb ein Stück von der Ferse ab, zwängte den Fuß in den Schuh, verbiß den Schmerz und gieng heraus zum Königssohn. (Grimm and Grimm 1997 [1980] [1857], 125)

> The maiden cut off a piece of her heel, forced her foot into the shoe, swallowed the pain, and went out to the prince. (Grimm and Grimm 2003, 83)

This example shows the succession of events as well as the use of parataxis, where sentences are juxtaposed and coordinated like building blocks. By contrast, Perrault uses sentences that are slightly longer, and rarely coordinates them using the same subject, instead favoring hypotaxis; there are a lot of subordinate clauses, especially of relative clauses. For example, Perrault characteristically places relatives at the beginning of a sentence:

> Sa Maraine qui la vit toute en pleurs, luy demanda ce qu'elle avoit. (Perrault 1980 [1697], 125)

> Her godmother, who saw her all in tears, asked her what was the matter. (Perrault 1729, 78)

> Cendrillon qui les regardoit, & qui reconnut sa pantoufle, dit en riant (Perrault 1980 [1697], 143)

> Cinderilla, who saw all this, and knew the Slipper, said to them laughing (Perrault 1729, 87)

> sa Maraine qui estoit Fée, luy dit (Perrault 1980 [1697], 125)

> Her godmother, who was a Fairy, said to her (Perrault 1729, 78)

This type of relative clause often brings an explanation of what is to come, where the narrator justifies an event before telling it. The same effect is also created in the text through the use of present participles. Syntax helps to distinguish between more and less important events.

In the Grimms' tale, the narrator does not give explanations but merely tells the story without intruding into the narrative. The Grimms even tend to erase causality markers so that it is up to the reader to reconstruct the causal links:

> Da brachte das Mädchen die Schüssel der Stiefmutter, freute sich und glaubte es dürfte nun mit auf die Hochzeit gehen. (Grimm and Grimm 1997 [1980] [1857], 121)
>
> *Then the girl brought the bowl to the stepmother, rejoiced, and thought she could now go along to the wedding.* (My translation)

In the above example, there is no doubt as to why the heroine rejoices, but translators have sometimes felt the need to restore an explicit causality, as in this example:

> Happy, because she thought she would now be allowed to go to the wedding, the maiden brought the bowl to her stepmother. (Grimm and Grimm 2003, 81)

The syntactic differences between an action-oriented and paratactic "Aschenputtel" and a narrative interrupted with descriptions and explanations as in "Cendrillon" is in part related to the different languages they were written in. And yet the 1801 German collection of *Feen-Mährchen* (Marzolph 2000) is in fact quite close to Perrault in regard to the length of the sentences, the relatives, and the connectors. Nor would it appear that the differences between Perrault's and the Grimms' tales boil down to a question of style, as they must in fact also be linked to the different conceptions of the genre and the different projects of their authors.

As mentioned above, the Grimms present the *KHM* as a work that aims to preserve folktales in their foreword to the 1812 edition. As such, it is part of a larger project to collect all kinds of folk poetry (*Volkspoesie*). For the Grimms, tales have a divine origin, and they only claim to be transcribing authentic folktales—nature's own voice—without adding any personal elements (see Tonnelat 1912, 198, and Jolles 1974, 222–23). It is thus, according to them, simplicity and purity that guarantee the authenticity of the tales (Grimm and Grimm 1997 [1980] [1857], 21–22). This explains why they do not use a narrator commenting on the story from a contemporary perspective. It also explains why the narrative is action driven, and proceeds as if there were no narrator at all. The morality is not even that of the narrator, but it ensues from the story: a character is rewarded because s/he is good and another is punished because s/he is evil. This is in line with the Grimms' vision of their tales; they have emanated from nature, so, to respect their alleged divine origin, they should not be told in a socially or historically determined voice. Indeed, in the light of this argument, the Grimms criticized their contemporaries' use of folktales:

> There is still no collection of this kind [the *KHM*] in Germany, one has almost always only used them as material to make larger narratives out of them that arbitrarily widen, transform, that which they could otherwise have been worth, always taking away from children what is theirs, without giving them anything in return. Even he who thought about them couldn't refrain from blending in manners of the poetry of the time. (Grimm and Grimm 1986 [1812], XVIII–XIX; my translation)

The Grimms made several changes to their tales in the successive editions of the *KHM*, but they argue that this was not to assimilate them into their own body of literary works, but in order to retrieve what they thought was a more authentic form.

Perrault, on the other hand, does not pretend to be what can anachronistically be referred to as a folklorist. The emphasis on the morals sets his tales in the framework of La Fontaine's fables (see, for example, Zuber 1997, 277). The word even appears in the title: *Histoires; ou, Contes du temps passé: Avec des moralités* (*Stories; or, Tales of Past Times, with Morals*). Perrault presents short texts with added morals in which a narrator links an apparently simple story to a view on his contemporary society. This is set in a literary tradition and he already did the same kind of work with "Le labyrinthe de Versailles" (see Escola 2005, 173–74; Adam and Heidmann 2010, 212–13). Perrault writes his tales for a society used to double meanings, and there is no doubt that they would get the "Morale très-sensée . . . qui se découvre plus ou moins, selon le degré de pénetration de ceux qui les lisent" ("very-sensible moral . . . which is being more or less disclosed depending on the degree of insight of those who read them"; Perrault 1980 [1697], foreword, my translation). In this game between the narrator and the reader, the narrator does not try to disappear but shows himself telling the story and intrudes on every occasion.

Conclusion: Text-Project-Context

A comparative textual analysis demonstrates how culture not only affects the ideology of the tales (that is, characters being punished or forgiven, and such), but also shapes the way in which the tales are told. While exemplifying this through a comparison of "Cendrillon" and "Aschenputtel," this article has also illustrated a way of studying culture through textual analysis. While it would be tempting to link episodes to cultural settings directly (in a text-context configuration), I have proposed a useful mediation through the tale-writing projects of the authors, thus establishing a text-*project*-context configuration. Indeed, authors create a literary project in positioning themselves inside a culture (a literary one, but also a historical, social, and ideological one); they refer to other texts and also engage with the debates of their times. Considering authors not only as part of a cultural setting but also as active operators who carry out a project in interaction with this cultural setting allows for a more nuanced understanding of the text, as well as the broader contexts it both reflects and contributes to. This also brings to the fore significant differences between the works of authors of the same period and country, such as the Grimms', Bechstein's, Brentano's, and the anonymous 1801 *Feen-Mährchen* collection, for example. While these projects share the same cultural background, they nevertheless allowed for the development of highly individualized projects. A comparison of the 1812 and 1857 editions of the *KHM* shows that even a "single" project such as the Grimms' evolved and changed.

Mediating through the tale-writing projects of Perrault and the Grimms also proved useful in the comparison of "Cendrillon" and "Aschenputtel." The highlighted differences between the texts did not lead to the conclusion that the French and German cultures are different, which would be both simplistic and reifying, as seen in the introduction, but were rather explained in the framework of the distinct projects the authors had in mind, and their different conception of the fairy-tale genre. "Cendrillon" emphasizes forgiveness and humorously rationalizes magic. Furthermore, the tale is double-voiced, with a pseudo-naive narrative voice overseen by a subtly ironic (or "enjoué") narrator. This reflects the development of the fairy tale as a literary genre, which emerged through literary games and experimentations at the end of the seventeenth century (Sermain 2005). In contrast, the concept of "folk" culture much discussed in Germany at the time informed the Grimms' project (see Mondon 2007). As they sought to transmit what they saw as "nature's voice" in a seemingly transparent or unmediated fashion, the Grimms could and would not use the kind of intrusive narrator we find in Perrault.

Stories like "Cendrillon" and "Aschenputtel" are numerous and widespread, and the various versions not only differ from culture to culture but also within each culture through various literary projects. This undoubtedly contributes to the richness of the fairy-tale genre.

Acknowledgments

I would like to thank Martine Hennard Dutheil de la Rochère and Gillian Lathey for helping me clarify the argument and brush up the English of this essay.

Notes

1. The violent punishment plays an important role for the Grimms, and this distinguishes their tale from Perrault's: "How meaningful is the feature completely missing in the French that the mean sisters for a short while deceive the king's son by violently shortening their feet to be able to put the shoes on, but are betrayed by the doves" (Grimm and Grimm 1997 [1980] [1857], 3: 301; my translation).
2. The Grimms even link the two adjectives in their dictionary: "In older language the use of *gut* [good] was limited within the religious-moral sphere to retain a specific religious meaning, which was later supplanted by *fromm* [pious], but still continues to be relevant in more modern times" (Grimm and Grimm 1854–1960, "Gut," V, A, 2; my translation).
3. Only since 1819; the term was not mentioned in the first edition.
4. The younger sister is said to be "pas si malhonneste que son aisnee" (not as impolite as her elder) in Perrault, and to have "noch ein wenig Mitleid im Herzen" (still had a little compassion in her heart) in Grimm.
5. In her study of reported speech in "Aschenputtel," Bottigheimer notes that the stepmother has more direct speeches in the 1857 edition than in the 1812 one, while the girls have fewer direct speeches. Aschenputtel is thus "silenced" (Bottigheimer 1987, 53).

References

Adam, Jean-Michel, and Ute Heidmann. 2010. *Textualité et intertextualité des contes: Perrault, Apulée, La Fontaine, L'héritier*. Paris: Classiques Garnier.

Aulnoy, Madame (Marie-Catherine) d'. 2004. *Contes des fées: Suivis des Contes nouveaux ou Les fées à la mode*. Paris: H. Champion.

Barchilon, Jacques. 1967. "L'ironie et l'humour dans les 'Contes' de Perrault." *Studi francezi* 32: 258–70.

Bechstein, Ludwig. 1845. *Deutsches Märchenbuch*. Leipzig: G. Wigand.

Benveniste, Émile. 1966. *Problèmes de linguistique générale* I. Paris: Gallimard.

Bottigheimer, Ruth B. 1987. *Grimms' Bad Girls and Bold Boys: The Moral and Social Vision of the Tales*. New Haven, CT: Yale University Press.

———. 1990. "Ludwig Bechstein's Fairy Tales: Nineteenth-Century Bestsellers and Bürgerlichkeit." *Internationales Archiv für Sozialgeschichte der deutschen Literatur* 2 (15: 55–88.

Escola, Marc. 2005. *Contes de Charles Perrault*. Paris: Gallimard.

François, Cyrille. 2011. "Fées et weise Frauen: Les faiseuses de dons chez Perrault et les Grimm, du merveilleux rationalisé au merveilleux naturalisé." In *Des* Fata *aux fées: Regards croisés de l'Antiquité à nos jours*, edited by M. Hennard Dutheil de la Rochère and V. Dasen, 259–78. Lausanne: Special issue of *Etudes de Lettres* 289 (3–4).

Furetière, Antoine. 1690. *Dictionnaire universel*. Rotterdam: Arnoud and Reinier Leers.

Grimm, Jacob, and Wilhelm Grimm. 1854–1960. *Deutsches Wörterbuch*. Leipzig: S. Hirzel.

———. 1869. *Contes allemands du temps passé: Extraits des recueils des Frères Grimm, et de Simrock, Bechstein, Franz Hoffmann, Musæus, Tieck, Schwab, Winter, etc. avec la légende de Loreley*. Translated by F. Frank and E. Alsleben. Paris: Librairie académique Didier.

———. 1986 [1812]. *Kinder- und Hausmärchen: Vergrösserter Nachdruck der zweibändigen Erstausgabe von 1812 und 1815 nach dem Handexemplar des Brüder Grimm-Museums Kassel mit sämtlichen handschriftlichen Korrekturen und Nachträgen der Brüder Grimm*. 2 vols. Edited by H. Rölleke and U. Marquardt. Göttingen: Vandenhoeck und Ruprecht.

———. 1997 [1980] [1857]. *Kinder- und Hausmärchen, Ausgabe letzter Hand* (1857). 3 vols. Edited by H. Rölleke. Stuttgart: Philip Reclam.

———. 2003. *The Complete Fairy Tales of the Brothers Grimm*. Translated by J. Zipes. New York: Bantam.

Jolles, André. 1974. *Einfache Formen, Legende, Sage, Mythe, Raetsel, Spruch, Kasus, Memorabile, Maerchen, Witz*. Tübingen: M. Niemeyer Verlag.

Maingueneau, Dominique. 2004. *Le discours littéraire: Paratopie et scène d'énonciation*. Paris: Armand Colin.

Marzolph, Ulrich, ed. 2000. *Feen-Mährchen: Zur Unterhaltung für Freunde und Freundinnen der Feenwelt. Volkskundliche Quellen*. Hildesheim: Olms.

Mondon, Christine. 2007. "Le mythe du peuple: De Herder aux romantiques de Heidelberg." In *Le peuple, mythe et réalité*, edited by Jean-Marie Paul, 17–27. Rennes: Presses Universitaires de Rennes.

Morgan, Jeanne. 1985. *Perrault's Morals for Moderns*. New York: Peter Lang.

Murphy, G. Ronald. 2000. *The Owl, the Raven, and the Dove: The Religious Meaning of the Grimms' Magic Fairy Tales*. New York: Oxford University Press.

Perrault, Charles. 1729. *Histories; or, Tales of Past Times, with Morals*. Translated by Robert Samber. London: J. Pote and R. Montagu.

———. 1967. *Contes*. Edited by Gilbert Rouger. Paris: Garnier.

———. 1980 [1697]. *Contes de Perrault*. Geneva: Slatkine Reprints.

Robinson, Orrin W. 2010. *Grimm Language: Grammar, Gender, and Genuineness in the Fairy Tales*. Amsterdam: John Benjamins.

Sainte-Beuve, Charles-Augustin. 1884. "Les Contes de Perrault [23 décembre 1861]." In *Nouveaux lundis*, vol. 1, 296–314. Paris: Calmann Lévy.

Sermain, Jean-Paul. 1987. "La Parodie dans les contes de fées (1693–1713): Une loi du genre?" *Biblio* 17 (33): 544–45.

———. 2005. *Le conte de fées: Du classicisme aux Lumières*. Paris: Desjonquères.

Tatar, Maria. 1987. *The Hard Facts of the Grimms' Fairy Tales*. Princeton, NJ: Princeton University Press.

Tonnelat, Ernest. 1912. *Les frères Grimm: Leur œuvre de jeunesse*. Paris: Armand Colin.

Uther, Hans-Jörg. 2008. *Handbuch zu den* Kinder- und Hausmärchen *der Brüder Grimm: Entstehung—Wirkung—Interpretation*. Berlin: W. de Gruyter.

Van der Toorn, Karel, Bob Becking, and Peter W. Van der Horst. 1999. *Dictionary of Deities and Demons in the Bible*. Leiden: Brill.

Zipes, Jack. 1989. *Beauties, Beasts, and Enchantment: Classic French Fairy Tales*. New York: New American Library.

Zuber, Roger. 1997. "Les *Contes* de Perrault et leurs voix merveilleuses." In *Les émerveillements de la raison: Classicismes littéraires du XVIIe siècle français*, 261–95. Paris: Klincksieck.

PLATE 1. Laced Glass Boot. Tyrol, Court Glasshouse, 1570–1590. Kunsthistorisches Museum, Vienna, KK 3386. Formerly in the collection of Ambras Castle.

PLATE 2. Bernard Perrot, Tabletop of Louis XIV's table, detail of hunting scene, 1668–81. Glass, brass and wood. Private collection. Photograph Sotheby's London.

PLATE 3. Bernard Perrot, Tabletop of Louis XIV's table, detail of Juno, 1668–81. Private collection. Photograph Sotheby's London.

PLATE 4. "Cinderella" print from woodcuts published by Hoffers, Rotterdam. Rijksmuseum, Amsterdam.

PLATE 5. "Cinderella" and "Puss in Boots" combined. R. J. Schierbrer. Rijksmuseum, Amsterdam.

PLATE 6. *Cendrillon: Une imagerie d'après le conte de Charles Perrault* by Warja Lavater. Maeght Éditeur, 1976, copyright © ProLitteris (Suisse) 2015. Used by permission of Cornelia Hesse-Honegger.

PLATE 7. *Kopciuszek* by Michał Rusinek, illustrations by Malgorzata Bieńkowska, graphic design by Grażka Lange, copyright © 2006 Jacek Santorski & CO. Used by permission of Michał Rusinek and Malgorzata Bieńkowska.

PLATE 8. Schermelé, Willy. 1943. *Asschepoester*. s.l.: s.n.

PLATE 9. Antoni Gawiński, *Bajki staroświeckie* (1928). Illustration by the author.

PLATE 10. Tadeusz Rychter. "Fairy Tale Fantasy Titled Cinderella," 1903. In the collection of Academy of Fine Arts Central Library in Kraków.

PLATE 11. Mieczysław Górowski. *Cinderella*, 1984. In the collection of Academy of Fine Arts Central Library in Kraków. Courtesy of Maciej Górowski.

PLATE 12. Adam Żebrowski. Prokofiev's *Cinderella*, 2010.

5

The Dissemination of a Fairy Tale in Popular Print

Cinderella as a Case Study

Talitha Verheij

There are countless adaptations of the Cinderella fairy tale nowadays, and the story is available in many different versions, languages and media. Over time this fairy tale became associated with children's literature, although often in a revised and transformed form. Many children, for example, know the adaptation of Perrault's version of Cinderella for the screen by Walt Disney. And if a child does not recall the story exactly by heart, he or she presumably recognizes Cinderella's name as referring to the well-known character. Many other fairy tales from the collection of Charles Perrault, such as "Little Red Riding Hood" or "Bluebeard," have become famous over time as well. However, the Cinderella tale turned out to be a surprisingly interesting case in the light of Dutch historical popularization processes, since popular prints of Cinderella developed in the opposite direction from that of the main developments in the literary production of fairy tales in the Netherlands. According to Certeau and Fiske, this is an example of how popular culture can speak against or oppose what the dominant culture provides (Certeau 1984; Fiske 1989).[1] In Dutch children's books tales were censored out of ideological considerations, but print publishers did not censor their print production and kept printing the original stories. In this respect they rejected attempts from the dominant culture to impose certain representations and conceptions upon (especially child) readers.

Throughout this essay I want to illustrate the dissemination of Perrault's version of the Cinderella fairy tale in Dutch popular print between 1700 and 1900. For this purpose, I will make use of research results from the University of Utrecht's Netherlands Organisation for Scientific Research (NWO) project "Popularisation and Media Strategies," in which researchers are currently analyzing the selection and adaptation processes of stories in popular print in the Netherlands in the eighteenth and nineteenth centuries. Cross-medial adaptation and appropriation, the "flows of content," "intermediality," or "remediation," are discussed in many media studies and literature studies by scholars such as Bolter and Grusin, Jenkins, Rajewski, or Ryan (Bolter and Grusin 1999; Jenkins 2006; Rajewski 2005; Ryan 2004). Of particular importance in my research is Jenkins's notion that popularization processes turned modern societies into convergence cultures. The scale and rapidity with which popularization takes place in our time (and in which stories are produced and disseminated with the help of new media) can be overwhelming. Nevertheless, on a smaller scale and with less speed, we observe this "flow of content" and these adaptation processes already in the eighteenth and nineteenth centuries. Part of the explanation for the popularization process lies not only in the story itself, but also in the conditions of the production and distribution of stories during the eighteenth and nineteenth centuries. My focus is on the lives and afterlives of stories in the Netherlands in popular, ephemeral media such as chapbooks, songs, almanacs, and, above all, penny prints.[2] Penny prints may be considered as the "new media" of their time since they played a central role in intermedial adaptations. Given its extensive production and wide dissemination, the penny print is an important research object for studying the knowledge and characteristics of Dutch popular culture.

Taking the Cinderella tale as a case study, I want to find out how we can explain the continual, time-crossing survival of certain "success stories." To discover this diachronic popularization, it seems crucial to analyze the processes of selection and adaptation. The adaptation of Cinderella in the medium of the penny print and the contextual print industry will be the primary objectives here. How did Cinderella "survive" in Dutch penny prints? Which version of the tale was popular? I will discuss the most important, dynamic developments in the print production of the eighteenth and nineteenth centuries: the emergence of a concentration of production and distribution processes. Finally, I will interpret the phenomena in the print industry and explain why Cinderella is an important case study in the context of my broader research project.

Penny Prints

Penny prints were large, plano sheets of paper (or broadsheets), with dimensions of approximately 12 by 16 inches (31 by 49 centimeters). The sheets were printed on one side and contained series of pictures (mostly woodcuts) with mainly rhyming captions of a few lines. Most of them were printed in black and white. Colored copies were colored by hand—or more precisely, by thumb.[3] The prints were sold for about one penny, or a cent in Dutch. They are therefore referred to as penny prints (Thijssen 2009, 37), or *centsprenten*. I have characterized the prints as "new media." They were novel in the sense that they brought oral and print culture together by re-telling old stories in a new way.

Compared to other popular genres, the production figures were massive. Penny prints were sought after not only because of their content but also because of their low price. Indeed, Jeroen Salman defines popular print as print that was (1) cheaply and massively produced, (2) cheaply priced, and (3) consumed by a large, widespread audience (Salman 1999). In order to earn money with products that have a very small profit, publishers had to sell great numbers of them. For instance, Stichter, a publisher in Amsterdam, sold about 277,000 prints in one year (1792), which is especially remarkable considering the fact that Amsterdam had about 180,000 inhabitants at that time. The market for penny prints had already flourished in the Dutch Republic during the seventeenth century, but reached its zenith in the eighteenth century, and Amsterdam (where other important publishers such as Lootsman, Van de Putte en De Groot were established) became its main production center. Therefore, the eighteenth century is often regarded as the "golden age" of penny prints.

In the Southern Netherlands (later Belgium) and other European countries such as France or Germany, the market for penny prints initially lagged behind that in the Northern Netherlands.[4] Nevertheless, different actors in the printing industry in the Northern and Southern Netherlands were strongly interconnected. Many eighteenth-century prints in Amsterdam were published with woodcuts manufactured by engravers of the Southern Netherlands during the sixteenth and seventeenth centuries. According to the collector Maurits de Meyer, firms in Amsterdam (such as Van Egmont, Kannewet and Rynders), in Rotterdam (such as Thompson), and in Zaltbommel (such as Noman) printed with woodcuts produced by the Antwerp woodcutter Jan Christoffel Jegher in the seventeenth century (Meyer 1962). In the nineteenth century, the heart of the industry shifted mainly to Rotterdam, Zaltbommel, Deventer, and eventually Belgium. However, the circulation of penny prints on the Dutch market remained extensive up to 1900.

In many cases, prints tell us more about contemporary daily life and culture than paintings. Obviously, caution is needed when interpreting images as accurate representations of historical culture, but penny prints can certainly inform us about, for instance, their own distribution methods. To give an example: there are many prints in which the print trade by peddlers is illustrated, such as the print of the Noman firm, in which a peddler is pictured with the caption: "I have prints and maps for sale, the piece or as a bundle" (Noman, no. 11). Prints were widely sold at markets and fairs, by peddlers in the city or country, retailers, and of course at regular bookshops. Taking into account the low price, even the lower classes were able to buy these penny prints. And if they could not afford them, they could still have a look at the prints displayed in the windows of bookshops or at market stalls (Borms 2010; Vanhaelen 2003). As a consequence, the prints were read by a large variety of people across boundaries of age, class, and place.

We can distinguish many different categories of penny prints. Since the beginning of print production in the fifteenth century, the prints exclusively contained religious themes, such as pictures of saints, Christ, or other biblical scenes. In the seventeenth century, publishers started to produce more profane series of prints, illustrating for instance scenes of daily life, of professions, the military, or of popular children's games. During the eighteenth and nineteenth centuries, prints with narratives increased. The origins of these stories often go back several decades, or even centuries. Others were adaptations of contemporary stories. The narrative prints are a unique cultural phenomenon. And the *Cinderella* print was one of them.

In order to hold their own against competition, publishers had to enlarge and update their print collections constantly. To understand how they sought to accomplish this, it is necessary to look closely at the production and distribution process of publishers and retailers. The Dutch production process of penny prints was very flexible. The images on the prints and the texts underneath them could be printed with the use of separate woodcuts and letters. Therefore, publishers could easily adapt and update their texts or quickly change the order of the images for a new issue.

Such changes in chronology or captions were common production strategies in the print industry and illustrate the flexibility of the production process. An example of that flexibility is the increased adaptation for children in the nineteenth century and the ways in which some prints were censored and edified for children. Many penny prints already addressed children explicitly in the eighteenth century, and popular stories frequently reached a young audience by print before they became part of the more formal children's literature.[5] This led to the scholarly assumption that children were the only buyers and consumers of penny prints.[6] However, this conclusion should be considered with caution. It is highly questionable, particularly for the eighteenth century, that children were the only potential buyers and consumers of penny prints. Angela Vanhaelen states justly that it would not have been a particularly profitable marketing strategy to single out certain buyers (Vanhaelen 2003). Another reason to question this "child assumption" is that penny prints often represented adult behavior and concerns, which appealed to a broad and adult audience (see, for instance, Borms 2010; Selm 1992; Thijssen 2009; Vanhaelen 2003; Vansummeren 1996).

Later, toward the nineteenth century, the publishing industry in general began to explore the market for children more specifically. Influenced by the Society of Common Benefit, founded in 1784, the attention to childhood and education grew substantially. According to the Society, the 1700s were considered to be an age of decline in the Netherlands, especially concerning morality and proper, civilized behavior. Thijssen claims that the society wanted to educate the ignorant, unvirtuous common man and children, and that this ideological aim was perfectly in line with the ideas of the Enlightenment (Thijssen 2009). Fairy tales and folk stories were considered to be too cruel and/or unedifying, especially for children. Morally inappropriate parts in children's books were removed or censored, and the traditional, often slightly cruel or banal penny prints were rejected by the Society.

But despite this prohibition, the Society also acknowledged that penny prints were an appropriate medium to disseminate ideas. They started to produce their own prints as instruments for ideological propaganda. In these series well-known stories were civilized and moralized. Thus the Society made efforts to ban and edify the traditional print series. Interestingly enough, the prints with fairy tales developed differently. The flexibility of the process and the increased pedagogic norms seemed to sense defeat in the face of the popularity of the original versions and the dominant position of some publishers in the production industry. The prints of the Cinderella tale are a perfect illustration of this phenomenon.

Cinderella

The first Dutch translation of Perrault's version of Cinderella appeared in 1754 and was published by Pieter van Os in The Hague. Cinderella was included in an illustrated collection of eight tales of Mother Goose, thus adopting the subtitle of Perrault's collection. After this debut on the Dutch market, many editions followed (especially in the nineteenth century), with about fifty editions of children's books containing the tales of Mother Goose. Many children's books combined the tales of Mother Goose, but there were also editions that contained the Cinderella tale individually. The first children's book containing the Cinderella fairy tale separately was published in 1830, by Hoffers in Rotterdam, and contained twelve woodcuts. Hoffers also produced a penny print of Cinderella and probably used the same woodcuts from that penny print for the production of the book (print production during 1820–37; publication of book in 1830). Publishers frequently used the wooden blocks they already had in stock. Those wooden blocks were often originally used to produce other popular material such as chapbooks, plays, pamphlets, or songbooks. Moreover, old wooden blocks were usually purchased by following generations of publishers and continued to be used decade after decade; some blocks circulated over the course of two centuries. The fact that the blocks over time got worn out and the quality of the prints decreased did not seem to bother the publisher or the audience.[7]

Hoffers's print (see color insert, plate 4) depicts the most popular version of Cinderella in the penny print industry. The print shows the story of Cinderella in twelve images with captions in rhyme and represents the version of the fairy tale by Charles Perrault. As we see, it contains the scenes where Cinderella works for her stepsisters, is not invited to the ball but is still able to attend thanks to the good deeds of the fairy godmother, dances with the prince, loses her shoe, and finally marries the prince. In the last picture, she forgives her stepsisters for their misbehavior. This print was copied many times, and it illustrates again that reusing wooden blocks, copying images from other publishers, and reprinting were very common production strategies. It was the most efficient, fast, and inexpensive way to enlarge an assortment of prints.[8] For many publishers it seemed to be a necessary offense to copy others in order to maintain their business position. Next to this version of Cinderella in twelve pictures, there were several other penny prints of the story known.

With their production of fairy tales the traditional print producers kept competing successfully against the Society of Common Benefit, which could not completely ban the traditional series. Publishers responded to the persistent popularity of the original fairy tales and seemed to escape the civilizing measures that were influencing literary production. In short, the print producers did not follow the norms that had been set by the society and kept presenting fairy tales in their original, uncensored versions.[9] Despite this relative "freedom," however, they all chose to produce the version of Perrault. It is indeed remarkable that none of the Dutch prints in the eighteenth and nineteenth centuries contained a version of Grimm, an observation that has not yet been satisfactorily explained. Was this because the Grimms lived and published later than Perrault? Or could the nonpopularity of the Grimms have to do with the fact that their more horrific version was considered to be inappropriate in the Northern Netherlands during the nineteenth century?

An example of the Grimms' harshness as opposed to Perrault's is the fate of the stepsisters. In Perrault's version of Cinderella, the stepsisters are not punished in the end. They show remorse, and in the last caption, the moral that "one shouldn't look down upon other, poorer or more common people" is explicitly stated. In the Grimm version, however, the sisters *are* punished. Birds peck out their eyes: one eye each when they go into the church for Cinderella's wedding, and the other one when they come out. Indeed, Perrault's version of Cinderella, with its happy end and explicit moral, is less offensive and perhaps more suitable for children. But that is not the explanation for the greater popularity of Perrault's Cinderella when compared to the reception of the Grimms' version. For one, cruelty is certainly not absent from Perrault or from the Dutch market; other fairy tales of Perrault contained as much or even more cruel elements than those of the Brothers Grimm. Examples of this are "Little Red Riding Hood" or the tale of "Hop o' My Thumb," in which murder and violence are rather shockingly illustrated. In general we observe that Perrault's versions—not those of the Brothers Grimm—of common fairy tales dominated the penny prints, even when Perrault's versions were more cruel or obscene.

Perrault's popularity in the Dutch penny print market can be explained in two distinct ways. First, it seems that stories became more fixed and standardized in penny prints than in other media. Publishers reprinted prints with the same wooden blocks and copied each other's work because it was cheaper, quicker, and easier. The commercial strategy of copying or reprinting, and an intermedial use of wood blocks, is more significant, because publishers could reach a wide audience with the same content simultaneously.[10] Since the valuable wooden blocks were often taken over by subsequent generations of publishers, we see a diachronic continuity occur in the production of narrative prints, with small differences and adjustments of the fabula or chronology (as a result of commercial or pedagogic considerations). Moreover, the prints with tales became even more standardized as distinct adaptations of the fabula or censorship did not take place. The possibilities for change were certainly not more limited than in other narrative prints or other media (due to the flexible production process), but once Perrault's version was popularized, publishers held on to it and were not eager to adapt and change their prints to the version of the Brothers Grimm.

In that way, fairy tale prints in particular developed differently from versions printed in contemporary children's books. Publication histories show that familiarity in children's books had to be reached through more proper, censored adaptations of the tales. The penny prints of fairy tales, however, stuck to the original versions of Perrault, whether they contained cruel or obscene scenes or not, and despite the fact that they were contested by the society.

An additional explanation that applies to many popular narratives might be the fact that prints had limited space, so it was especially necessary that the public recognized the story and could read the minimal captions in the right way. However, the necessity of standard captions and pictures for the sake of familiarity seemed to play a more marginal role in the production of fairy tales. Print publishers of tales were remarkably confident about the ubiquitous popularity of the stories and in some cases even decreased the space used by printing two tales on one page. An example of this is the print that combines the Cinderella tale with that of Puss in Boots (see color insert, plate 5). Both adaptations of the two fairy tales are fairly short in this example. The decision to retell the stories together in such short print versions only occurred within penny prints based on fairy tales. Publishers could choose this extremely truncated version because of the huge popularity of the tales, so it was not just a consequence of limited space on the print, but instead a strategic appeal to the popularity and collective knowledge of the tales.

Second, we can explain the dominance of the Perrault version by observing developments on the international market. In the 1840s and 1850s, many Dutch publishers ended their print production. The printing process became increasingly mechanized, and it was no longer profitable for them to produce in the traditional way.[11] They could no longer compete with the Belgian, French, and German publishers who gradually started to invest in new modern presses, such as the lithographic press, and to print on mechanically produced paper, which was much cheaper than traditionally manufactured paper. As a consequence, from the second half of the nineteenth century, the Dutch print market became dominated by a few large publishers based in other European countries, such as Brepols in Belgium and Pellerin in France. Again, the Cinderella tale proves to be an illustrative case. Due to increased concentration of production levels and the dominant position foreign publishers started to have in the Dutch market in the second half of the nineteenth century, their repertoire of stories increasingly dominated the market. And because these publishers (especially the French) produced prints with the Perrault version, this version continued to remain popular. Thus we can notice an increased continuity, despite the flexible possibilities in the production process of prints, of the fairy-tale version in prints.

Conclusion

Through adaptations in the mass medium of the penny print, publishers contributed to the persistent popularity of many traditional stories among a broad, diverse audience. By constantly reusing the same wooden blocks and thanks to the custom of copying, the same stories—and in this case, the same Cinderella version—were produced over and over again. Subsequently, the popular print industry was monopolized by a few large publishers who mainly produced the Perrault versions, which narrowed the available assortment even more.

Cinderella in the penny print is a perfect example of remediation and the implications that adaptations in (contemporary) new media have for the survival of stories in general and fairy tales specifically. I briefly referred to the increased concentration of publication in the popular literary field and the increasing dominance of international publishers on the Dutch market. I have demonstrated that selection and adaptation processes were dependent on the dynamic relation between the medium, its producers, and its public. It was the dynamic relation between those dominant actors that supported the choice and popularity of Perrault's version of Cinderella in the Netherlands. As already stated, modernity and processes of intermedial popularizations are often connected in media and literature studies. This case study validates the assumption that intermedial popularization already took place in the eighteenth and nineteenth centuries. My research makes it possible to unravel how fairy tales were made into popular culture over a longer time span than is indicated in existing research, and to see whether historical popular culture contains elements of a convergence culture. This article revealed just a few steps of my analysis, and by further exploring the characteristics of selection and adaptation in popular printing—how the stories make their way into the world—I will gain more insight into processes of cultural exchange in the eighteenth and nineteenth centuries. Not only will I discover more about "flows of content" and the dissemination of the Cinderella tale, but also the trajectories of many other stories from generation to generation, up to the present day.

Notes

1. See Harms (2013) for further analysis.
2. To construct the contemporary context, I analyze the way in which the stories engaged with larger cultural and ideological processes of identity, civilization, or modernization. How did the producers respond to the

demands of their changing public? These questions will be answered in other parts of my research.

3. This coloring was roughly done with two or three spots rather randomly pressed on the picture, which is why the method was called *à la manière hollandaise* (translated as "in a Dutch manner," and meaning rough and sloppy).
4. In these countries, the industry grew at least seventy-five years later than in the Northern Netherlands. The important Belgian publisher Brepols became acquainted with this widespread popularity of prints during his business travels to the Northern Netherlands.
5. C. F. van Veen even claims the prints were addressed to much younger children in the seventeenth and eighteenth centuries than late eighteenth- and nineteenth-century prints (Veen 1971, 20).
6. Penny prints are therefore also referred to as children's prints.
7. Borms gives a good example of such a damaged print from the publisher Van Egmont in Amsterdam. At the end of the eighteenth century, Van Egmont used the same blocks for his *Uilenspiegel* print that the publisher Van Ghelen had already used in 1580 (Borms 2010, 12).
8. Pirates often did not get punished for their actions. Patents were only applied for in specific cases and copyright laws first came into existence in the course of the nineteenth century. In 1815 the "Vereniging ter bevordering van de belangen des Boekhandels" (VBBB) was raised, a society that was concerned with the rights and interests of the publishing industry. The first copyright laws were acknowledged in 1817, but it took a while before the laws were clearly enforced. For rules about patents, see the work of P. G. Hoftijzer.
9. And many traditional folk stories as well, though some got censored.
10. In examining and discussing intermediality in my further research, as a mechanism of cultural exchange, I more closely define the aspects upon which stories and various adaptations of stories can be considered to be the same.
11. The largest firms that stopped their traditional production were Ulrich and Wijnhoven Hendriksen in 1849, Hoffers in 1840, Wendel in 1841, and Noman between 1840 and 1847 (Noman sold his wooden blocks to the Belgian publishers Brepols and Glenisson & Van Genechten).

References

Bolter, J. D., and R. Grusin. 1999. *Remediation: Understanding New Media.* Cambridge, MA: MIT Press.

Borms, A. 2010. *Centsprenten: Massaproduct tussen heiligenprent en stripverhaal.* Zwolle: Uitgeverij.

Certeau, Michel de. 1984. *The Practice of Everyday Life.* Berkeley: University of California Press.

Fiske, John. 1989. *Understanding Popular Culture.* London: Routledge.

Harms, Roeland. 2015. "Popular Culture and Penny Prints: How Eighteenth- and Nineteenth-Century Readers Indirectly Created Their Own Narratives." *Cultural and Social History* 12 (2): 217–34.

Jenkins, H. 2006. *Convergence Culture: Where Old and New Media Collide.* New York: New York University Press.

Meyer, Maurits de. 1962. *De volks- en kinderprent in de Nederlanden van de 15e tot de 20e eeuw.* Antwerpen: Scheltema and Holkema.

Rajewsky, I. O. 2005. "Intermediality, Intertextuality, and Remediation: A Literary Perspective on Intermediality." In *Intermédialités*, 6, 43–64. Montréal: Centre de reserche sur l'intermedialité.

Ryan, M. L., ed. 2004. *Narrative across Media: The Languages of Storytelling.* Lincoln: University of Nebraska Press.

Salman, Jeroen. 1999. *Populair drukwerk in de Gouden Eeuw: De almanak als lectuur en handelswaar.* Zutphen: Walburg Pers.

Selm, Bert van. 1992. *Inzichten en Vergezichten.* Amsterdam: Uitgeverij De Buitenkant.

Thijssen, J. G. L. 2009. *"Leerzame prentjens voor de jeugd": Schoolprenten van de Maatschappij tot Nut van 't Algemeen.* Utrecht: Uitgeverij Matrijs.

Vanhaelen, Angela. 2003. *Comic Print and Theatre in Early Modern Amsterdam: Gender, Childhood, and the City.* Aldershot, England: Ashgate.

Vansummeren, P. 1996. *Kinderprenten van Brepols.* Turnhout: Brepols.

Veen, C. F. van. 1971. *Drie eeuwen Noord-Nederlandse kinderprenten.* Den Haag: W. van Hoeve.

6

Moral Adjustments to Perrault's Cinderella in French Children's Literature (1850–1900)

Daniel Aranda

Introduction

"Cinderella or the little glass slipper" ("Cendrillon ou la petite pantoufle de verre") is the title given by Charles Perrault to the sixth tale he published in his 1697 book *Histoires ou Contes du temps passé, avec des moralités.* A century later, although "Perrault's undertaking is part of a worldly culture" (Escola 2005, 16), children's literature was in the making; it appropriated the text and began to spread it to child audiences. The belief that this particular tale is remarkably suited to such readers is obvious. Cinderella is almost always published in the incomplete collections of Perrault's tales or in fairy-tale anthologies and is often the subject of isolated publications in the form of booklets or picture books, or then again is integrated into alphabet primers. This practice is still in force today, as the story of the fallen—later to be rehabilitated—heroine is supposed to resonate with young readers. We will not repeat here the issue of the mediations that turned a mundane story into a tale for children. Let us remember that, according to Raymonde Robert, this mutation is "the story of a huge misunderstanding: it all happened as if the nineteenth century, and then the twentieth century, had taken at face value the assertion made by late seventeenth-century authors and critics that a fairy tale is not much more than an old wives' tale" (Robert 2002, 482).[1]

Yet such a textual transfer is not to be taken for granted, since children's literature publishers and the adapters they contract have to choose between two options, even though compromise solutions between the two are feasible. The first is to replicate Perrault's tale without any changes and thereby legitimize productions for youth by linking them to the prestige of classical literature. But then there is a risk of alienating young readers with a vocabulary and syntax they are unfamiliar with. The second option considers that "linguistically at least, these ancient texts needed some amendments to be made accessible to today's children" (Escola 2005, 12). But such a practice results in a composite text that owes some of its features to a second author. In this case, the paratext—title, subtitle, preface—hint most of the time that the story has been modified to that effect. However, some adaptations may also fail to mention Perrault's name although they have copied the text and even more frequently the events the author has imagined. The Cinderella story as imagined by Perrault then escapes its author and somehow falls into the public domain. Accordingly, to what extent are we still dealing with the Cinderella by Perrault, or with a production that cannot, in good faith, claim it bears the author's signature?

The issue proves to be even more complex when we observe that the changes implemented by the adapters are not limited to technical alterations. By this term we mean a mere lexical and stylistic transposition that retained the full sequence of actions reported by Perrault, while enabling nineteenth-century readers to have easier access to the story.

Perrault wrote "Cendrillon ou la petite pantoufle de verre," like all his other stories, for adult audiences, who were very familiar with court life. Transforming Perrault's text from a nineteenth-century perspective is also for children's literature to adapt to a radically different readership, not only in terms of its age but also of its social background as well as of the cultural context in which it operates. The adaptation of Perrault's "Cendrillon" is therefore also an ideological project and a moral one, aimed at achieving at least a partial readjustment of the values and practices offered to the young reader. Our purpose, therefore, is to identify and interpret these textual transformations—cuts, additions, interpolations, rewritten passages—to which children's literature subjects Perrault's tale, since these changes pursue a moral objective intended for its child readership. To carry out this comparison, two points need to be agreed on: on one hand, the boundaries of the corpus to be compared to Perrault's texts, and on the other the complex values that were at work in the 1697 "Cendrillon," which need defining if one wants to match the tale with the value systems offered by children's literature.

Regarding the first point, we have selected editions or reprints of "Cendrillon ou la petite pantoufle de verre" from the French productions published between 1850 and 1900. It is "after 1850 that publishers have expressly intended the *Contes de Perrault* for child readers. Indeed, it is only then that children are supposed truly to make up a separate category of readers" (Belmont 2010, 126). More generally, that period was also the first golden age of children's literature in France, which ensured a sufficiently large number of versions. In addition, that period, while far from the period that saw the publication of Perrault's text, is also very far from ours, which makes it easy for a twenty-first-century observer to spot the "values" that are being proposed. Moreover, this period spans two political regimes—the Second Empire and the Third Republic—and presents two competing types of publication, the Catholic and the liberal press, which may reveal shifts from one adaptation to another.

We consulted more than twenty versions of "Cendrillon" by Perrault from that period, which does not cover the entire referenced production but is a substantial sample of it. If we are not more accurate in our figures it is because the identification of a youth edition of Cinderella is not self-evident. It is not easy, particularly, to distinguish it from the "popular" versions of the story in the literature that used to be hawked at the time, because it does not specifically target a child readership, though not at all excluding it either. Out of that score of versions, about two-thirds conduct textual manipulations, but many of these are more technical than ideological, without ever overstepping the limit between the two. For example, the famous 1862 Hetzel edition, illustrated by Doré, is almost akin to the full text. However, though it keeps the subtitle and simply replaces "glass" ("verre" in French) with "vair" (a medieval fur derived from squirrel pelts) for reasons of pseudo-lexical accuracy, it removes the two versified morals, perhaps because of the greater difficulty for a child to understand a text in verse form. Another reason for this omission may be a desire to emulate the Grimms' fairy tales, which are much more recent, and which for their part explicitly target a child readership and are devoid of morals, which again links up with ideological considerations. Actually, our comparison will be based primarily on a half-dozen texts that ostensibly provide a corrective version of Charles Perrault's message.

But then again, what is this "message"? This is the second point that needs figuring out because, without it, it is totally impossible to identify ideological differences. Among the proliferation of interpretations prompted by Perrault's tales, we have chosen the one that is best suited to our purpose, that is, measuring shifts in the moral purpose of the tales, since internalizing ethical standards is the main objective of nineteenth-century youth literature. So we have opted for a Charles Perrault who turned his fairy tales into a means of defense and into an illustration of one way to live in society, which translated on his heroines' part into their courageously adhering to an ideal of sociability. "Cendrillon ou la petite pantoufle de verre" expresses what Marc Fumaroli, in his study "Les *Contes* de Perrault, ou l'éducation de la douceur," described as a "worldly culture" (Fumaroli 1998). When analyzing the tale titled "Les Fées," whose heroine's family situation and fate are very close to that in our story, Fumaroli discerns in it an apology for the powers of " 'worldly' softness that, as we observed earlier, includes so much innate grace, education and carefully coordinated initiation" (Fumaroli 1998, 475). This says a lot about how feminine that worldly ethics actually is at a time during the "women's quarrel" ("Querelle des femmes") when Perrault presents himself as the feminist opponent to a misogynistic Boileau. Perrault's heroines, including Cinderella, stand for flat opposition to misogyny, pedantry, and satirical cruelty, of the kind Boileau could be said to epitomize.

Based on these policy positions, the comparison of Perrault's Cinderella with avatars of the second half of the nineteenth century then reveals four sets of disjunctions that aim to reconstruct some of the behavior models available for children, which constitute the four successive points of our analysis. The first focuses on the implementation by children's literature of an infantilized heroine, in both senses of being younger and devalued. The second includes the elements that made for the emergence of a kind of Christian sanctifying suffering. The third set will describe the softening of feelings and emotional states considered as dangerous. Finally, we observe the way parents and public authorities are reclaiming control over events in these versions designed for the young.

An Infantilized Heroine

In Perrault, Cinderella is "a young daughter" or a "young girl" [*une jeune fille*] (Perrault 1967 [1697], 157)—one eligible for marriage as people used to say; the plot revolves around whether she would manage to emancipate herself from the serfdom she was subjected to by her family or find a husband. Insofar as the nineteenth-century versions we are looking at are designed for children, many of them tend to stage a younger heroine, to make her closer to their readers. Such rejuvenation is often implied, particularly through the recurring phrase "la petite Cendrillon," which is never found in Perrault's work, but regularly used in our corpus, both in stories and in a title such as *Le Livre des enfants sages: ABC de la petite Cendrillon* (1873). The epithet used to describe the heroine sounds like a rogue version of Perrault's subtitle ("La petite pantoufle de verre"). It has the advantage of simultaneously being a characteristic hypocoristic expression of a child's prattle, and as such indicates a positively young age only as an addition and indirectly, as it were. Indeed, a child character who marries is logically an untenable situation. Adapters are well aware of it, hence they wish to suggest marriage as an outcome rather than formally establish it. The result is disturbing indeed. We found only one version that poses Cinderella explicitly as a character who is not marriageable. In *Les soirées de Cendrillon*, the heroine is a real child, such "a cute little girl" [*une jolie petite fille*] (Hauteville and Wetzell 1878, 1). Logically, then, changing her age leads to transforming the plot altogether (see below).

Actually, this rejuvenation falls within ideological choice, not technical adaptation. In the nineteenth century, in fact, perhaps even more than in the twentieth century, many heroes (think of Jules Verne's) are adults in fiction intended for young readers. The explanation for such a rampant rejuvenation of Cinderella seems to be simply this: once a child again, the heroine can now, in our stories for the young, be deprived of some of the initiatives she takes in Perrault's tale.

Here we discuss the second meaning that we wish to give to the notion of infantilization: refusing to grant the protagonist the qualities of autonomy and responsibility she demonstrates in the 1697 tale. Perrault's Cinderella is indeed an active girl who, given her quasi-slave status, takes risks by traveling incognito to princely balls, and she does it by flaunting all the visible marks—of great wealth and high aristocratic status—that she actually does not have. Obviously, such a force of nature is not to some adapters' liking, and they are reluctant to offer young readers, and young female readers especially, a model of a female character who acts too freely and independently. This is the way we should understand the trend found in the nineteenth-century corpus: the point was to limit the initiatives the heroine would dare to take.

From this point of view, the "trying the slipper on" scene is significant. In Perrault, "Cinderella—who was watching [her stepsisters trying the slipper on], and knew it was her own—said laughingly: 'Let me have a go, it might fit me!' " [*Cendrillon qui les regardait, et qui reconnut sa pantoufle, dit en riant: "Que je voie si elle ne me serait pas bonne!"*] (Perrault 1967 [1697], 163). In some adaptations, that initiative the heroine takes has been kept, but with much more modesty on her part. For instance, in a version dating back to 1897, "Cinderella would look at their efforts with patient and smiling expectation" [*Cendrillon les regardait faire en souriant et attendait patiemment*] (Fauron 1897, 11). And a little further, the adapter adds: "she came to ask with shyness to be tested, too" [*elle vint timidement demander à tenter l'épreuve*] (Fauron 1897, 11). In another version, Cinderella "came shyly to ask with a smile: 'What about me, may I . . . ?'" [*s'avança timidement, et dit en souriant: "Et moi, que je voie . . . si je pourrai . . ."*] (Maugars 1865 [1852], 27). She patiently waits her turn, shyly, and speaks haltingly, and her laugh turns into a smile as well, all pointing in the same direction: a good girl ought to remain unassuming.

Yet two other adaptations go further, in that it is not Cinderella who asks to try the slipper; she merely accepts an invitation made to her by a third party. Thus in a version published in 1863 in the journal *La Semaine des enfants*, we read: "the slipper was therefore presented to her" [*on lui présenta, à elle aussi, la pantoufle*] (Anon. 1863, 303). And in an 1873 version, the gentleman himself asks Cinderella to take the test, and the humor is transferred from Cinderella to that gentleman: "the nobleman, for the sake of a laugh, also had Cinderella try on the slipper" [*le seigneur voulant plaisanter, fit aussi essayer la pantoufle à Cendrillon*] (Anon. 1873, 14).

It should be added that in Perrault's text, Cinderella evinces great activity in both happy and unhappy circumstances. At the end of the story, our protagonist "accommodated her sisters in her palace and wedded them both to great lords of the Court" [*fit loger ses deux sœurs au Palais, et les maria dès le jour même à deux grands Seigneurs de la Cour*] (Perrault 1967 [1697], 164). This is the last sentence of the story. But in an 1883 version, Cinderella's sisters' coordinated weddings are deleted (Anon. 1883, 62). In an 1897 version, the weddings are retained, but not as the last sentence of the story, since an epilogue was added that puts a damper on the heroine's generosity since the end of the story highlights her personal triumph (Fauron 1897, 14).

Such textual manipulations lead to a strange contradiction: Cinderella's active emancipation, as narrated by Perrault, often turns into the story of a sort of emancipation that she has to put up with, as it were. However, as we shall see, the idea of passivity is found in other adaptations and other sequences, through what might be called a Christian and sanctifying suffering.

A Christian Kind of Sanctifying Suffering

Perrault paints a crying Cinderella in one scene only, when the heroine watches her stepsisters driving off in their coach on their way to the ball. The words "cry" or "tears" are used three times:

> When she could no longer see them, she began to cry. Her godmother, who saw her all in tears, asked what the matter was. "I wish . . . I wish . . ." She was crying so hard she just could not finish. [*Lorsqu'elle*

> *ne les vit plus, elle se mit à pleurer. Sa marraine, qui la vit tout en pleurs, lui demanda ce qu'elle avait. "Je voudrais bien . . . je voudrais bien . . ." Elle pleurait si fort qu'elle ne put achever.*] (Perrault 1967 [1697], 159)

All adapters have retained the tearful scene, and they have even developed it or reused it at another time in the story. It agreed with a kind of sensitivity quite typical of the nineteenth century, when readers reveled in the evocation of characters—women in particular—who not only suffered but also displayed their pain in its physiological dimension as a means of representing the intensity and authenticity of the feelings characters experienced.

That is why some authors would not balk at amplifying such maudlin sentimentality in that very same scene: "Tears flowed . . . abundantly" [*Les larmes coulaient . . . abondantes*], one 1864 adaptation reads (Anon. 1864 [1858], 69). And in another version, it is said about the godmother: "Seeing her goddaughter so sad and unhappy, she said: 'Dry your tears, my child' " [*Voyant sa filleule si triste et si malheureuse, elle lui dit: "sèche tes pleurs, mon enfant"*] (Maugars 1865, 14). Another such adaptation proposes an incipit sentence that paints the heroine as an essential "cry-baby": "Little Cinderella would always be crying" [*La petite Cendrillon pleurait toujours*] (Anon. 1873, 6). Such uninhibited suffering was made out to be the emotional background that controls Cinderella's behavior throughout her adventures.

Compared with Perrault's text, the heroine's suffering, when it does not result in tears, is overrepresented in publications for the young. As for the scene when Cinderella's stepsisters are dolling themselves up, with her acting there almost as their servant, a picture book reports that "Cinderella, despite her sorrow, was advising [her stepsisters] about their dress" [*Cendrillon, malgré son chagrin, les conseilla dans leur toilette*] (Anon. 1860 [?]). Yet Cinderella's "sorrow" in this scene has been fabricated by the adapter. In the same way, one 1868 version asserts that "Cinderella was very humbled by their disdain" [*Cendrillon fut très humiliée de ce dédain*], when she feels neglected by the prince, who fails to invite her to the ball (Anon. 1868, 3). That indication is interesting because it presents an expression of suffering that Perrault never mentioned, and especially because of the suggested reason for her so-called suffering and humiliation. Nothing is more foreign to Perrault's heroines than snubbed vanity. It looks as if the adapter lent the heroine a defect that might justify her suffering, besides the injustice she has to put up with. Is it far-fetched on my part to interpret it as an attempt to burden the heroine with a sort of guilt, a kind of original sin, actually meant to legitimize the redemptive suffering she experiences?

Undoubtedly, the vast majority of editions for the young that take up Perrault's tale try to turn Cinderella into a Christian heroine, at least in the moral sense of the term, but with a bias for the kind of Christianity that was established in France in this second half of the nineteenth century. This was conservative or even reactionary, bent on regulating people's moral behavior as much as—or even more than—the Civil Code itself, and emphasizing the need to accept suffering in this world. In this regard, this Christianity for children is compatible with a watered-down form of romanticism, of the sentimental kind with its emphasis on the individual, which is so evident in our versions.

The fact is that many editions of the story—not only the officially Catholic ones for that matter—use a Sunday school vocabulary that is totally foreign to Perrault's text; they are pregnant with the idea of resignation as the right way to deal with suffering. In an already mentioned version, Cinderella is said to "hope, thanks to her resignation, to soften the evil sisters' mood" [*espérant, par sa résignation, adoucir le caractère de ses méchantes sœurs*] (Maugars 1865, 9). "The innocent girl was prepared to put up with anything" [*L'innocente souffrait tout*], another adaptation reads (Anon. 1864 [1858], 67).

Therefore, the godmother's intervention is the first to reinforce the heroine in her resignation, that is to say, to comfort her. In the same version we read that "her godmother, who loved her, had often secretly consoled her" [*sa marraine, qui l'aimait beaucoup, venait souvent en cachette la consoler*] (Anon. 1864 [1858], 69). In another adaptation, we read that "the good fairy godmother did her best to console her" [*la bonne fée fit de son mieux pour la consoler*] (Anon. 1869, 13). We must remember that in Perrault's version, Cinderella's godmother does not come to console her but to give her the material wherewithal to get to the ball. One version reads that the heroine "deserved, owing to her past sufferings, the happiness that awaited her" [*elle méritait, par ses souffrances passées, le bonheur qui l'attendait*] (Anon. 1868, 9). However, Perrault means that if Cinderella eventually finds happiness, it is not on account of her suffering but of her honesty, in the classical sense of the term, and in particular of that "good grace" [*bonne grâce*] that Perrault praised in the first moral of his story (Perrault 1967 [1697], 164).

It is worth noticing as well that these Christian virtues fit uneasily with the heroine's objective, which is, as in Perrault's story, to go to a ball and indirectly find a husband there. Although this obviously pertains to the worldly virtues of sociability as advocated by Perrault, that objective can only, in a context of rigorous morality, be deemed a frivolous activity.

Therefore, our adaptations result in a contradiction, in terms of the moral atmosphere of the story, if not in the very constitution of its heroine.

Hence the radical transformation of the text—dating back to 1878 and designed to provide a narrative framework to a collection of little stories—that is tacked on to Perrault's tale. Cinderella has now become that "pretty little girl" we mentioned in our first section, and her godmother is heard giving her the following explanation: "The hardships you are enduring will contribute to shape your character, and, if you manage to withstand them well, you will one day, I hope, turn into an accomplished young lady" [*les épreuves que tu subis en ce moment formeront ton caractère, et, si tu les supportes bien, tu seras un jour, je l'espère, une jeune fille accomplie*] (Hauteville and Wetzell 1878, 4). So our godmother, instead of acting as the helper that allows her goddaughter to attend the children's ball, keeps her at home and relieves the girl's melancholy by comforting her with nice pretty stories, one every evening. Perrault takes Cinderella along to explore a world that enables her to become emancipated, albeit in an elitist context. The 1878 narrative framework confines her to a strictly mental and carefully framed exploration. This author has not overcome the contradiction between marriage and the heroine's young age. This goes far beyond merely adapting a piece of writing.

The Softening of Feelings and Emotional States Considered Dangerous

Adapters consider the heroine's suffering, passivity, and resignation as useful trials, since they contribute to the edification of young readers. But they also develop a complementary component, the softening or sometimes even censoring of feelings, qualities, or attitudes evoked by Perrault, which, according to them, in the second half of the nineteenth century, are not suited to the age of the target audience, who must therefore be protected from them.

This applies to the way Cinderella's beauty is expressed. In his own account, Perrault emphasizes this feature, as the tangible manifestation of the heroine's moral mettle. When the sisters return from the first ball, for example, they tell Cinderella: "There came the most beautiful princess, the most beautiful ever to be seen" [*il y est venu la plus belle princesse, la plus belle qu'on puisse jamais voir*] (Perrault 1967 (1697], 161). If they underscore this point, of course, it is to humiliate Cinderella, who can only enjoy, along with the reader, their unwitting compliment. Yet one 1897 version puts a damper on that effect by making the assessment of aesthetic value less intensive and more distanced. This is what it becomes: "There was at the ball the prettiest person one can possibly see" [*il y avait au bal la plus jolie personne qu'il fût possible de voir*] (Fauron 1897, 8).

We find many examples of this kind. Perrault's phrase, "such a beautiful and amiable person" [*une si belle et si aimable personne*] (Perrault 1967 (1697], 161) is changed in an 1864 version into "such a gracious and amiable person" [*une si gracieuse et si aimable personne*] (Anon. 1864 [1858], 73). Similarly, the laudatory exclamation that welcomes Cinderella's arrival in the ballroom: "Oh, how beautiful she is!" ([*Ah, qu'elle est belle!*], Perrault 1967 (1697], 160) becomes, in another version: "how bright and magnificent she is!" [*qu'elle est brillante et magnifique!*] (Cantel 1870, 64). The second indication expresses a parade of beauty corresponding to a high social status, rather than natural qualities. In an 1883 version, the word "beautiful" [*belle*] is deleted twice, and on another occasion it is replaced by "pretty" [*jolie*] (Anon. 1883, 62). Such interpolations or deletions have one common goal: not to arouse the little reader's coquetry, in order to avoid instilling the sin of pride in her.

The same precautions can be noticed regarding the expression of love, a dangerous feeling that is not to be prematurely brought to young readers' attention, along with the gallantry games associated with it. During the second ball for example, Perrault describes the conversation between the prince and Cinderella: "The King's son was always by her side, and never ceased to whisper sweet compliments in her ear; the young lady was never bored, and forgot what her godmother had recommended" [*Le fils du roi fut toujours auprès d'elle, et ne cessa de lui conter des douceurs; la jeune demoiselle ne s'ennuyait point, et oublia ce que sa marraine lui avait recommandé*] (Perrault 1967 [1697], 162). But in an 1864 version, the gallant nature of their conversation is mitigated: "The King's son was always near her, and never ceased to compliment her" [*Le fils du roi fut toujours auprès d'elle, et ne cessa de lui faire des compliments*] (Anon. 1864 [1858], 75). It is even erased in this version: "The King's son was always by her side and kept talking with her" [*le fils du roi fut toujours auprès d'elle et ne cessa de l'entretenir*] (Anon. 1865 [1847], 42). In another 1865 version, the story removes the second episode of the ball, or rather merges both balls into one, thereby packaging together the compliments the prince rains on Cinderella (Maugars 1865, 20–21).

The same moderating maneuver takes place in the episode where the sisters narrate to Cinderella the events of the second ball. Perrault gets them to say, about the prince: "undoubtedly, he was deeply in love with the beautiful person" [*assurément il était fort amoureux de la belle personne*] (Perrault 1967 [1697], 163). Yet in an 1870 version, the sentence becomes:

"and he obviously wished to see again the person the little slipper belonged to" [*et qu'assurément il désirait revoir la personne à qui appartenait la petite pantoufle*] (Cantel 1870, 70). In another adaptation, the phrase becomes: "seemed to be very eager to see again the beautiful person" [*paraissait être fort désireux de revoir la belle personne*] (Anon. 1864 [1858], 77). An 1860 version removes the entire sentence altogether (Anon. 1860 [?]).

Let us point out one more interesting substitution of causality in an 1868 version. The reason for Cinderella's forgetting to come back home by midnight is said not to result from her gallant conversation with the prince, as Perrault specified, but from the most superficial euphoria generated by dancing in a luxurious setting:

> While Cinderella was becoming enthralled with the pleasure of dancing around such a brilliant world and around such magnificent reception rooms, bathing in an intoxicating music, she all of a sudden heard the strokes of midnight. [*Après s'être laissé entraîner par le plaisir de la danse au milieu de ce monde brillant et dans ces salons magnifiques retentissant d'une musique enivrante, Cendrillon entendit tout-à-coup sonner minuit.*] (Anon. 1868, 6)

That way the adapter "kills two birds with one stone": he does away with the love-courtship, deemed undesirable, and Cinderella is credited with a form of vanity, which immediately translates into the penalty for neglect and tardiness. Here again, the intention is to include a heroine in a scenario where the happy ending must be achieved by committing a mistake, however benign, and receiving atonement for it. Perrault's story and that mechanism are poles apart, indeed.

Although Cinderella is beautiful, and sensitive to the prince's soft words, she also adopts a behavior that, though evoked quickly by Perrault at the beginning of the story, does seem all the more important as it costs the girl her pejorative nickname: "Cinderella" or "Cucendron" (Perrault 1967 [1697], 158 and 162). When her work is finished, Cinderella would go to the fireplace and "sit in the ashes" [*s'asseoir dans les cendres*] (Perrault 1967 [1697], 158). That practice has been much discussed. Its morbid dimension cannot be overlooked: physical contact with a substance that is not noble; dead matter, which refers to the girl's mourning of her mother or of her giving up becoming a wife and mother one day. Still, several adapters have also diagnosed an almost pathological behavior, an incompatible one, to say the least, with the standards of hygiene that were beginning to emerge in the second half of the nineteenth century, which they did not wish to suggest in their adaptations. The difficulty lies in the fact that they cannot remove Perrault's indication, as it would make it impossible to understand the heroine's nickname, especially since it gave the story its title. Hence the compromise solutions that keep the importance given by the heroine to ashes but that cover up their disturbing potential. One adaptation explains that Cinderella remained "sitting close to the ashes" [*assise auprès des cendres*] (Maugars 1865, 8), and another version reads that the heroine "would spend all her time scrubbing, sweeping and sifting the ashes, which had earned the girl her nickname: Cinderella" [*passait sa vie à frotter, balayer, tamiser les cendres, ce qui l'avait fait surnommer Cendrillon*] (Fauron 1897, 1).

Parents and Public Authorities Reclaim Control over Events

In Perrault's tale, adult characters are assigned to an insignificant role, even when it comes to young people's parents. Cinderella's father and stepmother are mentioned at the beginning of the story and are not discussed throughout the rest of the text. Cinderella's stepsisters are therefore most responsible for the humiliations Cinderella endures, and the prince alone can be credited with raising the heroine from the ashes. That says a lot about how Perrault tells a story about young people and happenings among young people.

However, this is obviously considered as pernicious by many of our adapters, because it might suggest to young readers that, like the protagonists of the story, they can get on with their love lives as they please, away from parental control. It is to amend this defect that they strive to involve parents to a greater extent, Cinderella's as much as the prince's.

The most urgent task is probably to highlight Cinderella's father, who, in Perrault's story, is conspicuous by his absence and is described only as a weakling fawning to his second wife. Cantel maintains a reassuring image of a patriarchal society by deleting the sentence where Perrault explains that "his wife governs him entirely" [*sa femme le gouvernait entièrement*] (Perrault 1967 [1697], 158, and Cantel 1870, 55). Similarly, another adaptation rehabilitates him at the very end, "the father of the girl with the little glass slipper relished his unspeakable joy at seeing this happy change" [*le père de la jeune fille à la petite pantoufle de verre goûtait une joie indicible en voyant cet heureux changement*] (Anon. 1864 [1858], 78). Cinderella's father and stepmother need to be made to play a more active part, and the return from the first ball is a good opportunity. In the same 1864 adaptation, both adults intervene to narrate the evening: "The gentleman and his wife added their own praises of the mysterious unknown girl" [*le gentilhomme et sa femme renchérirent encore pour chanter les louanges de la mystérieuse inconnue*] (Anon. 1864 [1858], 74).

What is necessary regarding Cinderella's parents is all the more so as regards the prince's. In Perrault's tale, the loving young man confides in no one, and he alone "gets the town-crier to trumpet around the town" [*publier à son de trompe*] that he intends to marry the girl who could wear the slipper (Perrault 1967 [1697], 165). In contrast, in an 1865 version, he "told his mother that the only way to overcome his depression was to marry the beautiful stranger" [*déclara à sa mère qu'il ne guérirait qu'en épousant la belle inconnue*] (Maugars 1865, 25). The 1897 adaptation paints the prince's father as a confidant but also as an active protagonist:

> The king, his father, worried about his son's melancholy, and wanted to know the cause. When the young prince told him the reason for his sadness, the king got messengers to trumpet throughout all his kingdom that the heir to the throne, etc. [*Le roi son père, inquiet de cette mélancolie, voulut en savoir la cause. Lorsque le jeune prince lui eut confié le motif de sa tristesse, le souverain fit publier à son de trompe dans tout son royaume, que l'héritier du trône . . .*] (Fauron 1897, 8)

Note that the prince's love sickness, exploited in both these versions, is nowhere to be found in Perrault's tale, and originates from "Peau d'âne" ("Donkey Skin") by the same author. The advantage is that it reduces the prince's autonomy and justifies strengthening his father and mother's initiatives. They can be said to play for him the same role as Cinderella's godmother.

Adults also reclaim the course of events on the occasion of the wedding. With his usual simplicity, Perrault merely indicates about the prince that "a few days after, he married her" [*peu de jours après, il l'épousa*] (Perrault 1967 [1697], 164). However, the 1897 adaptation describes a proper, formal marriage proposal:

> The happy prince immediately renewed his offer of marriage. She agreed because, besides being handsome and brave, everyone agreed he had such goodness of heart. [*Le prince ravi lui renouvela aussitôt son offre de l'épouser. Elle accepta, car, outre qu'il était beau et brave, chacun vantait la bonté de son cœur.*] (Fauron 1897, 12)

In the 1864 version, things are also done "by the book" since the two families meet prior to the ceremony, and as for the prince, it is said that the marriage is celebrated "with the consent of his family" [*avec le consentement de sa famille*] (Anon. 1864 [1858], 79).

Perrault had wanted the story to unfold among young people behind closed doors, but he has been foiled in these versions, all the more so as many second-half-of-the-nineteenth-century versions demand that the love feelings that unite Cinderella and the prince are sanctioned by society as a whole, and by means of the institution of marriage, hence an occasion for great public rejoicing. Both solemn and popular, the young people's wedding is sometimes described at length, and creates "truly public happiness" [*allégresse vraiment publique*] (Anon. 1864 [1858], 80). The key, to our adapters, is to cancel in young readers' minds the notion that the two lovebirds could marry at their own convenience, without consulting anyone, in a sort of underground secrecy.

Conclusion

It is tempting, at the end of this investigation, to draw a sketch of the new Cinderella, as she emerges from these numerous adaptations of Perrault's tale. The heroine is a girl sitting on the fence between childhood and adolescence, prone to crying, and, owing to her resigned attitude, acting as a witness of her own emancipation more than playing an active part in it. Neither morbid nor exceptionally beautiful, she feels a sense of very pure inclination for her prince charming, and the two lovebirds' relationship is supervised and endorsed by the family as well as by society as a whole. Although, for lack of space, we have not been able to study the illustrations found in these adaptations, it should be noted that they often reinforce these developments. Indeed, many iconic representations of Cinderella sitting by the fireplace always exclude the possibility of a heroine placed "in ashes," as Perrault indicates. Similarly, the scene of tears and the wedding of two young people are willingly depicted with illustrations as well.

It should be borne in mind, however, that this sketch is the result of an accumulation of features scattered across several pieces of writing. Taken individually, the consistency of each adaptation is not threatened by an open clash between two conflicting value systems. On the whole, Perrault's worldly ethics, as described by Marc Fumaroli with reference to another story by the same author, are more or less laboriously recycled into a morality tale for nineteenth-century children. Let us beware we do not also commit an anachronism in reading Perrault's story. The story he tells of a woman's emancipation by marriage has no libertarian undertones akin to the movements that spread in industrialized countries in the 1960s: his is an elitist emancipation. Since his character is exceptional, she was bound, as such, to access the higher rank that was her rightful destiny.

The resulting children's versions are not content to censor aspects of Perrault's tale deemed undesirable. They outline what Gérard Genette calls a "transvalorization" (Genette 1982, 393) of the tale, that is to say, the substitution of one system of values for another. They bear the mark of a rigorist French nineteenth century that supports a character representing two populations under guardianship: women and children. Curiously, and subject to further scrutiny, the attempt to get Cinderella back into the fold does not appear more pronounced in religious editions than in "secular" ones, and not more so under the Second Empire than in the Third Republic. As Michele May explains about this period,

> The political interests of Catholic and secular publishers alike and their supporters became increasingly intense over the course of the century. Political fluctuations and social instability meant that children's books became a veritable battlefield for the hearts and minds of French children and their families. Ironically, however, both camps produced surprisingly similar literature. All publications developed for children emphasized correct behavior and social stability. (May 2010, 79)

The morality, ultimately a very homogeneous one, that emerges from all these adaptations is bourgeois and conservative, relying more on religion and family, and clearly reluctant to communicate in all its incisive freshness a story of female emancipation. In this respect, Perrault's vivid style, so ironic and falsely naive, contrasts with the very serious "bourgeois" earnestness found in our textual adaptations. Content and form coincide in both cases. "The whole thing is Christianized, moralities in verses are removed, and the text is rephrased and lengthened" (Nières-Chevrel 2009, 69). Perrault's story tells of the victory of sociability in all its forms, and especially in its love form. But in the context of a literature with mainly educational purposes, our adaptations rather seek to depict the victory of the child's obedience over adversity.

From this point of view, it must be recalled, in the second half of the nineteenth century, some texts intended for children are published that no longer portray a young person as "a being whose vices need silencing and passions smothering, an individual who must be eagerly educated and rigorously tamed" (Prince 2010, 41). Among French writers, Hector Malot, Jules Verne, or even, in some respects, Mme de Ségur, approach the child as a being who can be capitalized on, whose imagination and sensitivity can profitably be heightened. So it seems that our versions pertained in their time to a form of children's literature that is conservative. The editorial strategy that aims to build upon ancient texts by adapting them is one, it seems, whose first and foremost incentive is economic, yet it could also be said to be ideologically adverse to a formal or conceptual innovation. In this respect, one can only enjoy the unintentional irony of these versions by which our adapters prolong, as authors, the vexations her stepmother and stepsisters inflict on Cinderella.

Notes

1. All the translations are by Dominique Macabiès (Université des Sciences Sociales de Grenoble).

References

Anonymous. 1860 [?]. *Cendrillon: Livre d'images.* Épinal: Pellerin.

Anonymous. 1863. "Cendrillon." *La Semaine des enfants: Magasin d'images et de lectures amusantes et instructives* 451 (February 7): 303.

Anonymous. 1864 [1858]. "Cendrillon ou La petite pantoufle de verre." *Les Contes des fées par Charles Perrault: Édition revue pour les enfants chrétiens.* Limoges: Martial Ardant frères.

Anonymous. 1865 [1847]. "Cendrillon." *Les Contes des fées de Charles Perrault: Édition dédiée aux enfants.* Paris: Bédelet.

Anonymous. 1868. *Histoire de Cendrillon.* Wissembourg and Paris: Wentzel.

Anonymous. 1869. *Nouvel alphabet de l'enfance orné de gravures et suivi de l'histoire de Cendrillon.* Metz: Thomas, 1869.

Anonymous. 1873. *Le Livre des enfants sages: ABC de la petite Cendrillon.* Épinal: Pinot.

Anonymous. 1883. *Contes des fées pour les enfants.* Paris: Hinrichsen.

Belmont, Nicole. 2010. *Mythe, conte et enfance: Les écritures d'Orphée et de Cendrillon.* Paris: L'Harmattan.

Cantel, M. H. 1870. *Quatre contes de Perrault suivis de Histoire de Moutonnet.* Paris: F. Cantel.

Escola, Marc. 2005. *Contes de Charles Perrault.* Foliothèque. Paris: Gallimard.

Fauron, M. 1897. *Cendrillon ou la petite pantoufle de vair, conte, d'après Ch. Perrault.* Paris: Guérin.

Fertiault, François. 1859. *Les Contes de fées de Charles Perrault, revus et précédés d'une préface par F. Fertiault.* Paris: Vermot.

Fumaroli, Marc. 1998. "Les *Contes* de Perrault, ou l'éducation de la douceur." In *La Diplomatie de l'esprit*. Paris: Hermann.

Genette, Gérard. 1982. *Palimpsestes*. Collection Poétique. Paris: Le Seuil.

Hauteville d', and Wetzell, Mmes. 1878. *Les soirées de Cendrillon*. Paris: Lefèvre.

Maugars, A. 1865 [1852]. *Cendrillon*. Paris: Maugars, "Bibliothèque amusante des petits enfants."

May, Michele Ann. 2010. "The Republic and Its Children: French Children's Literature, 1855–1900." PhD diss., University of Illinois.

Nières-Chevrel, Isabelle. 2009. *Introduction à la littérature de jeunesse*. Paris: Didier Jeunesse.

Perrault, Charles. 1698 [1995]. *Histoires ou Contes du temps passé*. Paris: Barbin. Slatkine Reprints, J. Barchilon, ed., Geneva, 1995.

———. 1851. *Les Contes des fées*. Paris: Lecou.

———. 1866. *Contes des fées*. Paris: Bernardin-Béchet.

———. 1867 [1862]. *Les Contes de Perrault*. Paris: Hetzel.

———. 1867. *Contes des fées*. Paris: Delarue.

———. 1883. *Le Monde enchanté: Choix de douze contes de fées, précédé d'une histoire des fées et de la littérature féerique en France, par M. de Lescure*. Paris: Firmin-Didot.

———. 1884 [1865]. *Les Contes de Perrault, précédés d'une préface de J. T. de Saint-Germain*. Paris: Théodore Lefèvre.

———. 1893 [1853]. *Contes de fées, tirés de Charles Perrault, de Mmes d'Aulnoy et Le Prince de Beaumont*. 1893. Paris: Hachette.

———. 1894. *Contes*. Petite collection Guillaume. Paris: Dentu.

———. 1967 [1697]. *Contes*. Edited by Gilbert Rouger. Paris: Garnier Frères.

[———]. 1857. *Les Fées, Historiettes naïves et enfantines racontées par Claude Perrault* [*sic*]. Pont-à-Mousson: Haguental.

[———]. 1858. *Le Perrault des enfants*. Paris: Pagnerre.

[———]. 1873. *La Petite Cendrillon, conte des fées*. Épinal: Pinot.

[———]. 1883. *Cendrillon*. Livres illustrés pour les enfants. Lyon: Brun.

Prince, Nathalie. 2010. *La littérature de jeunesse*. Paris: Armand Colin.

Robert, Raymonde. 2002. *Le Conte de fées littéraire en France de la fin du XVIIe à la fin du XVIIIe siècle*. Paris: Champion.

II

~

Regendering Cinderella

7

Rejecting the Glass Slipper

The Subversion of Cinderella in Margaret Atwood's *The Edible Woman*

Rona May-Ron

Protofeminist Reimaginings of Cinderella

In a 1976 interview, Margaret Atwood stated that the Grimms' collection of fairy tales "was the most influential book [she] ever read" (Sandler 1990, 46). Atwood's deep involvement with the genre of fairy tales—her literary corpus is replete with direct references and indirect allusions to fairy-tale characters, plotlines, and motifs—has been discussed extensively by both folklore and Atwood scholars.[1] In various interviews Atwood has made her predilection for active and resourceful fairy-tale heroines, as opposed to passive and helpless ones, abundantly clear, thus affiliating herself with feminist critics who, in the 1970s, launched a critique of the patriarchal representation of women in fairy tales.[2] Moreover, she has expressed her dissatisfaction with popular versions of Cinderella in particular on several occasions, calling it a "conventional and re-done" story and, in a different interview, "a watered-down version" of those fairy tales that featured "quite active female characters" (Oates 1990, 71; Lyons 1990, 224). Despite this censure, the recurrence of the Cinderella topos in Atwood's writing attests to her recognition of its pervasiveness in Western culture—what Martine Hennard Dutheil de la Rochère calls "the Cinderella tale as cultural stereotype" (2009, 14)—and constitutes an acknowledgment of the constant critical vigilance it necessitates.

Atwood's repeated subversion of the tale continues a tradition begun by her literary foremothers. In *Fairy Tales and Feminism*, Donald Haase mentions feminist scholars who have investigated "the intertextual role of classic fairy tales in the works of nineteenth-century English women novelists," concluding that "such studies confirmed that these novelists used fairy-tale intertexts—in particular the well-known story of Cinderella—as subversive strategies to contest the idealized outcomes of fairy tales and their representation of gender and female identity" (Haase 2004, 20). From the latter half of the twentieth century to the present, Atwood has reinscribed and challenged diverse aspects of the Cinderella tale in her novels: the social devaluation of women who do not fit the mold, the binary distinctions between "good" and "bad" girls, the cultural silencing of women, the patriarchally regulated rivalry among women, the policing of women's bodies through naturalized disciplinary practices, the commodification and specularity of women as determined by the male gaze, and the phallocentric view of marriage as women's ultimate goal in life. By evoking and exploring these themes subversively, Atwood has created alternatives to the tale's traditional protagonist and plot. Stereotypes are not simplistically and didactically reversed in Atwood's novels; her heroines continuously oscillate between being readily pulled into the Cinderella vortex and struggling to break free from its undeniable power. Although not entirely relinquishing hope of being rescued by a prince, these fictional women have evolved beyond the conventional Cinderella insofar as they are self-reflexively conscious of the deeply embedded rescue wish that they have been socialized into internalizing and, subsequently, wrestle with its implications.

Atwood finished writing *The Edible Woman*, her first published novel, in 1965, and has called it a "protofeminist novel" because, as Fiona Tolan explains, she "located her novel within a pre-theorised discourse: a feminism that was yet to consciously identify itself as feminist" (Tolan 2007, 9).[3] Although admittedly influenced by the harbingers of second-wave feminism, Simone de Beauvoir and Betty Friedan, Atwood insisted that the "feminist" ideas articulated in her novel predated the academic discourse subsequently formulated by second-wave thinkers. As she herself put it, her ideas drew their inspiration from "the society by which she found herself surrounded" rather than an extant theoretical basis (Atwood 1982, 369). By the same token, Alison Lurie's 1970 article "Fairy Tale Liberation," which "sparked a . . . lasting debate about the relationship of women to fairy tales" (Haase 2004, vii), was published after Atwood, in *The Edible Woman*, reshaped the classic literary tale of Cinderella with its incumbent patriarchal ideologies. Although it would be remiss to attribute artificial starting points to theoretical discourses that inevitably evolve over long periods, even if only latently, before making their academic debut, I would concur with Tolan's claim that "frequently, it is apparent that Atwood's articulation of a theme predates the presence of that theme in feminist theoretical literature" (Tolan 2007, 8). Thus even before the debate regarding fairy tales as a site of gender production became a theoretical and academic one, Atwood's work challenged the patriarchal agendas prevalent in certain versions of the Cinderella story. Reiterating Atwood's self-proclaimed protofeminist stance serves to underscore that her literary depictions of feminist ideas, while seemingly commonplace by today's postfeminist standards, were avant-garde at the time they were first expressed.

Folklore scholarship shows that the tale of Cinderella numbers approximately eight hundred known variants, with the earliest dating as far back as ninth century China (Dundes 1982, 71). As Maria Tatar notes, "Cinderella has been reinvented by so many different cultures that it is hardly surprising that she is sometimes cruel and vindictive, at other times compassionate and kind" (Tatar 1999, 102). Drawing on Ruth Bottigheimer's comparative study of Cinderella variants, Tatar continues that "even within a single culture, she can appear genteel and self-effacing in one story, clever and enterprising in another, coy and manipulative in a third" (102). In France, Charles Perrault fashioned Cinderella into a paradigm of compliancy and virtue at the end of the seventeenth century; in nineteenth-century Germany the Grimm brothers silenced her;[4] and, in mid-twentieth-century America, Walt Disney transformed her into the epitome of cloyingly sweet female passivity. According to Jack Zipes, an intentional socializing strategy fueled Perrault and the Grimms, who pioneered the literary fairy tale in their respective cultures, and who promulgated, through these highly crafted stories, their ideas of femininity:

> Perrault's fairy tales which "elevate" heroines reveal that he had a distinctly limited view of women. . . . The task confronted by Perrault's model female is to show reserve and patience, that is, she must be passive until the right man comes along to recognize her virtues and marry her. . . . If she is allowed to reveal anything, it is to demonstrate how submissive she can be. (Zipes 1988, 25)[5]

As for the Grimms, their tales "contained sexist . . . attitudes and served a socialization process which placed great emphasis on passivity, industry, and self-sacrifice for girls" (Zipes 1988, 46). Finally, Jane Yolen sees in Disney's Cinderella "a coy, helpless dreamer, a 'nice' girl who awaits her rescue with patience and song" (Yolen 1982, 297). While Atwood's literary engagement with these variants is evident through her occasional direct references and indirect allusions to them, her writing often discloses a deeper apprehension of the tale as a potent cultural force that is greater than the sum of its literary and cinematic specimens.

In *The Edible Woman*, Atwood regularly alludes to Cinderella through the use of motifs, events, and symbols, thus creating a novel whose narrative frame and sociopsychological themes are analogous to the ATU 510A tale type. Her subversive use of the fairy tale as a core narrative structure and thematic basis serves to elucidate the protagonist's repudiation of traditional femininity in the novel. *The Edible Woman* opens when the protagonist, Marian, like many typical female Bildungsromans, is at a marrying age. A college graduate, Marian works at a firm that conducts marketing surveys in 1960s Toronto and is dating Peter, to whom she later becomes engaged. Once Marian accepts Peter's marriage proposal, she begins to gradually lose her appetite until she is unable to eat anything. Alongside this plot development, the narrative point of view shifts from first person to third person. Marian also commences an affair with another young man, Duncan, whose nonconformist character is a foil to Peter's straitlaced, aggressive, and phallocentric alpha-male mentality. Toward the end of the novel, when Marian decides to reject the marriage proposal she had initially accepted (by baking a woman-shaped cake and offering it to Peter, saying: "This is what you really wanted all along, isn't it?" [Atwood 1996a, 299–300], thus causing him to run away), she regains not only her appetite but also her narrative voice. *The Edible Woman* is a novel that engages with how women are objectified and consumed by patriarchal culture as well as with how the conventional trajectory of women's lives may not be the ideal formula for happily ever after.

Marian is presented as a Cinderella figure who seems to follow the life course of her fairy-tale alter ego: her way out of a mundane job is marriage. Atwood borrows two central, closely related motifs—flight and shoes—from the ATU 510A "Cinderella" story and employs them in her subversion of the tale. Whereas Cinderella's flight from the prince in Perrault's variant is the result of strict orders from her fairy godmother to return home before midnight (so as not to be revealed as a ragged cinder wench when the spell wears off), in Marian's story the flight stems from a genuine urge to flee rather than an external injunction to do so. Cinderella flees from the prince not because she is averse to the idea of marrying him, but, on the contrary, because she understands that if he sees her plain, unadorned self, it might jeopardize her chances of winning a marriage proposal. Marian, in contrast, flees from her "prince" in an earnest attempt to escape ensnarement in marriage—an attempt to preserve rather than conceal her "true" self. Likewise, Marian's shoe is not lost in the haste of flight but is deliberately discarded—suggesting that its owner does not wish to be confined within everything it symbolizes. Marian's resistance to the symbolic "glass slipper" additionally manifests itself in her unconsciously motivated loss of appetite, which functions as a rebellion against the radically restricted feminine role she is compelled to assume.[6] It should be noted that these acts of defiance are not executed unfalteringly throughout the novel. Marian reverts to an equally passive stance—and longs to be rescued—several times before the novel's end. But they do nonetheless demonstrate the struggle taking place within her psyche, and they serve to contest the fairy tale by challenging the snug, limiting glass-slipper femininity.

What exactly is it that Marian is fleeing? Critics who have written about *The Edible Woman* are in agreement that the novel's protagonist is repudiating a prescriptive, socially constructed femininity.[7] Atwood has two different characters in the novel explicitly accuse Marian of rejecting her femininity. The struggle that unfolds in the novel between the social obligation—internalized as a psychological need—to conform to a phallocentric ideal of femininity and the contrary desire to repudiate it is succinctly limned by Eleonora Rao: "*The Edible Woman* presents a feminine identity torn between society's expectations, which demand adherence to the traditional, devalued feminine role, and the need for self-realization" (1993b, 134). This is, in a nutshell, precisely the dilemma that Colette Dowling (1981) explores in *The Cinderella Complex*: women yearn for independence, but this yearning is often outweighed by a socialized fear of it. Thus they end up waiting passively for external forces to transform them rather than engendering their own autonomy. Dowling's book, published in 1981, speaks directly to, and of, the generation of women depicted in Atwood's novel.

There also seems to be a consensus among scholars regarding what constitutes the femininity that Marian struggles to reject. J. Brooks Bouson writes that "femininity, as Atwood dramatizes in *The Edible Woman*, is a male-assigned role" (1993, 27), and, according to Pamela Bromberg, Atwood suggests that "female narcissism proceeds from the internalization of the male gaze and imprisonment of the self in objectifying roles dictated by the dominant, patriarchal culture" (1988, 14). Such readings explicate Marian's motivation for rejecting the particular brand of femininity imposed upon her and her counterparts in the novel.

Of Glass Slippers, Female Anatomy, and Femininity

The symbolic equation of the shoe with femininity in the fairy tale, and in this particular reading of the novel, requires a brief exposition. Bruno

Bettelheim, in his psychoanalytic interpretation of the unconscious level of "Cinderella," points out that "a variety of folklore data supports the notion that the slipper can serve as a symbol for the vagina" (1989, 269). Thus, according to this line of reasoning, Cinderella's acceptance of the shoe constitutes an acceptance of her own femininity:

> He [the prince] symbolically offers her femininity in the form of the golden slipper–vagina: male acceptance of the vagina and love for the woman is the ultimate male validation of the desirability of her femininity. But nobody, not even a fairy-tale prince, can hand such acceptance to her. . . . Only Cinderella herself can finally welcome her femininity. . . . This is the deeper meaning of the story's telling that "she drew her foot out of the heavy wooden shoe and put it into the slipper, which fitted her to perfection." (Bettelheim 1989, 271)

Cinderella's obligation to assent to a male-constructed femininity situates Bettelheim on the same phallocentric continuum of female stereotypes of submissiveness that Zipes ascribes to Perrault and the Grimms. It is important that Cinderella "welcome her femininity" because only by doing so, according to Bettelheim, does she relieve the prince of his castration anxiety, which is a psychological manifestation of his socially constructed masculinity and "which would interfere with a happy marital relationship" (Bettelheim 1989, 271). Unlike her sisters in the Grimms' version, Cinderella does not need to mutilate herself to fit into the slipper; she is already the uncastrated, unbleeding, unthreatening woman. Furthermore, Bettelheim assures us, "by putting the slipper on her own foot and not waiting until the prince does it, she shows her initiative and her ability to arrange her own fate" (270). While I tend to agree with Bettelheim's notion that Cinderella's acceptance of the shoe symbolizes an acceptance of her femininity, I do not think it does so solely in the narrow psychoanalytic sense that he proposes. I believe it signifies submission to a broader socially sanctioned male-constructed femininity advocated by the tale's popularized versions. Moreover, I disagree that Cinderella's donning of the shoe denotes autonomy and agency. The shoe, especially Perrault's titular "little" glass slipper, stands for a kind of predetermined, fixed, constrained, and constraining social space—analogous to the narrow domestic sphere historically reserved for women—with very little room in which to wiggle. It is an inflexible, prefabricated mold that nullifies Cinderella's minor initiative of putting the shoe on herself, and, as such, its inexorable fixity negates her ability to "arrange her own fate." By slipping her foot into the shoe, Cinderella/Marian symbolically acquiesces to the prescribed, limited role of "Woman."

Thus welcoming this socially and psychologically imposed femininity acquires a problematic dimension when, in contrast to Bettelheim's sanguine phallocentric analysis, the fitting into the shoe is viewed as a *trap* rather than a triumph. In Bettelheim's interpretation, this "femininity," since it is necessary for ensuring the peace of mind of the castration-dreading man, is a patently male construct and is thus vital not for the psychological well-being of the woman herself but for that of her male partner. By consenting to a phallocentrically determined femininity, she is fulfilling a *male* desire. What she gains, as it were, from this acceptance is the "privilege" of being taken care of by a man who is not threatened by her because she does not represent a constant trigger for castration anxiety. Cinderella's feet, the only ones in the kingdom that fit into the diminutive slipper, are clearly smaller than average. From a feminist perspective, such little feet constitute a symbolic deprivation of independence because they signify a repudiation of physical as well as mental self-sufficiency: "once you're queen you won't have to walk any more" says the stepmother to the stepsisters in the Grimms' "Aschenputtel," as she hands a knife to each in turn (Grimm and Grimm 1983, 88).[8]

Like Aschenputtel, Marian flees from *The Edible Woman*'s version of Prince Charming, Peter, three times. As Atwood recasts Cinderella in this novel, shoes and feet gain a particular significance. The shoe motif culminates in a flight scene taken straight out of Cinderella. Marian and Peter are at the Park Plaza on a double date with Marian's flat mate, Ainsley, and Marian's old friend, Len. Peter's prince-charming persona is consistently touted throughout the novel, and in this "ball scene" Marian satirically demotes him to footman status: "Peter opened the plate glass door for me as he always does. Peter is scrupulous about things like that; he opens car doors too. Sometimes I expect him to click his heels" (Atwood 1996a, 66). The footman mannerisms may invoke Cinderella's arrival at the royal ball, as may the decor of the room where they are having drinks: "the square elegant room with its looped curtains and muted carpet and crystal chandeliers" (73). At the end of the chapter, when the two couples leave the Park Plaza, Marian breaks out into an unexpected flight: "On the street the air was cooler; there was a slight breeze. I let go of Peter's arm and began to run" (73). Just like Cinderella, Marian flees without any prior warning; just as the prince pursues Cinderella (in Perrault's version to the end of the staircase and in the Grimms' all the way to her father's house), so Peter pursues Marian. Marian's flight is a genuine attempt to escape a coercive conformity to the feminine mold; she thinks to herself: "All at once it was no longer a game. . . . It was threatening that Peter had not given chase on foot but had enclosed himself in the armour of the car . . . where was there to go?" (75).

In this novel, Peter—no less indoctrinated into patriarchal gender roles than Marian—represents the concept of traditional marriage, and that is one possible explanation of what Marian is fleeing.[9] In fact, in the next chapter, the day after his proposal, Peter confesses that he was unaware of his intention to propose: "I guess I've been running away from it," he says to her. In response, Marian thinks: "I had been too" (Atwood 1996a, 92). Whereas Bettelheim's reading of Cinderella's flight is that "her running away from the ball is motivated by the wish to protect herself against being violated, or carried away by her own desires" (Bettelheim 1989, 265), Marian seems to be evading not a physical violation but rather a violation of her subjectivity and independence.

The most striking similarity between Cinderella's flight scene and that of Atwood's novel is the loss of shoes. Shoes are "lost" in both texts, but the manner in which they are lost in the novel is significant and wholly consistent with Atwood's subversive rewriting of the fairy tale. Just as the Grimms' Aschenputtel has to overcome physical obstacles in order to evade the pursuing prince, which she does with much resourcefulness ("she . . . slipped into the dovecote" / "she climbed among the branches [of the pear tree] as nimbly as a squirrel" [Grimm and Grimm 1983, 86, 87]), so does Marian: "I pushed my way through a mass of prickly shrubberies . . . I took off my shoes and threw them over, then scrambled up, using branches and the uneven bricking of the wall as toe-holds" (Atwood 1996a, 76). Rather than accidentally losing a shoe in her flight, Marian *deliberately* takes off both shoes. This act is noteworthy for two reasons. Firstly, in Perrault's version, as in Disney's cinematic adaptation of Perrault's tale, Cinderella proves her ownership of the lost shoe by showing the prince/his emissary, respectively, the other slipper that she still has in her possession. Obviously, in order to facilitate her climb, Marian must take off both shoes. But symbolically, by doing so, Marian precludes the possibility that a remaining shoe will identify her as the owner of the stray slipper. Afraid that being caught will result in marriage, and that marriage, in turn, will mean conforming to what Rao terms "the traditional, devalued feminine role" (Rao 1993b, 134), Marian gets rid of the "evidence." More explicitly, "the presence of the 'other,' that is the other sex, in this novel is shown to leave no space for autonomy. It gives rise to objectification and unresolved conflicts for the woman" (Rao 1993b, 49). Therefore, by not leaving behind sloppy traces that may lead the prince to her, Marian attempts to protect herself from imminent violation and loss of self. Secondly, Marian does not inadvertently lose the shoes; she takes them off of her own volition. This detail again reinforces the notion that she is (still) an independent agent. She does not let fate happen to her but rather tries to have a hand (or a bare foot, as the case may be) in directing its course.

Atwood's subversion serves to contest the popularized Perrault/Disney version of the fairy tale without providing a one-dimensional alternative or resolution. She captures Marian's desire to break free and the simultaneous gravitation toward dependence on the "prince" by immediately providing a counteraction to the defiant and iconoclastic shoe scene. Ostensibly, Marian is taking charge of her own life, escaping from something she perceives to be a threat. However, immediately after this bold act: "I felt myself caught, set down, and shaken. It was Peter. . . . The relief of being stopped and held, of hearing Peter's normal voice again and knowing he was real, was so great" (Atwood 1996a, 76). Marian insists that she is fine and does not know what got into her. " 'Put on your shoes then,' Peter said, holding them out to me. He was annoyed but he wasn't going to make a fuss" (76).

Although Peter does not slip the shoes onto Marian's feet as befits a Prince Charming, he nonetheless insists that she put them on. Peter's annoyance accords with Bettelheim's slipper-vagina metaphor and its castration-anxiety implications: without her shoes Marian supposedly arouses castration anxiety in Peter because her bare feet imply that she does not fit into the shoes (which moments earlier, in her independence-asserting escape, she symbolically did not). This possibility suggests, in turn, that Marian may not possess the mandatory castration-free status—Bettelheim's prerequisite for successful marriages. But perhaps Peter, who a few pages later proposes to Marian, symbolically needs her to be wearing her shoes not for the purpose of avoiding the psychological trigger of the castration complex but rather as an act that signifies her capacity for containment, her fit-ability into the narrow confines of her forthcoming role as wife and mother. When Peter reprimands Marian for her "childish" behavior after running off, he "savagely" says to her: "The trouble with *you* is . . . you're just rejecting your femininity" (Atwood 1996a, 83). Marian's response to him is: "Oh, SCREW my femininity. . . . Femininity has nothing to do with it" (83; emphasis in original). Her defensive retort, coupled with the earlier act of deliberately removing her shoes, suggests that Peter is right: she *is* rejecting the putative femininity that society espouses. The very flight from marriage, symbolized by physical flight and by the refusal to be contained within prescriptive, symbolic shoes, is seen by the society that Peter represents as a repudiation of femininity: a "screw my femininity" indeed.

The two battling sides of the Cinderella complex are made manifest in this flight-and-rescue scene. In stark contrast to Marian's dizzy, uncertain, almost helpless, backward drop into Peter's arms: "I closed my eyes, knelt for a moment on the top of the wall, swaying dizzily, and dropped backwards" (Atwood 1996a, 76), her earlier scaling of the wall was confident, clear minded, calculated:

> In the darkness at the side of the house I paused to consider. . . . I could see something that was more solid than the darkness, blocking my way. It was the brick wall attached to the iron gate at the front; it seemed to go all the way around the house. I would have to climb it. (76)

The behavior that Atwood attributes to Marian finds an exact mirroring in Dowling's recounting of her own experience, almost as if the novel were a fictional reconstruction of the nonfictional study. Dowling describes how she was "hit with a wave of vertigo" one afternoon while working at the Brooklyn Museum. She soon realizes that these symptoms of dizziness "constituted a metaphor for an unarticulated but central question: Who will catch me if I fall?" (Dowling 1981, 64). Both Dowling and the fictional Marian exhibit physical symptoms that disclose their psychological state: they want to be caught by strong protective arms when they symbolically fall, which femininity-as-social-construct (through tales such as Cinderella) has convinced them that they will do once they attempt to stand alone. As soon as Marian realizes that she is, in fact, capable of standing on her own feet, unfettered by confining shoes, she retreats from her confident stance and yearns to be saved and protected by a man.

An oscillation between independence and dependence is depicted once again in Marian's second attempt at escape when she hides under Len's bed in his apartment.[10] As in her first flight, Marian's second act of rebellion is initially described in positive terms of triumphantly asserting her self-confidence: "I had dug myself a private burrow. I felt smug" (Atwood 1996a, 79). But, as in the wall-climbing scene, she quickly loses her nerve: "The position . . . was becoming more and more of a strain. . . . I began to wish they would hurry up and realize I had disappeared, so they could search for me" (79). Close on the heels of the impulse to escape comes the desire to be saved. Once again, Marian needs Peter's strong arms to rescue her by lifting the bed off her. Once again, an initially confident escape leads her, ambivalently, right back into Peter's arms. Atwood illustrates the Cinderella complex at work in the psyche of a young woman—through motifs and images that recall the tale—as the alternation between a self-reliant autonomy and an entrenched desire for rescue is dramatized in the scenes leading up to the marriage proposal.

Fleeing from the Prince: Marian's Rejection of Marriage

Prior to "Peter's final party"—the novel's last "ball"—Peter had suggested to Marian that she "might have something done with her hair. He had also hinted that perhaps she should buy a dress that was, as he put it, 'not quite so mousy' as any she already owned" (Atwood 1996a, 228). Cinderella's "mean apparel" and "nasty rags" (Perrault 1982, 16, 18), and "old gray smock" (Grimm and Grimm 1983, 84) will not do, and in a subversive and parodic move, rather than Cinderella's stepsisters and stepmother, it is the prince himself who tells Cinderella that she is not quite up to par. Just as Cinderella cannot go to the ball as she is, because that would not conform to the prince's (and society's) ideal of femininity, so Marian is also asked to work some magic and transform herself into a princess worthy of being the prince's consort, one capable of attracting his gaze and that of appreciative others. Thus in preparation for their engagement party, Marian summons a fairy godmother of sorts to transform her from her usual unadorned self. This triadic "fairy godmother" appears in the debased forms of a saleslady who sells her a short, red, sequined dress, a hairdresser who builds "her usually straight hair up into a peculiar shape embellished with many intricate stiff curved wisps," and her flat mate Ainsley as a makeup artist (Atwood 1996a, 230). Atwood de-glamorizes and demystifies the famous transformation scene in "Cinderella" and uncovers the machinations of objectification in various ways. Marian's metamorphosis into Peter's desired party girl is described as a crude, superficial process, quite antithetical to the enchanted atmosphere of transmutation in Perrault's tale and in Disney's animated adaptation. Moreover, Marian likens her treatment at the hairdresser's to a medical procedure in which she has no control over events: "she had felt as passive as though she was being admitted to a hospital to have an operation" (229). Even more telling is Marian's thought that "she didn't enjoy feeling like a slab of flesh, an object" (229). The magical metamorphosis, when stripped of its seemingly innocent fairy-tale charm, ultimately functions to objectify Cinderella for the benefit of the male gaze. Marian, in a subversive twist on Atwood's part, is a Cinderella figure who is conscious of the detrimental alteration as it is transpiring. When she looks at the row of women who are having their hair dried at the salon, she thinks to herself self-reflexively: "Inert; totally inert. Was this what she was being pushed towards, this compound of the simply vegetable and the simply mechanical?" (230). She is acutely aware that marriage will, as Dowling has phrased it, make her come "to a dead halt" (Dowling 1981, 7).

Despite this cognizance on Marian's part, the next paragraph begins with: "She resigned herself to the necessity of endurance" (Atwood 1996a, 230). Atwood's use of "necessity" and "endurance" clearly lend a satirical tone to the scene, for it is after all simply a visit to the beauty parlor, but the underlying sense of ambivalence is clear. Marian grapples with the Cinderella complex by resisting the fact that she is headed for inertia and passivity on the one hand and resigning herself to it on the other. While Marian's hair is being worked on, the urge to flee resurfaces: she thinks of herself as being "strapped into her chair—not really strapped in, but she couldn't get up and go running out into the winter street with wet hair and surgical cloth around her neck" (229). This notion of acquiescing to being metaphorically tied down is discussed in Marcia Lieberman's 1972 article "Some Day My Prince Will Come": the apparatus of acculturation in "Cinderella" ensures that "the girl who . . . submits to her lot, weeping but never running away, has a special compensatory destiny awaiting her" (Lieberman 1972, 194). Marian *is* tempted to run away yet again; however, she "submits to her lot," makes excuses, and ultimately undergoes the transformation that the prince has decreed. She is unhappy with the final result at the hairdresser's, thinking that "it made her look like a call girl," but she is resigned to it: "she had taken the leap, she had walked through that gilded chocolate-box door of her own free will and this was the consequence and she had better accept it. 'Peter will probably like it' . . . she reflected" (Atwood 1996a, 230, 231). She is, like the classic Cinderellas that have come before her, complicit in her own objectification.

Indeed, Peter, like the Prince Charming that he is, compliments Marian on her made-over look, thus endorsing her conformity to the socially prescribed feminine ideal. But much like the mask of Marian's "feminine role" that stands in opposition to her true feelings, her transformation into Peter's ideal woman renders her unrecognizable to herself. She thinks of herself as "a person she had never seen before" with "bare arms and barish dress and well-covered face" (Atwood 1996a, 244–45). Although she fits Peter's notion of what a "real" woman should look like, her gradually diminishing body and the external ornamentation that seems so alien to her make her cease to exist in her own eyes. As Cristina Bacchilega has put it, "by showcasing 'women' and making them disappear at the same time, the fairy tale thus transforms us/them into man-made constructs of 'Woman'" (Bacchilega 1997, 9).

After having fled from Peter twice before, on the night of their double date with Ainsley and Len, Marian runs away from a "ball" for the third time in the novel. With no prior warning, and without Peter even noticing, she slips out of his apartment during their engagement party. As in the previous two times, she is escaping out of the sheer fright that grips her at the thought of their impending matrimonial union. She feels that Peter, who has been taking pictures with his camera all night, is zeroing in on her, aiming to ensnare. She runs away because "she could not let him catch her this time. Once he pulled the trigger she would be stopped, fixed indissolubly in that gesture, that single stance, unable to move or change" (Atwood 1996a, 269). Losing her personal autonomy would be tantamount to a death sentence for her, as indicated by her referring to the camera button as a "trigger." "Shooting" her picture would be analogous to encasing her in the objectifying glass slipper, and marriage would bring her life to a dead halt.

Conclusion

Paradoxically, Atwood's subversion of Cinderella in *The Edible Woman* results in an ending that mirrors the ending of the classic fairy tale variants of Perrault/Disney and the Grimms. At the novel's close, its Cinderella figure is rescued, as she is in these popularized variants. However, it is not the prince who rescues her from enslavement to her wicked stepfamily; instead, she rescues herself from enslavement to a destructive concept of femininity. Marian isn't saved *by* the prince but rather *from* the prince. Cinderella's is a happy ending because she marries the prince; Marian's is a happy ending because she does not. As Atwood observes, "the comedy solution would be a tragic solution for Marian" (Gibson 1990, 12). Accordingly, Atwood called her first novel an "anti-comedy" because she succeeded in writing a comedy in which the heroine's triumph is not that she gets married, as the conventional comedy genre requires, but that she avoids doing so (Gibson 1990, 12). Marian excises the "prince," as well as the power he has over her, from her plot in the hopes of restoring and securing her subjectivity.

In the introduction to *Fairy Tales and Feminism*, Haase writes:

> Understood as a locus of struggle over cultural values and individual desires, the fairy tale actually invites thematic instability and contradictory impulses. Interpretations of classical and revisionist texts must be attentive to that struggle—that is, to the ambivalence with which women writers and other creative artists often approach the genre.

> Revisionist mythmaking, after all, enacts ambivalence by simultaneously rejecting and embracing the fairy tale. (Haase 2004, 30)

Atwood's critical distance detaches her from a personal engagement in "rejecting and embracing the fairy tale" but does ascribe this ambivalence to the fictional protagonist of her novel. That is, the locus of ambivalence lies not in Atwood the writer but in Marian the character, who simultaneously embraces and rejects the tale of Cinderella in her thoughts and actions. On the one hand, Atwood's revisionist novel undermines the ideologies of female passivity and limited gender roles that Perrault, the Grimms, and Disney espouse. Marian, unlike Cinderella, is ultimately an active and resisting agent who contests these roles. On the other hand, Marian still exhibits much of the gendered passivity found in these Cinderella variants. The novel's resolution also conveys this ambivalence. By ending the novel with Marian standing over her lover, Duncan, like a contented housewife with "a peculiar sense of satisfaction to see him eat as if the work hadn't been wasted after all," and smiling "comfortably" at him despite his complete disregard for her efforts, Atwood represents the difficulty of fully escaping the grip of the Cinderella complex (Atwood 1996a, 310). Even though Marian succeeds in chasing Peter away, thus supposedly upending the patriarchal order that threatened her autonomous existence, Atwood ends the novel with a scene that may be read as reestablishing traditional gender roles. Marian watches with contentment as the last of the cake vanishes "like a wink" into Duncan's mouth (310). The wink is, perhaps, Atwood winking at us. Marian has evaded the trap, but for how long? Her "choices remain much the same at the end of the book as they are at the beginning: a career going nowhere, or marriage as an exit from it," as Atwood herself has remarked (1982, 370). With this open—or, perhaps, closed—ending, Atwood subverts the resolution of the exemplary tale of Cinderella, transforming it into a cautionary tale for contemporary women.

Notes

1. Sharon Rose Wilson (1993), in *Margaret Atwood's Fairy-Tale Sexual Politics*, shows how Atwood regularly integrates fairy-tale intertexts in her writings; Shuli Barzilai (2000) discusses the tales of "Rapunzel" and "Bluebeard" in relation to Atwood's novel *Lady Oracle*; Vanessa Joosen (2011) addresses the parodic critique "aimed at sociopolitical fairy-tale criticism" in Atwood's prose poem "There Was Once" (59); and *Once upon a Time* is a recent essay

collection, edited by Sarah Appleton (2008), devoted to Atwood's engagement with myths, fairy tales, and legends.

2. Atwood discusses her favorite fairy tales in her interviews with Bonnie Lyons (1990) and Joyce Carol Oates (1990), stressing that the active resourcefulness of the heroes and heroines in these tales are what make them appealing to her. Atwood describes her connection to, and opinion of, the tales in interviews (Lyons 1990; Oates 1990; Sandler 1990) and in her critical writing, "Of Souls as Birds" and "Grimms Remembered," among others.
3. The novel was only published in 1969 because, according to Atwood, the publisher had lost the manuscript when it was first sent to him (Atwood 1982).
4. Ruth Bottigheimer's comparative analysis of "Aschenputtel" in the Grimms' published editions reveals that in their continuous editorial work the authors had gradually and systematically silenced their heroine. This was achieved when, in each subsequent edition of their collection, "direct speech . . . tended to be transferred from women to men, and from good to bad girls and women" (Bottigheimer 1987, 58). By the final edition of 1857, Cinderella is deprived of virtually all direct speech and the little that remains is "the unvarying incantations addressed to birds and tree" (63).
5. Although Perrault's attitudes toward women and their social roles were substantially more progressive than those writers belonging to the ancien régime school of thought, such as Nicolas Boileau, fairy-tale scholars have shown that Perrault's view of women was nevertheless highly conventional despite his "modernist" approach. Marina Warner acknowledges Perrault's protofeminist tendencies, but also points out that in his poem "L'Apologie des femmes," "Perrault, the champion of womankind, defender of old wives' wisdom, painting his paragon wife, invoked her perfect '*bouche enfantine*,' her childlike mouth—ignorance as virtue" (169). Likewise, Haase, refering to the same poem, calls it "a problematic text" because "Perrault used the authority of women only to legitimate the modernist position, having no real intentions of allowing women to exercise power in the public sphere" (2008, 739). Finally, as Barzilai (2005) shows in her review of Mererid Puw Davies's *The Tale of Bluebeard in German Literature*, presenting a "resolutely positive reading" of Perrault's gender politics in relation to women may be a projection of the reader's wishes more than it is an undebatable textual given (Barzilai 2005, 316).
6. Fiona Tolan, citing Gayle Greene, writes: "Marian's attempt to negate her body through starvation can be read, as Gayle Greene reads it, as a covert rebellion against a system that appropriates femininity as a commodity to

be consumed. Marian's anorexia, by this understanding, is a rejection of her femininity" (Tolan 2007, 17).

7. "*The Edible Woman*'s Refusal to Consent to Femininity" (Bouson 2000); "The 'Masquerade' of Femininity: *The Edible Woman*" (1993a); "The Two Faces of the Mirror in *The Edible Woman* and *Lady Oracle* (Bromberg 1988), to name a few.
8. On a more literal level, very small feet, as Chinese culture informs us, are a physical handicap that limits and restricts their owner; the feet and their ornate coverings serve to objectify women by turning them into aesthetic objects that are pleasing to the male gaze. They hardly liberate the women who are doomed to bear this disfigurement but rather confine them to a kind of prison where they may be gazed at.
9. In *The Edible Woman* female characters are not the only "victims" of a patriarchal construction of gender identity; men too—particularly the novel's Prince Charming, Peter—are at the mercy of the socially constructed models they feel compelled to emulate. In a wry comment, Alice Palumbo describes Peter as "merely the sum of the lifestyle tips he gathers from men's magazines" (2000, 74). Consequently, Peter has been indoctrinated to view himself as a rescuing prince no less than Marian has been programmed to think of herself as a passive woman in need of a male rescuer. Peter's view of marriage is clearly a result of the kind of masculinity society endorses and imposes on him. Statements attributed to Peter range from "he considered it unfair to marry . . . if you couldn't afford to support your wife," to "A fellow can't keep running around indefinitely. It'll be good for my practice too, the clients like to know you've got a wife; people get suspicious of a single man after a certain age, they start thinking you're queer or something" (114–15, 93). Peter's view of manhood is primarily defined by the code that "one may never do anything that even remotely suggests femininity. Masculinity is the relentless repudiation of the feminine" (Kimmel 1997, 229).
10. In the Grimms' "Aschenputtel," Aschenputtel hides in a (probably narrow) dovecote after her first flight, just as Marian's second attempt at escaping finds her in cramped quarters under Len's bed. Aschenputtel's second flight culminates in her making her way through branches and climbing a pear tree. Similarly, during her first flight Marian scales a wall with the help of branches.

References

Appleton, Sarah A., ed. 2008. *Once upon a Time: Myths, Fairy Tales, and Legends in Margaret Atwood's Writing*. Newcastle: Cambridge Scholars Publishing.

Atwood, Margaret. 1982. "An Introduction to *The Edible Woman*." In *Second Words: Selected Critical Prose*, 369–70. Boston: Beacon Press.

———. 1996a. *The Edible Woman*. New York: Bantam.

———. 1996b. "Grimms Remembered." In *The Reception of Grimms' Fairy Tales: Responses, Reactions, Revisions*, edited by Donald Haase, 290–92. Detroit: Wayne State University Press.

———. 1998. "Of Souls as Birds." In *Mirror Mirror on the Wall: Women Writers Explore Their Favorite Fairy Tales*, edited by Kate Bernheimer, 22–38. New York: Doubleday.

Bacchilega, Cristina. 1997. *Postmodern Fairy Tales: Gender and Narrative Strategies*. Philadelphia: University of Pennsylvania Press.

Barzilai, Shuli. 2000. "'Say That I Had a Lovely Face': The Grimms' 'Rapunzel,' Tennyson's 'Lady of Shalott,' and Atwood's *Lady Oracle*." *Tulsa Studies in Women's Literature* 19 (2): 231–54.

———. 2005. "Review of *The Tale of Bluebeard in German Literature: From the Eighteenth Century to the Present*, by Mererid Puw Davies." *Marvels & Tales* 19 (2): 313–16.

———. 2009. *Tales of Bluebeard and His Wives from Late Antiquity to Postmodern Times*. New York: Routledge.

Bettelheim, Bruno. 1989. *The Uses of Enchantment: The Meaning and Importance of Fairy Tales*. New York: Vintage Books.

Bottigheimer, Ruth B. 1987. *Grimms' Bad Girls and Bold Boys: The Moral and Social Vision of the Tales*. New Haven, CT: Yale University Press.

Bouson, J. Brooks. 1993. *Brutal Choreographies: Oppositional Strategies and Narrative Designs in the Novels of Margaret Atwood*. Amherst: University of Massachusetts Press.

———. 2000. "The Edible Woman's Refusal to Consent to Femininity." In *Margaret Atwood: Modern Critical Views*, edited by Harold Bloom, 71–91. Philadelphia: Chelsea House.

Bromberg, Pamela S. 1988. "The Two Faces of the Mirror in *The Edible Woman* and *Lady Oracle*." In *Margaret Atwood: Vision and Forms*, edited by Kathryn VanSpanckeren and Jan Garden Castro, 12–23. Carbondale: Southern Illinois University Press.

Dowling, Colette. 1981. *The Cinderella Complex: Women's Hidden Fear of Independence*. New York: Pocket Books.

Dundes, Alan, ed. 1982. *Cinderella: A Casebook.* Madison: University of Wisconsin Press.

Dutheil de la Rochère, Martine Hennard. 2009. "Queering the Fairy Tale Canon: Emma Donoghue's *Kissing the Witch.*" In *Fairy Tales Reimagined: Essays on New Retellings*, edited by Susan Redington Bobby, 13–30. Jefferson, NC: McFarland.

Gibson, Graeme. 1990. "Dissecting the Way in Which a Writer Works." In *Margaret Atwood: Conversations*, edited by Earl G. Ingersoll, 3–19. Princeton, NJ: Ontario Review Press.

Grimm, Jakob, and Wilhelm Grimm. 1983. "Ashputtle." In *Grimms' Tales for Young and Old: The Complete Stories*, translated by Ralph Manheim, 83–89. New York: Doubleday Anchor Books.

Haase, Donald, ed. 2004. *Fairy Tales and Feminism.* Detroit: Wayne University Press.

———, ed. 2008. *The Greenwood Encyclopedia of Folktales and Fairy Tales.* Westport, CT: Greenwood Press.

Joosen, Vanessa. 2011. *Critical and Creative Perspectives in Fairy Tales: An Intertextual Dialogue between Fairy-Tale Scholarship and Postmodern Retellings.* Detroit: Wayne State University Press.

Kimmel, Michael S. 1997. "Masculinity as Homophobia: Fear, Shame, and Silence in the Construction of Gender Identity." In *Toward a New Psychology of Gender*, edited by Mary Gergen and Sara Davis, 213–19. New York: Routledge.

Lieberman, Marcia K. 1987. " 'Some Day My Prince Will Come': Female Acculturation through the Fairy Tale." In *Don't Bet on the Prince: Contemporary Feminist Fairy Tales in North America and England*, edited by Jack Zipes, 185–200. New York: Routledge.

Lurie, Alison. 1970. "Fairy Tale Liberation." *New York Review of Books*, December 17, 42–44.

Lyons, Bonnie. 1990. "Using Other People's Dreadful Childhoods." Interview with Margaret Atwood, in *Margaret Atwood: Conversations*, edited by Earl G. Ingersoll, 221–33. Princeton, NJ: Ontario Review Press.

Oates, Joyce Carol. 1990. "My Mother Would Rather Skate Than Scrub Floors." Interview with Margaret Atwood, in *Margaret Atwood: Conversations*, edited by Earl G. Ingersoll, 69–73. Princeton, NJ: Ontario Review Press.

Palumbo, Alice M. 2000. "On the Border: Margaret Atwood's Novels." In *Margaret Atwood: Works and Impact*, edited by Reingard M. Nischik, 73–86. New York: Camden House.

Perrault, Charles. 1982. "Cinderella, or the Little Glass Slipper." In *Cinderella: A Casebook*, edited by Alan Dundes, 14–21. Madison: University of Wisconsin Press.

Rao, Eleonora. 1993a. "The 'Masquerade' of Femininity: *The Edible Woman.*" In *Strategies for Identity.*

———. 1993b. *Strategies for Identity: The Fiction of Margaret Atwood.* New York: Peter Lang.

Sandler, Linda. 1990. "A Question of Metamorphosis." Interview with Margaret Atwood, in *Margaret Atwood: Conversations*, edited by Earl G. Ingersoll, 40–57. Princeton, NJ: Ontario Review Press.

Tatar, Maria, ed. 1999. *The Classic Fairy Tales.* New York: W. W. Norton.

Tolan, Fiona. 2007. *Margaret Atwood: Feminism and Fiction.* New York: Rodopi.

Warner, Marina. 1996. *From the Beast to the Blonde: On Fairy Tales and Their Tellers.* New York: Noonday Press.

Wilson, Sharon Rose. 1993. *Margaret Atwood's Fairy-Tale Sexual Politics.* Jackson: University Press of Mississippi.

Yolen, Jane. 1982. "America's Cinderella." In *Cinderella: A Casebook*, edited by Alan Dundes, 296–304. Madison: University of Wisconsin Press.

Zipes, Jack. 1988. *Fairy Tales and the Art of Subversion: The Classical Genre for Children and the Process of Civilization.* New York: Methuen.

8

Fairy-Tale Refashioning in Angela Carter's Fiction

From Cinderella's Ball Dresses to Ashputtle's Rags

Martine Hennard Dutheil de la Rochère

According to Marina Warner, "the fairy tale grew up in 1979" (2014, 141) with the publication of Angela Carter's *The Bloody Chamber and Other Stories*, which started a fashion for adult fairy tales that lasts to this day. The coming of age of the genre began when Carter translated French fairy tales during the summer of 1976, and the translation-(re)creation dynamic was a key to the author's literary practice. The present article exemplifies this two-fold process by analyzing Carter's Perrault-based translation for children, "Cinderella: or, The Little Glass Slipper," from *The Fairy Tales of Charles Perrault* (1977), in counterpoint with "Ashputtle *or* The Mother's Ghost," her Grimm-based retelling of the story for grown-ups published in *The Virago Book of Ghost Stories* (1987), and reprinted posthumously in *American Ghosts and Old World Wonders* (1994 [1993]). In "Cinderella: or, The Little Glass Slipper" Carter dusts off the worldly and humorous French text to transmit an emancipatory message to young girls about the importance of self-fashioning, while "Ashputtle *or* The Mother's Ghost" explores the ambivalence of mother-daughter relations in a darker mode and mood. Carter started out by "freshening up" the classic fairy tale for children for Victor Gollancz, and went on to respond to anonymous folk versions that she had discovered in the course of her research and found "much much more interesting and infinitely ruder" than the stories cleaned up for the nursery, as she put it in an interview with John Bailey shortly before her untimely death (Carter 1998b, 38).[1] She explains that *The Bloody Chamber* collection was inspired by her translation of French *contes* and by a lesser-known folktale tradition that would give a new impulse and direction to her writing, and shape her understanding of literary creation as emerging from the interplay of reading and (re)writing:

> Reading is just as creative an activity as writing, and most intellectual development depends upon new readings of old texts. I am all for putting new wine in old bottles, especially if the pressure of the new wine makes the old bottles explode. (Carter 1998b, 37)[2]

Since every reader is a potential author who can tease out new meanings in old texts, translation and rewriting are two distinct, and yet inseparable, activities that reveal Carter's acute attention to linguistic, textual, and cultural differences. The bottle metaphor draws attention to the profoundly transformative impact of active reading that renews our understanding of the familiar tales, challenging expectations and certainties, and thwarting efforts to contain meaning in favor of an open-ended process of ever-renewed interpretation and (re)creation.

The mutable identity of Cinderella thus exemplifies the recent "creative turn" disrupting the old-fashioned binaries and hierarchies of original text versus poor copy in favor of a new understanding of translation as refashioning, whose differences from an already elusive "original" are not only inevitable but also meaningful and productive. One of the most influential proponents of this paradigm shift is Susan Bassnett, for whom "it is absurd to see translation as anything other than a creative literary activity, for translators are all the time engaging with the texts first as readers and then as rewriters, as recreators of that text in another language . . . Translation was a means not only of acquiring more information about other writers and their work, but also of discovering new ways of writing" (Bassnett 2006, 174). The fact that translators not only play a key role in cross-cultural exchanges but also in the emergence of new literary trends and cultural formations has become more and more apparent in recent years (see Simon 1996; Venuti 2008 [1995]; France and Gillespie 2008, 2010, 2005, 2006, forthcoming).[3] A critical inquiry into the "invisibility" of the translator has notably led to the (re)discovery of key figures who contributed to the revival and renewal of texts, genres, and literary forms, and hence to a reappraisal of the role of translation in the elaboration of innovative poetics. Many authors have indeed placed the activity of translation at the heart of their creative process, either by translating their own writings or by translating other texts that fed into their own work, like Angela Carter. After André Lefevere, translation is considered here as a modality of rewriting that forms a continuum with Carter's famous "stories about fairy stories" in *The Bloody Chamber* and beyond.[4]

In the present case, it is tempting to draw on the metaphor of dress to describe Carter's translation of Perrault's "Cendrillon ou la petite pantoufle de verre," where dressing figures so prominently, in counterpoint with her much bloodier retelling of the tale as a ghost story in "Ashputtle *or* The Mother's Ghost." Ben Van Wyke nevertheless cautions against the platonic model of representation that underlies the familiar metaphor critiqued by Nietzsche (Van Wyke 2010). While the Cinderella tale suggests the image of translation as a new dress, then, it also questions it inasmuch as Cinderella *is* what she wears; this undermines the belief in an alleged essence or unchanging nature of the tale conventionally represented by its "type" in the Aarne-Thompson-Uther Folktale Index.

The Folklorization of Perrault in English: The Two-Faced Cinderella, or Perrimm and Grimmault

Carter believed in the emancipating role of education and reading. She praises Perrault's "fables of the politics of experience" in "The Better to Eat you with," because they carry a pragmatic message of worldly instruction that children can learn from: "We must cope with the world before we can interpret it" (Carter 1998c, 453). But in her rewritings, Carter harked back to a folk tradition associated with the Grimms' *Kinder- und Hausmärchen* where she found deeper anthropological and psychological insights.

The Bloody Chamber contains variations on the familiar tales of Bluebeard, Beauty and the Beast, Sleeping Beauty, and Little Red Riding Hood, among others. Surprisingly, however, Cinderella is absent from the collection, even though Carter had originally planned to include a "very primitive, very archaic" version of the Cinderella story (Dutheil de la Rochère 2013, 263). In marked contrast to the lighthearted tone of her translation of Perrault for children, Carter's "Ashputtle *or* The Mother's Ghost," published much later, focuses on the macabre and cruel elements of the Grimms' folktale. In *American Ghosts and Old World Wonders* (1994 [1993]), the threefold structure of the text hints at the tale's openness for interpretation and reinterpretation. Subtitled "three versions of one story," "Ashputtle" inspires three retellings: "1. The Mutilated Girls," "2. The Burned Child," and "3. Travelling Clothes."

While the motif of dress links the translation and the rewriting, it also draws attention to radical differences in treatment, tone, style, and significance. In her translation of Perrault for children, Carter chooses to convey the full title of Perrault's "Cendrillon ou la petite pantoufle de verre," as if to stress the difference between Perrault's text and the Disneyfied stereotype, or the connection between the heroine and her marvelous glass shoe: "Cinderella: or, The Little Glass Slipper." She even adopts the distinctive punctuation of Robert Samber's first English translation of Perrault in *Histories or Tales of Past Tales, with Morals* (1729). Carter probably read Samber's translation in Iona and Peter Opie's *The Classic Fairy Tales* (1974), which she describes as "a beautiful coffee table book" in her notes and lists in the select bibliography of *The Fairy Tales of Charles Perrault*. The long title and unusual punctuation of her retranslated fairy tale pays homage to the early translator while also emphasizing the specific nature and purpose of her *new* translation, as the dust cover of *The Fairy Tales of Charles Perrault* makes clear ("newly translated by Angela Carter"). Her rewriting of the tale, "Ashputtle *or* The Mother's Ghost," on the other hand, takes as its starting point Ralph Manheim's retranslation of the Grimms' *Kinder- und Hausmärchen*, which Carter was also familiar with. In her journal, Carter mentions a photocopy of "Ashputtle" from Ralph Manheim's acclaimed translation of *Grimms' Tales for Young and Old*.[5] Manheim's "literal" translation of the Grimms' collection was first published in New York by Anchor Press/Doubleday in 1977, and in London by Victor Gollancz (Carter's own publisher) in 1978. Manheim explains in the preface that he wanted to capture the "authentic" folktale voice that was lost when the tales were softened and bowdlerized for children. He describes his new translation as an attempt to be "faithful to the Grimm brothers' faithfulness" to their oral sources, adding that he has "tried to use a simple, natural language" to convey (or, rather, reconstruct) the voices of the individual storytellers, whether "mysterious, elegiac, hushed-and-frightening, poetic, whimsical, rowdy, solemnly or mock-solemnly moralizing, and so on" (Grimm and Grimm 1983, 1). Carter's literary project echoes Manheim's inasmuch as she aligns herself with an oral storytelling tradition that she seeks to honor. Her "Ashputtle *or* The Mother's Ghost" even begins with a quote from Manheim's "Ashputtle," whose gloss serves as a prologue for her two subsequent retellings of the tale, thereby exemplifying the idea of close reading and textual analysis as a preliminary basis for new creation.

In *The Classic Fairy Tales*, which also influenced Carter's perception of the genre, Iona and Peter Opie stress the antiquity and ubiquity of pre-Perrault versions of Cinderella; they note its many "parallels from different countries" collected in the nineteenth century onward, and observe that "Perrault's story, for all its wit and compassion, is a worldly and somewhat sentimentalized version of older and darker stories, which have many strange undertones" (Opie and Opie 1974, 13). In several versions, they observe,

"Cinderella and the Fairy Godmother." Reversible head by Rex Whistler, ca. 1935, reproduced in *The Classic Fairy Tales* (Opie and Opie 1974).

"the magical assistance the heroine receives comes to her from the spirit of her dead mother" (13). The Opies also underline the cruelty of the tale, which puts a lot of emphasis on Ashputtle's suffering and graphically depicts the mutilation of the stepsisters before and after the heroine's ultimate triumph. They note that similar tales have been collected in various parts of the world, including a Chinese version dating back to the ninth century AD.[6] The folklorist Andrew Lang, whose work Carter also knew quite well, similarly contrasts Perrault's "civilized" *conte*, where Cinderella forgives her mean stepsisters, to the Grimms' "savage *Märchen*," which contains two gruesome scenes involving mothers: the bloody cutting of the toe and heel of Ashputtle's rivals suggested by their own mother, and their blinding by the protective and vengeful mother/bird on Ashputtle's wedding day.[7] In Manheim's translation: "But the shoe was too small and she couldn't get her big toe in. So her mother handed her the knife and said: 'Cut your toe off. Once you're queen, you won't have to walk any more.' " The girl cut her toe off, forced her foot into the shoe, gritted her teeth against the pain, and went out to the king's son" (Grimm and Grimm 1983, 88). But the bird draws the prince's attention to the "blood spurting" (88), and one after the other the false brides are returned home. To punish them for being "wicked and false" (89), both sisters are blinded by doves.

The Classic Fairy Tales captures the double legacy of the tale in a striking image chosen to illustrate the introduction. While the playful magic of disguise and magical transformations is central to modern notions of Cinderella informed by Perrault's witty and urbane fairy tale, Carter unearths and responds to the Grimms' gloomy, creepy, and bloody folktale. From translation to rewriting, the focus shifts from pretty dresses, resourceful godmother, and happy ending to the ambivalent presence of the dead mother who returns in the shape of a bird to help and avenge—but also to haunt—the persecuted heroine. In the first retelling, upon finding her stepsister's cut-off toe in the fireplace, Ashputtle "feels both awe and fear at the phenomenon of mother love. Mother love, which winds about these daughters like a shroud" (Carter 1994 [1993], 115).

"Cendrillon ou la petite pantoufle de verre" and "Cinderella: or, The Little Glass Slipper": From the Making of a Princess to Dressing Up

Perrault's "Cendrillon ou la petite pantoufle de verre" mocks both the bitter competition to win a prince's hand and the obsession with fashion at the court of Louis XIV. In contrast to Disney's movie, however, Perrault's moral explicitly distances itself from the conventional praise of female beauty and stresses the role of fine manners and education instead:

Moralité	**Moral**
La beauté pour le sexe est un rare trésor, *De l'admirer jamais on ne se lasse;* *Mais ce qu'on nomme bonne grâce* *Est sans prix, et vaut mieux encor.* *C'est ce qu'à Cendrillon fit avoir sa Marraine,* *En la dressant, en l'instruisant,* *Tant et si bien qu'elle en fit une Reine:* *(Car ainsi sur ce Conte on va moralisant.)*[8] *Belles, ce don vaut mieux que d'être bien coiffées,* *Pour engager un cœur, pour en venir à bout,* *La bonne grâce est le vrai don des Fées;* *Sans elle on ne peut rien, avec elle, on peut tout.*	Beauty is a fine thing in a woman; it will always be admired. But *charm* is beyond price and worth more, in the long run. When her godmother *dressed* Cinderella up and told her how to behave at the ball, she instructed her in charm. Lovely ladies, this gift is worth more than a fancy hairdo; to win a heart, to reach a happy ending, *charm* is the true gift of the fairies. Without it, one can achieve nothing; with it, everything. (Carter 1977, 95–96, italics mine)
(*Contes*, 177–78)	

Perrault's first moral values *bonne grâce* over and above beauty. According to Antoine Furetière's dictionary (1690) *bonne grâce* combines affability, amiability, and kindness. *Grâce* is defined as something that is pleasing (attitude, appearance, dress, conversation) but also what conforms to good taste, polite manners, and reason (*faire un conte de bonne grâce*).

The meaning of *bonne grâce* also extends to the effect of these qualities on a prince or a king. According to the *Dictionnaire de l'Académie française* (1694): "On dit, *Estre en grace auprés du Prince, ou de quelque personne puissante,* pour dire, Y estre en consideration, en estime. *Bonnes-graces,* se dit dans le mesme sens. *Il est dans les bonnes-graces du Roy. Il a perdu les bonnes-graces du Prince.*" Associated with the appearance, attitude and behavior of court ladies, *bonne grâce* is therefore a strong marker of power and influence at court. In the fairy tale, it is the proper training and connections provided by the fairy godmother that ensure the fairy-tale heroine's success and royal marriage, even more than her great beauty. Perrault thus places nurture over good looks, showing that it is essential to master the codes of the aristocratic ethos and courtly milieu in order to marry a prince. The tale may even nod to Perrault's contemporary, Madame de Maintenon (1635–1719), who was born Françoise d'Aubigné (apparently in the Niort prison), married the poet Scarron, and later became governess of the king's illegitimate children. She secretly married Louis XIV in 1683, and apparently exerted a great influence on the king by promoting morality, piety, and austerity. Although posterior to Perrault, another famous Cinderella-like figure was Jeanne Antoinette Poisson, known as Madame de Pompadour (1721–1764), who was educated from childhood to become Louis XV's mistress and secured titles of nobility for herself and her relatives, like the fairy-tale heroine. Translating from a late twentieth-century perspective colored by her feminist sensibility, Carter picks on the idea of education and personality to challenge the beauty myth (usually associated with the fairy tale) and praise natural *charm* as the new locus of magic. In keeping with modern expectations about the genre and Carter's own values, the moral focuses on love over social advancement, and plays with the idea of the storyteller as a fairy godmother who gives good advice to her young readers.

Because fairy tales tend to be read ahistorically, a phenomenon reinforced by simplified editions and bowdlerized adaptations, the worldliness of Perrault's fairy tale is seldom perceived by the average reader. But Carter's close attention to the French text enabled her to perceive and modernize its down-to-earth wisdom in her translation. Perrault's wry humor gives way to child-friendly, optimistic, and humorous advice to young girls. In this sense, Carter's message is not so alien from Perrault's aim to transmit a "very sensible moral" (une "Morale très sensée") in the preface of *Histoires ou contes du temps passé*, though of course the translator makes it speak to her own time, context, and concerns. The translator aligns herself with the tradition of the pedagogical tale for children shed of its moralizing tone and normative purpose, while meeting the readers' expectations about the genre. Her "happy ending" is about love ("to win a heart") and no longer about what it takes to make a royal match.

We note that Perrault stresses the role of experienced and well-connected women in the making of a princess or a queen. Because she has been trained (*en la dressant*) to attract a prince's attention, Cinderella gets a prince as her "prize" with the help of her godmother. Carter mistranslates the French *dresser* (trained) as *dressed* (clothed), which shifts the focus from the good manners acquired by the girl in the hands of her godmother to her striking apparel. This reflects Carter's insights into identity as self-fashioning brilliantly developed in her cultural criticism and articles gathered in *Shaking a Leg: Collected Journalism and Writings* (Carter 1998c). The motif of the "dressing-room" thus runs through Carter's writings across genres and periods.

In "Ashputtle *or* The Mother's Ghost," however, Carter activates the actual meaning of the French word *dresser* as the brutal training of an animal to obey and do one's bidding. The tale becomes an occasion to reflect on ruthless mothers shaping generations of Cinderellas to fulfill their own ambitions: the stepmother, the narrator notes in the first retelling, "is prepared to cripple her daughters" (Carter 1994 [1993], 115), and the dove stays close to Ashputtle at the ball "pecking her ears to make her dance vivaciously, so that the prince would see her, so that the prince would love her, so that he would follow her" (115). "Ashputtle *or* The Mother's Ghost," then, captures the darker sociopsychological significance of the tale as it raises the issue of intergenerational transmission and the reproduction of behavioral patterns from mothers to daughters. The shift from "Cinderella: or, The Little Glass Slipper" to "Ashputtle *or* The Mother's Ghost" then arguably hinges on a word, *dresser*, whose meaning slips from dress and fashion to the brutality of the Grimms' *Märchen*.[9] Carter's rewriting, in other words, can be seen as a corrective (or redress) to her translation.

In her foreword to *The Fairy Tales of Charles Perrault*, Carter links Perrault and Grimm, claiming that "Perrault's sources stemmed from the lore of the same kind of country people who told stories to Jacob and Wilhelm Grimm in Germany a hundred years later" (Carter 1977, 16), but she also contrasts "the savagery and dark poetry of Grimms' 'Household Tales' with Perrault's elegant, witty and sensible pages" (17). Carter's translation of Perrault's "Cendrillon" favors simple grammatical forms, syntax, and vocabulary. This child-friendly strategy is also consistent with the style of folktales. Some details of Carter's translation of Perrault even seem to reflect the pressure of the Grimms' tale. Thus Cinderella's mother is said to be dead, which is only implied in Perrault's text, where the father simply remarries. Another shift has to do with class, with Perrault's noble *gentil-homme* becoming an ordinary *man* in Carter's translation, and so closer to the Grimms' *reicher Mann*. The grammar of Carter's text reflects the stark conflict that opposes women for the possession of a rich husband. Like Manheim, Carter resorts to repetitions, possessive forms, and symmetrical constructions: the second wife has "two daughters *of her own*," whereas the first wife "had given him [Cinderella's father] a daughter *of his own*" (Carter 1977, 83; italics mine). "Ashputtle *or* The Mother's Ghost" even starts with a close textual analysis of the opening of Manheim's "Ashputtle" ("A rich man's wife fell sick and, feeling that her end was near, she called her only daughter to her bedside and said . . ."; Grimm and Grimm 1983, 83):

> Although the woman is defined by her relation to him ("a rich man's wife") the daughter is unambiguously hers, as if hers alone, and the entire drama concerns only women, takes place almost exclusively among women, is a fight between two groups of women—in the right-hand corner, Ashputtle and her mother; in the left-hand corner, the stepmother and *her* daughters. (Carter 1994 [1993], 110)

While Carter's translation of Perrault's text sends an optimistic message to young girls about the pursuit of happiness with the help of benevolent, worldly-wise, and experienced female helpers, her rewriting focuses on the more ambivalent role played by mothers who take control of their daughter's lives and manipulate them like dolls or puppets to do their bidding: "the girls, all three, are animated solely by the wills of their mothers" (Carter 1994 [1993], 111). Their motivations are complex, ranging from personal ambition and desire for revenge to concern for their daughter's economic security once they are dead and gone. Whereas Carter's translation of Perrault warns young girls that there is more to the seduction game than a "fancy hairdo," then, the rewriting set in an immemorial past reflects on what binds one generation of women to the next.

Quarreling over Cinderella, or Carter's Dressing Down of Bettelheim

Carter's retranslation of Perrault took place at a time when the fairy tale was debated among feminists and accused of reinforcing patriarchal norms and values. Snow White, Sleeping Beauty, and Cinderella in particular were seen as perpetuating stereotypes of femininity that went against the progressive ideals promoted by the women's liberation movement (see Zipes 1986; Haase 2004; and Joosen 2011). Sarah Gamble has observed that the feminist Carter "uncovers a deeper, more subversive history of the fairy tale, bringing to the surface not only what Warner terms its 'harshly realistic core' but also 'the suspect whiff of femininity' from which it has never been completely dissociated," even though "her reclamation of the position of female storyteller does not lead her to the exoneration of the female gender from complicity with—and even an active perpetuation of—the circumstances of its own oppression" (Gamble 2008, 27). Another influential interpretive framework for the fairy tale was Bruno Bettelheim in *The Uses of Enchantment* (1976), with whom Carter declared she was "quarreling furiously," probably because he contends that "the rescuers fall in love with these heroines because of their beauty, which symbolizes their perfection" (Bettelheim 1976, 277).[10] As is well known, Bettelheim devotes a long chapter to Cinderella, which he presents as a story about "sibling rivalry." He sums up several versions of the tale, including the ancient Chinese tale that associates sexual attractiveness with small feet. He admits, however, that "neither in Basile's story nor in the much more ancient Chinese tale is there any mention of Cinderella being mistreated by her siblings" (Bettelheim 1976, 246). This is probably why Carter, who was critical of the reductive nature and sexist bias of Bettelheim's psychosexual readings, chose to focus on mother-daughter relationships instead in the prologue to her own retellings. Significantly, the stepsisters are absent from her own takes on the stories "The Burned Child" and "Travelling Clothes."

In his reading of the Grimms' tale, Bettelheim predictably associates the striking image of the bloody shoe with the bleeding vagina as a manifestation of castration anxiety. Like Anne Sexton's ironic take on "Ashputtle" in *Transformations* (1971), Carter's anthropologizing rewriting interprets the motif no longer as an abstract Freudian symbol but as the painful physical mutilation perpetrated by mothers on their own daughters to secure a princely marriage for them. She even makes bitter fun of the sexist bias of psychoanalytical discourse when Ashputtle's stepmother is described as "brandishing the carving knife, the woman bear[ing] down on her child, who is as distraught as if she had not been a girl but a boy and the old woman was after a more essential portion than a toe" (Carter 1994 [1993], 115). By focusing on the blood and the pain foregrounded in the folktale, Carter uses the vivid image of the mutilated foot bleeding in the tiny shoe to symbolize the brutal consequences of a patriarchal order perpetrated by women—allegedly in the name of love and social conformity. The shoe is no longer a magical "petite pantoufle de verre," but a much more disquieting "old world wonder" and another variation on the bloody chamber motif.

Dressing Mother Goose: Eating Mamma or Puns and Pumpkins

How, then, did "Ashputtle *or* The Mother's Ghost" come into being? In Carter's understanding (and as the bottles metaphor suggests), literary creation involves a constant decanting and transformative process. Accordingly, she mixed Perrault and Grimm when she connected the magical scene of the godmother's changing the pumpkin into a golden coach (Perrault) with Ashputtle's orphan state (Grimm). In her notes for "Ashputtle *or* The Mother's Ghost," Carter indicates that the first version of her own story (its seed, as it were) was based on a pun. On a page titled "Eating Mamma," she picks the episode of the pumpkin transformed into a stage coach and even quotes the passage in French: "Va dans le jardin et apporte-moi une citrouille. Cendrillon alla aussitot [*sic*] cueillir la plus belle qu'elle peut [*sic*] trouver."[11] In her commentary Carter astutely makes a connection between Cinderella's lack of family (or "kin") with the magic pumpkin. She muses over the word *pumpkin*, whose suggestive form becomes perceptible only through the detour of the French text, as Carter observes herself:

> The godmother asks the girl to fetch a pumpkin; poor orphan Cinderella, out she goes to fetch the only fruit that never wants for family because its "kin" go everywhere with it, as suffix, as indelible second syllable although this point is lost in French, of course.[12]

The pumpkin/kin pun therefore becomes a key creative device, through associations of ideas that function like an umbilical cord linking Perrault's and the Grimms' texts, their union (crossing, or cross-breeding) generating the idea of pregnancy, mothering, and reproduction central to the rewriting: Carter makes an "analogy between pumpkin and woman's belly ('full of seeds')" and jots down another one between the "belly of the mother" and a pumpkin "pie." Carter thus locates magic in language, which becomes especially productive in translation because it has the power to *re-enchant* language.

One idea leading to another, Carter moves from the "pregnant" fruit to baking a pumpkin pie as equivalent to "eating a mother"; the pie becomes a cheerful "invocation of the mother," a homey "meal of motherhood," and even "a kind of transubstantiation" that harks back to ancient ceremonies where the participants consume the body of a venerated ancestor, as in the Eucharist. The kitchen itself becomes a "space of welcome, odorous and warm, place of time and metamorphosis, the womb, that mysterious, moist, magical vessel—the alembic of flesh."[13] The hearth, Cinderella's dwelling place, is no longer associated with the heroine's degradation and misery but with cooking as analogous to pregnancy and, symbolically, creativity; just as women's bodies have the magic power of baking babies in their "oven," the kitchen is a distinctly female space where new versions of the familiar tales are cooked up. This echoes Carter's understanding of the storytelling tradition as a domestic art in the preface of the collection she edited for Virago: "Who first invented meatballs? In what country? Is there a definitive recipe for potato soup? Think in terms of the domestic arts. 'This is how *I* make potato soup'" (Carter 1990, x).

Cooking indeed strengthens the connection with storytelling as a metaphor for female production, in keeping with traditional fairy-tale imagery. The story of Cinderella, however, took a new and unexpected turn when "Ashputtle *or* The Mother's Ghost" was reprinted in *American Ghosts and Old World Wonders*, which Carter put together when she was dying from lung cancer. Transposed into a new geographical and cultural setting, Perrault's pumpkin, and the association of the pumpkin pie with the mother's belly found in Carter's notes, now evokes the American festival of Halloween, the festival of the dead, and thus becomes a meditation on the author's own legacy. The significance of the tale shifts from the pregnant belly of the pumpkin to the coffin that turns into a coach, from cooking and eating to giving birth and dying; from Cinderella to Ashputtle, ashes to ashes, dust to dust.

After a Fashion: From Translation to Rewriting, Literary Mother to Daughter

One of the most striking differences between Cinderella and Ashputtle is the identity of the helper figure: from the benevolent fairy godmother in Perrault to the mother reincarnated as a bird in Grimm. As Carter observes in "Ashputtle *or* The Mother's Ghost," "The mother's ghost dominates the narrative and is, in a real sense, the motive center, the event that makes all the other events happen" (Carter 1994 [1993], 111).[14] This introduces a generic shift from the humorous *conte merveilleux* to the macabre and cruel *Märchen* that Carter reads as a ghost story, drawing our attention not only to the mutability of the fairy tale but also to its inherent hybridity in the endless process of linguistic and cultural translation. In "Travelling Clothes," the last rewriting that is literally a kind of *envoi*, the dead mother visits her daughter and kisses her scars away, gives her a red dress (her own blood?), and addresses her: "I had it when I was your age" (Carter 1994 [1993], 119). The girl puts on her mother's gifts: the red dress and the "worms from her eyesockets" that have "turned into jewels" (119). The familiar motifs of the "beautiful dresses" and the "diamonds and pearls" (Grimm and Grimm 1983, 84) associated with the fairy tale are fused with the macabre (and often omitted) scene of the pecking of the eyes at the end of the Grimms' tale, but transmuted by Carter into something hauntingly beautiful and uncanny.

Like Perrault's female contemporaries who initiated the fashion for the *conte de fées*, Carter liked to posture as a modern-day, irreverent, and worldly-wise fairy godmother drawing from personal experience to advise and "instruct" the young girls to whom she addressed her translations, and the older ones to whom she destined her rewritings.[15] "Ashputtle *or* The Mother's Ghost" retells the story of Cinderella in markedly different forms and styles, but it always places as its focus the figure of the dead mother found in the folk tradition. The tripartite structure of the rewriting reflects the writer's awareness of the changing meaning of the story. A mother comes back to help her daughter find a suitable husband, dictating her fate and imposing her will. Their relationships are complex, a mixture of love and conflict, complicity and rivalry, self-denial and self-affirmation, identification and independence. The same applies to literary creation that unfolds in the interplay of repetition and difference, and where intergenerational transmission necessarily involves transformation and even opens up the possibility of liberation from prewritten scripts. The last retelling, "Travelling Clothes," fuses the bloody shoe (Grimm) and the magical coach (Perrault) into a new motif: the coffin, with which the tale ends. The shoe, which symbolizes female confinement in marriage (or female destiny as involving marriage and childbearing) becomes analogous with death in an image that gives a macabre twist to Sexton's simile in *Transformations*: "Her foot fits the shoe like the corpse fits the coffin!" (Sexton 1971, 116).[16]

When Carter decided to include "Ashputtle *or* The Mother's Ghost" in *American Ghosts and Old Wonders*, the story begins to resonate with the secondary meaning of the mother's *will*, no longer as determination but as testament. Condemned by lung cancer, Carter seems to meditate on her role as a literary mother returning in ghostly fashion through the magic of writing. She stages herself as a maternal figure taking leave of her reader-daughter(s), inviting us to use the gifts she has bestowed on us in order to become better, closer, and more attentive readers, and in turn make the story our own. In the last, enigmatic, ambiguous, and open-ended retelling, a mother asks her daughter to step inside her coffin. The girl refuses at first, but the mother insists:

> "I stepped into *my* mother's coffin when I was your age."
>
> The girl stepped into the coffin although she thought it would be the death of her. It turned into a coach and horses. The horses stamped, eager to be gone.
>
> "Go and seek your fortune, darling." (Carter 1994 [1993], 119–20)

Once again, the genesis of the tale gives a clue to the creative process and the point of the retelling. In the typewritten draft of her "Ashputtle *or* The Mother's Ghost," Carter scribbled at the top of the page: "escape the same fate."

Ad-dress

Carter's translation and rewriting draw attention to marked differences between the literary and the folk traditions, but a comparative analysis also reveals cross-cultural connections and hybridizations as the tale travels across time and space. Like many authors, translators, illustrators, and editors of the tale, Carter distinguished but also subtly amalgamated different versions, in a more or less deliberate fashion, thereby stressing the creative force of linguistic and cultural translation.[17] Carter's translation of Perrault's worldly and humorous *conte* communicated a matter-of-fact message to young girls about how to get on in the world and marry happily, while "Ashputtle *or* The Mother's Ghost" became an occasion to explore the enigmatic nature of "mother love." Carter's Grimm-based rewriting nevertheless contains traces of the French *conte* that Carter had translated, starting with its title; when "Cendrillon ou la petite pantoufle de verre" turns into "Ashputtle *or* The Mother's Ghost," the name Ashputtle signals a shift to the folk tradition, and yet the syntax of the title is still modeled on Perrault's French text. The mutable identity of the fairy-tale heroine thus draws attention to the palimpsest quality of the tale, and to the multiple refashionings of the Cinderella story as the source of its/her renewed life and ongoing appeal.

Notes

1. http://www.bbc.co.uk/archive/writers/12245.shtml, June 25, 1991: 12:00–12:50. Last accessed September 6, 2014.
2. This contradicts a passage from Mark 2:22 in King James Bible (Cambridge edition): "And no man putteth new wine into old bottles: else the new

wine doth burst the bottles, and the wine is spilled, and the bottles will be marred: but new wine must be put into new bottles."

3. For an overview of the French fairy tale in translation, see Lathey 2010, chap. 3.
4. Feminist translation theory and practice greatly contributed to changing its image as a creative activity (see Simon 1996). As I argue in *Reading, Translating, Rewriting: Angela Carter's Translational Poetics* (2013), the modalities of translation in Carter's work extend to cross-generic and intermedial transposition as central (trans)creative strategies. This article is based on the last chapter of the book *Giving Up the Ghost* (Wayne State University Press, 2013).
5. Angela Carter Papers, British Library, MS 88899/1/82.
6. Echoing Andrea Dworkin in *Woman Hating* (1974), Carter made the connection between the Chinese Cinderella story "Hieh-Sien" (mentioned by both Lang and Opie) and the custom of footbinding in "Ashputtle *or* The Mother's Ghost": "Ashputtle's foot, the size of the bound foot of a Chinese woman, a stump. Almost an amputee already, she put her tiny foot in it [the bloody shoe]" (Carter 1993, 116).
7. Carter cites Andrew Lang's edition of *Perrault's Popular Tales* (Lang 1888) in *The Fairy Tales of Charles Perrault* (1977). In his abundant notes, Lang refers to the ritual of bodily mutilation to fit beauty standards in the Chinese custom of foot-binding. In her introduction to *The Virago Book of Fairy Tales*, Carter highlights the multiple versions of the tale, "the basic plot elements of the story we know as 'Cinderella' occur everywhere from China to Northern England" (Carter 1990, xv). "Ashputtle *or* The Mother's Ghost" can be seen as an imaginative reconstruction of "ur-versions" of the tale in the manner of folklorists. As Lorna Sage aptly points out, however, for Carter, "There's no core, or point of origin, or ur-story 'underneath,' just a continuous interweaving of texts" (Sage 2001, 74).
8. In Perrault, the stepsisters are almost exclusively described in moral terms: they are haughty and proud, like their mother, but also rude, mean, and far less beautiful than Cinderella in spite of their elaborate clothes (but not ugly, as in Disney's film). They are also pettily cruel with Cinderella, giving her an insulting nickname, making fun of her inadequate clothes, and laughing and rejoicing at her miserable condition. The tale ends happily with a royal wedding and Cinderella's forgiveness as exemplifying "bonne grâce."
9. The second section about the burned child living in the ashes was published in *Cosmopolitan* in July 1987 and in *Merveilles et Contes* (vol. 1, no. 2, 1987). The full text was anthologized in *The Virago Book of Ghost Stories*

(1987), and included a few years later in *American Ghosts and Old World Wonders* (1993). The heretogeneous collection contains seven stories that Angela Carter collected or completed before her death in 1992. It includes an unfinished screenplay as well as short prose pieces that blur the boundaries between genres, and between fiction and critical or cultural analysis.

10. Interviewed by John Haffenden, Carter famously declared that *The Bloody Chamber* collection was in part the result of "quarreling furiously with Bettelheim" (Haffenden 1986, 84).
11. Angela Carter Papers, British Library, MS 88899/1/82.
12. Ibid.
13. Ibid.
14. See Cristina Bacchilega's discussion of Carter's take on Ashputtle in *Postmodern Fairy Tales*. Michelle Ryan-Sautour also stresses how the text "weaves together the genealogy of the Cinderella tale with questions of motherhood and ultimately generates allegory about culture and authorship" (Ryan-Sautour 2011, 34). The collective dimension partly accounts for Carter's attraction to "fairy tales, folk tales, stories from the oral tradition," such narratives reflecting "the most vital connection we have with the imaginations of the ordinary men and women whose labour created our world" (Carter 1990, ix).
15. Cinderella's godmother in Perrault reminds her of "women of independent means who've done quite well for themselves, one way and another, and are prepared to help along a little sister who finds herself in difficulties. It's little May West comforting the young girl who's been seduced and abandoned in *She Done Him Wrong*: she gives her nice clothes and good advice. . . . 'We all need a fairy godmother of some kind or another,' says Perrault sagely. Hard work and ingenuity, virtue and beauty are all very well. But somebody's got to run the racket" (Carter 1998a, 454).
16. Anne Sexton's "Cinderella" comically stresses the horror of the mutilation and bloody shoe ("amputations don't heal like a wish"), and yet when Cinderella tries on the famous slipper: "This time Cinderella fit into the shoe / like a love letter into its envelope." Carter, however, explores the idea of slipping one's foot into a blood-filled shoe, and the disturbing juxtaposition of romance and gore in the Grimms' version of the tale.
17. Karen Seago (2006) sees this merging of the French and German traditions in the course of the nineteenth century as "one of the most important features of the tale's reception in England" (180).

References

Bacchilega, Cristina. 1997. *Postmodern Fairy Tales: Gender and Narrative Strategies*. Philadelphia: University of Pennsylvania Press.

Bassnett, Susan. 2006. "Writing and Translating." In *The Translator as Writer*, edited by Susan Bassnett and Peter Bush, 173–83. New York: Continuum.

Bettelheim, Bruno. 1976. *The Uses of Enchantment: The Meaning and Importance of Fairy Tales*. New York: Vintage.

Carter, Angela. 1979. *The Bloody Chamber and Other Stories*. London: Penguin.

———. 1994 [1993]. *American Ghosts and Old World Wonders*. London: Vintage.

———. 1998a. "The Better to Eat You With." In *Shaking a Leg*, 451–55.

———. 1998b. "Notes from the Frontline." In *Shaking a Leg*, 36–43.

———. 1998c. *Shaking a Leg: Collected Journalism and Writings*. London: Vintage.

———, ed. 1990. *The Virago Book of Fairy Tales*. London: Virago.

———, trans. and foreword. 1977. *The Fairy Tales of Charles Perrault*. London: Victor Gollancz.

Dutheil de la Rochère, Martine Hennard. 2013. *Reading, Translating, Rewriting: Angela Carter's Translational Poetics*. Detroit: Wayne State University Press.

France, Peter, and Stuart Gillespie, eds. Vol. 1: 2008; Vol. 2: 2010; Vol. 3: 2005; Vol. 4: 2006; Vol. 5: forthcoming. The Oxford History of Literary Translation in English. Oxford: Oxford University Press.

Gamble, Sarah. 2008. "Penetrating to the Heart of the Bloody Chamber: Angela Carter and the Fairy Tale." In *Contemporary Fiction and the Fairy Tale*, edited by Stephen Benson, 20–46. Detroit: Wayne State University Press.

Grimm, Jacob, and Wilhelm Grimm. 1983. *Grimms' Tales for Young and Old: The Complete Stories*. Translated by Ralph Manheim. New York: Anchor Books (Doubleday, 1977; Gollancz, 1978).

Haase, Donald, ed. 2004. *Fairy Tales and Feminism: New Approaches*. Detroit: Wayne State University Press.

Haffenden, John. 1986. "Angela Carter." In *Novelists in Interview*. London: Methuen.

Joosen, Vanessa. 2011. *Critical and Creative Perspectives on Fairy Tales: An Intertextual Dialogue from Fairy-Tale Scholarship and Postmodern Retellings*. Detroit: Wayne State University Press.

Lang, Andrew. 1888. *Perrault's Popular Tales*. London: Oxford Clarendon.

Lathey, Gillian, ed. 2006. *The Translation of Children's Literature: A Reader*. Clevedon, England: Multilingual Matters.

———. 2010. *The Role of Translators in Children's Literature: Invisible Storytellers*. New York: Routledge.

Lefevere, André. 1992. *Translation, Rewriting, and the Manipulation of Literary Fame*. London: Routledge.

Opie, Iona, and Peter Opie, eds. 1974. *The Classic Fairy Tales*. London: Oxford University Press.

Perrault, Charles. 1981. *Contes*. Edited by Jean-Pierre Collinet. Paris: Gallimard (Folio Classique).

Ryan-Sautour, Michelle. 2011. "Authorial Ghosts and Maternal Identity in Angela Carter's 'Ashputtle *or* The Mother's Ghost: Three Versions of One Story.'" *Marvels & Tales* 25 (1): 33–50.

Sage, Lorna. 2001. "Angela Carter: The Fairy Tale." In *Angela Carter and the Fairy Tale*, edited by Danielle Roemer and Cristina Bacchilega, 65–82. Detroit: Wayne State University Press.

Seago, Karen. 2006. "Nursery Politics: Sleeping Beauty and the Acculturation of a Tale." In *The Translation of Children's Literature: A Reader*, edited by Gillian Lathey, 175–89. Clevendon, England: Multilingual Matters.

Sexton, Anne. 1971. *Transformations*. Boston: Houghton Mifflin.

Simon, Sherry. 1996. *Gender in Translation: Cultural Identity and the Politics of Transmission*. London: Routledge.

Van Wyke, Ben. 2010. "Imitating Bodies and Clothes: Refashioning the Western Conception of Translation." In *Thinking through Translation with Metaphors*, edited by James St. André, 17–46. Manchester: Saint Jérôme.

Venuti, Lawrence. 2008 [1995]. *The Translator's Invisibility: A History of Translation*. New York: Routledge.

Warner, Marina. 2014. *Once upon a Time: A Short History of Fairy Tale*. Oxford: Oxford University Press.

Zipes, Jack, ed. 1986. *Don't Bet on the Prince: Contemporary Feminist Fairy Tales in North America and England*. London: Routledge.

9

Multiple Metamorphoses, or "New Skins" for an Old Tale

Emma Donoghue's Queer Cinderella in Translation

Ashley Riggs

Fairy-tale plots often revolve around metamorphosis, and the Cinderella tale is no exception. We are all familiar with the heroine of the Grimm brothers' "Aschenputtel" or of Charles Perrault's "Cendrillon." Whether aided by a dove, as in Grimm, or by a fairy godmother, as in Perrault and in subsequent Disney productions, she is doubly *transformed*: from the daughter of an aristocrat or a rich man into a dirty and oppressed maid, abused by her stepmother and stepsisters, and then into a beautiful, glamorous princess and wife, when she is rehabilitated and marries the prince.

Popular tales like Cinderella have inspired countless rewritings and adaptations, especially in response to the feminist movement, and they have therefore undergone significant metamorphoses themselves. For example, Emma Donoghue, a self-proclaimed lesbian author, revisits Cinderella in "The Tale of the Shoe," which opens her 1997 collection, *Kissing the Witch: Old Tales in New Skins*.[1] The tale departs dramatically from familiar versions of Cinderella to challenge both the prior texts and prevailing cultural norms. When it is translated into French, it is transformed once again through notable and surprising alterations as it passes into a new language, culture and context.

"The Tale of the Shoe," or "Queering" Cinderella

Donoghue's "The Tale of the Shoe" "queers" the tale in the various senses of the term (see Dutheil de la Rochère 2009a, 65–66). As Martine Hennard

Dutheil de la Rochère observes, "queer" has multiple meanings: not only homosexual but also "of obscure origin, denoting a state of malaise or discomfort, eccentric"; moreover, the verb "to queer" is "linked to the act of questioning."[2] Donoghue indeed questions conventional representations of gender roles and of desire as conveyed by Perrault, the Grimms, and Disney by redefining two quintessential elements of the fairy tale: magic and metamorphosis. Magic is deployed not in the service of beauty and upward social mobility, but to transform the physical and emotional world of the Cinderella figure, develop her sense of self, and confer upon her a new, homosexual identity that provides love, comfort, and fulfillment. Thus the celebration of heterosexual unions through the happy endings of the prior versions is also radically transformed, while the reader, in turn, is subtly encouraged to revise her own views on societal norms regulating beauty, social status, romantic relationships, and even age differences.

Donoghue clearly refers back to the canonical versions by Perrault and Grimm, but also to her literary foremothers, other rewriters like Anne Sexton, Olga Broumas, and Angela Carter. She honors the contributions of her predecessors by redeploying certain motifs and inscribing her work within a female fairy-tale tradition; at the same time, she departs dramatically from the conventional heteronormative plot (Dutheil de la Rochère 2009a). She also employs another strategy that emphasizes the mutability of the fairy tale: she uses transitional or, as Jennifer Orme (2010) calls them, intradiegetic pages to illustrate how fairy tales lend themselves to repeated transformation, and to connect the rewritten tales in her collection in a narrative chain. Through the similarly constructed dialogues that appear on each transitional page, a character from one story goes on to become the narrator of the next one, and this process repeats itself until the end, when the reader is called upon to carry on the tradition. In this way, a community of women builds, shares, renews, and extends the narrative chain in a potentially never-ending process. Thus, in line with the literary project announced in the collection's title, Donoghue gives not only the heroine but also the tales themselves a *new skin*.

The Tale in Translation: A New Context, a New Frame, a New Skin

In order to examine the French translation of Donoghue's tale by Valérie Cossy, "Le conte de la chaussure," I have employed an approach to translation criticism developed by Lance Hewson (2011). This approach allows analysis of text and translation on multiple levels and provides the critic with terminology for describing the translational effects observed and how they are likely to shape the reader's impressions and understanding of the translated text. These effects are divided into three types of *voice effects*, which occur when translational choices alter the voices of narrators or protagonists, and three types of *interpretational effects*, which change the way the reader is likely to interpret the text. In comparison with the source text, the critic may find certain voices embellished, rendered less salient or remarkable, or significantly transformed, for example. S/he may identify choices that open up avenues of interpretation, close them down, or encourage interpretations that differ from those inspired by the original. I have used Hewson's terminology in detail elsewhere (Riggs 2014); for the purposes of this article, I will employ less specialized language as I summarize the effects of the translational choices observed in the excerpts of text and translation chosen for analysis.

This comparative approach sometimes conflicts with another key perspective in translation studies, the "creative turn" (Bassnett and Bush 2006; Perteghella and Loffredo 2006), which considers each text as an independent piece of writing whose meaning is creatively co-constructed by reader, author (with the translator fulfilling each of these roles successively, in the case of the translated text), text, and context. The present study, while comparative, also seeks to highlight aspects of the translation that creatively produce and enrich meaning within the new culture and context in which the text appears. The two positions can perhaps be reconciled using Lawrence Venuti's notion of "resistant translation," whereby

> the translator seeks to reproduce whatever features of the foreign text abuse or resist dominant cultural values in the source language, yet this reproductive effort requires the invention of analogous means of signification that are doubly abusive, that resist dominant cultural values in the target language, but supplement the foreign text by rewriting it. (Venuti 1992, 12)

Such a position allows the critic to identify and to value elements that contribute to "queering" the text—essential in this particular case since, while not necessarily only linguistic, they "abuse or resist dominant cultural values"—while recognizing the inevitable variability of meaning "as differential plurality" (Venuti 1992, 12).

When comparing a text and its translation, it is important to observe both the textual and the paratextual characteristics of each publication. The Swiss/French journal *Hétérographe, revue des homolittératures ou pas* is the new context in which the translation of Donoghue's Cinderella rewriting appeared in 2009. Because its composition, purpose, and readership differ

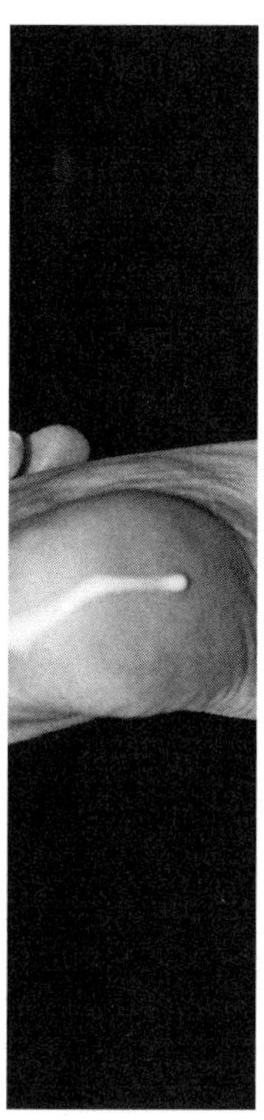

Image from *Hétérographe* 1 (2009): 21. © Lara Lemmelet. Reproduced with the permission of the photographer, Lara Lemmelet.

from Donoghue's collection of interlinked tales, it thus constitutes another manifestation of a "new skin." Indeed, the French translation, "Le conte de la chaussure," is accompanied by a variety of other writings (short fiction, poems, essays, book reviews, an interview, and so on). It is also framed by sensual black-and-white photographs interspersed among the texts in the journal. They show not clearly identifiable surfaces of skin, sometimes with a milky fluid running over them, evoking both deliberately ambiguous bodies, and sex.

Interestingly, the image that falls after the last page of "Le conte de la chaussure" evokes the heel of a foot, photographed from below, with a trail of a milky substance dripping over the back of it. Hence a link created with the "chaussure" (shoe) of title and intertext, and with the "talon" (heel) of the stepsister cut off in the Grimms' version of the tale. These suggestive images are "interleafing" signs that replace the transitional pages of Donoghue's collection, adding an erotic twist to the tale and a visual representation of the emblematic foot of the heroine. Like the texts they join together, the images contribute to "queering" the publication. Furthermore, both *Hétérographe* and its publisher have set out a clear aim of defending sexual minorities and promoting experimental literature and art. The journal's mission statement evokes "artistic work" and three objectives: to "destabilize boundaries," "deconstruct gender power relations," and "broaden the discussion on bodies."[3]

The translator of "The Tale of the Shoe," Valérie Cossy, is a professor of gender studies at the University of Lausanne and a member of the editorial committee of *Nouvelles Questions Féministes*, a review founded in 1981 by Simone de Beauvoir (among others) with a clear feminist agenda. Cossy has studied translation and reception extensively, and the main focus of her work is the status of the heroine in literature. Thus the formation of specific feminist literary and critical traditions in different cultural contexts, and the representation of gender roles and gender stereotypes, are central to her teaching and research. Her awareness of, and training in, these areas undoubtedly inform her translation work as well, while her contribution to a review with a clear queer agenda testifies to her interest in new developments in postfeminist studies.

A Comparative Analysis of "The Tale of the Shoe" and "Le conte de la chaussure"

Unlike the Cinderella tales by Perrault and the Grimms and unlike Disney's popularized film versions, "The Tale of the Shoe" is told in the first person. The main character has lost her mother, and her grief, which is a feature of the Grimms' version, is accentuated in the opening lines of the tale. In contrast, the negative female relationships represented by the stepfamily and present in the best-known versions of the tale are removed; Donoghue's version focuses instead on the personal trajectory of the narrator from despondency to self-fulfillment through her encounter with the fairy godmother. The heroine of Donoghue's tale and the sisters of the Perrault, Grimm, and Disney versions are conflated, enabling the author to "undo" one aspect of the conventional good/evil binary opposition on which the well-known versions rely; that of the good, virtuous girl *versus* the evil stepsisters. The evil women are in fact replaced by internalized voices that harass the heroine and destroy her self-esteem. The girl's hopelessness and her problematic relationship to language illustrate her depression, self-hate, and deviation from society's expectations. From the opening lines, the protagonist's grief and physical discomfort evoke yet another meaning of "queer":[4]

> Till she came it was all cold.
>
> Ever since my mother died the feather bed felt hard as a stone floor. Every word that came out of my mouth limped away like a toad. (Donoghue 1997, 1)
>
> *Avant qu'elle n'arrive, le froid régnait partout.*
>
> *Depuis que ma mère était morte, mon lit de plumes ressemblait à un sol en pierre. Les mots qui sortaient de ma bouche étaient aussi disgracieux que des crapauds.* (Cossy 2009, 17)

In the English text, the movement of limping away and the animal (toad) chosen as the point of comparison combine to provide a vivid and negative image. As Dutheil de la Rochère (2009b) points out, the animal clearly recalls Perrault's own "Les fées" / "The Fairies," known as "Toads and Diamonds" in English, in which the wicked sister of the Cinderella figure is condemned by a fairy in disguise to spit toads and snakes whenever she speaks. In the French translation, the choice of "étaient aussi disgracieux que" (were as ugly as) makes the comparison more abstract and thus less visually striking than the original. Readers of the French translation are likely to see the toad as ugly but not to observe the abject nature of both the toad's movement and the girl's "every word." In addition, the plural "les mots" (the words) does not emphasize each individual word as the English does. At the same time, "disgracieux" echoes Perrault's moral about the importance of "bonne grâce," so that the intertextual echo with his "Cendrillon" is maintained. The adjective also underscores the new heroine's striking departure from the conventional beauty and grace of the familiar Cinderella figure. The *tangibility* of the girl's grief, desperation, and suffering is nevertheless attenuated. The other comparison in the paragraph, of the feather bed with the stone floor, is a surprising or "queer" feature indeed. In the French, this comparison shows similar effects to the previous one due to the more vague and abstract "ressemblait à" (resembled), which puts less emphasis on the *hardness* of the feather bed. Again, the French does not insist as forcefully upon the physical manifestations of the girl's mental and emotional pain. Furthermore, the first line, "avant qu'elle n'arrive, le froid régnait partout" (before she arrived, the cold reigned everywhere), with the added punctuation that lengthens and slows, and the choice of "régner" (to reign), show embellishment. The tale's opening becomes more literary and more contemplative, but also attenuates the final, physical impact of "cold." Given the choices discussed here, Donoghue's strategy of using both fairy-tale imagery[5] and sensory references to depict emotions as physical sensations[6] and to emphasize the power of touch (including sexual intimacy) may become less visible in the translation as a whole.

Soon after, an older female stranger comes to the girl's aid. This figure will allow her to forge a new identity, to reject the roles prescribed for her and to "come out" as a lesbian. The older woman is also the repository for the story's magic. Indeed, her features herald the lesbian relationship as a source of the marvelous, as demonstrated by an amusing and suggestive comparison of her little finger with a magic wand whose ability "to do spectacular things" (Donoghue 1997, 6) might be read to include giving sexual gratification. The older woman provides the girl with various dresses that are likened in the text to "new skins" and takes her to the ball multiple times. The comparison (below) highlights the shift Donoghue makes from the focus on dress, and hence appearance, in all of the well-known versions of Cinderella, to an emphasis on skin and the body. During one of the visits to the ball, the description of the dress hints at the start of the heroine's transformation, the change in her identity and self-image. But this impression is not as pronounced in the French:

> That night my new skin was red silk, shivering in the breeze. (Donoghue 1997, 6)

> *Cette nuit-là, c'est une soie rouge tremblant dans la brise qui me tint lieu de nouvelle peau.* (Cossy 2009, 19)

The emphatic introduction ("c'est une" / it was a) of "soie rouge" (red silk) and the addition of the expression "tenir lieu de" (to serve / act as), reduce the impression of the *equivalence* of the "red silk" and the "new skin," obscure the idea that they are one and the same, and hence attenuate the sexual implication of "going to the ball." Furthermore, a comma is added. This change, like the fronting of both "soie rouge" and "tremblant dans la brise" (trembling in the breeze), slows our discovery of the "nouvelle peau." I would argue that the altered syntax, together with the lesser insistence on equivalence just mentioned, mutes the erotic undertones present in the image of the exposed, shivering "new skin." There may even be an attenuation of some of the associations one could make between the color—raw skin, a skin, or a self that is very much alive, open and ripe for experience—and the skin's exposure to the elements ("the breeze") that seems to indicate its vulnerability to, or readiness for, a (sexual) awakening.

As the protagonist's repeated visits to the ball are described, the reader discovers a key difference between this girl and the Cinderella figure s/he remembers from earlier versions: while Donoghue's character wants to attend the ball and respects the rituals and behavior connected to it, she also expresses her awareness of (and developing repulsion for) the role she is supposed to play:

> I knew just how I was meant to behave. (Donoghue 1997, 4)

> *Je savais exactement tout ce que je devais faire.* (Cossy 2009, 18)

The girl's use of "meant" in fact constitutes an important repetition; it echoes an earlier occurrence, where it was translated by "censée":

> And then, because I asked, she took me to the ball. Isn't that what girls are meant to ask for? (Donoghue 1997, 3)

> *Et puis, parce que je lui demandai, elle m'emmena au bal. C'est ce que les filles sont censées demander, non?* (Cossy 2009, 18)

One might therefore expect to find "censée" again in French, rather than "devais" ("Je savais exactement comment j'étais censée me comporter" / I knew exactly how I was meant to behave). The elimination of this key repetition means there is less emphasis on the discrepancy between the social expectation and the girl's own desires. It is interesting to note that repetition is also a crucial feature of fairy tales and is reproduced in the English but often avoided in the translation.

As the scene continues, the protagonist's revulsion develops and is even accompanied by vomiting, a moment of bathos that is certainly *not* what one expects to find in a fairy tale. Immediately afterward comes a comical scene in which the not-so-charming prince proposes to the main character but the heterosexual romance loses all appeal:

> Out on the steps he led me, under the half-full moon, all very fairytale. His long moustaches were beginning to tremble: he seemed like an actor on a creaking stage. As soon as the words began to leak out of his mouth, they formed a cloud in which I could see the future. (Donoghue 1997, 6)

> *Il me conduisit au sommet des marches, sous une demi-lune, tout à fait le style conte de fées. Ses longues moustaches se mirent à trembler; il ressemblait à un acteur sur une scène qui grince. Dès que les mots commencèrent à tomber de sa bouche, ils formèrent un nuage dans lequel je pus voir l'avenir.* (Cossy 2009, 19–20)

Like the abject limping toad in the opening lines of the tale and the vomiting in response to the prince's proposal, the phrase "leak out" is disturbingly visual and arouses disgust. In French, however, with the lexical choice of "*tomber*" (fall), the negative physical connotation is softened and our image of the prince changes: he is hesitant, shy, and uncertain but lacks the repellent character conveyed by "leak," which made him seem repugnant and even suggested he might not be in control of his physical functions. The reader of the French is likely to develop a different, and certainly less negative, impression of the prince than the reader of the English. In addition, in the first sentence, the French normalizes a syntax that is deliberately, markedly, and poetically inverted in English, "out on the steps he led me." In "tout à fait le style conte de fées," "tout à fait" does not translate "all" (all the elements of the scene) but rather overtranslates "very." These choices seem to temper the mocking tone of the author's narrator; nevertheless, the French text makes explicit the traditionalism and artificiality of fairy-tale conventions.

Although the girl is hounded by the internal voices to accept the prince and thus embrace a socially acceptable—that is, a heterosexual—identity, she instead returns to the older woman. She momentarily *loses her words* in a symbolic representation of her lack of a proper language or prior tale fit to express her newly discovered self. Her solution is to reach out, and this ambiguous movement, through which she may be seeking both the words appropriate to her feelings *and* physical contact with the woman with whom she is falling in love, can be read as evoking touch, skin, eroticism, and the emergence of a new, queer self.

> I must have dropped all my words in the bushes. I reached out. (Donoghue 1997, 7)

> *J'avais dû perdre tous mes mots dans les buissons. Je fis un effort pour les retrouver.* (Cossy 2009, 20)

The French sentence "Je fis un effort pour les retrouver" (I made an effort / tried *to find them*) is both longer and more explicit than "I reached out." It removes an ambiguity: did the girl reach out to retrieve the words, or did she reach out toward the woman she loves? It also leaves out a possible reason for the action: the girl may well have *physically extended* her arm toward the other woman, unlike in French, because she could not speak to her. This corresponds to Donoghue's focus on the sense of touch as intimately linked to desire. The English, then, conveys multiple possible actions, thereby calling upon the reader to question and interpret and also reinforcing the queer character of the text. The translational choice in French, however, provides a sole interpretation of the scene to the reader of the translation.

The all-important symbol already evoked in the title, the shoe, is addressed again in this scene. In all the best-known versions of Cinderella, the shoe secures the heterosexual union and hence the happy ending. The girl's emphatic tossing of the shoe into the bushes represents her conscious rejection of the traditional outcome and its constraints. Her dramatic, defining gesture is highlighted by the style of the English text:

> I threw the other shoe into the brambles, where it hung, glinting. (Donoghue 1997, 8)

> *Je jetai la deuxième chaussure dans les ronces où elle s'accrocha scintillante.* (Cossy 2009, 20)

With the absence of commas in the French, after "ronces" and especially after "s'accrocha," this final image of the discarded shoe, presented in English as if a camera has done a long, close-up shot of it, may appear less pointed and dramatic. The integral analysis of text and translation shows that changes in punctuation often cause alterations in the French; most common are the insertion and removal of commas, which significantly alter the perceived speed and rhythm of the narrative and thereby the intensity of the drama. However, the alliteration achieved in the French ("sh" / "s") constitutes stylistic embellishment that may be read as "retrieving" this emphasis on the shoe through different means. Moreover, in both texts, the poetic imagery whereby the shoe becomes part of the landscape, almost a shining moon, is equally present and effective.

When the older woman asks about the shoe, the girl justifies her discarding of it:

> It was digging into my heel, I told her. (Donoghue 1997, 8)
>
> *Elle me blessait au talon, lui dis-je.* (Cossy 2009, 20)

The physical pain caused by the shoe is tantamount to the pain caused by being forced to squeeze into a heterosexual mold. While the lexical choice "blessait" (from the verb *blesser*: to hurt) is of a slightly higher register and slightly more abstract than the phrasal verb "digging into," it certainly conveys violence; after all, *blessés de guerre* is a familiar phrase evoking war injuries. Thus at this important moment in the story, the translation continues to evoke painful constraint and maintains both the link with and the implicit critique of the Grimms' version, in which the stepsisters voluntarily endure the suffering that this protagonist rejects, by cutting off pieces of their feet.

At the end of the tale, the scene in which the two women become a couple includes another significant feature related to *words*, which is transformed in translation. The alterations revolve around the term "spelling":

> Her finger was spelling on the back of my neck. (Donoghue 1997, 8)
>
> *Son doigt traçait des signes dans ma nuque.* (Cossy 2009, 20)

"Spelling" is translated as "traçait des signes" (drew signs/symbols). It is important to note that a similar construction using the verb *tracer* (to draw/trace) had been chosen in French for an earlier scene involving drawing, in which the women's romance had not yet begun or was only in its very earliest stages:

> Our fingers drew pictures in the ashes on the hearth, vague shapes of birds and islands. (Donoghue 1997, 4)
>
> *Nos doigts tracèrent des dessins dans la cendre du foyer, de formes vagues d'oiseaux et d'îles.* (Cossy 2009, 18)

Thus, at the end of the tale, the somewhat childlike action of drawing, producing only "vague" images, evolves; it is *transformed* into the more advanced ability to spell, to use language, *and* to love, and this ability is passed on to the Cinderella figure by the older woman. Moreover, the traditional fairy tale *spell* is broken, and a new, liberating spell is cast. In the French, rendering "spelling" as "traçait des signes" creates a new association with the earlier "traçait des dessins" ("drew pictures"). This choice can be viewed in contrasting ways. Insofar as it places the action of spelling on a par with the action of drawing, it may be seen to mask the progression toward a more advanced form of communication and expression and toward a new, queer identity. The disappearance of "spelling" also removes an explicit association with the words that the girl had "dropped" and that the stranger is literally giving back to her as she simultaneously "spells out" a new role for the Cinderella figure. With "signes" (signs) we don't see as distinctly the evolution from the realm of "vague shapes" to that of words, nor the girl's acquisition of a language to recognize, admit, and express her love. In addition, without a close equivalent of "spelling," which is linked to *word* construction through its meaning and to the recently dropped "words" through its position in the sequence of events, the reader may be less likely to recall the prince's words and the girl's own toad-like words at the beginning of the tale. The reader may also be less likely to interpret the retrieved, spelled words, infused with intimacy since they are inscribed on the erotically sensitive "back of the neck," as a desirable antidote to the prince's awkward and abhorrent "leaked" ones and to the Cinderella figure's earlier "limping" ones.

Nevertheless, the choice of "signes" in the French has fascinating and fruitful consequences both in light of Donoghue's subtle reference to "casting a spell," and in light of the new context of publication. The term "signe," like "spell," goes *beyond* the realm of words to that of magic in that it evokes mystical signs designed to summon supernatural aid or intervention. Thus in the French as in the English, the fairy godmother figure works her magic to cure the heroine's suffering and to provide her with a new ending. The girl's early efforts to "picture a future" (Donoghue 1997, 2) are finally realized through the magical intercession of love and of touch. Moreover, "signes" could be interpreted as a metatextual comment, tied in with the reorientation of the tale, the shift from words to images reflecting the new frame in which the story appears and in particular the photographs featured in *Hétérographe*. It could be seen to reference this tale as "artistic work" and explicitly as a translation accompanied by other diverse texts, "driven by" the effort to "destabilize boundaries" and "to deconstruct gender power relations," to quote *Hétérographe*'s mission statement. According to such a reading, resemanticization[7] of the English word "spelling" mirrors, and is mirrored by, the resemanticization of the tale.

Finally, the two women leave together in an ending that contrasts sharply with the familiar "happily ever after" fairy-tale finale:

> So then she took me home, or I took her home, or we were both somehow taken to the closest thing. (Donoghue 1997, 8)

> *Alors à ce moment, elle m'emmena à la maison, ou je l'emmenai à la maison, ou d'une façon ou d'une autre nous fûmes toutes les deux emmenées à ce qui nous tint lieu de maison.* (Cossy 2009, 20)

Egalitarian and understated, deliberately blurred yet suggestive of sexual union due to both the choice of expression ("the closest thing") and its brevity, the final lines suggest a new beginning more than an ending. Another, more negative interpretation is equally valid, however: that we observe a wry wink at the present state of affairs, that is, a society in which the characters must *settle* for "the closest thing" because it is not yet entirely acceptable for two women to establish a romantic relationship, a *true* "home," together. Incorporating such ambiguity and leaving room for contradictory interpretations is indeed characteristic of queer writing.The relative prolixity of the French does not lead to marked translational effects, nor does it alter the possibility of multiple and conflicting interpretations. Moreover, the association potentially constructed with "tint lieu de nouvelle peau" (see above) by the phrase "tint lieu de maison" is a felicitous one, since both the girl's *nouvelle peau* and *nouvelle maison* are bound up with her *nouvelle*, homosexual identity that has taken form progressively throughout the tale.

Donoghue's ending includes another significant alteration: in this union, wealth and status are totally irrelevant. In relation to this economic dimension, it is interesting to note that the rags-to-riches motif found in Perrault, the Grimms, and Disney and so often called into question by fairy-tale rewriters was already subtly criticized in Donoghue's version when the protagonist stated "I was a girl with my fortune to make" (1997, 4), but the pecuniary connotation and thus the critique were softened in translation with the more abstract, loftier choice of "*destin*" (destiny/fate; Cossy 2009, 18) for "fortune." The resulting narrowing of potential interpretations is a common translational effect, both in the excerpts discussed here and in the integral analysis.

"Queering" the "Happily Ever After" in English and in French: New Skins, New Pages, New Possibilities?

In the final line of the tale, we also encounter the kind of metamorphosis highlighted by Jack Zipes (2000, xix) and related to the symbol of the home:

> Th[e] pursuit of home accounts for the utopian spirit of the tales, for the miraculous transformation does not only involve the transformation of the protagonist but also the realization of a more ideal setting in which the hero/heroine can fulfill his or her potential.[8]

In Donoghue's tale, such a "miraculous transformation" has indeed occurred: with her discovery of love and her acceptance of her new identity, the young protagonist has changed, and a kind of new "home" has materialized for her, "a more ideal setting" (that "maison," or "the closest thing") "in which" she "can fulfill . . . her potential." Other transformations occur in turn. First, the "ideal setting" of the Perrault, Grimm, and Disney Cinderella tales has been transformed,[9] becoming a loosely defined, open space where the (homosexual) heroine can thrive, rather than a closed "happily-ever-after" formula located within marriage and heterosexual coupling. This openness is characteristic of the "queering" process, which provokes questions and reveals the existence of unexplored potential rather than providing clear, defined, and fixed messages, endings, or answers. The traditional heterosexual closure of the well-known Cinderella versions has been effectively subverted or "queered." Second, at the level of the collection as a whole and as foretold by the collection's title, "old tales" have been given "new skins" through the process of rewriting. Skin, here, is metaphorical, but these new stories are of course comprised of concrete pages upon which the new roles and realities have been inscribed. Skin and page are thus subtly linked by Donoghue in an analogy that in fact echoes a prior reality: long ago, texts appeared on vellum, a parchment made from the skin of a calf. Through the association of "oldness," "newness," skin, page, and rewriting, Donoghue highlights not only the history and the continuity of fairy tales but also their capacity for renewal. Moreover, the process of rewriting, when defined as "entering an old text from a new critical direction" (Rich 1975, 90), is logically also one of "queering," since the act of throwing "the old" *into question* is at the center of the operation. Third, the very multiplication of the women-centered, rewritten tales in the collection obliges the reader to recognize her own expectations and desires as culturally, socially, and discursively defined and offers her, too, multiple new possibilities for identification. Like Cinderella herself, like fairy tales, like our notions of ideal settings and ideal endings, the reader can also be transformed.

The French translation of the tale within its new constellation of texts and images offers the readership of *Hétérographe* similar possibilities. The French version is not radically divergent from the original, and an effective recontextualization is achieved via the "new skin"/new pages of the French-language publication, especially given the links established within *Hétérographe* among body, eroticism, queerness, and the striking, sexualized images. As I argue elsewhere (Riggs 2014), this recontextualization may in fact point to a shortcoming of Hewson's model: its seeming inability to account for the potential "authorization" of a new, different text *by* the original text and context themselves, especially when they mobilize a queer approach emphasizing openness, mutability, re-visioning and rewriting.[10] Moreover, Valérie Cossy may have sought to highlight, at some points in her text, the studied simplicity of Donoghue's style and to avoid a more flamboyant, camp aesthetic that would have risked enclosing Donoghue's rewriting in another kind of "shoe," or stereotype.

Sometimes, however, specific translational choices *within* the French text itself, by attenuating both the "queering" strategies and the criticism, also temper the subversive power of the text. As we have seen, humor, bathos, mockery, and eroticism are sometimes diminished. Ambiguity is undone. Punctuation and syntax are often normalized, and repetition avoided. Some associations and intertextual echoes disappear while others are created. According to the critical perspective adopted here, such alterations are undeniably felicitous when they convey the mocking, ironic, or critical nature of the voices and the "queerness" of the text, and when they reflect the relationship between text and paratext, but less so when they detract from these elements. The observations made here, together with other analyses of three tales from Angela Carter's *The Bloody Chamber* and their translations, suggest that translators of rewritings sometimes tend to focus on plot to the detriment of stylistic devices and deviations from normative grammar, syntax, and language. Are the translators of these rewritings unconsciously referring to their conception of what constitutes a literary fairy tale in their culture and language, despite the deliberate departure from the traditional notions of fairy tale by the rewriters? Do the translators feel that they cannot bend the conventions of the target language, since they do not consider themselves as authors in their own right, and refuse to adopt a more "resistant" approach? Whatever the reasons may be, the partial attenuation that we have observed of some of the queer elements within Donoghue's tale is surprising and contrasts with the stated mission of the French-language publication and the framing of the text.

At the same time, text, translation, and context engage in a queer dialogue, just like the shifting narrators of *Kissing the Witch*. "The Tale of the Shoe" dramatically transforms various elements of prior Cinderella plots, as we have seen, especially through its foregrounding of the sensual, its depiction of the process of self-realization, and its promise of alternative, queer identities and endings—or rather, new beginnings. In turn, in Cossy's translation, the spelling of words becomes the drawing and transmission of magic signs, enhancing one of the central themes of Donoghue's tale: the magical and redemptive power of love and touch. The erotic connotations of the tale, if sometimes softened in the translation, are retrieved by the photographs interspersed throughout the journal. These ambiguous, sensual images contribute to queering all of the accompanying content, including "Le conte de la chaussure." Through their multiple metamorphoses, then, text, translation, and context provide a succession of "new skins" to the "old" Cinderella tale. The changes introduced also push the reader to recognize, question, and potentially reject culturally constructed expectations and desires. Together, text, translation, and context self-consciously remind us of the constantly shifting nature of text, meaning, identity, and sexuality, em*bodying* change and demonstrating, indeed, the reader's own capacity for transformation.

Acknowledgments

I am grateful to the editors and reviewers of this volume for their careful readings and valuable suggestions.

Notes

1. The collection was first published by Hamish and Hamilton (London) earlier the same year, under the shorter title *Kissing the Witch*.

2. These are my translations. Martine Hennard Dutheil de la Rochère's French text in *Hétérographe* (2009a) is an essay (a translation-adaptation) based on her contribution to Susan Redington Bobby's (Dutheil de la Rochère 2009b) edited volume *Fairy Tales Reimagined*, and it acts as a companion piece to Valérie Cossy's translation of Donoghue's tale into French. Dutheil de la Rochère was a member of the *comité de soutien* of the journal until *Hétérographe* ceased publishing in spring 2012.
3. http://heterographe.com, last accessed on May 23, 2015.
4. As Dutheil de la Rochère (2009b, 14) points out, the meaning of "queer" denoting "the state of feeling ill or bad," even queasy, is also thematized in Donoghue's rewriting.
5. For example, "the small sounds of the mice," presupposed by the definite article and therefore referring the reader back to prior Cinderella versions, "were getting on my nerves" (Donoghue 1997, 6); also see the discussion of the finger/magic wand below.
6. Touch is subtly linked with taste and hearing, more than with vision. We see this, for example, in "she put her tiny finger over my mouth" (Donoghue 1997, 3; the gesture may also foreshadow kissing and therefore subtly evoke the title of Donoghue's collection) and "she put one hand over my ear" (5); the girl can "hear surprise" on the older woman's breath" (7) because they are standing so close together.
7. "Resemanticization" refers to the process by which a given form takes on new meaning. It is based on the idea that meaning is not predefined, but constructed. Context is a key factor in the construction of meaning.
8. Dutheil de la Rochère (2009b, 25) also quotes this passage. My own reading therefore unfolds in a Donoghue-like fashion, both based on and yet departing from her article stressing female literary and critical genealogies.
9. In fact, the very notion of "ideal" has been subtly interrogated.
10. This would be more in keeping with the "creative turn" in translation studies.

References

Bassnett, Susan, and Peter Bush, eds. 2006. *The Translator as Writer*. New York: Continuum.

Cossy, Valérie, trans. 2009. "Le conte de la chaussure." *Hétérographe: Revue des homolittératures ou pas* 1: 16–20.

Donoghue, Emma. 1997. *Kissing the Witch: Old Tales in New Skins*. New York: Harper Collins.

Dutheil de la Rochère, Martine Hennard . 2009a. "Cendrillon est amoureuse (de la fée marraine)." *Hétérographe: Revue des homolittératures ou pas* 1: 64–69.

———. 2009b. "Queering the Fairy Tale Canon: Emma Donoghue's *Kissing the Witch*." In *Fairy Tales Reimagined: Essays on New Retellings*, edited by Susan Redington Bobby, 13–30. Jefferson, NC: McFarland.

Hewson, Lance. 2011. *An Approach to Translation Criticism:* Emma *and* Madame Bovary *in Translation*. Philadelphia: John Benjamins.

Orme, Jennifer. 2010. "Mouth to Mouth: Queer Desires in Emma Donoghue's *Kissing the Witch*." *Marvels & Tales: Journal of Fairy-Tale Studies* 24 (1): 116–30.

Perteghella, Manuela, and Eugenia Loffredo, eds. 2006. *Translation and Creativity: Perspectives on Creative Writing and Translation Studies*. New York: Continuum.

Rich, Adrienne. 1975. "When We Dead Awaken: Writing as Re-Vision." In *Adrienne Rich's Poetry*, edited by Barbara Charlesworth Gelpi and Albert Gelpi, 90–98. New York: Norton.

Riggs, Ashley. 2014. "Thrice upon a Time: Feminist Fairy-Tale Rewritings by Angela Carter and Emma Donoghue, and Their French Translations." PhD diss., University of Geneva/University of Lausanne, Switzerland.

Venuti, Lawrence. 1992. Introduction to *Rethinking Translation: Discourse, Subjectivity, Ideology*, edited by Lawrence Venuti, 1–17. New York: Routledge.

Zipes, Jack. 2000. "Towards a Definition of the Literary Fairy Tale." In *The Oxford Companion to Fairy Tales: The Western Fairy Tale Tradition from Medieval to Modern*, edited by Jack Zipes, xv–xxxii. Oxford: Oxford University Press.

10

Home by Midnight

The Male Cinderella in LGBTI Fiction for Young Adults

Mark Macleod

> 9 pm on a November Saturday. Joni, Tony and I are out on the town. Tony is from the next town over and he needs to get out. His parents are extremely religious. It doesn't even matter which religion—they're all the same at a certain point, and few of them want a gay boy cruising around with his friends on a Saturday night. So every week Tony feeds us bible stories, then on Saturday we show up at his doorstep well versed in parables and earnestness, dazzling his parents with our blinding purity. They slip him a twenty and tell him to enjoy our study group. We go spend the money on romantic comedies, dimestore toys, and diner jukeboxes. Our happiness is the closest we'll ever come to a generous God, so we figure Tony's parents would understand, if only they weren't set on misunderstanding so many things. Tony has to be home by midnight, so we are on a Cinderella mission. With this in mind, we keep our eye on the ball. (Levithan 2003, 1)

In the opening scene of David Levithan's young adult novel *Boy Meets Boy* (2003) the as yet unnamed narrator, Paul, exemplifies the process of oral reappropriation observed by Zipes (2002, 197) in which the literary appropriation reenters oral discourse in a semantic shift determined by the changing cultural context. This chapter is concerned, not with the explicit adaptations or parodies of Cinderella for young readers, such as Babette Cole's *Prince Cinders* (1987), Helen Ketteman's *Bubba, the Cowboy Prince* (1997), Sandi Takayama's *Sumorella* (1997), and Roald Dahl's "Cinderella" in *Revolting Rhymes* (1982), or with film parodies such as Jerry Lewis's "Cinderfella" (1960), Todrick Hall's gay "CinderFella" (2012), or CollegeHumor's

"Tinderella" (2014). It explores, instead, tropes of the Cinderella story that have become so deeply embedded in Western narrative tradition that their provenance does not need to be explained. In any case, as Graham Anderson argues (2000, 18), the allusion to specific fairy-tale characters or place names does not point to adaptation: the real evidence is in narrative structure.

For Rob Baum (2000, 69) the lack of clear provenance in the popular imagination means that the Cinderella story approaches the functional status of myth. Its potential for contingent meaning results in its being repeatedly pressed into service by such social movements as feminism, although as Karlyn Crowley and John Pennington (2010) demonstrate, adaptation can take the plot a long way from the classic texts of Perrault and Grimm. The proliferation and brevity of references to Cinderella, however, demonstrate how deeply this tale is embedded in the imagination. Furthermore, as Linda Hutcheon (2006) points out, the adaptation process simultaneously challenges and confirms the stereotype. This is the reason that fairy tales generally, and "Cinderella" in particular, have been appropriated by feminist narrative and theory: they inscribe and also contest ideals of feminine passiveness and appearance. Scholars such as Bruno Bettelheim (1976, 236) and Anderson (2000, 23) endorse the Opies' view that "Cinderella" is the best known and best loved of fairy tales, and in their discourse analysis of *Grimm's Fairy Tales*, Lori Baker-Sperry and Liz Grauerholz find that the tales "that have been reproduced the most (*Cinderella* and *Snow White*) are precisely the ones that promote a feminine beauty ideal" (2003, 722). Even more pervasively than "Some day my Prince will come"—the popular theme song from Disney's *Snow White*—traditional retellings of Cinderella imply that youthful beauty, fashionable clothes, filial obedience, patient subservience to a man, and heterosexual marriage are the keys to a woman's happiness.

Since the late twentieth-century LGBTI rights movement began as the corollary of feminism, it is not surprising to find adaptations of Cinderella in LGBTI narratives for teens. For the readers, and some writers, of these adaptations, the 1950 Disney film is the primary source of the Cinderella story. Disney's reorientation of fairy tales from male-centered European to female-centered American texts has been well documented (Stone 1975; Zipes 1995; Lyon Clark 2003), and the appeal of the marginalized female protagonist as a metaphor for oppressed and unacknowledged sexuality is clear. In the context of emotionally charged headlines about both the threat and inevitability of "marriage equality," fairy-tale adaptations in fiction challenge readers with the idea that sexual diversity is a new story, but at the same time an ancient story, and perhaps not as improbable or unreasonable as it may at first appear, after all.

Although Marcia Lieberman (1986, 192) points out that the Norwegian Cinderlad chooses his position, the contemporary gay male Cinderella is in some ways structurally related to the male Cinderellas from Havelok the Dane to Harry Potter and beyond, identified by scholars and folklorists (Cosquin 1918, 193; Thompson 1958, L101; Stone 1975, 44; Salisbury 1997). The shyness and youthfulness of this "improbable hero," as Stith Thompson calls him, may signify his lack of power. His physical appearance and naïveté may signify his essential goodness and the potential for romance, and initially he may have neither courage nor strength. But these apparent traits are not his by choice. His limitations constitute a spell that has been imposed on him. To some extent, then, he functions as the female Cinderella does insofar as his role is determined by the male-dominated society (Anderson 2000, 159). Unlike the female Cinderella, however, he is not the ostensible object of heterosexual male desire. In LGBTI narratives the male Cinderella's challenge is to break through the spell of silent inaction and assert his sexuality, which is equated with his true identity. The question of whether LGBTI sexuality is a lifestyle of personal choice, or a genetic imposition, is, of course, central to the continuing public conversation about LGBTI rights.

From the outset, the spectrum of sexuality represented as "LGBTI" is problematic, however, as Maria Pallotta-Chiarolli (2005), Jayne Caudwell (2006), and Eric Anderson (2009) demonstrate in their work on sport and sexuality. The label assumes a commonality of concerns that cannot be sustained the further one works into it. The issues confronting transgender children, for example, are not the same as those confronting children who identify as gay or lesbian. Martine Hennard Dutheil de la Rochère (2009) demonstrates the insights to be gained from a queer reading of "Cinderella" that exposes and interrogates the sexist assumptions of the literary canon. On the other hand, queer theory now extends into areas that have little to do with sexuality, and as a critical framework it has become so broadly applicable—and inoffensive—that it is losing its political edge. That is the reason for the use of "LGBTI" here, rather than "LGBTQ" (Queer/Questioning) or the excessive LGBTQQIA. The constant addition to the "alphabet soup" (Ring 2012) threatens to collapse the political project into self-deprecating humor. Identifying as LGBTI can still be a daily matter of life and death in many communities. This is particularly acute for boys questioning their sexuality in a heteronormative male-dominated culture. For these reasons this paper limits the questions it raises to teen fiction that is identified as gay male related, and it immediately acknowledges

Judith Butler's (1990) and Eve Sedgwick's (1990) contesting of the essentialist assumptions in doing so.

Although physical sexual interaction is reported at much younger ages, the age of participants in LGBTI children's literature is positioned closer to legal ages of consent—generally sixteen to eighteen—due to the potential use of these texts in the classroom and school library, where they are subject to censorship by adults. An explicit instance of this disparity occurs in Alex Sanchez's novel *Rainbow Boys* (2001). Nelson "the school fag" is in his senior year of high school and is the subject of eroticized bullying, but he is secretly hopeful and fearful of what turns out to be his *first* penetrative sexual experience at the age of sixteen. Similarly, Bobby, the gay footballer narrator of Bill Konigsberg's *Out of the Pocket* (2008), spends most of that novel wondering what it would be like *if* he ever had sex with another boy—and yet he is seventeen. To follow Sedgwick and Butler and define the sexuality of such characters as performative is therefore hypothetical, as far as physical interpersonal sex goes, and the text tends to focus instead on appearance and identity.

The emphasis on identity is not unique to LGBTI texts, however. Jody Norton (1999) sees reductive essentialism as deeply embedded in literature for children and teens overall.

> As a discipline and as a body of texts, children's literature continues to operate on the basis of an outmoded binary paradigm of gender, in part because psychiatry, the social sciences, legal theory, education, and the humanities continue to function, for the most part, as though it had not already been clearly demonstrated that there are neither two sexes and two genders, nor two sex/genders. (Norton 1999, 417)

This binary paradigm is inscribed in the simple gender role reversals of countersexist texts produced by feminism—mainly for younger readers—from the 1970s, although Maria Nikolajeva observes that in Swedish young adult novels of the early 1980s, male characters play conventionally female roles (2006, 19). But to identify later US characters as male Cinderellas is not to feed the popular culture stereotype that gay men wish to be, or wish to dress as, women. Maria Tatar acknowledges that fairy tales "place a premium on surfaces" (2012, 119), and in the retellings derived from Perrault, the Cinderella story offers support for those young readers who imagine that changing their appearance will change their identity. While physical appearance is significant in the Grimms' version, the acknowledgment of Cinderella's inner goodness is far more important.

Although boys might be expected to dismiss a story about three sisters, a fairy godmother, ball gowns, and glass slippers, Ella Westland (1993) finds her ten- to eleven-year-old male respondents interested in the story and generally sympathetic to the prince. But what are the values embedded in the narrative that allow boys to position themselves as Cinderella herself? Because the abjection of women is so deeply inscribed in fairy tales, both Linda Parsons (2004, 139) and Karen Wohlwend (2009, 58) observe girls at play disrupting stereotypes in the Cinderella story. Referring to the construction of gender in Cinderella, David Maines says:

> When boys and girls hear the Cinderella narrative, they hear it in slightly different ways, with different listening frames. Maybe it means that Cinderella bonds to others and that Prince Charming dominates—that both boys and girls hear this and that the Cinderella narrative is really a dialectical tension in which males and females are simultaneously brought together and set apart. (1996, 102)

Norton (1999) extends the point about gender positioning. Arguing that tales such as "Cinderella" constitute a space that transchildren can inhabit imaginatively without feeling judged, she defends contemporary adaptations and parodies against the condemnation of traditionalists such as Dorothy Butler, because they offer a transforming fantasy that ends at midnight, or with the conclusion of the text. Its temporariness is therefore reassuring. Is this temporariness an appeal for boys questioning their sexuality? Most protagonists in children's literature are male, and we take it for granted that girls can relate to them, so Norton challenges the assumption that boys will not read across gender:

> If this form of gender transitivity is acceptable, why not also encourage further flights of the gendered imagination: for example, reading Cinderella as a male-bodied character, or Robin Hood (like Peter Pan) as a female-bodied one, and explaining that some children (and adults) identify fundamentally (not just transiently) across sex/gender lines; or drawing attention to alternatively gendered beings like fairies, who are not always represented as clearly either masculine or feminine? (Norton 1999, 421)

A minority of queer-identifying or curious boys may read Cinderella in the specific way Norton is suggesting, as a diva fantasy about frocking up and being the most talked about guest at the ball. For the majority, however, the story is not really about dressing up and going out. There are several questions that the Cinderella story might help young readers address. What is the relationship between appearance and reality? Is transformation possible and can it be permanent? Is the goal of transformation the acceptance of others, or self-acceptance—or both? Can it be achieved without help, and if not, who can be relied on for support: family, friends, or unknown members of the community? Can a romantic attraction survive if it transgresses social conventions? The Cinderella story as the Grimms tell it is about being marginalized and finally having your true worth acknowledged. These are the significant values the male Cinderella shares with the female character of the source tales: equivalents of ugly sisters, a glass slipper, and metamorphosed animals may or may not be involved.

As a story of transformation Cinderella is indeed about the external transformation of the protagonist, but, more importantly, it is about the internal transformation of the *audience* within the narrative and the broader audience of its implied readers. Cinderella's inner goodness is unchanged throughout most versions of the story. Even when she has the opportunity to humiliate her sisters by giving them a bad hair day, she resists it. Her clothes and shoes, even the transformed pumpkin, rats, and mice, do not change Cinderella herself, but they do change the way others see her—so much so that her sisters don't recognize her.

How does this emphasis determine the reading of Cinderella tropes in LGBTI texts? Whereas in the early development of young adult fiction, the expression of a character's gay sexuality was not realized, or was punished by the displaced death of a family member, a friend, or a pet, the male Cinderella story since the late 1990s offers the fictional possibility of public expression and acknowledgment. This is partly due to antidiscrimination laws, to the increased presence of LGBTI presenters and characters such as Ellen DeGeneres and *Will & Grace* on mainstream television and in film, and to a network of clubs in US schools called the Gay-Straight Alliance, which began in California in 1998 and became national in 2005 (http://gsanetwork.org/about-us/history). In the Alex Sanchez novel referred to earlier, *Rainbow Boys*, and Brent Hartinger's *Geography Club* (2003), the queer male protagonist is attracted to the sports jock. This sports jock is the masculine paradigm that the protagonist cannot be, but he is the catalyst for the protagonist's tentative steps toward claiming his own subjectivity by "coming out." His coming out rite of passage is a public occasion at the climax of the narrative. In novels such as *Geography Club*, he attends his first meeting of the school's Gay-Straight Alliance. More frequently, however, the climax is the end-of-school dance known as "prom night." Both are images of a liberated society. Acceptance by members of the Gay-Straight Alliance, or attending prom night with a same-sex partner, provides, in a colloquial sense, the fairy-tale ending that some LGBTI characters and readers dream of: their "fabulous Cinderella moment" (Boyer 2004, 17). It is interesting that referring to the temporary relevance of clothing, Marina Warner uses the expression "come out" to describe Cinderella's appearance at the ball in traditional tellings, although she is probably drawing on the language of debutante balls in the past.

> The prince does not see someone different at the ball, he sees the true beauty, who has "come out," acknowledged her state and put aside her disguise. This is why, in popular imagery, Cinderella remains equally lovely, whether in rags or riches. (Warner 1988, 148)

Appearance is assumed to be more significant by the sports jocks around the gay male Cinderella, however. The way he talks, looks, and moves, as well as the words he uses, are equated with his identity. There is no other reality, such as the male Cinderella's feelings, under this surface. *Geography Club* opens with the protagonist Russel Middlebrook in the locker room after PE and the homophobic bully, Kevin, yelling out for shampoo. He says that Russel is the kind of guy who always has shampoo, just as he always has clean undies. This feminizes Russel by positioning him outside the team of "real" boys. Here, the jock is the potential Prince, but he also plays the ugly sisters' role of harassing the male Cinderella. In other novels, gangs of homophobic bullies play the role of Cinderella's sisters. Kevin's awareness of the state of Russel's underwear anticipates his own outing later in the novel as the mysterious "GayTeen," who Russel encounters in a chatroom and agrees to meet at the playing field after dark. When Kevin decides by the end of the novel that he needs to keep his sexual interest in men hidden after all and can therefore only be a friend, not the lover that Russel desires, he has a team to go back to. Russel has referred to him earlier as Baseball Jock Incorporated (20). Kevin says that, while he sympathizes with boys such as Russel and Brian, whose sexuality is acknowledged throughout the school, being popular is too important to him to risk coming out. Russel's sense of abjection is ameliorated only by joining the school's Gay-Straight Alliance.

Although the whole point of the Gay-Straight Alliance is that attenders are not identified sexually as either gay or straight, onlookers and even some members assume that if a student is at the meeting, he must be gay. While not entirely free of the old stereotypes, therefore, the male Cinderella experiences his coming out at the Gay-Straight Alliance as the hypothesis of an ideal society that would recognize his true worth and empower him.

Because a dance is inherently more dramatic, however, the prom night novels add the element of fun to this political image of empowerment. In the closing scenes of films such as *My Best Friend's Wedding* (1997), *In & Out* (1997), and *Monsoon Wedding* (2001), the dramatic tensions around sexual diversity are resolved in dancing, much as Ellen DeGeneres's trademark dancing with her audience functions at the beginning of her daily television talk show. Like the Gay-Straight Alliance meeting in LGBTI young adult fiction, the dance floor is a site in which stereotypes are contested. Given contemporary dance styles, individual students may be alternately dancing alone, with another student regardless of gender, or in a group; the only constant is that the dialogue between bodies is constantly changing. Dance is a rare and climactic image of sexuality as performative in these texts. The celebration of freedom on the dance floor, however, is contrasted with the power of gender stereotypes in the weeks leading up to prom night and in the crowning of the Prom King and Queen.

The object of the three-day feast or ball in Perrault and the Grimms is the identification of a bride for the Prince, so Cinderella and her sisters attend without partners and are unchaperoned. Going to the ball with a partner would defeat the whole purpose. But the gay male Cinderella's abjection is inscribed in the much-discussed question of who will accompany him to prom night. Tatar argues that we keep recycling the Cinderella story "to manage our cultural anxieties and conflicts about courtship and marriage" (2012, 121). Although her inference is about heterosexual anxieties, it is even more relevant to those whose exclusion from the conventions of courtship and marriage is a hotly contested political issue. In his study *Kings and Queens: Queers at the Prom*, David Boyer says:

> Prom shines a spotlight on coupling and romance, forcing queer teens to publicly confront an attraction that until very recently, society basically condemned. (Boyer 2004, 3)

Going to the prom alone is not an option, because it would identify the gay male Cinderella as a loser in a society where heterosexual coupling is expected. In that sense, the prospective royal suitor who will embrace and pursue the male Cinderella is the assembled school community. That is who the protagonist must win over.

The question of whether he has the courage to arrive at the prom with a male partner occurs so frequently that it is now a cliché of US young adult fiction. It originates with *Reflections of a Rock Lobster*, the 1981 memoir of Aaron Fricke, the first student to sue his school for the right to take his male partner to prom night, and it is revived by cases such as that of transgender female-to-male student Cinthia (Tony) Covarrubias, running for Prom King in Fresno California in 2007 (Letellier 2007, 13).

The image is popularized in season 2, episode 20, of the TV series *Glee*, when drama student Kurt Hummel is voted Prom Queen (2011). Kurt at first refuses to accept the coronation, but with the help of his partner, Blaine, changes his mind and accepts the chance to be a role model. David Karofsky—the closeted gay sports jock, who has bullied Kurt—is crowned Prom King, but he cannot face coming out and dancing with Kurt. In the crowning of two boys as Prom King and Queen, the society's heteronormative values are both contested and reinscribed in prom night. The script acknowledges that the archaic Prom Court, which traditionally chooses the Prom King and Queen, is metonymic rather than parodic, when Kurt invokes the new Duchess of Cambridge, the future "Queen of England." He accepts the crown and says to the crowd on the dance floor, "Eat your heart out, Kate Middleton!"

In the *Rainbow Boys* sequels, *Rainbow High* and *Rainbow Road*, and in such novels as *Out of the Pocket* or Lee Bantle's *David Inside Out* (2009), however, the situation in earlier novels is inverted and the male Cinderella is the sports jock himself. The narrator of *David Inside Out* is a runner, as is Sean, the boy he is in love with. He repeatedly succumbs to sexual encounters with Sean, only to be rejected immediately afterward. Heidi Eng (2006) points out that despite the homosocial behavior evident on the playing field and in the dressing room, homoerotic desire and practice in sports are silenced. The jock enjoys the challenge of experimenting, but when heteronormative silence is restored, the male Cinderella is doubly vulnerable and isolated, because the jock denies that it ever happened, or says the experiment proved to him that he's "not like that." The male Cinderella is now out, but still alone. When the jock himself is the male Cinderella, on the other hand, the story is about the price he will pay if his true nature becomes public. He may gain the acknowledgment of other gay students, but he will lose his sports scholarship, the support of adult authority figures such as his coach, and the rest of the team—none of whom, of course, is less than 100 percent heterosexual. The sports are generally those that project body images of orthodox masculinity, such as swimming, athletics, wrestling, or team sports such as baseball, basketball and football—particularly the body contact codes. And typically there is at least one highly charged scene in the locker room.

Anderson (2009) asserts that the range of masculinities now acceptable in the sporting arena contests Raewyn Connell's concept of "hegemonic masculinity," although the university population Anderson bases his research on cannot be regarded as typical. The continuing newsworthiness of such headlines as "US Soccer Star 'Comes Out' as Gay" (Masters 2013) challenges Anderson's conclusion. Sedgwick rejects the identity politics of the 1970s–1980s, and Butler (1990) and Julia Creet (1994) are among the critics who challenge the coming out story, because it assumes that sexuality is essentialist rather than performative. However, young adult fiction appears to be stuck with the idea that sexuality is defined by what the character *is*, rather than what he or she *does*. This is due not just to the age of the protagonists referred to earlier, but to the brutal taxonomy of the schoolyard and—despite all the emphasis on achieving a personal best—to the predominance of competitive sport, which labels participants as winners and losers, strong and weak, masculine and feminine. Competitive sport persists beyond the schoolyard as a bastion of the essentialist sexism that confronts the protagonist, and as a metaphor in corporate and public discourse.

Bobby Framingham, the star football player who is the narrator of *Out of the Pocket*, expresses the choice starkly between essentialist and performative sexualities in the opening chapter, when he finally says hello to the fellow athlete he has dreamed about.

> As I walked past him, I recognized for the first time that what had been just dreams meant something; someday I might act on those dreams with another guy. That maybe I'd have a date with someone, and that someone would be male. And then I would be considered gay. (Konigsberg 2008, 10)

For most of the novel, Bobby's fear of losing a football scholarship and the approval of his coach and teammates determines his inaction. Then he meets the out student Bryan, who says if Bobby wants to be in a relationship with him, then he must take action and come out publicly.

Brent Hartinger (2009) asserts that the coming out novel is finished and that sexuality is now incidental rather than central to the LGBTI narrative, and this indeed describes the changing emphasis in his own recent fiction. Publishers' lists, however, make it clear that generally, like the happily choreographed celebration of diversity in the television series *Glee*, Hartinger's assertion is based on aspiration, rather than fact. Thomas Crisp (2009, 336) argues that the major role played by homophobia in contemporary narratives limits their potential to make a radical break with heteronormative stereotypes, so the male Cinderella anticipating his entrance at the formal dance still has fictional potential.

Novels by Hartinger, Sanchez, and Levithan, however, contest not just political opposition but also the relevance of heteronormative fictional models. In *Rainbow Boys*, when Kyle comes out to his mother, her loving response surprises him, and his father's anger doesn't. But when the ultra-jock Jason drops in, ostensibly so that Kyle can coach him in math, Kyle's father is delighted to learn that he is a jock and says he has told Kyle to spend more time hanging out with athletic boys, presumably since this will make a man of Kyle. Here the implied author invites the reader to enjoy a conspiratorial laugh at the conventional assumption of what hanging out with athletic boys might entail. When Jason first kisses Kyle, Kyle immediately grasps at the heterosexual cliché and whispers that he loves him—a mistake that causes Jason to panic and retreat. Later, when Nelson allows himself to have his own first sexual encounter, unprotected with a man he has just met in a chatroom, he too makes an almost pathetic attempt to reassure himself with a narrative cliché: "even if Brick was HIV positive, they could take care of each other. Wasn't that what lovers were for?" (149–50). The danger here is urgent and physical, however; it is not merely a failure of narrative models.

Although by the third novel of Sanchez's trilogy, *Rainbow Road*, when the champion basketballer Jason is comfortable enough with his sexuality to take his lover Kyle on a road trip across the country to California, where he has been offered a sports scholarship, it is significant that as they set out, they ostracize Nelson for dyeing his hair pink. The unpartnered Nelson's flamboyant camp behavior becomes the scapegoat that, by contrast, normalizes their own relationship. The somewhat melodramatic treatment of Nelson's unprotected sexual initiation may be explained, if not excused, by the socializing function of all children's literature identified by scholars such as John Stephens (1992) and Perry Nodelman (2008). Jack Zipes sees such countercultural fairy-tale tellers as attempting to "transform the civilizing process" (1983, 179). Although the implied author of *Rainbow Road* celebrates the rite of coming out, he also highlights its potential risks.

However, the departure from realist fictional models in novels by David Levithan (2003) and David LaRochelle (2005) and in the animated feature film *ParaNorman* (2012) indicates that the anxiety embedded in the male Cinderella trope may be diminishing. The revelation that the heavily muscled jock Mitch in *ParaNorman* is gay has been praised as a significant moment in animated film, because the main point is that he is a footballer who just happens to be gay. Gay scriptwriter Chris Butler says that the revelation of Mitch's sexuality was:

> important to us. We were telling a story that was fundamentally about intolerance. We believed that it was important to have the strength of our convictions. (Butler 2012)

On the other hand, the late positioning of this revelation is ambiguous. It comes, as Chris Butler says, in a kind of punch line to the narrative. Courtney the cheerleader asks Mitch if he would like to see a movie. He says yes and that she will like his boyfriend and that his boyfriend will be really happy, because he loves chick flicks. This may be taken as supporting Anderson's and Hartinger's assertion that identifying as gay is now incidental. On the other hand, the positioning may be read as a coming out: the delay making this revelation a big deal indeed in a film for young audiences. And conservative reaction has been predictable.

> You knew it was only a matter of time before the gay community, which has successfully integrated gay characters into every possible form of entertainment for adults, targeted children. . . . If they really were "brave" they'd announce from the start that Mitch was gay and see just how many parents would take their children to see this movie. (Bigelow 2012)

The appearance of the male Cinderella at prom night in David LaRochelle's novel *Absolutely, Positively NOT* is similarly ambiguous. Steven, the narrator, partners his mother to square dancing every week, has a poster of Speedo-clad Superman on his bedroom wall, and tries to deny that he finds his teacher, Mr. Bowman, physically attractive. He is bullied and called a "faggot" by other boys in the changing room. Then on an ice-fishing trip with his father, Steven broaches the subject of his lack of sexual interest in girls:

> "Did you always want to date girls?"
>
> My dad looked up from the hole.
>
> "As opposed to dating what, Steven? Gorillas? Of course I always wanted to date girls. . . . You're a DeNarski. The DeNarski men have always been a hit with the ladies." (LaRochelle 2005, 89–91)

In the absence of support from his family, the male Cinderella in LGBTI young adult fiction turns to a best friend who is often female, a coach, or a teacher. In a desperate bid to prove to himself that he is "absolutely, positively NOT gay," Steven forces himself to date girls for a month and feels a complete failure until one of them, Rachel, admits that she and her family have known he was gay for a while. She proposes setting up a Gay-Straight Alliance at school to support Steven and is prepared to sue the principal if he tries to block it. But Steven is the one who blocks it, because he can't handle the exposure.

An alternative Cinderella moment looms when Steven's mother encourages him to attend the school dance. Despite his argument with Rachel over the Gay-Straight Alliance, he again confides in her. She is his totally supportive fairy godmother, and he tells her is going to the dance with Kelly.

> Rachel's eyes widened to the size of small planets
>
> "Kelly Markovitch? All-state quarterback? Way to go, Steven! When you come out, you really come out!" She tapped a finger lightly on my chest. "You know, I've always suspected that half the football team was gay."
>
> "Not Kelly the football player. Kelly your dog." (LaRochelle 2005, 141–42)

The only reason Steven is going to the dance is to shut his mother up. Just as Nelson's extreme stereotype behavior allows his gay friends to appear "normal," Kelly the golden retriever (a blond) becomes the displaced object of the fury that would have greeted any human male partner Steven might have taken to the dance. Steven's partner may be a dog, but she is at least female.

> Our table was darkened by a shadow roughly the size and shape of a water buffalo. It was Mr. Cheever, our vice principal.
>
> "Get that filthy animal out of here," he growled.
>
> Kelly growled back.
>
> "And get it out now, before it attacks someone. . . . I am not about to let some smart aleck kid disrupt this school event. I want that dog out, and I want it out NOW!" (156–57)

The vice principal's objections are overtaken by the other students' desire to pet Steven's date, because it is so cute. Although the memory of the ugly bullying earlier in the novel is temporarily overtaken by this farcical Cinderella moment at the dance, the subtext is ambiguous. It hinges on sexist (and species-ist) colloquial double meanings of the word "dog" in English: an unattractive female, and a disloyal or criminal male. Because Steven's partner is literally, if not metaphorically, a dog, the scene therefore both parodies and confirms the homophobia that has prevented Steven from identifying himself as gay throughout the narrative. Like the narrator's pun quoted at the beginning of this chapter, "we keep our eye on the ball" (Levithan 2003, 1), and the double entendre above, "My dad looked up from the hole" (LaRochelle 2005, 89), the joking here takes the heat out of such awkward moments, but at the same time it confirms Heather Milne's argument that gay male fiction cushions and sanitizes lived urban experiences to a degree that fiction about heterosexual teens does not (2013, 177). It could be argued that the intention is to give the ostracized gay protagonist a future, but the joking clearly derives from a hegemonic perspective that allows the male Cinderella an easier time than his female counterpart, who is the object of Perrault's moralizing.

The celebratory comic gaytopia of David Levithan's *Boy Meets Boy* (2003) is in sharp contrast to the uncertain resolution of the comedy in *Absolutely, Positively NOT*. As indicated earlier, *Boy Meets Boy* opens with the narrator, Paul, aware that he and the other students must get their friend, Tony, home by midnight, like Cinderella. In this alternate reality, Paul first has his own sexuality confirmed when at the age of six he sees that his teacher has written on his kindergarten report card, "Paul is definitely gay and has very good sense of self" (8), and when in third grade he makes a successful run for class president with the slogan "Vote for Me—I'm Gay." The daring of this utopian vision is exhilarating, with sexuality being declared in early childhood and the anxiety of coming out made irrelevant. But it's in the figure of Infinite Darlene, the six-foot-four quarterback who wears drag and becomes homecoming queen, that *Boy Meets Boy* collapses the distinction between the gay-identifying character and the football jock. For all the novel's good-natured high energy, which sweeps aside any question of paradox in the phrase "gay sports jock," this character confronts directly the conservatism of middle America.

Like Paul, Infinite Darlene is blissfully free. Tony, however, is the male Cinderella from the oppressively religious family, who watch and suspect his every move. If his family allowed it, he would identify as gay. So to him, Infinite Darlene the drag queen, who embodies enough orthodox masculinity to be celebrated as a star quarterback, is a wonderful fantasy character that he himself could never be. The plot centers on Tony's desire to go to the dance with the other students, who occupy varied positions along the spectrum of sexual diversity. The major question for Tony's parents is, who will be his date? He can't go alone, and they would never accept the narrator Paul, because that would mean Tony is gay. So the students devise a strategy that ensures that he can have his Cinderella moment in the final chapter. They turn up to collect Tony and tell his parents that each one of them is his date: boys and girls, of varying sexual identities, all acting as one.

The utopian vision here is a long way from the anxiety of attending a Gay-Straight Alliance meeting, or making an entrance at prom night with a same-sex partner or even a dog. But in a tacit acknowledgment that the school dance may not be totally free of stereotyping when they eventually get there, Tony and all his dates stop on the way to the gym and dance in a clearing in the woods, liberated by the natural environment and the darkness, temporarily both alone and together in all the possible combinations of a triumphant gay fairy tale. Here they are "home," and the night has only just started. It might end at midnight, but it is a triumphant Cinderella moment for the whole society.

References

Anderson, Eric. 2009. *Inclusive Masculinity: The Changing Nature of Masculinities.* New York: Routledge.

Anderson, Graham. 2000. *Fairytale in the Ancient World.* London: Routledge.

Baker-Sperry, Lori, and Liz Grauerholz. 2003. "The Pervasiveness and Persistence of the Feminine Beauty Ideal in Children's Fairy Tales." *Gender and Society* 17 (5): 711–26.

Bantle, Lee. 2009. *David Inside Out.* New York: Henry Holt.

Baum, Rob. 2000. "After the Ball Is Over: Bringing *Cinderella* Home." *Cultural Analysis* 1: 69–83.

Bettelheim, Bruno. 1976. *The Uses of Enchantment.* London: Thames and Hudson.

Bigelow, William. 2012. "'ParaNorman' Slips in First Openly Gay Animated Character." Breitbart.com. August 29. http://www.breitbart.com/Big-Hollywood/2012/08/29/paranorman-first-gay-animated-character.

Boyer, David. 2004. *Kings and Queens: Queers at the Prom.* Brooklyn, NY: Soft Skull Press.

Butler, Chris. 2012. "Why *ParaNorman* Featured the First Gay Character in an Animated Film." Interview with D. Anderson-Minshall. *Advocate*,

November 29. http://www.advocate.com/arts-entertainment/dvds/2012/11/29/why-paranorman-featured-first-gay-character-animated-film.

Butler, Judith. 1990. *Gender Trouble: Feminism and the Subversion of Identity*. New York: Routledge.

Caudwell, Jayne, ed. 2006. *Sport, Sexualities, and Queer/Theory*. New York: Routledge.

Cole, Babette. 1987. *Prince Cinders*. London: Hamish Hamilton.

CollegeHumor. 2014. "Tinderella: A Modern Fairy Tale." YouTube. http://www.collegehumor.com/video/6948903/tinderella-a-modern-fairy-tale.

Connell, Raewyn. 1995. *Masculinities*. Cambridge: Polity.

Cosquin, Emmanuel. 1918. "Le 'Cendrillon Masculin.'" *Revue des Traditions Populaires* 33: 193–202.

Creet, Julia. 1994. "Anxieties of Identity: Coming Out and Coming Undone." In *Negotiating Lesbian and Gay Subjects*, edited by Richard Henke and Monica Dorenkamp, 179–99. New York: Routledge.

Crisp, Thomas. 2009. "From Romance to Magic Realism: Limits and Possibilities in Gay Adolescent Fiction." *Children's Literature in Education* 40 (4): 333–48.

Crowley, Karlyn, and John Pennington. 2010. "Feminist Frauds on the Fairies? Didacticism and Liberation in Recent Retellings of 'Cinderella.'" *Marvels & Tales* 24 (2): 297–313.

Dahl, Roald. 1982. *Revolting Rhymes*. Illustrated by Quentin Blake. London: Jonathan Cape.

Dutheil de la Rochère, Martine Hennard. 2009. "Queering the Fairy Tale Canon: Emma Donoghue's *Kissing the Witch*." In *Fairy Tales Reimagined: Essays on New Retellings*, edited by Susan Redington Bobby, 13–30. Jefferson, NC: McFarland.

Heidi Eng. 2006. "Queer Athletes and Queering in Sport." In *Sport, Sexualities, and Queer/Theory*, edited by Jayne Caudwell, 49–60. New York: Routledge.

Fricke, Aaron. 1981. *Reflections of a Rock Lobster*. Boston: Alyson.

Hall, Todrick. 2012. "CinderFella." July 27. https://vimeo.com/46462576.

Hartinger, Brent. 2003. *Geography Club*. New York: HarperTempest.

———. 2009. "Brent's Brain: The Website of Writer Brent Hartinger." www.brenthartinger.com, accessed December 21.

Hutcheon, Linda. 2006. *A Theory of Adaptation*. New York: Routledge.

Ketteman, Helen. 1997. *Bubba, the Cowboy Prince*. Illustrated by James Warhola. New York: Scholastic.

Konigsberg, Bill. 2008. *Out of the Pocket*. New York: Dutton.

LaRochelle, David. 2005. *Absolutely, Positively NOT*. New York: Scholastic.

Letellier, Patrick. 2007. "Transactions: A Transgender News Update." *Lesbian News* 32 (11): 13.

Levithan, David. 2003. *Boy Meets Boy*. New York: Alfred A. Knopf.

Lieberman, Marcia K. 1986. " 'Some Day My Prince Will Come': Female Acculturation through the Fairy Tale." In *Don't Bet on the Prince*, edited by Jack Zipes, 185–200. Aldershot, England: Gower.

Lyon Clark, Beverly. 2003. *Kiddie Lit*. Baltimore: Johns Hopkins University Press.

Maines, David R. 1996. "Gender, Narrative, and the Problematics of Role." *Michigan Sociological Review* 10: 87–107.

Masters, James. 2013. "US Soccer Star 'Comes Out' as Gay." CNN.com. February 18. http://edition.cnn.com/2013/02/15/sport/football/robbie-rogers-football-gay-u-s-.

Milne, Heather. 2013. "Isolation, Exploration, Affirmation: Dominant Patterns in Four Books for Gay Teens." *Jeunesse: Young People, Texts, Cultures* 5 (1): 171–78.

Nikolajeva, Maria. 2006. "New Masculinities, New Femininities: Swedish Young Adult Fiction towards the Twenty-First Century." In *Changing Concepts of Childhood and Children's Literature*, edited by Vanessa Joosen and Katrien Vloeberghs, 17–29. Newcastle: Cambridge Scholars Press.

Nodelman, Perry. 2008. *The Hidden Adult: Defining Children's Literature*. Baltimore: Johns Hopkins University Press.

Norton, Jody. 1999. "Transchildren and the Discipline of Children's Literature." *The Lion and the Unicorn* 23 (3): 415–36.

Pallotta-Chiarolli, Maria. 2005. "We're the X-Files: Bisexual Students 'Messing Up Tidy Sex Files.'" In *Sexuality, Sport, and the Culture of Risk*, edited by Keith Gilbert, 7–36. Oxford: Meyer and Meyer Sport.

Paramount Pictures. 1960. *Cinderfella*.

Parsons, Linda T. 2004. "Ella Evolving: Cinderella Stories and the Construction of Gender-Appropriate Behavior." *Children's Literature in Education* 35 (2): 135–54.

Ring, Trudy. 2012. "LGBTQQIA." *Advocate*, August 22. http://www.advocate.com/arts-entertainment/advocate-45/2012/08/22/lgbtqqia.

Salisbury, Eve. 1997. "(Re)dressing Cinderella." In *Retelling Tales*, edited by Thomas G. Hahn and Alan Lupack, 275–92. Rochester, NY: Boydell and Brewer.

Sanchez, Alex. 2001. *Rainbow Boys*. New York: Simon and Schuster.

———. 2003. *Rainbow High*. New York: Simon and Schuster.

———. 2005. *Rainbow Road*. New York: Simon and Schuster.

Sedgwick, Eve Kosofsky. 1990. *Epistemology of the Closet*. Berkeley: University of California Press.

Stephens, John. 1992. *Language and Ideology in Children's Fiction*. New York: Longman.

Stone, Kay. 1975. "Things Walt Disney Never Told Us." *Journal of American Folklore* 88 (347): 42–50.

Takayama, Sandi. 1997. *Sumorella: A Hawai'i Cinderella Story*. Illustrated by Esther Szegedy. Honolulu, HI: Bess Press.

Tatar, Maria, trans. 2012 [2004]. *The Annotated Brothers Grimm*. New York: W. W. Norton.

Thompson, Stith. 1958. *Motif-Index of Folk-Literature*. Bloomington: Indiana University Press.

Warner, Marina. 1994. *From the Beast to the Blonde: On Fairy Tales and Their Tellers*. London: Chatto and Windus.

———. 1988. "The Wronged Daughter: Aspects of Cinderella." *Grand Street* 7 (3): 143–63.

Westland, Ella. 1993. "Cinderella in the Classroom: Children's Responses to Gender Roles in Fairy-Tales." *Gender and Education* 5 (3): 237–49.

Wohlwend, Karen E. 2009. "Damsels in Discourse: Girls Consuming and Producing Identity Texts through Disney Princess Play." *Reading Research Quarterly* 44 (1): 57–83.

Zipes, Jack. 1983. *Fairy Tales and the Art of Subversion*. London: Heinemann.

———. 1986. *Don't Bet on the Prince*. Aldershot, England: Gower.

———. 1995. "Breaking the Disney Spell." In *The Politics of Film, Gender, and Culture*, edited by Elizabeth Bell, Lynda Haas, and Laura Sells, 21–42. Bloomington: Indiana University Press.

———. 2002. *The Brothers Grimm: From Enchanted Forests to the Modern World*. 2nd ed. New York: Palgrave Macmillan.

11

"I'm sure it all wears off by midnight"

Prince Cinders and a Fairy's Queer Invitation

Jennifer Orme

As fairy-tale scholars know, the fairy tale owes its long life and continued proliferation in a variety of media to its inherent and seemingly inexhaustible ability to adapt to ever shifting social and cultural contexts and to any genre that catches its fancy (see Greenhill and Matrix 2010). In the realm of children's literature, and particularly in picture books, Cinderella is often invited to slip into different outfits, or even different physical forms, and bring her ever-popular and well-known motifs with her to attend the revisionists' ball. On the sidelines, gossiping about Cinderella's latest form, her ride, her prince, and even her magical helpers, we literary critics and folklorists watch like eagle-eyed chaperones, paying close attention to the subtle and sometimes not-so-subtle interplay between traditional and contemporary political and cultural concerns the fairy-tale guests bring to the party.

As Vanessa Joosen has demonstrated in *Critical and Creative Perspectives on Fairy Tales* (2011), "retellings and criticism participate in a continuous and dynamic dialogue about the traditional fairy tale, yet they do so on different terms" (3). The terms of feminist critical interventions into the fairy-tale realm are well established, well documented, and ongoing (see especially Haase 2004), but the interactions between fairy tales and lesbian/gay and queer literary criticism are comparatively recent (Dutheil de la Rochère 2009; Orme 2010; Turner and Greenhill 2012; Duggan 2013; and Seifert 2015). Moreover, the three critical perspectives are closely related and often their threads intermingle. Here I tease out some of the ways feminist, lesbian/gay, and queer approaches are distinct from each other and demonstrate their relations and differences through three close readings of one Cinderella revision: Babette Cole's 1987 picture book, *Prince Cinders*.

The first reading sees the book as a response to the feminist fairy-tale debates that were happening at the time of its publication. The second takes a lesbian/gay critical literary position that grows out of feminist concerns and examines assumptions about the relationships between gender and sexual identity and the coding of homosexuality in the text. The third interpretation proposes a queer reading that focuses less on character representation and more on the destabilizing potential of internal textual contradictions that adhere to the ostensible aims of the book itself.

As Mandy Merck, Naomi Segal, and Elizabeth Wright say in *Coming Out of Feminism* (1998), " 'queer' emerges from the closet of insult, but also from the egg of 'lesbian and gay' as well as the womb of feminism" (4). Because of this close relationship, feminist, lesbian/gay, and queer literary perspectives tend to slip into and out of each other's purview. However, there are differences in their objects of attention (the representation of women, gay and lesbian subjects, and textual transgressions of gendered and sexual norms respectively). Therefore, the goals of these approaches and what is at stake are also related but distinct.

In their introduction to the collection of essays *Over the Rainbow: Queer Children's and Young Adult Literature* (2011), Michelle Ann Abate and Kenneth Kidd differentiate between their uses of the terms:

> Recognizing the difficulty of such designations, we use "lesbian/gay" to designate the first wave of academic work on same-sex topics (lesbian/gay studies) as well as the first wave of children's books with same-sex focus or component (lesbian/gay children's literature). "Queer" is highly elastic and linked with the advent of queer theory and queer studies in the academy. We use "LGBTQ" to indicate lesbian/gay/bisexual/transgendered/queer people. (2011, 9n1)[1]

Abate and Kidd's designations are helpful, but they do not go quite far enough for my project. Recognizing that "queer" is elastic and linked to academic discourses tells us of its origins and relationships, but does not clarify what the elasticity encompasses or what queer theory and queer studies *do*. I follow their uses of "lesbian/gay" and "queer," but I am not concerned here with demonstrating the kinds of academic work that has been done on gay/lesbian or queer subjects and texts. Rather I demonstrate what I see as important differences between them within literary studies, and I extend Abate and Kidd's designations to include the kind of feminist critique I will employ.

Part of the difficulty in delineating clear distinctions between the terms comes from the close historical and methodological relationships between the three approaches. This closeness has led to sometimes confusing and inconsistent uses of "queer" to mean anything from its older sense of "odd" or "strange" or "outlandish," to shorthand for LGBTTIQQ2SAAP subjects, to very specific type of reading practices. In a hope to avoid the polarizing debates that have occurred around the issue of the term "queer" (see McKee 1997; Halperin 2003; Marcus 2005; Schneiderman 2010; and Halley and Parker 2011), I propose here a clarification of how I use it in this article. I agree with Tison Pugh, who argues for a view of queerness "not as a synonym for *homosexuality* but as a descriptor of disruptions to prevailing cultural codes of sexual and gender normativity" (Pugh 2011, 6). Lesbian/gay and feminist literary criticisms are methodologies with a utopian drive toward equality and inclusion that is politically important and still very necessary. Queer literary theory is still political, of course, but more amorphous and difficult to pin down. Queer is concerned with how texts construct and deconstruct cultural norms as they relate to intersecting forms of desire and control. We might say that feminist and lesbian/gay work toward a politics of inclusion and unity and queer works toward a politics of transgression and unassimilablity. And yet the three can and often do sit happily side by side, occasionally slipping into each other's space, using each other's tools and slipping back again.

Both within fairy-tale studies and more broadly, feminist critique has been established and institutionalized as a reading practice for longer than either lesbian/gay or queer and as such has a longer history and more methodological and theoretical branches. I am interested in one relatively narrow, but still influential, form of feminist literary criticism of fairy tales that focuses on the representation of female characters and femininity in fairy-tale texts. As exemplified by Marcia Lieberman's polemic call to arms, "Some Day My Prince Will Come: Female Acculturation through the Fairy Tale" (1972), this type of criticism is based upon a notion of gender as ideologically constructed. Fairy tales are singled out as being particularly influential on female identity formation (see Haase 2004; Joosen 2011, esp. 50–53), but constructions of masculinity are rarely considered. Key are issues of voice and visibility; female competition and the centrality of masculine figures, even *in absentia*, to tales about women; and the ways the feminine tends to be marginalized and devalued within patriarchal literary fairy-tale traditions.

Similarly, lesbian/gay literary criticism looks at the representation of lesbian/gay characters, both explicitly articulated as such and covertly implied through homosocial relations that can be read as homosexual. Like the type of feminist literary criticism above does for woman centered themes and representations of sexism, lesbian/gay criticism of children's literature identifies and explicates gay and lesbian characters and/or their often overwhelming absence as well as themes related to homosexuality such as homophobia (Jenkins 1993 and 1998). As with some feminist literary theory, lesbian/gay often works through identity politics and is utopian in its aims. Its intention is to bring lesbian/gay subjects into the literary conversation, not as marginal figures, tokens, or stereotypical or monolithic representations of Otherness, but as complex, fully formed subjects whose experiences are as multifaceted and varied as presumed heterosexual literary characters are.

Queer literary theory is less identitarian than feminist and lesbian/gay literary criticism and more deconstructive—it looks for gaps, fissures, and contradictions that both create and sustain a text's effects but also reveal nonnormative gender positions and desires that make the text's normative ideologies possible in the first place. In her discussion of the tensions between lesbian/gay inclusive picture books and more anarchic queer ones, Melynda Huskey argues that "while foregrounding homosexuality . . . robs the picture book of its queerness, seeking it where it 'isn't' establishes it most fully" (2002, 68). She goes on to point out that by

> stepping outside that interpretive circle that needs homosexuality to be normal, and which consequently must render it as abnormal, we enter the connotative realm, the elusive, impossible-to-deny because impossible-to-prove world of implication. (Ibid., 69)

Reading texts queerly, she implies, means moving away from the search for gay and lesbian subjects, which necessarily always marks them as in opposition to the normal of assumed heterosexuality, and instead reveling in the implicit transgressive possibilities inherent in the text. Further, adapting Lee Edelman, she asserts that

> queerness does not name an identity but can only ever disturb one. To read child characters queerly may not, in fact, be the same thing as reading children's literature queerly. Reading children's literature queerly means reading for its non-normativities more broadly. (Ibid., 123)

I have conceptualized this broader reading practice elsewhere (Orme 2010, 2012, 2015) as accepting the "queer invitation" offered by the contradictions and destabilizations inherent in many fairy tale revisions.

Prince Cinders critiques both feminine and masculine hegemonic norms, and it encodes gay male abjection; in doing so, and perhaps inadvertently, it creates queer space. That space comes into existence in the dissonances between the text's surface ideological purpose as feminist fairy-tale revision and its ironic stance as parody of the best-known versions of Cinderella.

Prince Cinders

Babette Cole is a British author who has been writing and illustrating children's picture books since the 1970s. She is known for an irreverent sense of humor, for absurd and grotesque illustrations, and for taking on so-called sensitive topics such as "the facts of life" (*Mommy Laid an Egg*, 1993); death (*Drop Dead*, 1997); divorce (*Two of Everything*, 1997, UK title, *The Un-Wedding*, 1998, US title); and puberty (*Hair in Funny Places*, 2000). In addition to *Prince Cinders*, Cole has written three original fairy-tale princess books: *Princess Smartypants* (1986), *Long Live Princess Smartypants* (2005, US title *Princess Smartypants Rules*), and *Princess Smartypants Breaks the Rules* (2009).

It could be argued that many of Cole's picture books are queer. They privilege the playful, anarchic, absurd, and disruptive; her characters are caricatures, outlandish, ridiculous, and often grotesque; and their adventures tend to transgress the bounds of childhood purity and innocence so desired by adults for children's literature.

Prince Cinders is one such book. On the first page we are introduced to Prince Cinders himself who is depicted and described as "not much of a prince" because he is "small, spotty, scruffy and skinny" (Cole 1987). He wears worn and patched jeans, a white shirt, and often a white apron and untied trainers. He is fair-haired and wears a small crown to signify his princely status (as do all of the other royal characters). His three brothers are described as "big and hairy" throughout the text and are nearly identical large men with black locks, moustaches, and wide, sly grins reminiscent of 1980s heartthrob Tom Selleck, a slightly less butch Sylvester Stallone, or even Queen front man Freddy Mercury. They tease Cinders about his looks and make him do all of the housework while they drive off to the disco in their two-seater convertibles with their identical blond princess girlfriends.

While his brothers are off at the disco, a dirty fairy arrives (via the chimney) to grant Cinders three boons. She transforms a tin can into a car (although it is a dinky car); she transforms Cinders's ratty jeans and apron into a suit (although it is an anachronistic bathing suit); finally, she transforms

Cinders himself from small and scruffy to big and hairy like his brothers (although in his big hairiness Cinders takes the form of a giant monkey or ape). The fairy then sends Cinders off to the ball, but because he is too large to fit through the door of the disco, he goes to the bus stop to return home. There he encounters the Princess Lovelypenny who is frightened of his big monkeyness. As the clock strikes midnight he transforms back to his old shape and, believing he has saved her from the beast, Lovelypenny calls out to him, but he runs away so quickly that he "even lost his trousers in the rush" (Cole 1987). Lovelypenny uses the princely trousers to mount her husband-search and, when they are found to fit him, the two marry and Prince Cinders lives "in luxury happily ever after" (ibid). But happily ever after is not the end of the story because Lovelypenny has "a word" with the fairy who, on the last page, delivers retribution upon Cinders's brothers.

Feminism and Gender Critique

The importance of feminist criticism to fairy-tale studies cannot be overstated, as Donald Haase argues in *Fairy Tales and Feminism* (2004): "Awareness of the fairy tale as a primary site for asserting and subverting ideologies of gender is evident throughout the genre's history" (vii). However, Marcia Lieberman's "Some Day My Prince Will Come" (1972) can be said to be the beginning of the feminist fairy-tale debates of the late twentieth century (see Harries 2001; Haase 2004; Joosen 2011). These debates, which were part of a liberal feminist discourse about the representation of women in literature, centered on the question of whether fairy tales were good for girls. Lieberman and others, such as Andrea Dworkin (1974) and even Simone de Beauvoir years earlier (1953), argued that no, they were not good for girls because women and girls were represented as passive objects of beauty fit only to wait for their princes. These arguments were so powerful that, as Joosen demonstrates, "aspects of Lieberman's argument can still be discerned in the attitude to the traditional fairy tale expressed in many fairy-tale retellings. They still surface in recent texts—especially, though not exclusively, those intended for children" (Joosen 2011, 50), and she notes that many of the older revisions that sprang from these arguments, such as Cole's *Princess Smartypants* and *Prince Cinders*, are "still being reprinted and used in classrooms" today (ibid).

The primary concern of early rewritings in response to these critiques was to create strong, active, intelligent female protagonists for fairy tales aimed at a child audience. Sex reversals of characters as well as gendered-trait reversals were and are common techniques to make fairy-tale picture books more acceptable to parents concerned with gender inequality. Simply making girls into a rescuing princess and/or giving girls "masculine" gender traits and behaviors, such as creating and implementing rescue plans, physical acts of bravery, and athleticism, are assumed to be enough to make feminist icons of them. *Prince Cinders*'s ostensible purpose is in line with other fairy-tale revisions produced in the 1980s and 1990s in response to critical scholarship on the genre (Joosen 2011). Like his sisters, such as *The Paper Bag Princes* (1980, Robert Munch) and *Princess Smartypants*, as well as numerous others, *Prince Cinders* performs gender reversals and exaggerations to critique gender norms.

Princess Lovelypenny is reminiscent of other revised princess characters in children's picture books. She is blond and skinny, with sticky-uppy hair and a crown, and wears a leopard print pantsuit. Her name indicates that she is both beautiful (Lovely) and rich (penny), as does her coat of arms, which pictures two blond princesses in pink tutus facing each other across the shield of three pennies over a treasure chest. These blond princesses, and through them Lovelypenny herself, are linked to fairy magic by the little wings on their backs. Lovelypenny is typical of the gender-reversal style revision; she is active, independent, and perceptive (excepting the moment of her meeting with the prince when she mistakenly believes he has saved her from a giant monkey). After she provides Cinders with his happily ever after by marrying him, she also instigates a punishment for Cinders's big hairy brothers by whispering something to the fairy about them.

Where the majority of progressively minded fairy-tale revisions in this period written and marketed specifically to a child audience and their parents concentrated on creating strong, independent, and active heroines, *Prince Cinders* performs a more radical transformation by placing a male character in the role of innocent persecuted hero in a tale popularly conceived as centering on a girl's social rise though marriage. As a parody of well-known Cinderella tales by the likes of Perrault and Disney, *Prince Cinders* is one of the few fairy-tale revisions of the 1980s and '90s to interrogate gender norms of masculinity and the ways that hypermasculinity, as privileged form of male gender identity, can be as limiting and potentially damaging to young boys as the hyperfeminine passivity of fairy-tale heroines is argued to be to girls. Cinders is both a figure of fun and reader identification because he is not masculine enough, while his brothers are set up as paragons of '80s beefcake. They are handsome and strong and have sports cars and pretty blond girlfriends. The "message" would seem to be that it is okay to be a "small, spotty, and skinny" boy, while also suggesting that the paragon of masculinity is flawed and lacking, selfish and bullying. The reversal here is not quite the same as it is in books that play with gender performance reversal for girls and allow girl characters to have agency. Cinders is not terribly clever (or at least he does nothing to imply that he has a clue) and is very passive. He is so shy that he runs away the first time a girl speaks to him and then, unlike all of the other princes in the neighborhood, he does not even line up to try on the pants and win the princess. Rather, he just happens to be standing about (pants-less) with a broom when Lovelypenny commands that he try on them on.

The humor of the tale and its critiques are played out visually and textually via the irony of seeing a boy do women's work (cleaning) and being shy and passive in contrast to the hypermasculine aggression, strength, and physicality of his brothers. The book clearly critiques assumptions about masculinity and femininity, but it does so only as a joke. The absurdity of the tale does not, ultimately, challenge binary assumptions about gender; it merely exaggerates and reverses them for a brief time. By the end of the tale, Cinders is shown lying back on a divan as Princess Lovelypenny feeds him grapes from the vine. The text reads: "So Prince Cinders married Princess Lovelypenny and lived in luxury, happily ever after" (Cole 1987). Grammatically it is only Cinders who lives happily ever after, Lovelypenny's happiness no longer seems to be much of a concern. In this way, *Prince Cinders* employs those early, somewhat simplistic reversal techniques and thus also demonstrates some of their failings. For example, the book offers only two models of masculinity, passive and clueless or aggressive and clueless. As Tina L. Hanlon says,

> Babette Cole's *Prince Cinders* and *Princess Smartypants* are full of role reversals and male-bashing, with outspoken feminist princesses who rescue their prince or defend themselves from undesirable suitors and monsters. Although some of these clever girls merrily dance or drive off into the sunset alone, the accomplishments and rewards of these independent heroines are severely limited by the portrayal of emasculated opponents and suitors who are so easily duped and so undeserving. (Hanlon 1998, 145)

What results is a faux-feminist gender reversal that sets up men as either helpless, dopey, and timid (and therefore in need of care by active, intelligent women), or as aggressive, stupid, and venal (and therefore to be rejected by women outright).

In addition, as Deborah Thacker points out, both Cole's *Princess Smartypants* and *Prince Cinders* "challenge gender stereotyping but retain the conventional binary of passive/active" (2001, 14n4). Furthermore, this passive/active binary is reversed back by Lovelypenny's own desire. Lovelypenny's declaration states explicitly that the man *who wears the pants* will win her as a prize: "The Princess Lovelypenny Decrees that she will marry whoever fits the trousers lost by the prince who saved her from being eaten by the Big Hairy Monkey. Fitting sessions begin today/P.L" (Cole 1987). This decree, along with the image of Cinders's happily ever after with Lovelypenny, who has changed her leopard-print pantsuit for a toga and her role as hero seeker for a role as domestic servant, give Cinders's desires and happiness precedence. The marriage signals a reversal back to hetero-patriarchal dominance and offers Cinders a way out of his oppressed state by permitting him to take on a normative gender identity via normative gender relations. Once he gets the girl, he is no longer treated like one.

Gender and Sexuality

Cinders is physically small and weak, unable or unwilling to defend himself from his brothers, and is most often pictured doing domestic chores. Cinders's gender identity is something he wishes to escape by becoming just like his brothers, big and hairy. His success in escaping a life of women's work comes about with no thanks to his own actions, or even a magical transformation into a paragon of gender normativity; Cinders's success is due entirely to his entrance into the heterosexual matrix via Lovelypenny's husband hunt.

Lovelypenny is the agent through which Cinders's heterosexuality is both created and affirmed. If he does wear a shadowy mark of homosexuality via his association with women's work, women's wear (the apron), his perusal of magazines that feature near-naked bodybuilders, and a disinclination to talk to pretty girls, this mark is erased by his marriage and placement firmly within normative gender and sexual relations with Lovelypenny. The mark does not disappear altogether though; it is transferred indelibly onto his big hairy brothers.

The story does not end with Cinders and Lovelypenny's marriage. Once their domestic arrangements have been settled, Lovelypenny has "a word" with the fairy about Cinders's brothers, and on the last page of the book the brothers have been magically transformed into "house fairies," who "flitted around the palace doing the housework for ever and ever" (Cole 1987).

Although the word "punishment" is not used in the text, that this transformation is an act of retribution for the brothers' belittling of Cinders and making him into a feminized domestic servant is apparent. This is underscored by the absurdity of the caricatured Tom Sellecks with their moustaches, chest, arm, and leg hair and muscular physiques swathed in diaphanous white dresses with little green wings, which they use to flit about unhappily, with the signifiers of women's work such as feather dusters in their hands and colossal frowns on their faces.

Homophobic hilarity at the transformation of the villains into fairies works along the lines of the catharsis of the punishment of villainy, and particularly the punishment of women's transgressions of heteropatriarchy, in other Cinderella variants. In the Grimms' final 1857 version of Cinderella, for example, the wicked stepsisters are physically tortured by having their eyes plucked out by birds at the wedding (Zipes 2003, 84). Here the equivalent punishment is to have the big hairy brothers transformed into fairies, thus implying that homosexuality is a punishment akin to torture.

Gay male sexuality in cultural production is most often coded as a form of femininity via camp outrageousness, or associations with the signifiers of femininity. Although George Chauncey points out that the term "fairy," in the early days of the twentieth century, did not necessarily take part in the "heterosexual-homosexual binarism that governs our thinking about sexuality today" (1994, 48), the term has been associated with effeminate males since at least that time.

The term *fairy* at the turn of the century, argues Chauncey, was not a term of division

> between "heterosexual" and "homosexual" men, but between conventionally masculine males, who were regarded as men, and effeminate males, known as fairies or pansies, who were regarded as virtual women, or, more precisely, as members of a "third sex" that combined elements of the male and female. (Ibid.)

The final punishment upon the heteronormative brothers is not only to have their masculinity ridiculed but also to be transformed into members of a "third sex." Today, as Chauncey notes, the heterosexual/homosexual binary has overshadowed more complex gender distinctions, and "fairy" is an unequivocal epithet for an effeminate gay man, even in children's literature. Children's literature, and especially picture books, tends to avoid sexuality at all costs, while at the same time, paradoxically, tacitly assuming that all children are heterosexual (Bruhm and Hurley 2004; Pugh 2011). *Prince Cinders* subverts these norms by actively raising the issue of homosexuality via the figure of the domestic male house fairy.

So *Prince Cinders* fails on both progressive counts; it is neither a very successful feminist text, nor is it LGBT friendly. It reaffirms gender norms by providing the male hero, even if he is skinny and spotty, with a willing wife who erases the taint of effeminacy by serving him and wanting him to "wear the pants." The hypermasculine big hairy brothers are punished for their arrogance and bullying by being transformed, against their will, into symbols of effeminate gay masculinity, thus putting their initial gender identities and their sexuality into question—and getting a laugh by doing it.

Queer

Lee Edelman has argued that,

> If queerness marks the excess of something always unassimilable that troubles the relentlessly totalizing impulse informing normativity, we should expect it to refuse not only the consolations of reproductive futurism but also the purposive, productive uses that would turn it into a "good." (Dinshaw et al. 2007, 189)

In this quotation Edelman is discussing the idea of "queer temporality," his reference to "reproductive futurism" is linked to the conceptual, theoretical "Child" as emblem of futurity as opposed to any real children or even literary children. Shifting Edelman's argument to textual queerness in a children's picture book relocates queer unassimilability to literature. Unlike the progressive political goals of feminist and lesbian/gay literary criticism, then, queer literary critique is not interested in declaring a text as "good" or "bad" for children, women, or LGBT subjects. Rather, it seeks to find the ways that these evaluations can be elided in favor of unrecoupable disruption.

In some ways *Prince Cinders* does take part in the purposive and productive drive to be "good." The book does perform a critique of absurdities of gender hegemony through the creation of an active girl in Lovelypenny and of a wimpy but worthy male hero in Cinders. In these ways it may be said to take part in emancipatory identity politics and the desire to make a better world through children's literature and specifically revisionist fairy tales. The fact that it fails in this goal does not detract from its intentions and, in fact, may be a way into the book's queerness.

Judith Halberstam offers another way of thinking about resistance to a politics of unassimilability and the totalizing effects of normativity through what she calls "queer failure" (2011). Following James C. Scott (1987),

Halberstam discusses queer failure as a kind of "weapon of the weak." Halberstam includes "feigning incompetence" as a tool for the

> practice of stalling the business of the dominant. We can also recognize failure as a way of refusing to acquiesce to dominant logics of power and discipline and as a form of critique. As a practice, failure recognizes that alternatives are embedded already in the dominant and that power is never total or consistent; indeed failure can exploit the unpredictability of ideology and its indeterminate qualities. (88)

The figure most closely related to queer failure in *Prince Cinders* is the dirty fairy who is a marginalized and disruptive outsider. She arrives in a cloud of ash (more like an untimely Christmas elf than either the more common fairy godmother or the traditional cinder-girl of *Prince Cinders*'s pre-texts), sporting a dusty school uniform plus wings and a magic wand. She is significantly smaller than both Cinders and Lovelypenny, which, in conjunction with her school uniform, denotes her as a younger child who is still in training. Her apparent youth, the wings that signify her fairy-ness and stars on the Alice-band in her hair and on her wand that are in the shape of the Star of David, code her difference and outsider status. She is aligned with Cinders and Lovelypenny by her whiteness and sticky-uppy blond hair, but she is also a child, still in school, Jewish, nonroyal, and nonhuman. She is the only character in the book whose gender performance is minimized and whose sexuality is left ambiguous; she is also the queer figure in the text.

The dirty fairy takes on the role of the conceptual Child so derided by Edelman, and that Michael Cobb refers to when he argues,

> the rhetorical "nature" of queer theory, and the rhetorical "nature" of queers, reminds us that engagement with the political, cultural, and symbolical fields requires figures that can disfigure, that can undo, identities and politics that seem natural, inevitable, and sacred—those identities, in many ways, made possible by the Child. (Cobb 2005, 124)

In *Prince Cinders* it is the fairy who disfigures and undoes naturalized gender identities and sexual politics.

The fairy's first task as magical helper is to produce a version of the little red corvette that denotes masculine sexuality and power, yet she creates, not the cool cars of the big hairy brothers, but a *dinky*-car (pun intended). The small size creates another kind of joke; she minimizes this icon of masculinity to a child's toy but may also be making a sly comment on Cinders's virility. She also misinterprets the male suit, a signifier of power, wealth, and status, by dressing Cinders in not just any swimsuit but an anachronistic full-piece red-and-white striped absurdity, thus transforming Cinders's rags into a clownish costume. If the clothes make the man, this fairy's view of masculinity is a little queer. Finally, her last transformation is a fundamental and parodic mis-reading of the desirability of big hairiness as masculine ideal by equating this type of masculinity with beastliness. Cinders becomes a beast, but Cole's text preempts Beauty and the Beast interpretations; he does not need the tears, kisses, or the true love of Lovelypenny to transform him back into a prince. Instead, as the fairy surmises, it will just wear off. More importantly, he does not even recognize his apelike transformation; when monkey-Cinders looks into the mirror he sees a carbon copy of his brothers standing before him, grinning widely. Cinders is unable to recognize the fairy's signs of masculinity as exaggerated campy silliness and happily goes off to the disco.

Unlike Cinders, the fairy does recognize that she gets the signifiers of masculinity wrong, but she goes ahead with her spells with only brief exclamations of: "Drat!" "Crumbs!" and "Rats!" after each transformation and then dismisses the whole problem with a nonchalant, "Wrong again, but I'm sure it all wears off at midnight" (Cole 1987). The fairy's original intentions are less important than her attitude toward her spells. She acknowledges she's got something wrong, but is blasé about her failure. She knows she has failed in her task to create a normative masculine specimen and instead has created a giant monkey in a red-and-white striped bathing suit trying to drive a dinky-car, but she lets him go to the ball anyway. Her failed spells serve to destabilize symbols of masculine privilege and dominance by presenting them as childish, outdated, and beastly.

Even after his transformation back into a boy, Cinders is never completely recuperated into gender normativity. He remains skinny and spotty, and while he replaces his apron with a tie and his muscle magazine with a doting wife, he is pictured as a feminized object of desire in the final image in which he is draped over a divan like countless female models in classical painting[2] (though he wears more clothes than they generally do). His brothers, on the other hand, are transformed from paragons of dominant masculinity and into the binary opposite that makes the status of their previous incarnations as paragons possible.

The fairy's transformation of the brothers in the end suggests that she does have some control over her powers, and that she is fully aware of the effectiveness of her punishment and its consequences. It also raises the possibility that her previous failures were not failures at all but deliberate subordinations. The queerness of her final retributive move is in its form, but also in its permanence and its placement in the text. The spell cannot be undone, the big hairy brothers will remain house-cleaning fairies, symbols of male homosexuality, for ever and ever.

The book begins and ends with marginalized male figures, ridiculed and ridiculous, irredeemable. The failed transformations of the fairy's spells on Cinders are also failures in that they don't "take"; unlike most Cinderellas, whose beauty is revealed once they've been cleaned up a bit, Cinders appears unchanged at the end. The fairy's final spell *does* take though, and with a vengeance. The queer here is in the fairy's refusal, or inability, to reproduce the codes and signs of heteromasculinity properly. Further, in her decision to transform the heterosexual, hypermasculine males into signifiers of homosexuality, she leaves them as hybrids; they keep their physical attributes and attitudes, but their clothing, their social place and standing are altered. Finally, the fairy's queer intervention is immutable. The "for ever and ever" of the last line will not allow the big hairy brothers to rehabilitate, reassimilate, return to "normal," or make beefcake house fairies a new norm.

The queer move by the fairy at the end of the book is not "good"—the brothers will not "learn their lesson" and return to their previous state but altered for the better. The last spell upon the brothers, and upon us, is disruptive and irresolvable. Final closure happens with this moment. With this image the dirty fairy has queered the brothers, whether they like it or not, and there is no escape for them from a queer existence, ever after.

Prince Cinders does not succeed in creating a feminist happily ever after for women, and it does not even imagine a happily ever after for gay men. It briefly reverses gender hierarchy but ultimately reinforces normative gender representations and heteronormativity. At the same time, it also creates a space around the dirty fairy that is unassimilable and troubles the totalizing impulses and common assumptions about fairy tales (and children's literature) as utopic. It denies the purposive productive "good" of a progressive liberal gender ideology by exploiting its own homophobia through the fairy's queer failures (or refusals) to understand and support gender and sexual stability and, unlike Cinder's transformations, this spell will not simply wear off.

Notes

1. Since the publication of Abate and Kidd's book, the LBGTQ acronym has expanded, especially in activism and community projects, to be more

inclusive. As of this writing variations on LGBTTIQQ2SAAP (Lesbian, Gay, Bi, Transgender, Transsexual, Intersexed, Queer, Questioning, Two Spirited, Ally, Asexual, Pansexual) are often used and/or shortened to LGBT+. In discussing cultural productions of the late twentieth century, however, it seems relevant to recall that dominant discourses (such as children's literature) considered the world to be made of two sexes, two genders, and two sexualities.

2. Thanks to Anne Duggan for pointing out the resemblance of Cinders's pose to an odalisque. The comparison of Cinders to an eroticized and exoticized Oriental Other presents further layers of queer interpretive possibilities.

References

Abate, Michelle Ann, and Kenneth Kidd. 2011. Introduction to *Over the Rainbow: Queer Children's and Young Adult Literature*, edited by Michelle Ann Abate and Kenneth Kidd, 1–11. Ann Arbor: University of Michigan Press.

Beauvoir, Simone de. 1953. *The Second Sex*. Translated by H. M. Parshley. New York: Knopf.

Bruhm, Steven, and Natasha Hurley, eds. 2004. *Curiouser: On the Queerness of Children*. Minneapolis: University of Minnesota Press.

Chauncey, George. 1994. *Gay New York: Gender, Urban Culture, and the Making of the Gay Male World, 1890–1940*. New York: Basic Books.

Cobb, Michael. 2005. "Childlike: Queer Theory and Its Children." *Criticism* 47 (1): 119–30.

Cole, Babette. 1986. *Princess Smartypants*. London: Puffin Books.

———. 1987. *Prince Cinders*. London: Puffin Books.

———. 1993. *Mommy Laid an Egg!; or, Where Do Babies Come From?* London: Jonathan Cape.

———. 1996. *Drop Dead*. London: Jonathan Cape.

———. 1997. *Two of Everything*. London: Jonathan Cape, 1997. Published as *The Un-Wedding*. New York: Knopf, 1998.

———. 1999. *Hair in Funny Places: A Book about Puberty*. London: Random House.

———. 2005. *Long Live Princess Smartypants*. London: Penguin, 2004. Published as *Princess Smartypants Rules*. New York: Putnam.

———. 2009. *Princess Smartypants Breaks the Rules*. London: Puffin.

Dinshaw, Carolyn, Lee Edelman, Roderick A. Ferguson, Carla Freccero, Elizabeth Freeman, Judith Halberstam, Annamarie Jagose, Christopher Nealon, and Nguyen Tan Hoang. 2007. "Theorizing Queer Temporalities: A Roundtable Discussion." In "Queer Temporalities," edited by Elizabeth Freeman. Special issue, *GLQ: A Journal of Lesbian and Gay Studies* 13 (2–3): 177–95.

Duggan, Anne E. 2013. *Queer Enchantments: Gender, Sexuality, and Class in the Fairy-Tale Cinema of Jacques Demy*. Detroit: Wayne State University Press.

Dutheil de la Rochère, Martine Hennard. 2009. "Queering the Fairy Tale Cannon: Emma Donoghue's *Kissing the Witch*." In *Fairy Tales Reimagined: Essays on New Retellings*, edited by Susan Redington Bobby, 13–30. Jefferson, NC: McFarland.

Dworkin, Andrea. 1974. *Woman Hating*. New York: Plume.

Greenhill, Pauline, and Sidney Eve Matrix, eds. 2010. *Fairy Tale Films: Visions of Ambiguity*. Logan: Utah State University Press.

Grimm, Jacob, and Wilhelm Grimm. 2003 [1857]. "Cinderella." In *The Complete Fairy Tales of the Brothers Grimm*, 3rd ed., translated by Jack Zipes, 79–84. New York: Bantam.

Haase, Donald, ed. 2004. *Fairy Tales and Feminism: New Approaches*. Detroit: Wayne State University Press.

Halberstam, Judith. 2011. *The Queer Art of Failure*. Durham, NC: Duke University Press.

Halley, Janet, and Andrew Parker. 2011. Introduction to *After Sex? On Writing since Queer Theory*, edited by Janet Halley and Andrew Parker, 1–14. Durham, NC: Duke University Press, Ebrary.

Halperin, David M. 2003. "The Normalization of Queer Theory." *Journal of Homosexuality* 45 (2): 339–43.

Hanlon, Tina L. 1998. "'To Sleep, Perchance to Dream': Sleeping Beauties and Wide-Awake Plain Janes in the Stories of Jane Yolen." *Children's Literature* 26 (1998): 140–67.

Harries, Elizabeth Wanning. 2001. *Twice upon a Time: Women Writers and the History of the Fairy Tale*. Princeton, NJ: Princeton University Press.

Huskey, Melynda. 2002. "Queering the Picture Book." *The Lion and the Unicorn* 26 (1): 66–77.

Jenkins, Christine A. 1993. "Young Adult Novels with Gay/Lesbian Characters and Themes, 1969–92: A Historical Reading of Content, Gender, and Narrative Distance." In *Over the Rainbow: Queer Children's and Young Adult Literature*, edited by Michelle Ann Abate and Kenneth Kidd, 147–63. Ann Arbor: University of Michigan Press.

———. 1998. "From Queer to Gay and Back Again: Young Adult Novels with Gay/Lesbian/Queer Content, 1969–1997." *Library Quarterly* 68 (3): 298–334.

Joosen, Vanessa. 2011. *Critical and Creative Perspectives on Fairy Tales: An Intertextual Dialogue between Fairy-Tale Scholarship and Postmodern Retellings*. Detroit: Wayne State University Press.

Kidd, Kenneth. 1998. "Introduction: Lesbian/Gay Literature for Children and Young Adults." *Children's Literature Association Quarterly* 23 (33): 114–19.

———. 2011. "Queer Theory's Child and Children's Literature Studies." *PMLA* 126 (1): 182–88.

Lieberman, Marcia R. 1972. "'Some Day My Prince Will Come': Female Acculturation through the Fairy Tale." *College English* 34 (3): 383–95.

Marcus, Sharon. 2005. "Queer Theory for Everyone: A Review Essay." *Signs* 31 (1): 191–218.

McKee, Alan. 1997. "Fairy Tales: How We Stopped Being 'Lesbian and Gay' and Became 'Queer.'" *Social Semiotics* 7 (1): 21–36.

Merck, Mandy, Naomi Segal, and Elizabeth Wright, eds. 1998. *Coming Out of Feminism?* Oxford: Blackwell.

Orme, Jennifer. 2010. "Mouth to Mouth: Queer Desires in Emma Donoghue's *Kissing the Witch*." *Marvels & Tales* 24 (1): 116–30.

———. 2012. "Happily Ever After . . . According to Our Tastes: Jeanette Winterson's 'Twelve Dancing Princesses' and Queer Possibility." In *Transgressive Tales: Queering the Grimms*, edited by Kay Turner and Pauline Greenhill, 141–60. Detroit: Wayne State University Press.

———. 2015. "A Wolf's Queer Invitation: David Kaplan's *Little Red Riding Hood*." In "Queer(ing) Fairy Tales," edited by Lewis C. Seifert. Special issue, *Marvels & Tales* 29 (1): 87–109.

Pugh, Tison. 2011. *Innocence, Heterosexuality, and the Queerness of Children's Literature*. New York: Routledge.

Schneiderman, Jason. 2010. "In Defense of Queer Theory." *Gay and Lesbian Review*, January 1. http://www.glreview.org/article/article-447/.

Scott, James C. 1987. *Weapons of the Weak: Everyday Forms of Peasant Resistance*. New Haven, CT: Yale University Press.

Seifert, Lewis C., ed. 2015. "Queer(ing) Fairy Tales." Special issue, *Marvels & Tales* 29 (1).

Solis, Santiago. 2007. "'Snow White and the Seven Dwarves' Queercripped." *Hypatia* 22 (1): 114–31.

Thacker, Deborah. 2001. "Feminine Language and the Politics of Children's Literature." *The Lion and the Unicorn* 25 (1): 3–16.

Turner, Gay, and Pauline Greenhill, eds. 2012. *Transgressive Tales: Queering the Grimms*. Detroit: Wayne State University Press.

12

Cinderella from a Cross-Cultural Perspective

Connecting East and West in Donna Jo Napoli's *Bound*

Roxane Hughes

Donna Jo Napoli's novel *Bound* (2004) makes literal and metaphorical connections between past and present, East and West, and ancient China and modern-day America through the Cinderella tale. By weaving together Duan Chengshi's ninth-century Chinese tale of Yexian[1] and the Grimms' "Aschenputtel" from *Kinder- und Hausmärchen* (1847), Napoli draws attention to the connected histories of East and West as manifested in the fairy-tale tradition and uncovers textual, historical, and cultural links for the Cinderella story beyond the European context. She locates the Yexian tale in Ming China, when foot-binding became a prominent custom among Chinese women from the middle and upper classes, and thus associates the small feet of the heroine of the Yexian tale with the mutilation of the stepsisters' feet in "Aschenputtel" through the motif of foot-binding.

By intertwining the Chinese and the German tale, *Bound* engages with recent debates on sexual politics in a culturally diverse and globalized world, highlighting shared histories of female oppression in the name of beauty ideals in patriarchal societies across borders.[2] Napoli is not alone in using the fairy tale to address crippling beauty ideals, the role of mothers in perpetuating oppressive traditions, and the rivalry that opposes young women and their mothers in the competition for a suitable husband. Angela Carter's "Ashputtle *or* The Mother's Ghost" (1993), a threefold retelling of the Grimms' story that imaginatively recovers the cultural roots of the folktale and explores its sexual politics, similarly examines female mutilation and disabling motherly love.[3] Reading *Bound* in relation to this kindred text foregrounds Napoli's attempt to reconcile respect for cultural difference with a progressive agenda. Napoli negotiates this double bind by dramatizing foot-binding and other oppressive bonds with an attempt to redefine *binding* in a positive manner.

"The oldest Cinderella story I could find was from China," Napoli explains. "Now, come on, once you realize that, suddenly you're in the world of foot-binding. The ideal of beauty for a long time in China was the foot so small it could sit in your palm like a lotus blossom. So I became quickly convinced that Cinderella had to have originated in China at or after the point when foot-binding was introduced."[4] *Bound* follows the general plotline of Chengshi's Yexian tale,[5] but takes place in a different setting that allows this connection between the beauty ideal of tiny feet and the Cinderella story as it is known in the West. To make foot-binding a central element of her rewriting, Napoli transposes the Yexian tale from its pre-Qin and Han southern Chinese environment to Ming northern China (2004, 185–86). The Yexian tale, originally set in the third century BC, could not have had a heroine with bound feet. Textual evidence situates the beginning of foot-binding in late Tang (AD 618–907) and early Song (960–1279) dynasties—shortly after Chengshi's tale was published.[6] The Ming dynasty (1368–1644) is conversely characterized by a spread of foot-binding amid middle- and upper-class women, especially among the Han population that governed China. Furthermore, the Ming dynasty makes the love story between a wealthy prince and a low-class girl more plausible. Inspired by the emperor of the Ming dynasty who believed in merit over privilege and who rose from peasantry to his imperial position thanks to his excellence in battle against the Mongols, Napoli locates her retelling of Cinderella at a crucial moment in the history of China.[7]

To further the link between this crippling custom and Chengshi's ur-Cinderella tale, Napoli fleshes out the Yexian plot and invents two stories that are directly related to foot-binding. The first presents Yexian's father as a progressive man who, in Napoli's rewriting of the tale, refuses to bind his daughters' feet because he needs their help in his pottery shop, but also to privilege their intellectual and artistic development. At a time when women were confined to the domestic sphere and refused an education, Napoli depicts the father as an independent-minded figure. After his death, however, his principles are not followed by his second wife, who decides to bind her biological daughter's feet to assure a good marriage and a better future for her, which she, as a widow, cannot grant her.[8]

The other side narrative of Napoli's novel calls attention to the forms that female oppression takes in various social and cultural contexts. It revolves around the story of Wei Ping, the stepsister of Xing Xing (the Yexian/Cinderella figure), whose feet are bound by her mother despite her late father's wishes. Wei Ping suffers excruciating pain from having her feet bound years too late. Despite the stepmother's effort at binding her feet as tightly as she can to make up for the years "lost" as a result of the father's decision, Wei Ping's feet remain too large to secure a good marriage match. Postponing foot-binding hindered the shrinking of a girl's feet and restructuring of the bones that would enable her to reach the "ideal" size of the three-inch-long golden lotus: "if she had her feet bound at the age of six when Stepmother had first proposed it to Wu," the narrator explains in Napoli's novel, "her feet would be small enough to fit in a man's hand like a golden lotus blossom, and she'd already undoubtedly be betrothed" (2004, 7). Wei Ping's feet, which are "already as long as the full spread of Stepmother's fingers, much longer than Xing Xing's [unbound] feet" (8), make her both unattractive and unmarriageable.

The painful binding process Wei Ping endures speaks of the pressure of conformity on a girl's body and mind. Instead of empowering her socially, her feet are merely disabling and debilitating. Wei Ping is unable to walk and has to move from her bed to the *kang* (the central piece of furniture in the house where one can sit or even lie down) while kneeling on two stools, putting the weight of her body on each of her knees alternatively. Moreover, "When Xing Xing washed her half-sister's foot bandages, she had to scrub hard to get the bloodstains out. And lately Wei Ping's feet oozed a foul-smelling yellow liquid that seemed to drain away her energy" (10–11). The deformation of the bones as well as the putrefaction of the skin caused by the tight bandages renders the pain unbearable: "I hang my legs over the bed so that the pressure of the bedstead behind my knees will dull the pain. You have no idea how bad it is," says Wei Ping to her sister (33). Wei Ping finds comfort, however, in the belief that her feet are shrinking day after day, and in the hope of a good marriage.[9]

The account of Wei Ping's excruciating pain her crippled feet cause, as well as her disillusionment when unable to marry, functions as a parallel narrative to the rags-to-riches story of Xing Xing, whose feet are left unbound to serve as a slave in her stepmother's household. The more privileged daughter suffers the agony of bound feet in the name of beauty and marriage, while the hard-working and humiliated servant escapes physical mutilation. It is, however, the feudal society Xing Xing lives in that metaphorically wraps tight bandages around her feet. She is not only bound to her cruel stepmother and sister, but also to loneliness, to a life of subservience and servitude as well as to shame due to her lowly social status. Napoli's focus on foot-binding, be it literal of metaphorical, thus stresses the custom's sociocultural implications.

The side story of Wei Ping departs from Chengshi's tale in which Yexian's sister is rarely mentioned,[10] but resonates strongly with the Grimms' "Aschenputtel." The mutilation of the stepsisters' feet in the German tale invites a connection between the Chinese Cinderella story and foot-binding, which Angela Carter also makes in a subsection of her own rewriting, "Ashputtle *or* The Mother's Ghost." Carter notes that the Grimms' version of the tale invites a symbolic reading as a "story about cutting bits off women, so that they will fit in" (Carter 1995, 391). Carter dramatizes the mutilation scene in "Aschenputtel" to explore women's brutal (and bloody) competition to secure a husband for their daughters and the crippling beauty ideals that this fierce rivalry inspires.[11] Napoli furthers this link by emphasizing the sisters' competition caused by their desire to marry the prince, already present in "Aschenputtel." Wei Ping, whose bound feet remain too large, looks at her sister's unbound, yet amazingly small, feet with contempt. Xing Xing's feet are, in the first part of the novel, a constant source of mockery and belittlement: "No one cares about your feet," Wei Ping mutters, "no one will find you a husband" (Napoli 2004, 5, 6). Wei Ping's mocking tone, however, says much about the jealousy and envy provoked by the unusual smallness of Xing Xing's feet and the personal pride she takes in them, thereby foregrounding the potential threat she poses to her sister. Competition among female siblings was high in a society in which a woman's chance to marry into a higher social class or as first wife depended on her small feet and her filiation.

Napoli also dramatizes women's internalization of social norms and beauty ideals in the episode where a pet raccoon bites off Wei Ping's putrefying left toe. The mother, blind to the pain of her daughter, chops off the corresponding right toe with a cleaver to render the two feet symmetrical and smaller. The scene alludes to the Grimms' "Aschenputtel," in which the stepmother orders her two daughters to mutilate their feet in order to fit into the tiny slipper:

> "Hau die Zehe ab: wann du Königin bist, brauchst du nicht mehr zu Fuss zu gehen." (Grimm and Grimm 1996, 126)

> "Cut the toe off; once you're queen, you won't have to walk any more," says the mother to the first daughter. (Dundes 1982, 28)

This is reiterated when the mother commands her second daughter to cut off a piece of her heel to fit the tiny shoe.[12] The two daughters obey their mother's command, force their bloody feet into the shoe, and walk to the prince masking their pain.[13] In Napoli's *Bound*, the mother explains to Wei Ping the necessity of cutting the healthy foot in similar terms: "Your left foot will be smaller than your right now," she said, "So if you want me to act properly, I must do it fast. . . . You are not the first girl in China to lose a toe on a bound foot. . . . Let's be smart, Wei Ping; now your feet will be much smaller than we'd dared to hope" (Napoli 2004, 41–42). Wei Ping is dazed and does not react. Her passivity contrasts with her mother's appearance after beating the raccoon to a bloody mass of "brains and lungs and intestine and fur" (40). Her "blood-spattered" face looks "crazed" "as she ripped at the shredded bandages on Wei Ping's left foot" (40). The woman has "a monster face twisted with [a] monstrous idea," Xing Xing observes (42).

Napoli's stepmother figure recalls Carter's who, as if she were "after a more essential portion than a toe," "is prepared to cripple her daughters" to gain a son-in-law (Carter 1995, 393). Napoli's central motif of foot-binding echoes the enigmatic nature of "mother love" in Carter's rewriting that captures a mother's willingness to compromise her daughters' physical integrity to conform to social ideals and economic security. Carter thereby questions the Grimms' simplistic opposition of the "good mother" who comes to the heroine's rescue in the shape of a bird and the "bad" one who inflicts pain on her daughters: "mother love" indeed "wind[s] about these daughters like a shroud" (393). The daughter is reduced to an "amputee" and, metonymically, to the fetishized "stump" encased in the bloody shoe, this "hideous receptacle, this open wound, still slick and warm as it is" (394), that turns into a coffin at the end.[14] The blood, symbol of "death-in-life," as Francisco Vaz da Silva explains (2008, 3: 128), highlights the cruel initiation young girls must go through in order to marry and discloses the crippling effect of imposed beauty and social ideals on a woman's body. In this respect, the mutilated foot becomes in Carter's tale a metaphor for the consequences of the patriarchal ideology for female bodies and mother-daughter relationships.

Similar to Carter, Napoli questions the emotional and psychological bond between mother and daughter created by the transmission of crippling ideals of feminine beauty and the prospect of a wealthy husband, and further shows the destructive aspect of a mother's "love" as motivated by rivalry for men. This can be seen in the connection between Wei Ping's feet and Xing Xing's fish, presented as prey to both the raccoon and the stepmother's cleaver. The fish, like the raccoon, is introduced into the household by Xing Xing and serves as a distraction for her crippled sister before the stepmother kills it. Wei Ping's comments about her bound feet at the beginning of the novel are often comically interwoven with statements about the fish's growth. Turning her head to cover her lie when asked about her sister's shrinking feet, Xing Xing looks divertingly at the bowl containing the fish. By stating matter-of-factly that "the beautiful fish had grown so much, it could barely turn around" (Napoli 2004, 33), the narrator directs the reader's attention away from Wei Ping's feet, following Xing Xing's eyes turned toward the fish to avoid her sister's inquiring gaze. This prefigures the raccoon's attack. Recognizing the raccoon's carnivorous instinct and fearing for her beloved fish, Xing Xing moves the bowl outside to prevent the hungry raccoon from eating the fish, which ironically bites off the sister's toe instead.

As Wei Ping's toes are bitten off by the raccoon and further mutilated by the mother, the fish—the reincarnation of Xing Xing's dead mother—falls prey to the stepmother's cleaver. After a long absence, Xing Xing returns to the pond behind the house to visit the fish. When she steps into the water and swims with it, she feels that they are "like mother and child": "The beautiful fish was the reincarnation of Mother. They were together again, at last" (Napoli 2004, 117). The reunion between Xing Xing and her symbolic mother points to the protection that the figure of the mother represents for her. The fish, which has "grown enormous" (121),[15] stresses the magical and developing bond between Xing Xing and her mother and becomes as a result an increasing threat for Wei Ping's future. This danger embodied by the fish resonates with "Aschenputtel," where the mother's spirit is reincarnated as a dove that helps Aschenputtel go to the ball, but also calls the prince's attention to the sisters' bloody shoes before blinding the stepsisters as a punishment for their cruelty.[16] When she senses the presence of a rival in the magical fish, the stepmother decides to sever this threatening tie.

Napoli's allusion to the Grimms' version is further reinforced if we read her rewriting in the light of Carter's understanding of "Aschenputtel." Carter sees in the story two mothers fighting for the possession of a "hypothetical son-in-law," through the use of their daughters "as instruments of war or as surrogates in the business of mating" (Carter 1995, 391). Carter accordingly puts the mother's ghost at the center of her rewriting. Likewise, Napoli uses the fish as a central element of the plot to account for the development of Xing Xing's character and to capture the two mothers' rivalry over men as well as contrasted strategies to empower their daughters. By butchering the fish/mother with the same cleaver that she used to mutilate her daughter's feet, the stepmother chops to destroy the symbolic curse cast on her daughter's bound but still large feet, as well as to sever the metaphorical tissues linking mother and daughter. By separating mother and daughter, she wants to get rid of her husband's first wife, deprive Xing Xing of the strength bestowed by her mother's spirit and therefore eliminate the threat that the latter represents.

Just as the bloody slippers provide evidence of the stepmother's deception at the end of the Grimms' tale, the mutilation of Wei Ping's feet and the dismemberment of the fish tell against the stepmother in *Bound*. By chopping both feet and fish, flesh and magical meat, she unwittingly participates in Xing Xing's gradual empowerment. It is in response to her stepmother's transgressive act that Xing Xing gains a voice. Realizing that the fish they had just eaten for dinner—a fish that was cut unusually and alarmingly small—was her befriended fish of the pond, she angrily asks her stepmother: "Did you fool the fish into thinking you were me? . . . What knife did you use? The cleaver? . . . It must have been hard to kill such a large fish, to cut up all the flesh. And then the task of getting rid of it must have exhausted you" (Napoli 2004, 139). While Yexian, Aschenputtel, and even Carter's "mother's daughter" (1995, 393) are mute at the end of the tale, Napoli's modernized Xing Xing rebels against her stepmother's acts and condemns her for her cruelty. In *Bound*, it is no longer the reincarnated spirit of the mother who points to the stepmother's deception, but the assertive heroine herself.

Furthermore, the physical changes on Wei Ping's body fail to have the desired effect. As Napoli states, "only the front of her foot could get in, of course" (2004, 178), alluding to both the mutilation accomplished by her mother and the cutting of the sister's big toes to fool the prince in the Grimms' tale. The intertextual reference becomes even more obvious when Wei Ping's own mother tries on the shoe and fails the test. Napoli's modern take on an old story thus serves to caution against modern canons of female beauty promoting bodily transformations.

Another contemporary twist on the mother-daughter relationship introduced in Napoli's novel is Xing Xing's stepmother's adding her own name to the list of potential brides to try on the shoe. Her competition against her own daughter echoes present-day anxieties about older women as rivals of younger ones. Although she claims that she does so for her daughter's sake, because "it would be the best life for Wei Ping" (Napoli 2004, 171), her prayer to the ancestors reveals that she places her own dream of wealth above her daughter's interest and future. She no longer desires a son-in-law or even the son she never had, but a new husband:

> I'd never marry an ordinary man. But this is different. No one would want me to give up such a chance. It's a prince, after all. A prince. I've heard he lives across an arched stone bridge—marble, not the wooden bridges of the countryside—behind vermilion walls, with statues of elephants outside the gates. (171)

Nevertheless, Wei Ping sides with her mother instead of defending her half-sister, suggesting that the mother-daughter bond is very strong, just as Xing Xing will not be separated from her mother even in death.

The stepmother's dream of the prince's palace and wealth vanishes. Unable to fit into the tiny shoe that would make the dream come true and change their future, mother and daughter are both erased from Napoli's rewriting. In contrast to the Yexian tale, in which the stepmother and daughter are killed by flying stones of unexplained origin and buried in the Tomb of Regretful Women (Chengshi 2012, 124) where offerings were made to the goddess of matchmakers, the ending of *Bound* refuses narrative closure for Wei Ping and her mother. Although not involving further mutilation, the two women's misfortune is reminiscent of the Grimms' tale in which the stepmother is left to wander and the daughters are blinded by doves who pierced their eyes in retribution for their cruelty.

In contrast to the crippling bond connecting the stepmother and Wei Ping, Napoli presents the nurturing, protective, and enabling tie that binds Xing Xing to her dead mother. While the novel criticizes the maiming of the body, as well as the bondage and dependence on men in which these women live under patriarchy, encapsulated in (foot-)binding, it also proposes a more positive definition of binding as a bond of love and equality within the traditional marriage plot structure. The happy ending to the Yexian-Cinderella tale, however, neither undermines the institution of marriage nor the ideals of feminine beauty; Xing Xing's natural beauty and small feet, as well as her other accomplishments, do not deviate from the prescribed romance plot.

Napoli paradoxically celebrates this positive mother-daughter bond through the gift of the tiny "golden lotus" slippers. In "Ashputtle *or* The Mother's Ghost," Carter had already associated Ashputtle's foot with that of "a Chinese woman, a stump. Almost an amputee already, she put her tiny foot in it" (1995, 394). This description turns the culturally valorized "tiny foot" of the heroine into an abject "stump." In Napoli's novel, Xing Xing's small feet magically enter her mother's golden lotus slippers. In contrast to Carter's stump-like feet, Xing Xing's are exquisitely small, recalling Yexian's abnormally small feet once shod in the slippers she receives from the fish bones. Magically adapting to the heroine's unique foot size, Yexian's lost slipper fascinates the people of the Tuo Han Kingdom:

> The cave people sold the shoe to the Tuo Han kingdom, which was then obtained by the king. The king commanded his subjects to try on the shoe, but the shoe became a cùn [about 3 cm] smaller when even the smallest feet tried it on. (Chengshi 2012, 124)

This arouses wonder in the kingdom and beyond. In addition to fitting only Yexian's feet, the small slipper is surprisingly light:

> It (the shoe) was light as a feather and made no sound when walking on stone. (Chengshi 2012, 124)

Compared to a feather, the shoe in Chengshi's tale is so light that she can walk with almost supernatural grace.

Likewise, Xing Xing's feet fit magically into her bound-footed mother's tiny lotus slippers. Rather than criticizing the ostensive damage and pain mutilation caused, Napoli draws attention here to the enabling potential of a female legacy transmitted from one generation to the next. The inherited tiny slippers no longer symbolize mutilation, but the strength that a woman can acquire thanks to bonds of love:

> Mother had not walked gracefully. No woman with bound feet walked gracefully, no matter how sexy that irregular swing of the hips was thought to look. Yet the shoes seemed to exude grace, as though anyone who wore them could walk through fear, through cruelty, and come out standing strong. Mother was trying to help Xing Xing stand strong by saving these shoes for her. That was it, of course. (Napoli 2004, 154)

The tiny slippers come to represent beauty, grace, and resistance as Xing Xing's mother's legacy to her daughter.

On a metaphorical level, the shoes Napoli created for Xing Xing's mother point to her indebtedness to the Chinese and German fairy-tale traditions, through Chengshi and the Grimm brothers respectively. The emblematic shoe stands for Napoli's rewriting of the Cinderella tale, which clothes anew the feet of her predecessors across boundaries of time and culture. By figuratively covering the altered foot/tale, Napoli's shoe gives a sense of uniqueness and beauty while nevertheless alluding to the bindings and deformation it conceals. The double connection between Napoli's literary heritage and her heroine's maternal inheritance is shown through the transformation of Xing Xing when she wears her mother's golden slippers and through the multiple layers of intertextual references that this scene discloses. By putting her foot in her mother's shoe, Xing Xing is born anew:

> Her breath suspended, Xing Xing gingerly tried one foot in a shoe. It nestled there like a chick under her mother's wing. . . . She put the

> other one on and walked softly around the cavern room. Then she went more quickly. Then she danced. With her feathered cloak, she felt ready to take flight. She twirled and laughed, gratitude practically breaking her heart. (Napoli 2004, 154)

The shoes protect Xing Xing's bare feet, a maternal enclosure further epitomized by the protective image of her feet nestled as a chick under her mother's wing. Mirroring the development of a chick guided by its mother, she progresses from walking to dancing and ultimately to a metaphorical takeoff. Wrapped in a feathered cloak and wearing shoes that Chengshi had described as light as a feather, she changes into a metaphorical bird ready to take flight. This transformation also alludes to the golden lotus slippers that, by rendering a woman's legs longer and thinner, gave the illusion that she was "overcoming gravity," "flying up to the sky" or even "floating on clouds" (Wang 2002, 9). The tiny shoes and Xing Xing's illusory flying movement promise another type of binding that is no longer crippling but enabling.

Giving pain in conjunction with maternal care, foot-binding created a special emotional and psychological bond between mother and daughter that it is often difficult to comprehend. This strong tie is represented by the lotus shoes that mothers made and gave to their daughters on the binding day. As Dorothy Ko explains,

> On the daughter's footbinding day, she received her first gifts of lotus shoes from her mother. From then on, the mother would teach her one by one all the necessary skills to be a good woman, beginning with sewing and shoe-making. Shoes thus have special emotional meanings to a woman beyond the material aspect. We may say that votive shoes are expressions of her religious devotion, and the first binding shoes are a mother's labor of love. (Ko 2001, 69)

The lotus shoes function as a daughter's rite of initiation into womanhood and mark the reciprocal and intimate exchange between a mother and her daughter outside the bounds of male control ("our bodies and labor make us women, she might have said to her daughter, and our bodies and labor are the ties that *bind* us in a female kinship that no men can undo" [Ko 2001, 63; my emphasis]). Ko further explains how the lotus shoes acted as a "material extension of [a woman's] body and her medium of communication" (69). The binding, the shoemaking, and the embroidery were performed in the intimate space of women's quarters. Similarly, the designs, motifs, and characters embroidered on the shoes were used by women to communicate with one another. Each pair of lotus shoes tells a unique story about its makers and owners that contemporary focus on the flesh and bones of the custom have tended to obscure (Ko 2001, 97).[17]

Napoli's choice of making Yexian's tiny slippers into lotus shoes can be read in relation to the complex intertwined story of motherly love and transmission of female culture (and not merely as a symbol of patriarchal domination and mutilation). The bound shoes Xing Xing inherits from her mother signify the mother's ongoing nurturing presence and materialize an emotional bond between mother and daughter that not even death can sever. If, in the context of fairy tale, the shoe can be read as symbolizing female imprisonment in marriage and child bearing, as Martine Hennard Dutheil de la Rochère interprets Carter's retelling (Dutheil de la Rochère 2013, 294), Napoli uses it to represent more positive intergenerational and (cross-)cultural bonds in *Bound.*

Also, Xing Xing's transformation into a metaphorical bird after fitting her mother's shoes alludes to the reincarnation of the mother's spirit as a dove in "Aschenputtel." While it is the mother/dove that helps Aschenputtel overcome trials, from the sorting of the beans to the granting of wishes and to the final revelation of the sisters' betrayal, Xing Xing becomes a dove herself in *Bound*, figuratively taking on the role of the emblematic mother. Napoli, conversely to Chengshi's, the Grimms', and even Carter's rewriting, slowly turns her heroine into an emancipated figure who outgrows her mother's nurturing presence in order to fulfill her own destiny.

The Cinderella figure in the Yexian tale, in "Aschenputtel," as well as in Carter's "Ashputtle *or* The Mother's Ghost" fits the shoe and marries the prince without, however, being granted a voice. In Chengshi's Yexian tale, Yexian marries the king as soon as she tries on the shoe, changes into her radiant jade clothing, and tells him the whole story:

> Yexian then appeared in her green silky coat, walking hesitantly in her slippers. She looked like a heavenly person. She then told the whole story to the king. The king brought back to the kingdom the fish bones, which had granted all of Yexian's wishes. . . . When the king arrived in the Tuo Han kingdom, he took Yexian as his high-ranking wife. For a year, the greedy king incessantly asked the fish bones for treasure and jade. (Chengshi 2012, 124)

It is the king who returns to the kingdom with Yexian and the fish bones, makes of Yexian his wife, and ultimately uses the fish bones for his own ends. English translators have claimed that Yexian became the king's "first wife" (Jameson 1982, 77), "chief wife" (Waley 1947, 229), or "primary wife" (Mair 2005, 365). However, the phrase Chengshi used does not necessarily mean "first wife." Yexian could have become one of the king's concubines, but of a relatively higher social status.[18] In this respect, although Yexian is said to occupy a higher position than wives in general, she remains potentially one among other concubines at the king's court, diminishing therefore her empowerment at the end of the Yexian tale.

In the Grimms' tale, even though Aschenputtel is not a "passive creature awaiting deliverance," since she asks her father for a twig, "plants it, waters it, tends it, and then tells the tree to shake and shower her with silver and gold," as Harriet Goldberg states (in Zipes 2000, 97), she remains silent at the end. It is the prince who asks her to try on the shoe despite the stepmother's protest and declares her as the right bride, after the series of deception he witnessed: "Das ist die rechte Braut!"; a declaration and confirmation that are further accentuated by the dove's proverbial song:

> Rucke di guck, rucke di guck,
> Kein Blut in Schuck:
> Der Schuck ist nicht zu klein,
> Die rechte Braut, die führt er heim. (Grimm and Grimm 1996, 127)

> Look, look!
> No blood in the shoe!
> The shoe's not too small.
> He's bringing the right bride home. (Dundes 1982, 29)

The mother's spirit, reincarnated in the dove, not only gives voice twice to the series of deceptions performed by the stepmother—"Rucke di guck, rucke di guck, / Blut ist im Schuck: / Der Schuck ist zu klein, / Die rechte Braut sitzt noch daheim" (Grimm and Grimm 1996, 126)[19]—but also triumphantly proclaims her own daughter as the right bride.

Aschenputtel's silence is also emphasized in Carter's rewriting of the tale. Ashputtle, the "mother's daughter" (Carter 1995, 391), seems to exist only through her mother's will, words, and actions. The mother, reincarnated as a dove, speaks for her daughter at the end of the tale. She tells the prince to "Let Ashputtle try" (394), and denounces the sisters' deceitful mutilation before proclaiming her triumph: "Look! . . . Her foot fits the shoe like a corpse fits the coffin! See how well I look after you, my darling!" (394). Ashputtle no longer appears as a beautiful fairy-tale princess, but is reduced to the "stump" of her foot and the squelching sound that it makes when she slips it into the bloody shoe—"this open wound" (394). The trial of fitting the foot into the shoe has become in Carter's words, "an ordeal in itself" (394), giving an altogether different perspective on the heroine's triumph, which, of course, is first and foremost her mother's.

Moreover, the comparison of Ashputtle's feet in the tiny slippers with a corpse in a coffin echoes the previous connection of the mother's love winding like a shroud. This imagery gives an ironic and sinister twist to the romance plot at the end, as it foregrounds both the deadly relationship that binds the daughter to her ghostly mother and the marriage prefiguring death. Indeed, the mother's oppressive declaration of possessive love and nurturing presence contrasts with the coffin-like shoes that encase Ashputtle's stumps stained by the blood of the mutilated sisters. This episode outlines for her a darker future than her mother is willing to admit, a future in which she does not seem to have much say, as a creature being passed along from her mother/dove to the prince.

By making Xing Xing the main character of *Bound* and by having the heroine assert herself at the end, Napoli presents the mother-daughter relationship in positive terms, and she likewise rehabilitates the figure of the father, stressing his role on the girl's education and self-development in the teaching of calligraphy and poetry. This also resonates with contemporary debates about the role and involvement of fathers in the education of children (see Pattnaik 2013; Flouri 2005; or Biller 1993), and with a growing interest in (a)typical parental roles in fairy tales and American fiction for young adults (see Crew 2002).

Xing Xing, already well versed and skilled in calligraphy (art helps her bear her condition), gradually learns to speak up. She tells the truth to the doctor about her sister's situation, thereby breaking the bond of secrecy she had made with her stepmother: "In her whole life Xing Xing had never said so many words to anyone," the narrator comments. "Xing Xing said the whole truth. She loved telling it. The telling made her feel energized and strong, ready for anything" (Napoli 2004, 93). She slowly learns to express herself and speak her mind, even with the prince. Xing Xing does not wait for the prince to make the first move but directly asks to try the shoe on and challenges the prince in an open debate:

> "If I were a prince," said Xing Xing . . . "I'd want an answer directly from my subject, not via a representative—especially one not chosen by the subject herself."
>
> . . .

> "But look at you," he said. "You're far from a prince."
>
> . . .
>
> "Justly spoken. . . . And padded clothing can make one appear fatter and, so wiser than he is."
>
> . . .
>
> "I think you just insulted me."
>
> "Or perhaps I teased you. . . . Did you not suggest that looks tell the worth of a person, when you clearly don't believe it yourself?"
>
> "You're certainly not subservient, whether you make a show of bowing or not." And he laughed. "All right, then. Did you go to the cave festival, Impertinent One?" (Napoli 2004, 179–80)

By talking back to the prince, she develops a voice of her own. Likewise, she wittingly asks the prince to look beyond appearances, which is of course a key theme in the tale.

The shoe-fitting episode is followed by a funny exchange between Xing Xing and the prince. The prince, stunned by her beauty, "breathlessly," yet matter-of-factly, says, "I like your clothes," to which she answers wittingly, "And I like yours. . . . Especially your funny hat" (181–82). This exchange is mirrored when she fits the shoe and transforms punningly from the "impertinent" into the "pertinent one" (182). Whereas the prince kneels in front of her and tells her she is *his* wife, Xing Xing refuses easy submission to the prince's wishes and regains control of the situation by retorting: "Is that an offer? . . . We haven't even exchanged names" (182). The romantic encounter between prince and princess-to-be in the fairy tale is gently mocked, with the heroine leading the game. No longer silent and obedient, she encourages the prince to conform to her wishes. He willingly answers to her query and exchanges names—a mere formality—as well as accepts her marriage conditions.

> "There are important things about me that you need to know," said Xing Xing.
>
> "Let me hear them."

> "I don't want to be bought or sold," said Xing Xing.
>
> "Neither do I."
>
> "I can read and write," said Xing Xing.
>
> "So can I."
>
> "My feet are not bound."
>
> "I noticed," said the prince.
>
> "I have no dowry."
>
> "I need none," said the prince. (183–84)

By highlighting the fact that Xing Xing's feet are unbound despite the golden slippers, Napoli winks at the series of deceptions that conclude the Grimms' "Aschenputtel." In addition to reclaiming her unbound feet, Xing Xing emphasizes her education and accomplishments, her refusal to be subdued, and her lack of dowry; the prince has to acknowledge this before he can marry her. Her self-assertion is counterpointed by the prince's mocking short answers that underline the absurdity of the system that regulates patriarchal society.

By departing from the conventional ending in which the heroine silently accepts the prince's marriage proposal, Napoli does not propose the triumph of the female protagonist over her male counterpart, but points instead to the necessary collaboration between the sexes. It is in their combined effort to modernize traditional gender roles and transform social relations that Xing Xing and the prince set a more progressive and egalitarian basis for their relationship through marriage. "And it's bound to be better," Napoli concludes, "with a companion who knows how to be tender, a companion you may grow to cherish" (184). Referring to Xing Xing's fate, yet addressing the reader in an apostrophe, Napoli offers a broader understanding of what marriage can be if the romantic fairy-tale-like ending and its ironic happily-ever-after female submission to the prince are replaced by a modern relationship that sets the stage for the next generation.

The intertextual connections linking *Bound* to the Chinese and German versions of the tale, as well as to Carter's retelling, emphasize Napoli's reworking of the motif of binding in the Cinderella story across cultural and temporal boundaries. Napoli's approach to both the fairy-tale tradition and the custom of foot-binding does not evade the ambivalent role of women in perpetuating crippling beauty ideals in the name of social conformity, but unlike Carter, Napoli ultimately celebrates bonds of love over oppressive family, social, and cultural strictures.

Acknowledgments

I am grateful to Martine Hennard Dutheil de la Rochère and Marie Emilie Walz for their generous feedback and comments on earlier drafts of this paper, to Donna Jo Napoli for kindly answering my e-mails about the making of *Bound*, to Guo Xiaohui for her help in locating and translating Duan Chengshi's Chinese text, and to Ryan Hughes for proofreading the piece.

Notes

1. Chengshi's (2012) Yexian tale was published in his collection of miscellanies titled *You yang Zazu*. For more information concerning this collection of fantastic tales, see Li Xueqin and Lü Wenyu. 1996. *Siku da cidian*. Vol. 2. Changchun: Jilin daxue chubanshe, 2174. There are three major English translations of Chengshi's Yexian tale: R. D. Jameson (1982) was the first to provide an annotated translation; Arthur Waley, in 1947, offered a slightly more detailed translation followed by comments on the Chinese tale; and more recently, Victor H. Mair presented yet another translation in his coedited *Hawai'i Reader in Traditional Chinese Culture* (2005). For further study about contemporary renderings of Chengshi's Yexian tale, consult Louie's (1982) children's book *Yeh-Shen* and its animated adaptation *Yeh-Shen: A Cinderella Story from China*, released by CBS Storybreak in 1985. Another cinematographic adaptation, *The Year of the Fish*, was directed by David Kaplan and released in 2007. See Zipes (2010).
2. The resurging interest in foot-binding during the feminist movement of the 1970s and '80s in the United States influenced contemporary representations of foot-binding and inspired reflections on the practice as symbolizing universal female subjugation, as in Dworkin (1974) and Daly (1978).
3. Foot-binding is a prominent topic in contemporary American works, including Emily Prager's "A Visit from the Footbinder," in Prager (1982); See (2005); Namioka (1999); and Harrison (2001). Many Chinese American women writers have used foot-binding in their writings as a trope for their move from oppression to liberation in the United States, and as a means to reconnect symbolically with their female ancestors. For sociohistorical

works, see Yung (1995) and Yung (1999). For literary works, consult Chang (1996), Wang Ping's poetry collection *Of Flesh and Spirit* (1999), and her short story "Lotus" in *American Visa* (1994). My ongoing doctoral work focuses on representations of foot-binding in Chinese American history, literature, theatrical performances, and museum displays.

4. The reason for making foot-binding an integral part of *Bound* was communicated to me by Donna Jo Napoli in an e-mail dated February 7, 2014.
5. Chengshi's Yexian tale narrates the rags-to-riches story of a girl who escapes her servitude with the help of a fish. At the death of her parents, Yexian is left in the hands of her wicked stepmother who keeps her in bondage. Her only distraction is a fish that lives in the pond behind their house, and whom she visits and feeds daily. When the connection between Yexian and the fish becomes stronger, the stepmother kills the fish and cooks it. Yexian, while mourning the disappearance of her friend, receives a visit from a person from the sky who reveals to her the cruel deed committed by the stepmother and informs her of the magical nature of the fish bones she can collect from the cesspit. She collects the bones and receives from them resplendent clothing and golden slippers in order to attend the upcoming cave festival. During the celebration, she is forced to run away when her stepsister recognizes her, and in her rush, she drops one of her slippers, which is then found and sold to the king of the neighboring kingdom. The shoe is tried on the foot of each woman in the kingdom, but to no avail. It is once the king's attendants visit the neighboring cave region that they find Yexian. Conversely, to Yexian who marries the king, her stepmother and stepsister are killed by flying stones. They are then buried and worshipped as goddesses of matchmakers. The king uses the fish bones to grant his wishes, but the magic ends after a year. The king then buries the fish bones by the sea with gold. The tale ends with the burial place being looted by the king's troop and washed away by the waves.
6. Due to a lack of archeological evidence on the beginning of foot-binding, what we know about the practice is based on textual records such as Chinese myths, poems, and paintings that appeared during the late Tang and early Song dynasties. Twelfth-century author Zhang Bangji situates its beginning at the end of the Tang dynasty at the court of Emperor, and poet, Li Yu (r. 961–75). He recounts how Li Yu made a special six-foot-high lotus-shaped stage out of gold for his favorite concubine and gifted dancer, Yao Ning. She was ordered to bind her feet with white silk in the shape of the crescent moon and dance for the court. The women at Li Yu's court were said to have bound their feet in imitation. The custom seems to have spread, however, at the end of the Song dynasty among upper-class

women, although records concerning foot-binding are infrequent before the eleventh century (Wang 2002, 31).

7. Personal e-mail communication with Napoli dated February 7, 2014.
8. Napoli's emphasis on the stepmother's role in propagating foot-binding resonates strongly with contemporary depictions of women's involvement in the custom. For instance, Emily Prager's short story, "A Visit from the Footbinder," dramatizes the difficult choices mothers have to make in order to secure a good future for their daughters. In a conversation with his wife, Lord Guo Guo refutes men's implication in the binding of their daughters' feet. In response to his wife's accusation of having crippled her daughter, Lord Guo Guo retorts incredulously: "Men took from you your ability to walk? . . . 'It is the man who pulls the binding cloth to cripple a daughter's feet? No man could do a thing like that. No man could bear it' " (Prager 1992, 29). Lady Guo Guo, like the stepmother in *Bound*, settles on the binding of her young daughter's feet although her husband has shown his lack of interest in her final decision and action: "These are women's things, your affairs, wife, not mine" (29).
9. The pain foot-binding causes has drawn the attention of writers and scholars in the West since the late nineteenth century, and has dominated accounts of the custom at the medical, historical, and fictional levels ever since. For depictions of foot-binding written at the turn of the twentieth century, see Alicia Little's memoirs *Intimate China* (1899) and *In the Land of the Blue Gown* (1902), as well as John Macgowan's *How England Saved China* (1913). For later historical and oral accounts, consult Howard Levy's "Painful History of the Lotus Hooks," and his interviews with bound-footed women "Ladies of the Bound-Foot Era," in his *Chinese Footbinding* (1966). The two documentaries *Small Happiness: Women of a Chinese Village* (Carma Hinton and Richard Gordon, 1984) and the more recent *Footbinding: In Search of the Three Inch Golden Lotus* (Yue Qing Yang, 2004) similarly draw attention to the pain endured by bound-footed women. For fictional representations see Lisa See (2005), and Prager's short story "A Visit from the Footbinder" (1982).
10. Yexian's half-sister in Chengshi's tale is mentioned twice: when she recognizes Yexian at the cave festival and when she is killed at the end with her mother. Other (Indo-)Chinese versions, however, revolve around the conflicting stories of two siblings. See Ting (1974).
11. The connection between the stepsister's foot mutilation in "Aschenputtel," Duan Chengshi's ninth-century Yexian tale, and the practice of foot-binding is also made in an exhibition titled *Grimm's Anatomy: Magic and Medicine*, at the Mütter Museum of the College of Physicians of Philadelphia, on

display since 2012 (http://muttermuseum.org/exhibitions/grimms-anatomy-magic-and-medicine-1812-2012/). This exhibition organized for the bicentennial anniversary of the Grimms' *Kinder- und Hausmärchen* (1812) approaches "Aschenputtel" from an interdisciplinary perspective, as it brings together the Grimms' fairy tales and the *real* deformed bodies that these folktales evoke. "Aschenputtel" is presented through the motif of foot-binding: the episode of the stepsisters' foot mutilation is juxtaposed to the display of an amputated and preserved bound foot. This specimen exposes the material and physical consequences of maiming practices on the human body that may have inspired the tale. *Grimm's Anatomy* is discussed at greater length in my ongoing doctoral work.

12. "Da reichte ihr die Mutter ein Messer und sprach: 'Hau ein Stück von der Ferse ab: wann du Königin bist, brauchst du nicht mehr zu Fuss zu gehen'" (Grimm and Grimm 1996, 126).
13. The Grimms' 1857 version reads: "Das Mädchen hieb die Zehe ab, zwängte den Fuss in den Schuh, verbiss den Schmerz und ging heraus zum Königssohn," and for the second: "Das Mädchen hieb ein Stück von der Ferse ab, zwängte den Fuss in den Schuh, verbiss den Schmerz und ging heraus zum Königssohn" (Grimm and Grimm 1996, 126).
14. For a more detailed analysis of Carter's "Ashputtle *or* The Mother's Ghost" and the ambivalence of "mother love," see Dutheil de la Rochère (2013). Prager formulates a similar critique in "A Visit from the Footbinder." The binding of the young protagonist's feet by a professional foot-binder calls attention to the mother's perpetuation of these crippling social ideals for the sake of her daughter's social conformity and material security. Recalling the turtle dove that reveals the wrong brides' mutilated feet and bloody shoes at the end of "Aschenputtel," Pleasure Mouse's "tiny shoes are stained with blood as were her dreams of ladyhood" (Grimm and Grimm 1996, 37).
15. The fish, which is said at the beginning of Chengshi's Yexian tale to be about 2 cùn long (one cùn being a unit of length of about 3 cm), approximates the size of an adult man when the stepmother kills it. Yexian's tiny slipper is equally measured in cùn when tried on to the feet of the women in the Tuo Han kingdom. As the transliterated Chinese text reads: "The cave people sold the shoe to the Tuo Han kingdom, which was obtained by the king. This latter commanded his subjects to try on the shoe, but the shoe became a cùn smaller when even the smallest feet tried it on" (Chengshi 2012, 124; my translation).
16. While the connection between the fish and the mother's spirit is obvious in *Bound*, it is not the case in the Yexian tale. Although Vanessa Joosen claims that the fish stands for the reincarnation of the deceased mother

(Vaz da Silva 2008, 1: 201), no textual evidence justifies this interpretation. Nothing is said about the identity of the fish and of the ungendered being, which magically appears to Yexian after the fish is killed. By using a character that represents "human being, person," to qualify this creature coming down from the sky, Chengshi has left its gendered identity ambiguous (2012, 124). Napoli's association of the fish with the mother's spirit therefore reflects the pressure of the Grimms' tale.

17. Concerning the communicative function of the shoe, see Ko's chapter "The Speaking Shoe" in *Every Step a Lotus* (2001, 97–130), and Wang Ping's section on "Nu Shu" in *Aching for Beauty* (2002, 161–73).
18. Personal e-mail communication with Guo Xiaohui dated February 21, 2014.
19. "Look, look! / There's blood in the shoe! / The shoe's too small. / The right bride's still at home" (Dundes 1982, 28).

References

Beauchamp, Fay. 2010. "Asian Origins of Cinderella: The Zhuang Storyteller of Guangxi." *Oral Tradition* 25 (2): 447–96.

Biller, Henry B. 1993. *Fathers and Families: Paternal Factors in Child Development*. Westport, CT: Auburn House.

Carter, Angela. 1995. "Ashputtle *or* The Mother's Ghost." In *Burning Your Boats: The Collected Short Stories*, 390–96. London: Chatto and Windus.

Chang, Pang-Mei Natasha. 1996. *Bound Feet and Western Dress: A Memoir*. Mew York: Doubleday.

Chengshi, Duan. 2012. *You yang Zazu*. Beijing: Shangaiguji Chubanshe.

Crew, Hilary S. 2002. "Spinning New Tales from Traditional Texts: Donna Jo Napoli and the Rewriting of Fairy Tale." *Children's Literature in Education* 33 (2): 77–95.

Daly, Mary. 1978. *Gyn/Ecology: The Metaethics of Radical Feminism*. Boston: Beacon Press.

Dundes, Alan, ed. 1982. *Cinderella: A Casebook*. New York: Garland.

Dutheil de la Rochère, Martine Hennard. 2013. *Reading, Translating, Rewriting: Angela Carter's Translational Poetics*. Detroit: Wayne State University Press.

Dworkin, Andrea. 1974. *Woman Hating*. New York: Dutton.

Flouri, Elini. 2005. *Fathering and Child Outcomes*. Hoboken, NJ: Wiley.

Grimm, Jacob, and Wilhelm Grimm. 1996. "Aschenputtel." In *Kinder- und Hausmärchen*, edited by Hans-Jörg Uther, 120–28. Munich: Eugen Diederichs Verlag.

Harrison, Kathryn. 2001. *The Binding Chair; or, a Visit from the Foot Emancipation Society*. New York: Random House.

Jameson, R. D. 1982. "Cinderella in China." In *Cinderella: A Casebook*, edited by Alan Dundes, 71–97. New York: Garland.

Ko, Dorothy. 2001. *Every Step a Lotus: Shoes for Bound Feet*. Berkeley: University of California Press.

Levy, Howard. 1966. *Chinese Footbinding: The History of a Curious Erotic Custom*. New York: W. Rawls.

Louie, Ai-Ling. 1982. *Yeh-Shen—Cinderella Story from China*. Illustrated by Ed Young. New York: Philomel.

Mair, Victor. 2005. "The First Recorded Cinderella Story." In *Hawai'i Reader in Traditional Chinese Culture*, edited by Victor Mair, Nancy Shatzman Steinhardt, and Paul R. Goldin, 362–67. Honolulu: University of Hawai'i Press.

Namioka, Lensey. 1999. *Ties That Bind, Ties That Break*. New York: Delacorte Press.

Napoli, Donna Jo. 2004. *Bound*. New York: Simon Pulse.

Pattnaik, Jyotsna, ed. 2013. *Father Involvement in Young Children's Lives: A Global Analysis*. London: Springer.

Prager, Emily. 1982. *A Visit from the Footbinder and Other Stories*. London: Vintage. 11–39.

See, Lisa. 2005. *Snow Flower and the Secret Fan*. New York: Random House.

Ting, Nai-Tung. 1974. *The Cinderella Cycle in China and Indo-China*. Helsinki: Academia Scientiarum Fennica.

Vaz da Silva, Francisco. 2008. "Blood." In *The Greenwood Encyclopedia of Folk Tale and Fairy Tales*, edited by Donald Haase, 1: 127–28. 3 vols. Westport, CT: Greenwood Press.

Waley, Arthur. 1947. "The Chinese Cinderella Story." *Folklore* 58: 226–38.

Wang, Ping. 1994. *American Visa*. Minneapolis, MN: Coffee House Press.

———. 1999. *Of Flesh and Spirit*. Minneapolis, MN: Coffee House Press.

———. 2002. *Aching for Beauty: Footbinding in China*. New York: Anchor Books.

Yung, Judy. 1995. *Unbound Feet: A Social History of Chinese Women in San Francisco*. Berkeley: University of California Press.

———. 1999. *Unbound Voices: A Documentary History of Chinese Women in San Francisco*. Berkeley: University of California Press.

Zipes, Jack, ed. 2000. *The Oxford Companion to Fairy Tales: The Western Fairy Tale Tradition from Medieval to Modern*. Oxford: Oxford University Press.

———. 2010. *The Enchanted Screen: The Unknown History of Fairy-Tale Films*. New York: Routledge.

III

Visualizing Cinderella

13

Revisualizing Cinderella for All Ages

Sandra L. Beckett

Cinderella as a Crossover Text

The classic versions of Cinderella were actually crossover texts, that is, works appreciated by both children and adults. Charles Perrault penned "Cendrillon ou la petite pantoufle de verre" ("Cinderella or The Little Glass Slipper") with a dual audience of adults and children in mind. "Cendrillon" can be appreciated on one level by very young children, but the author addresses adults in his ironic social commentary. Although Perrault's tales were told among cultured, upper-class adults at the end of the seventeenth century, the author clearly includes children in his target audience. His collection *Contes du temps passé avec des moralités* (*Tales of Times Past with Morals*), better known as *Contes de Ma Mère L'Oye* (*Tales of Mother Goose*), was attributed to his youngest son, Pierre Perrault d'Armancour, who was seventeen at the time of their writing and refers to himself as "a Child" in the preface dedicated to "Mademoiselle," Louis XIV's nineteen-year-old niece Elisabeth Charlotte d'Orléans (Perrault 1997, 19). Jacob and Wilhelm Grimm's "Aschenputtel" was published in 1812 in *Kinder- und Hausmärchen* (*Children's and Household Tales*), a collection of fairy tales intended to appeal to all Germans, young and old alike. In a letter to Arnim on January 28, 1813, Jacob stated that the volume was not targeted at children, though it made him happy to know they were reading it (in Shavit 1986, 21). Subsequent editions were modified in light of this young readership, but the preface to the second edition warned that some parents might still find certain parts inappropriate for children. Neither Perrault's nor the Grimms' collections were meant to constitute children's books. For many years, however, Cinderella was relegated, along with other fairy tales, to the nursery and the children's library. Widely considered a children's favorite of the fairy-tale canon, Cinderella has been the subject of thousands of illustrated books for children. Its status as a cherished "children's story" was enhanced by Walt Disney's popular 1950 film adaptation, inspired by Perrault's version. Today the tale of Cinderella is once again considered appropriate for all age groups. Over the past few decades, writers and illustrators around the world have been restoring the tale to a crossover audience. This chapter examines a few of the many retellings published since the 1970s that use the art of visual storytelling to target a crossover audience of both children and adults.

Abstract Cinderellas

In the 1970s, two artists used a visual code reminiscent of Russian constructivism and the Bauhaus to offer highly original retellings of Perrault's "Cendrillon." The Swiss artist Warja Lavater has gained an international reputation with her innovative accordion-style *imageries* (see Beckett 2012, 32–33, 42–46, 66–67). Lavater refers to the elementary visual code based on colors and forms as "pictorial language" or "pictograms" (Lavater 1993, 186), and the only text is the legend on the flyleaf at the beginning. These versatile books can be read in a conventional manner as double-page spreads or they can stand, allowing all the pages to be viewed simultaneously. Between 1965 and 1982, Lavater published a series of six *imageries* with the French publisher Maeght to pay homage to Charles Perrault; *Cendrillon: Une imagerie d'après le conte de Charles Perrault* (Cinderella: An imagery adapted from a tale by Charles Perrault) was the fourth tale published in the series in 1976.

A comparison of the legends of Lavater's first tale, *Le Petit Chaperon Rouge*, and her *Cendrillon* illustrates the increased number, diversity, and complexity of the symbols used in the later tale. Whereas Little Red Riding Hood is a simple red dot (all the tale's other characters are also single-colored dots), Cinderella is an elegant silver dot encircled with black and blue. In certain scenes, the icon is completely splattered with black to represent the cinders of the hearth. Some of Lavater's signs take on a symbolic meaning. The malevolence of the stepmother is suggested by the black dot, undoubtedly her black heart, at the center of the red circle; in the subsequent illustrations the darkness almost completely overshadows the red. The two stepsisters are merely smaller versions of their mother, although the black center is not as pervasive. A few icons are slightly more figurative: the fairy godmother has a wand and the prince is a richly decorated triangle with a mustache made of protruding swirls (that seem to droop when he is unhappy). Even attributes are listed in the legend, including Cinderella's gown and slippers. The elaborate nature of this tale's visual language is well demonstrated by the scene depicting Cinderella's arrival at the ball. In a colorful swirl of orange gown, the fairy-tale heroine enters the ballroom, where the prince is surrounded by golden dot-guests and flanked by the ornamented icons of the stepsisters. The king's small triangular servants and soldiers stand at attention by the entrance, while the elaborate, gold-crowned dots of the king and queen occupy a dais, and the simple dots of the proletariat gather outside the line that represents the palace walls.

Lavater uses the technique of folding to create dramatic effects and shifting perspectives. A close-up of Cinderella and the prince dancing is followed by a long view encompassing the entire ballroom, where the whole court watches the couple. The artist also sets up striking contrasts between light and dark, as the illuminated palace is replaced by the shadowy night outside and then the even blacker interior where the heroine sits once again in the hearth covered in cinders. By altering the size of certain icons, the artist can focus attention on a character or motif, or heighten the drama or suspense. Cinderella's small figure is marginalized in the darkness of the hearth as one of her stepsisters tries on the slipper, but roles are reversed in the subsequent double folds, where the spotlight is on Cinderella, and the stepsisters and stepmother are relegated to the dark, cinder-covered world. The tiny dots of the stepfamily are left behind as Cinderella and the prince set out for the palace, and they remain small at the wedding ceremony, where attention is focused on the much larger icons of the happy couple. Despite the abstract code, it is clear to all that Cinderella and the prince are embracing. The final image resembles an aerial view taken by a camera that recedes to leave the couple to enjoy their happy ending in privacy. Lavater even manages to instill her abstract images with playful humor. The unfurled dress and the two slippers abandoned in the trees seem to humorously suggest that the bedding of the bride is underway. However, such sexual innuendos will probably only occur to adult viewers.

Lavater's *imageries* are expensive art books printed from original lithographs and brought out by a publisher that is first and foremost a well-known Paris art gallery. The Galerie Maeght also sells her works unfolded and mounted as artworks to be hung on the wall. Children have nonetheless appropriated Lavater's expensive artist's books. The artist was initially astonished when she learned that children liked and apparently understood these tales published in luxury editions, sold in museums and art galleries, and bought chiefly by collectors of artist's books. She would later claim, however, that the pictorial language of her *imagerie* appeals to all ages (Lavater 1991, 44). Teachers and librarians have repeatedly confirmed the appeal of her tales with children, who particularly appreciate the interactive nature of these book-objects. The success of her artist's books with a young audience eventually led to a CD-ROM project in the 1990s. In 1995, thirty years after the publication of the first tale in the series, Lavater's innovative works were also turned into an award-winning digital film.

In 1975, the French comics artist Jean Ache (pseudonym of Jean Huet) used a similar visual code, which he referred to as "narrative abstraction," to illustrate Perrault's "Cendrillon" in *Le Monde des ronds et des carrés* (The world of circles and squares), published in Japan. Although his rendition of the tale appeared one year before Lavater's, the Swiss artist had been using her visual code to illustrate fairy tales since the 1960s. Like Lavater, Ache had interpreted other classic tales using his pictorial language. *Le Monde des ronds et des carrés* also contains "Le Petit Chaperon Rouge," while a book published in France in 1974, titled *Des carrés et des ronds: Fables et contes*, included two other Perrault tales. Despite the resemblance of the innovative visual codes used by the two artists, Ache's book is more conventional than Lavater's wordless *imagerie*. Ache also provides a legend at the beginning of the story, but his book adopts the standard codex form and it contains Perrault's text on the rectos in both French and Japanese, as well as a brief bilingual caption under each illustration. Ache's shapes are not limited to squares and circles, as the title seems to suggest, and his legend is far from exhaustive, since it includes only the characters and "the carriage with its horses, its footman, and its four lackeys."

Lavater's and Ache's representation of Cinderella as a partially blue dot sprinkled or smudged with black is strikingly similar. However, Lavater depicts Cinderella sitting in a dark, cold, ash-filled rectangular fireplace, whereas the square fireplace beside which Ache's heroine sits is full of hot, red and yellow, triangular flames. Ache effectively uses squares, rectangles, and triangles to create a decor of floors, walls, curtains, and stairs, stretching the shapes out as necessary to give perspective to the illustrations. From the lower left-hand corner of one image, Cinderella's eyes follow, "as long as possible," the stepsisters who make their way toward the horizon on the way to the ball. The illustration of a golden-haloed Cinderella dancing gracefully with her quadrilateral prince at the ball is a particularly striking composition of colors and shapes. So, too, is the scene in which Cinderella flees the ball, losing her shoe on a long staircase. Whereas Lavater represents Cinderella's shoes as separate icons (they are perhaps also suggested by the blue oval shapes within the dot that signifies the heroine), Ache cuts a small blue pie shape from his Cinderella circle to constitute the lost shoe. The Japanese publisher obviously felt Ache's unusual book required paratextual explanations, which are targeted at older readers. The author of the introduction initially thought that Ache's plan to publish a children's book "with only squares and circles" was "a typical French joke," but on receiving the "beautiful" book, he realized that it renewed the illustration of "overexposed stories" and recognized the intelligence of children (Ache 1974, 3). The afterword also begins by acknowledging how strange this picture book must seem to readers, since there are only "○s △s □s," and how different the unique illustrations are from "the childish pretty pictures" they are familiar with. Its author states that children may understand the book better than adults, thus recognizing, as many experts do today, that child readers are often more visually literate than their adult counterparts. Through the use of a visual code based on geometrical shapes, Lavater and Ache retell the story of Cinderella in a manner that is accessible to children while appealing strongly to adults.

Cinderella à la Zurbarán

When the French publisher Hatier asked Kelek to illustrate Perrault's tales, she had initially been reluctant to do what had been done so many times before. The black French artist succeeded, however, in finding an original approach for her illustrated edition of Perrault's *Contes*, published in 1986. She revisualizes Cinderella and the other fairy-tale characters through the prism of classical painting. The self-taught artist, who was a regular visitor to museums, describes her method in terms of a voyage "down the ages on the iconographic level" (Kelek 2001). The illustrations for each tale are inspired by different artists from a wide range of styles and periods. Her subtle and sophisticated allusions to past masters tend to be in a playfully parodic mode. The brief afterword describes the artist as an "impertinent" fairy; her magic allows her to move from century to century, creating "du neuf avec de l'ancien" (new with old), just as Perrault himself had done several centuries earlier. Kelek's single full-page illustration for "Cendrillon ou la petite pantoufle de verre" focuses on the iconic slipper of the subtitle. Her fairy-tale heroine is inspired by one of the many female saints painted by the Spanish artist Francisco de Zurbarán. The seventeenth-century artist, who was more or less a contemporary of Perrault, devoted himself almost entirely to religious works. The painting that Kelek appropriates is his *Saint Ursula*, completed in 1650. Associating the fairy-tale heroine with a saint may seem quite fitting, as the kindly, charitable nature of Perrault's Cinderella, who generously forgives her vicious stepsisters, seems nothing short of saintly. However, the choice of intertext clearly reflects a parodic intention: Kelek questions the idealistic saintliness of this cruelly mistreated young girl. Despite the more severe hairstyle, Kelek's Cinderella is a rather seductive young woman. The cloak over her left shoulder is now of a blood red color more suited to Little Red Riding Hood, and she gazes boldly, perhaps even provocatively, over her shoulder directly into the eyes of the viewer. The arm that holds an arrow in the original is now lowered, elegantly gloved, and carries a folding fan, a symbol of feminine flirtation.

Kelek's recasting of past masters is highly sophisticated and can only be fully appreciated by a very cultured adult audience. The artist does not generally choose the parodied works from the repertoire of familiar iconic art works, and she often superposes multiple allusions that are not necessarily to works by the same artist or from the same period. In this case, the Cinderella who wears Saint Ursula's seventeenth-century shoes is transplanted into a neoclassical setting dominated by a fairly faithful rendition of the Italian marble font of a kneeling angel in Copenhagen's Church of Our Lady. The work known as *Baptismal Angel Kneeling* (1839) is by the internationally renowned Danish sculptor Bertel Thorvaldsen, the only non-Italian with a work in Saint Peter's Basilica. The mystical intensity that characterizes Zurbarán's naturalistic paintings of saints seems to be transferred from Cinderella to the marble sculpture. If, as Jean Perrot suggests, the statue is an "icy and ecstatic double of the sensual young woman" (Perrot 1991, 41), this allusion reinforces the parody of the saintly/angelic qualities of Perrault's heroine. It is also possible that Kelek is ironically replacing the fairy godmother who watches over Cinderella in Perrault's tale with a stone guardian angel who stares unseeingly over the fleeing heroine. The fact that the small vignette on the tale's title page shows the bust of the stone angel would seem to support Jean Perrot's hypothesis of a double. Perhaps Kelek suggests ironically from the outset that such a paragon of virtue could never be a flesh and blood girl. Even cultured adults interested in the fine arts can easily overlook some of the artist's refined intertextual play. Kelek does not expect her readers to decode the references and rightly claims that the pictures "work without the references" (Kelek 2001). Thus the artist's sophisticated visual rendition of Cinderella remains accessible to children.

Recontextualization

Kelek used a form of recontextualization to retell Cinderella in a single plate in an illustrated collection of Perrault's tales. Many illustrators publish illustrated editions of only Cinderella that recontextualize the tale into an entirely different period or culture. In order not to be influenced by all the illustrations of the story that had come before, Roberto Innocenti uses this approach in his *Cinderella*, which was published to wide international acclaim in 1983. The work was commissioned by the Swiss-born illustrator Étienne Delessert, a pioneer of the modern picture book, for the collection "Il était une fois" (Once upon a time), which had strong crossover appeal. Innocenti's *Cinderella* is often considered more appropriate for high school students than children, and it is greatly appreciated by adults for its rich decor. Convinced that the fairy-tale world is not far away and long ago, Innocenti sets tales in a specific time and place, in this case the Roaring Twenties in England.[1] The decadent glamour of that era is a modern-day substitute for that of Louis XIV's court at Versailles. Perrault's text appears in a framed box that is either inserted into the illustrations or appears on a facing page with a small vignette. Innocenti's depiction of interiors, furniture, art, and costumes of the 1920s era are richly detailed and historically accurate, reflecting art deco architecture and flapper-style clothing. Certain details can be appreciated by attentive readers of all ages: the blind gentleman walking down the street toward the children playing blind man's bluff, the lizard-like features of the footman, and the coachman's rat-like face with its large moustache and buck teeth. More subtle allusions may only be decoded by older readers: the playful reference to the Cartesian nature of the godmother's magic in the numerous preliminary sketches scattered about the room or the statue of Cupid who points a drawn, arrowless bow at the smitten couple dancing in the pavilion.

In the narrow framed panel on the title page, the heroine seems to foresee her own happy ending, as her reflection in the water shows her dressed in the gown she later wears to the ball. The words of the fairy-tale incipit, which also constitute the title of the collection, are isolated above another narrow framed panel in the striking page layout that is adopted for all the series' tales. Some of Innocenti's illustrations fill gaps in the familiar text. The illustrator draws attention to the passive father who remains conspicuously absent in the verbal narrative: a man tips his hat chivalrously to the stepmother and her daughters in their fashionable fur-trimmed coats and flapper hats, while Cinderella, scantily dressed in a poor shawl and wearing a washerwoman's scarf over her hair, scrubs laundry immediately below them on a cold winter day. In the initial illustrations, the frivolous activities of the stepsisters and the indolent indulgence of the stepmother, who is usually depicted with at least one bottle of alcohol, are contrasted with Cinderella's drudgery. Set above the framed text are small vignettes that highlight, punctuate, or add a detail. Innocenti has a gift for creating striking angles and interesting perspectives, as in the bird's-eye view from the window or the close-up of Cinderella's shapely leg during the shoe fitting. Innocenti's final vignette is a kind of postscript devoted to the one character

whose fate is not mentioned by Perrault. The stepmother sits alone by the window on a cold winter day smoking, drinking (five empty bottles sit or lie on the floor beside her), and reading Innocenti's *Cinderella.* The mise en abyme of his own book, which is open at the previous double spread recounting Cinderella's happy ending, underscores the not-so-happy ending of the stepmother. The smiling stepsisters are present at the wedding with their new husbands, but the stepmother is visibly absent from the sepia plate that takes the form of a black-and-white photograph in a photo album.

Innocenti is not content merely to illustrate Perrault's tale. He has explained that the recontextualization was intended to show that this universal archetype is not limited by her time. In doing so, Innocenti also demonstrates that her story transcends ages.

A Canine Cinderella

William Wegman uses photographs of his Weimaraners to transform the timeless tale into "a classic for our time," according to the blurb on the jacket flap of his *Cinderella*, published in 1993. The humorous retelling was brought out by Hyperion, the general-interest book publishing division of the Walt Disney Company. Unlike the works examined thus far, this book also retells the text, although it does not deviate greatly from the classic tale. Inspired by Perrault's version and undoubtedly by the Disney adaptation, Wegman infuses the tale with witty, tongue-in-cheek humor. The book's appeal for all ages lies, however, in the whimsical visual interpretation of the tale offered by the internationally renowned American photographer who had already made a name for himself with his humorous signature 20 x 24 Polaroid photographs of his dogs. Wegman uses the same photographic process in the collection of picture books titled Fay's Fairy Tales, after the dog that, along with her offspring, provides the fairy-tale cast. The same year the book was published, the Museum of Modern Art (MoMA) in New York mounted an exhibition titled *William Wegman's Cinderella* (May 13–July 6, 1993). Wegman's rendition of the tale retains the conventional page layout of illustrated books, that is, text on the verso and illustration on the recto, but, like Innocenti's, the text is often accompanied by small vignettes. These reflect elements of the illustration on the facing page or, more frequently, add a glimpse of events from a different, often contrasting perspective.

The poses and deadpan expressions of the canine characters, as well as the costumes and settings, recast the familiar tale in a very funny light. Fay, as the wicked stepmother, lounges languorously on the sofa with a fox stole draped around her neck, while a sad-looking Battina/Cinderella, dressed in a drab gingham house dress, goes about her updated chores, vacuuming the rug of a circa 1940s living room. Wegman's anthropomorphized Weimaraners are not without a certain resemblance to some of Perrault's human/animal characters, notably the comic hero Puss in Boots. However, the kitschiness of Wegman's minimal sets and the tastelessness of the garish clothing and wigs contrast humorously with the elegant Versailles-like decors and stylish costumes described in Perrault's tale of Cinderella. There is something comically grotesque about the hybrid creatures that Wegman creates by giving the Weimaraners human limbs. Wearing a disheveled dark wig and an orange chiffon dress, the stepmother points an admonishing, manicured finger at readers as she stares boldly into the camera. The elder stepsister thrusts a huge human foot with red toenails in the direction of the dainty little glass slipper. The fact that Cinderella is spared the grotesque-looking human limbs seems to suggest her genuineness and unaffectedness, although the prince is also given human hands. The underlying social satire in Wegman's version reflects that of Perrault himself, although it is conveyed in a less subtle manner that is more accessible to younger readers.

The transformation scene is particularly amusing, as it almost appears as if the fairy godmother's magic has backfired. The "charming rat" painted realistically on the backdrop becomes a Weimaraner wearing only a hat in the role of a "debonair footman." The dog in the small vignette on the facing page could be either the fairy godmother or the footman. The six liver-colored puppies that replace Perrault's "six dappled grays" are described as "the most noble, spirited coach horses in the land." Many of the witty remarks in the rather lengthy text seem targeted more at adults than children. The narrator informs readers that Cinderella speaks "perfect Old French," but the prince's shyness is eased when she regains her "genteel but not so pretentious" normal voice. Wegman plays with the glass slipper motif, revisiting the question of the material by adding the mocking explanatory comment: "They were not the kind of glass slippers that could break or could cut you." Wondering later where Cinderella learned to gracefully dance a gavotte, a minuet, a sarabande, and then "the daring waltz, all the rage amongst those in the know," the narrator states that she seems "transported by her special glass slippers," which we know also "glow." The magic qualities that the narrator seems to attribute to the fairy-tale heroine's slippers may evoke Dorothy's ruby slippers in Disney's 1985 film *Return to Oz*, but the latter's iconic slippers are undoubtedly a blend of Perrault's glass slippers and Andersen's red shoes. Adults will note the strong touch of irony in the decidedly unhappy expressions on the faces of the happy couple in

Cinderella, 1993 © William Wegman, from *Cinderella* by William Wegman (Hyperion).

the final wedding portrait. Wegman's playful treatment of themes and motifs appeals to a wide audience, however. A *Publisher's Weekly* review pronounced the book for "all ages," and Hyperion would eventually refer to works such as Wegman's as "multipurposed books" intended for a crossover audience (Rosen 1997, 28).

Graphic Innovations

Since 2000, a number of authors and illustrators have retold Cinderella in innovative picture books that explore the genre as a unique art form. In 2001, the Norwegian author and illustrator Fam Ekman published *Skoen* (The shoe, 2001), a beautiful, large-format picture book illustrated in her distinctive, bold graphic style that combines various media, including pencil, paint, and collage. In this whimsical retelling for all ages, Cinderella and her prince are not reunited until their golden years. Ekman brings to this highly original reworking of the classic tale her distinctive, naive, rather grotesque characters that are a curious blend of expressionism and cartoons. An elderly junk dealer, portrayed with a single ear and sausage-like nose that evokes Perrault's "Les souhaits ridicules" ("The Ridiculous Wishes"), engages a prim and proper-looking cleaning lady to bring order to his home, cluttered with years of collecting. Over coffee, the cleaning lady relates the story of her past. Ekman plays humorously with the motifs and themes of the familiar story, which is thus embedded in a sequel of sorts. There is an allusion to Perrault's "Les Fées" ("The Fairies"; a.k.a. "Diamonds and Toads") in the story of her childhood. A stream of toads hopped out of the mouth of the cruel stepmother, who refused to accept her as a daughter, but confessed she needed a "cleaning girl." It seems this Cinderella was destined to clean for the rest of her life. Ekman links the motifs of cleaning and shoes by including among the many jobs given to her by the vicious stepsisters that of "polishing their shoes three times a day." In a very striking illustration, Ekman draws all eyes down to the huge shoes on the grotesquely large feet of the two ugly stepsisters, who tower over the small figure holding the shoe brush in the bottom corner. The heroine herself is seen only from the back, and her face is quite indistinct later as she does the stepsisters' hair. When her face is revealed—only twice in profile—it is certainly not that of the stereotypical fairy-tale beauty. Both she and the prince are rather homely and unassuming characters. Cinderella tacks remnants of cloth together to make a dress for the ball and wears the same scarf in which she cleans the house. The head of the exhausted Cinderella who sags in a chair at home talking to the ladle and the wall is strikingly similar to that used in

the ballroom scene, just as the heads of the stepsisters seem to be identical to those in the previous illustration and even in the earlier plate, where their hair is hidden by hats. The characteristic blending of media is used very effectively to show that all attention is focused on Cinderella at the ball, where her prominent, colorful figure overshadows the small black-and-white figures in the background. Although the text and illustrations are relegated to separate pages in *Skoen*, this is a highly sophisticated postmodern picture book that appeals to all ages, as do all of Ekman's groundbreaking books.

Text and image become inseparable in the Cinderella story published in Poland in 2006 by the author Michał Rusinek and the illustrator Malgorzata Bieńkowska. The graphic design of *Kopciuszek* (Cinderella) was done by the talented Polish illustrator Grażka Lange. Like Ekman's *Skoen*, this version retells the story in both text and image. It was the third book in the innovative collection Niebaśnie (un-fairy tales), created to retell classic tales in a new light. These subversive reworkings address very current, controversial topics, in this case the power of the media and its reinforcement of gender stereotypes. In the first line of the tale, the narrator explicitly addresses an audience of both children and grownups. This modern retelling presents Cinderella as a fashion-conscious neat freak, while the stepsisters are portrayed as unruly girls with bad manners, a penchant for junk food, and a complete indifference to their personal appearance. Whereas the ugly stepsisters are depicted as naive, childlike collages made out of brown paper, roughly cut pieces of paper, and sloppily applied paint, Cinderella is an elegant figure composed largely of careful cutouts from women's magazines (of the type she herself reads avidly). In this version, the ball is held by a financial shark who wants to marry off his son, the fairy godmother is replaced by the television (advertising a new clothing rental store called "The Fairy"), and the slipper is a trendy Nike. With her brilliant, magazine-produced smile, such as can only be seen in commercials, the fashionable Cinderella charms the businessman's son, but just as he is about to propose, she sees the clock and swears, since her rented dress has to be returned by midnight. A string of very similar looking girls stretches across two double spreads, a sampling of the more than one hundred girls who, in answer to the father's advertisement, queue with an identical Nike in hand. The author and illustrator poke fun at the conventional fairy-tale happy ending. Cinderella makes no attempt to establish her identity, but simply faints, and the passive businessman's son marries the first girl in the line despite her nastiness. He doesn't seem like much of a catch himself because the narrator informs readers of his indifference to women. A new happy ending is supplied: Cinderella becomes a radical feminist, not unlike her stepsisters, having learned the lesson expressed in the tale's very explicit moral: "If somebody wants to be like everybody, she usually is like nobody." The final endpapers offer the recurrent image of a single rather conventional shoe, but the front endpapers provide an array of very diverse Cinderella slippers, including a Nike cutout superposed on the drawing of a heel. In this post-modern picture book, text, illustrations, and graphic design work together to tell a narrative with crossover appeal. The mixed media techniques used range from childlike drawings and collages to sophisticated cutouts from fashion magazines. The loud, brazen text, which seems to imitate the voice of media, is interspersed with ironic comments in a smaller, less obtrusive text, which target an older audience. This highly original retelling of Cinderella presents a powerful message about the influence of the media and its reinforcement of gender stereotypes in today's world, a message intended for young and old alike.

In 2005, the Swedish cartoonist, children's book artist, and graphic novelist Joanna Rubin Dranger published a unique work titled *Askungens syster och andra sedelärande berättelser* (Cinderella's sister and other cautionary tales). Cinderella is actually the subject of three of the seven tales in the lengthy book of 380 pages. The unusual Swedish book has been called a graphic novel for adults, but according to Rubin Dranger herself it is really a collection of "graphic short stories" addressed "mainly at adults."[2] She explains her interest in this particular fairy tale in the preface of the book, where she discusses her own reading of Disney's *Cinderella* at the age of seven. The story bothered her because she did not empathize with "pretty, angelic Cinderella," but rather with the ugly sisters, "tied to their mother's apron strings, jealous, self-centered, with their big noses and their great big feet." The author concludes: "Something had gone wrong, and it never struck me that the problem might lie with the fairy tale itself." In the tale that gives its title to the collection, Rubin Dranger retells the Disney version from the perspective of one of the mean and ugly stepsisters, whom she portrays as a kind of self-confident Madonna or Lady Gaga figure. As the subtitle, "an automythological tale," suggests, the author explores the autobiographical genre in the third version, "Lyckostpulvret" (Happiness-Powder), which presents the fairy-tale heroine as an innocent, kindhearted girl, whose "difficult, unfair and loveless childhood" has caused a "neurotic condition." The arrival of the Good Fairy with some "happiness-powder" provides a very tongue-in-cheek happy ending. The second version, "Askungen: En nyillusterad Grimm-klassiker" (Cinderella: A re-illustrated Grimm classic) is of particular interest here, as it retains the classic text—in this case the Grimms' version as told in the Swedish translation by Britt G. Hallqvist, while at the same time telling a very different story by means of an original graphic novel style. According to the author, the tale is "illustrated as far from the Disney version as possible."[3] The conventional text-image relationship of the illustrated book is completely undermined in this work, which shows clearly why Rubin Dranger does not consider herself an illustrator but rather a "visual storyteller" (Larsson 2008). Direct speech from the classic tale is integrated into the illustrations in the form of speech bubbles, beginning with the dying words of Cinderella's mother, who tells her to be "good and pious," a recommendation that Rubin Dranger plays with ironically in the visual narrative. The dying mother is not depicted romantically as a beautiful woman, but rather as a ghastly, wasted figure in a modern hospital bed. The dialogue takes on new meaning in these lively, humorous pictures, as in the frame in which one of the stepsisters asks: "Is the stupid goose to sit in the parlour with us?" (Rubin Dranger 2005, 109). The remaining text often appears in a conventional manner on an otherwise blank page, followed by one or more very unconventional wordless illustrations. Sometimes the text is accompanied with black silhouettes reminiscent of shadow theater or a framed image or multiple images.

Rubin Dranger seems to turn the classic tale completely upside down by portraying an ugly Cinderella and beautiful stepsisters. In actual fact, however, her depiction of the stepsisters is faithful to the Grimms' text, where they are described as "beautiful and fair of face" (Rubin Dranger 2005, 102), an image apparently erased from the collective memory by the Disney version. The images question the ideal of beauty that is conveyed in classic tales, as well as that which still dominates in contemporary society. The prince, modeled after the American singer Prince, prefers the chunky, tattooed Cinderella to her slim, beautiful sisters. At the ball, one of the stepsisters looks strikingly like the Disney Cinderella. The heavy black border that frames the images creates the effect of a screen, even before readers discover that Cinderella herself has composed the tale on a laptop. Two images at the beginning and end create a frame story and set this tale clearly in the age of digital media. The frame story also adds a metafictive dimension, which questions and subverts the classic tale. Under the watchful eye of Frida Kahlo, this modern Cinderella refuses to be the victim and tells a very different version of her story. The images often blatantly contradict the verbal narrative: Cinderella's displeasure as she thanks her father for the hazel twig, her feigned weeping, her fury when her stepmother refuses to allow her to attend the ball, and her anger when they abandon her at home. She is definitely not the submissive, meek Disney Cinderella. The contradiction between text and image is a constant source of humor. This

"Askungen: En nyillusterad Grimm-klassiker" from *Askungens syster och andra sedelärande berättelser* by Joanna Rubin Dranger, copyright © 2005 Bonnier. Courtesy of Joanna Rubin Dranger.

chunky Cinderella is certainly not the "little stunted kitchen-wench" her father calls her. The foot mutilation episodes become rather absurd, as the stepsisters' dainty feet can hardly be too big for Cinderella's slipper. The final image brings readers back to the frame story. Cinderella's contented smile as she considers the final image of her story on her laptop screen belies her "good and pious" nature. The word "slut" has been written repeatedly on multiple images of the bleeding stepsisters on the page she contemplates with visible pleasure. The stepmother is also cast in a new light, as she brings Cinderella a snack and considers, with consternation, the ghastly image on the screen.

Conclusion

The crossover appeal of these versions of Cinderella is largely due to the media and techniques used to retell the well-known story. Since the 1970s there has been a shift away from conventional "illustration" toward new forms of visual storytelling. Warja Lavater insisted on the fact that it was not her intention to "illustrate," but rather to "draw" books that "tell stories by means of visual codes" (Lavater 1993, 186). The Swiss artist stated categorically: "I am above all an author, and what I do is not illustration" (Lavater 1991, 45). Her words sound remarkably similar to those pronounced by Joanna Rubin Dranger almost three decades later in 2008. Although she holds a position of professor of illustration, Rubin Dranger does not want to be called an illustrator but rather "a visual storyteller." Like Lavater, she insists: "I do not think the word illustration is adequate for what I do" (Larsson 2008). In the 1970s, Warja Lavater and Jean Ache retold "Cinderella" with an experimental visual code that can be read in a different manner by each reader, allowing readers of all ages to engage in the storytelling process. In the 1980s, the more traditional illustrated books of Kelek and Roberto Innocenti used recontextualization to create multilayered versions that have appeal for all ages. William Wegman also brings an original visual approach to a more traditional-style illustrated book through the medium of photography in his 1990s recasting of the tale. The picture-book retellings of Fam Ekman and Malgorzata Bieńkowska in the 2000s use the innovative, multimedia graphic experiments of the postmodern picture book to achieve crossover appeal. Over the past few decades, the story of Cinderella is being retold in an exciting range of groundbreaking, multilayered visual narratives. Rubin Dranger's graphic short stories constitute one of the latest of many innovative experiments with graphic storytelling that have brought new life to what the Japanese author referred to in the 1970s as an "over-exposed" story. The American artist and illustrator Tom Feelings, who refers to himself as a storyteller in picture form, sees picture books as "a natural extension of [the] oral tradition" and therefore capable of reaching young and old alike. He writes: "Telling stories through art is both an ancient and modern functional art form that enables an artist to communicate on a large scale to people young and old" (Feelings 1995). In our technological age of visual media, artists from many fields are exploring the art of visual storytelling in order to revisualize an age-old tale for a contemporary audience of all ages.

Notes

1. Some recontextualizations are less subtle and include paratextual elements to assist in decoding. These works do not have the same broad appeal as Innocenti's. Lynn Roberts and David Roberts's use of an Art Deco decor in their 2001 picture-book retelling is clever but more contrived than that of Innocenti. Their *Cinderella* is subtitled "An Art Deco Love Story" and contains a postscript in the form of an "illustrator's note" that acknowledges the influence of "movie stars, magazine covers, and art of the 1920s and '30s." The illustrator identifies the artists whose paintings are imitated and provides some guidelines for readers interested in trying to identify the sources of the wallpaper, furniture, pottery, and fashion designs. The detailed representation of an era explains the book's appeal with some adults and the fact that it was chosen as the inspiration for the animated Christmas windows of the department store Smith and Caughey in Auckland in 2009. Steven Guarnaccia's *Cenerentola* (Cinderella), published with Corraini in 2013, is subtitled "una favola alla moda" (a fashionable tale) and sets the fairy tale in the world of high fashion. The designers and the creations that inspire the wardrobe of Guarnaccia's characters are identified on the endpapers, a key that even adult readers will require.
2. E-mail, October 20, 2012.
3. E-mail, October 21, 2012.

References

Ache, Jean. 1974. *Le monde des ronds et des carrés: Fables et Contes*. Illustrated by Jean Ache. Paris: Balland.

Beckett, Sandra L. 2012. *Crossover Picturebooks: A Genre for All Ages*. London: Routledge.

Ekman, Fam. 2001. *Skoen*. Oslo: J. W. Cappelens Forlag.

Feelings, Tom. 1995. *The Middle Passage: White Ships/Black Cargo*. Introduction by John Henrik Clarke. New York: Dial Books.

Guarnaccia, Steven. 2013. *Cenerentola: Una favola alla moda*. Mantova: Corraini.

Kelek. 2001. Telephone conversation with Sandra L. Beckett, June 25.

Larsson, Therese. 2008. "Joanna Rubin Dranger, bildberättare" (interview). *Fokus* 5, September.

Lavater, Warja. 1976. *Cendrillon: Une imagerie d'après le conte de Charles Perrault*. Paris: Adrien Maeght.

———. 1991. "Tête à tête: Entretien avec Warja Lavater." Interview by Bernadette Gromer. *La Revue des livres pour enfants* 137–38 (Winter): 40–49.

———. 1993. “Perception: When Signs Start to Communicate.” In *The Faces of Physiognomy: Interdisciplinary Approaches to Johann Caspar Lavater*, edited by Ellis Shookman, 182–87. Columbia, SC: Camden House.

———, after Charles Perrault. 1995. *Imageries*. Six animated films. Paris: Cinquième Agence.

Perrault, Charles. 1983. *Cinderella*. Illustrated by Roberto Innocenti. Mankato, MN: Creative Company.

———. 1986. *Contes de Charles Perrault*. Illustrated by Kelek. Paris: Hatier.

———. 1997. “À Mademoiselle.” In *Contes de ma mère l'Oye*. Illustrated by Gustave Doré. Folio Junior Édition Spéciale. Paris: Gallimard.

Perrot, Jean. 1991. *Art baroque, art d'enfance*. Nancy: Presses Universitaires de Nancy.

Roberts, David, and Lynn Roberts. 2001. *Cinderella: An Art Deco Love Story*. London: Pavilion.

Rosen, Judith. 1997. “Breaking the Age Barrier.” *Publishers Weekly*, September 8, 1997, 28–31.

Rubin Dranger, Joanna. 2005. *Askungens syster och andra sedelärande berättelser*. Stockholm: Bonnier.

Rusinek, Michał. 2006. *Kopciuszek*. Illustrated by Malgorzata Bieńkowska. Graphic design by Grażka Lange. Warsaw: Jacek Santorski.

Shavit, Zohar. 1986. *Poetics of Children's Literature*. Athens: University of Georgia Press.

Wegman, William, with Carole Kismaric and Marvin Heiferman. 1993. *Cinderella*. New York: Hyperion.

14

The Illustrator as Fairy Godmother

The Illustrated Cinderella in the Low Countries

Jan Van Coillie

Without doubt, illustrators strongly influence the way we imagine fairy tales. For most of today's children, Cinderella looks like a Disney star, with long eyelashes and blond hair, ending up in the arms of her Prince Charming.

Throughout the centuries, scores of illustrators and film producers visualized the tale of Cinderella, affecting the imagination of every new generation. In this article I study how this tale was visualized in the Netherlands and Flanders from 1850 till the present. Of the 379 versions I could trace, I studied seventy-six in detail, paying attention to both text and illustrations. These editions were randomly chosen, spread over time. Forty-three were based on Perrault and thirty-three on Grimm, though the line between them is not always very clear, as fifteen editions mix elements from both sources. I only included translations and adaptations of which the plot is more or less a faithful rendering of the source text's plot. This means that I excluded "new stories inspired by" the fairy tale (Seago 2008) and parodies.

Three questions guided my research: How do the illustrations relate to the texts, how do they visualize the fairy tale, and how do the editions function as cultural texts? The first question focuses on the relation between text and image. Answering the second question, I concentrate on the visual means by which the illustrators visualize the characters and the relations between them. I focus on Cinderella, the prince, and the stepmother and stepsisters. In dealing with the third question, I examine what culturally determined values, norms, opinions, and images the illustrators convey.

The Relation Text—Illustrations

Most studies of the visual representation in children's books focus on the relation between pictures and words in picture books. Nikolajeva and Scott (2001) developed an elaborate model, containing five categories that describe the interaction between text and image. When both modes of communication present the same information, they call the interaction "symmetrical." When one mode fills in gaps, left by the other, the relation is complementary. With "enhancement," the pictures significantly amplify or reinforce the verbal story or vice versa. The researchers are especially interested in the "counterpoint" mode, which is used when "words and images provide alternative information" (Nikolajeva and Scott 2001, 17). The dynamics of the interaction is increased, provoking multiple readings and interpretations. "Contradiction" can be seen as an extreme form of counterpoint, when text and image (seemingly) take the story in opposite directions.

In most books with fairy tales, the synergy between text and illustrations is much weaker than in the picture books Nikolajeva and Scott studied. Instead of picture books, these fairy-tale books are called "illustrated books": the illustrations have a decorating rather than an "essential" function (Van der Pol 2010, 22). However, it is important to realize that illustration always implies selection and interpretation. Consequently, the distinction between the various modes of symmetry, complementarity, and enhancement cannot be taken to be too rigid.

The illustrator selects not only the textual scenes he illustrates, but also the characters, objects, and so on featuring in these scenes. Therefore, the researcher must not only pay attention to what is depicted, but also to what is not. These "omissions" may be revealing from an ideological point of view, as the hidden ideology may well become clear from what is not shown. The illustrator not only selects, but also interprets, as he necessarily has to concretize what the text tells or describes. Even when the text mentions that Cinderella has blond hair, the illustrator must fill in how long, how thick her hair is. Evaluative words and words that name feelings or character traits leave even more room for interpretation. When the text mentions that Cinderella is beautiful or modest, the illustrator has to make this beauty and modesty concrete.

Gaps, Frames, and Clichés

In fairy tales descriptions are mostly highly restricted, causing many "gaps"—instances in the text where information is missing. Every individual reader (and by extension every illustrator) may fill in these gaps in his own way (Iser 1974, 280). In doing this, he uses what Iser calls "mental images" (178), also known as "frames," defined by Lakoff (2004, xv) as "mental structures that shape the way we see the world." López (2002) stresses the cultural dimension of frames, defining them as "structures of knowledge that represent the world view of a particular society, that is, its beliefs, values and emotions, its prototypes of people and things, of sequences of situations and events, its social scenarios and the metaphorical and metonymical structure of thought" (López 2002, 312).

Illustrators thus make use of frames while interpreting fairy tales. These can be "visual" frames, allowing them to infer visual details that are not mentioned in the text, but also "interpersonal" frames, such as mental models of the relationship between family members or lovers and "generic" frames, prototypes of people such as "the modest girl" (López 2002, 316). It may be clear that frames are both individually and collectively determined. Well-known collective frames are ideologies. They include larger-scale systems of ideas such as democracy and more "intimate" cultural ideas, dealing with gender, sexuality, and race (Parsons 2011, 113). For McCallum and Stephens, for whom the ideology of literary texts "inheres in framing" (McCallum and Stephens 2010, 364), fairy tales are used ideologically "by presenting desirable models of human personality, human behavior, interpersonal relationships, social organization, and ways of being in the world" (361). It is interesting to investigate whether the illustrations used in the various Cinderella versions support this tendency to socialize children in this way.

Ideologies tend to be taken for granted (Hollindale 1988). For that purpose, they use images and frames that are repetitive, resulting in stereotypes, defined by Amossy and Herschberger-Pierrot (1997, 26) as "the images in our head that mediate our relation with reality. They are made-up representations, preexistent cultural schemes, by means of which every person filters the changing reality" (my translation[1]). In literary texts, stereotypes take the form of clichés and stock characters. Because fairy tales are so widely distributed and have been translated, adapted, and illustrated time and again, they may be expected to provide us with many clichés and to "perpetuate societal standards" (Alfred Corn, quoted in Robins 1998, 101).

The Language of the Illustrator

Apart from the question of how text and image are interrelated, this study wants to answer the question, which means do the illustrators use to give shape to their interpretation? This requires a model that allows us to analyze the "language" of the illustrator. *Reading Images: The Grammar of Visual Design* by Gunther R. Kress and Theo Van Leeuwen (1996) offers an extensive taxonomy for analyzing visual language. Central concepts in their work are "composition," "perspective," and "visual symbols." Composition encompasses the relative size of the object, color and contrast, foregrounding, and focus. Perspective, such as the bird's-eye view, manipulates the reader's interpretation of characters and objects and the relations between them. According to Serafini (2011, 346), visual symbols "represent ideas that are conventionalized through their use in sociocultural contexts." They function as clichés, such as the fireplace in Cinderella, symbolizing the location to which women were condemned in the middle-class ideology.

The present analytical model integrates the central concepts of Kress and Van Leeuwen in the classification developed by Kris Nauwelaerts (2008) for the analysis of picture books. Nauwelaerts distinguishes illustrative, formal, and graphic characteristics. Illustrative characteristics include figuration, expression, styling, setting, attributes, and visual symbols. Figuration refers to external proportions (the relative size of objects, people, and animals) and internal proportions (for example, a head that is too small in proportion to the body). Expression, in turn, refers to body language (mimics and posture).

Formal characteristics comprise color and contrast, contour lines, foregrounding, and focus, volume effect, technique, and texture. They can exert a strong manipulative and emotional effect. Dark colors, for instance, can enhance suspense, a bird's-eye view can suggest loneliness, and by zooming in on a telling detail or bringing an object to the fore, the illustrator can give it more importance.

Graphic characteristics include layout and trim area, the integration of text and illustration, graphic framing, and typography (fonts, typefaces). The frames or borders around the picture select what is pertinent to be included and what is not. Frame breaking triggers the imagination and enhances the dynamics of the picture (Scott 2011).

Cinderella: The Synergy of Inner and Outer Beauty

What does Cinderella look like? Neither Perrault nor Grimm provides us with a single detail about her physical appearance. Perrault merely tells us that she is a hundred times more beautiful than her stepsisters. In the Grimm version the prince is immediately struck by her beauty. Cinderella's looks are therefore a textual gap that grants illustrators almost complete freedom. Still, in 82 percent of the studied versions, Cinderella has blond hair. Obviously, most illustrators' frames of a beautiful woman include blond hair, most likely under the partial influence of previous illustrations. Warner points out how this frame of the blond beauty reaches back to Ancient Greece (Warner 1994).

Sometimes the illustrator's freedom is restricted by the translator, who may add details on Cinderella's appearance. In some versions she has "shiny golden hair" (Cramer 1925[2]) or "beautiful golden hair" (Heuninck 1984). Whatever the case may be, Cinderella always has fine features and a slim face, at least when she is portrayed as a young woman. Some illustrations indeed depict Cinderella as a child, an image that contrasts with the text and with adult expectations and that betrays a strong adaptation by the illustrator to his or her child audience.

A remarkable example is *Asschepoester in het cirque Carré* (Anon. ca. 1875). Here, Cinderella and her stepsisters are wearing adult clothes and have adult faces, but their body proportions are those of children.[3] The version by Dick Bruna from 1966 was an international success. In his typical minimalist style, he portrayed Cinderella as a toddler. The representation of Cinderella as a young child is also typical of many editions, published by commercial, international publishers. *Mijn mooiste Fabeltjesboek* (Anon. 1987) clearly shows this sentimentalized child image, portraying Cinderella with wide-set eyes, a tip-tilted nose, and a tiny mouth. The strongly abridged text abounds with diminutives.

Just like for Cinderella's physical appearance, we hardly find any details about her clothes in the texts by Perrault and Grimm. Even though some translators give more details, the illustrators are still free to make their own designs. Consequently, Cinderella's apron, as well as her ball gowns, looks quite different through the years. Still, clichés abound in the illustrations of the ball gowns, most of which are wide crinolines. Modern designs are very rare; they obviously do not fit in the frame of the fairy-tale princess. In *Liesje in het Dromenland* (Anon. ca. 1915) Cinderella's fin-de-siècle dress strangely contrasts with the medieval costumes of her sisters, accentuating the moral contrast between them. Not only contemporary but also "naturalized" dresses are exceptional. In just two of the studied versions, Cinderella is depicted with a typical Dutch cap and clogs.

There is no doubt that Cinderella's character is exemplary. For Perrault she is of unparalleled obedience and sweetness, and the brothers Grimm repeat three times that she is "fromm und gut." Perrault links her outer to her inner beauty, telling us she is "aussi bonne que belle." Moreover, her behavior proves that she is utterly diligent and docile. She withdraws into the kitchen whenever she is ordered to and she helps her sisters, even though they cruelly mistreat her. As John Stephens (1992, 140) states, "ideologically, she represents a model of perfect wifehood—she is beautiful but abject, and she is available but submissive." Many of the older translations (before 1950) make these traits explicit and even intensify them. Moreover, these central virtues are repeatedly stressed in the illustrations, making the image of the modest and diligent Cinderella a most powerful cliché.

The selection of the scenes in the illustrated books is quite telling: in 36 percent of the studied books, Cinderella is shown while doing household chores; in 40 percent, one can see her helping her stepsisters doing their hair or dressing up. Very often her modesty is visually accentuated through her posture and facial expressions. In the kitchen, her dejected look and drooping shoulders suggest sadness or resignation but also passiveness or submissiveness. Moreover, again and again, she is surrounded by objects associated with household chores: the kettle over the fire and the broom.

One of the first Dutch editions of the Grimm tales (Anon. 1861) puts the kitchen scene literally in the center. The book is illustrated with "arabesques," pictures showing different scenes on small vignettes around a central image (Freyberger 2009, 126–51). On the illustration accompanying Cinderella, the central part shows Cinderella near the fireplace, while the surrounding vignettes illustrate scenes such as the heroine at her mother's grave or in the company of the prince, who hands her the slipper.

A much-discussed version from the second half of the nineteenth century is the rhymed Cinderella by the popular poet Jan Pieter Heije (Burgers and Kroon 1865). Heije's text abounds with evaluative adjectives and nouns, stressing the typical bourgeois virtues of Cinderella. She is "pious" (*vroom*), "humble and good" (*nedrig en goed*). Her greatest virtues are "mercy," "pity," and "modesty" (*barmhartigheid, meêlij en zedigheid*). Half of the illustrations depict the heroine while she is putting those virtues into practice: cleaning the floor on her knees with dustpan and brush, helping her stepsister, or feeding a poor beggar woman. The final illustration contains a remarkable addition: a cat with an escutcheon (with tongs and ash scoop) and a ribbon that says "Humilitas" ("Humility"), a strong visual symbol for the tale's central message.

In some versions, the title or subtitle stresses the central virtue. In *Asschepoetster of Nederigheid beloond* (Anon. 1875), Cinderella's main virtue has been made explicit, "Nederigheid" meaning "humility." Her name has been changed too, the second part "*poetster*" meaning "cleaning lady." On the first illustration, Cinderella is sitting next to the fireplace, with kettle, broom, and pumpkin. The name *Asschepoetster* also appears on the front page of the version with text by Miss Van Osselen-Van Delden (Anon. 1904). The final sentences of this book unveil the prince's preference for the domestic Cinderella. When the prince and Cinderella are married, he is sometimes said to ask his "dearest Cinderella" to put on her old clothes again. In this version, Cinderella is called "Ella Edelzwaan" (Ella Nobleswan).

Often, Cinderella's patience and modesty are stressed in contrast with her stepsisters' vanity and mockery. In *Sprookjes van Moeder de Gans* (1916) Rie Cramer exploits the effects of figuration and expression. She draws Cinderella on her knees, adjusting her stepsisters' dresses and carrying buckets while her stepsisters are poking fun at her. She looks small, while her stepsisters' haughtiness is stressed by having them break through the frame. Willy Schermelé (1943) accentuates the central motives in another way: he places the text in frames with decorative edges, containing the main characters and visual symbols like a broom (for Cinderella) and a fan (for the stepsisters). Froukje van der Meer (1944) modernizes the setting, but still stresses Cinderella's virtues as a good housewife and a caring sister: she shows Cinderella ironing her stepsisters' clothes.

Cinderella and the Prince: Between Modesty and Seduction

Neither Perrault nor Grimm gives any information about the appearance, clothes, or character of the prince. Perrault does emphasize his courtly conduct and blind love and Grimm his jealousy (the prince allows no one else to dance with Cinderella). Again, the illustrators, having a free hand, produce very different representations. Clichés, however, continue to abound, resulting in recurring "typical" elements, such as the crown and the trousers in Spanish style.

Not only do the same attributes pop up time and again, but also the same scenes, the most popular one being the prince or his servant handing Cinderella her slipper (it occurs in 64 percent of the studied versions). In this scene, Cinderella's and the prince's glances are particularly interesting, since they tend to reveal the artist's vision on gender relation. Perrault wrote nothing about the way the prince and Cinderella look at each other, but Grimm mentions that Cinderella bows before the prince and then stands up, while the prince looks at her.

In almost all the illustrations that depict this scene, Cinderella looks down demurely, avoiding eye contact. In the texts accompanying this crucial scene, Cinderella's modesty is formulated explicitly time and again. "A humble child sees itself beloved,[5] it says in the poem next to the illustration

Drupsteen, Wilhelmina. 1907. *Asschepoester. Het oude sprookje.* Amsterdam: D. Coene.

in *Nieuwe gedichtjes op de vertellingen van moeder de Gans* (Anon. ca. 1851). On the picture by Wilhelmina Drupsteen from 1907, Cinderella has become a prototype of shyness. In the text opposite the illustration, she is called a "child" twice, in line with the phenomenon of "infantilization," typical of that period. On an illustration by Rie Cramer from 1925, Cinderella not only modestly glances down, but also gently touches her lips with her finger. The prince stares at her longingly, one knee bent.

While sentimentality and infantilization were rampant during the first decades of the twentieth century, this condescending view became even more obvious in the commercialized, international editions that appeared after 1950. In *Assepoester: Mijn mooiste sprookjes* (Ramon 1991) Cinderella's shyness is accentuated by her posture: she sits down, her ankles crossed and her hands pressed against the seat of her chair.

While almost all illustrators emphasize Cinderella's modesty (not only in her relation with the prince, but also as a kitchen maid), there are some artists who bring out another side: her seductiveness. Since it is quite uncommon for a children's book to make statements about manifestations of femininity, the illustrator's decision to do so may be conscious or—much more likely—unconsciously determined by different frames. It is no coincidence that this image turns up more frequently during the years 1900–1950, when art nouveau exerted an important influence on children's books illustrations. In this art movement, the images of the fatal woman and tricky seductress were popular (Fahr-Becker 1997, 85). When Rie Cramer (1925) depicts Cinderella running down the stairs, she gives her a seductive look. Willy Schermelé (1943) shows both sides of Cinderella. When she meets the prince at the ball, she looks seductively over her shoulder, her head slightly tilted, touching her lips with a fan. However, when the prince asks her to dance, she looks down demurely. (See color insert, plate 8.)

In more recent times Sebastiaan Van Doninck (2012) puts Cinderella's sensuality openly in the picture. She is wearing a see-through dress, so that you can see her white knickers and her breasts.

Physical contact was a taboo in the editions for a long time. Even while dancing, Cinderella and the prince kept a safe distance. When, during the 1980s, they got closer together, the physical attraction is often toned down by making her more childish and by using romantic clichés. In *Assepoester* (Anon. ca. 1985) both the prince and Cinderella look like young teenagers. The prince is wearing a toy sword. As always, he is taller than his beloved, looking down on her. In another commercialized edition (Ramon 1991), clichés abound in the costumes, haircuts, and last but not least the doll's faces. On the cover Cinderella and the prince are holding each other tight, but their eyes do not meet. This romantic approach is bound to determine the reader's expectations.

However different the pictures of the prince may be, they all show a slim, handsome, young, white male. Or at least almost all of them. Those rare illustrations that deviate from this cliché, and consequently from the expectations of most of the public, question the ruling ideology in a confronting manner.

In the etchings by Gustave Doré (originally from 1867), which were very popular in the Netherlands well into the twentieth century, the prince is an old, lecherous man. Moreover, the court is represented by caricatures.

Van Doninck, Sebastiaan. 2012. *Het Grote Grimm Boek*. Vertaald door Kristien Dreesen. Tielt: Lannoo.

Doré's pictures contain a sharp critique on court life (Gheeraert 2007). Remarkably, in the 1890 edition with text by Schenkman (Doré 1890), the caption does not focus on the dancing couple, but on the ladies "peeping" at Cinderella with envy.

In more recent editions, the prince looks much more common. Annemie Heymans (1982) draws him on top of the stairs, so that he looks small in his white, open shirt. Thé (1996) pictures him in military uniform, but even when he gently carries Cinderella in his arms, he looks slender. Sebastiaan Van Doninck's interpretation from 2012 surprises the reader, as he pictures the prince as a huge, dark colored man, confronting us with our white, Western way of framing the fairy-tale prince.

The Stepsisters and Stepmother: Pride Punished or Forgiven

Clearly, the stepmother and stepsisters are Cinderella's antipodes. Perrault writes that the stepsisters were exactly like their mother, who was the proudest and most haughty woman that was ever seen ("*la plus hautaine et la plus fiere qu'on eut jamais veuë*"). Unlike Cinderella's clothes he does describe theirs in detail. Obviously, the stepsisters were fashionably dressed, wearing tight corsets, a velvet dress with English embroidery, a coat with gold flowers, a wig and a bonnet with lace strips. Closely following Perrault's description, most illustrators base their costumes on the French court fashion of his time, though they rarely keep the details he provides (and which many translators omit). These seventeenth- and especially eighteenth-century costumes with huge wigs, wasp waists, and wide crinolines easily lend themselves to parody.

As for the stepsisters' looks, Perrault just mentions their small waists. Again, he gives the illustrators almost a complete freedom to fill in the gaps. In some versions the stepsisters look quite pretty, in others neutral, but in most they are very ugly, linking outer and inner ugliness. Occasionally, the ugliness of the stepmother and stepsisters is made explicit. The stepmother tops everyone. In most books she is depicted as being far more terrifying than her daughters. Daan Hoeksema (1907) depicts her as a vicious hag who towers high above Cinderella, a twig in her hand, ready to beat her. Adolf Münzer's stepmother looks like a true witch, with dark skin, a wart on her cheek, a large hooked nose, and a mean look (Münzer 1905). Over time, she becomes more and more of a cliché, culminating in Walt Disney's utterly mean version, which became part of the collective memory.

At the end of the nineteenth century, the first caricatures of the stepsisters turn up. They are in line with the growing importance of humor in children's literature at the time (Van Coillie 2007, 352). In Agatha's pantomime picture book version (Anon. 1893), the contrast between the fat and the lean stepsister reinforces the humorous approach. In Anna van Gogh-Kaulbach's *Asschepoester* (Anon. 1913), one of the first children's books with photographs, the stepsisters are transvestites.

Froukje Van der Meer (1944) strongly manipulates the spectator by means of color, expression, posture, and perspective. By making the stepsisters look aside, their noses in the air, Van der Meer accentuates their vanity. The contrast between the bright colors of their dress and the black skirt of the stepmother puts extra emphasis on the latter's malicious character, which is further emphasized by her stern look and her towering cap. The text reads: "They were terribly proud and vain."[6]

During the 1980s, the stepsisters are frequently depicted in their underwear, taboo breaking being a popular form of humor in children's books in those days. Thé (1996) works with the humor technique of the caricature, giving the one sister extremely fat and the other extremely long feet. In the text Jacques Vriens explicitly mentions the stepsisters' ugliness: "Well, it was not so difficult to be prettier than Rosa and Agniet. The two girls were very ugly. Rosa had a big pimple on her nose and Agniet had two huge floppy ears."[7]

Anonymous. 1913. *Asschepoester*. Verteld door Anna van Gogh-Kaulbach. Amsterdam: Allert de Lange.

While Perrault does not mention anything about their looks, the brothers Grimm write that the stepsisters are beautiful, with fair faces, but evil and dark hearts. The word "*weiss*," indicating the color of Cinderella's face, is loaded with meaning. It has been translated in many different ways as "white," "fair," or "pale," but has been omitted in most versions. It is most probably no coincidence that in his translation of 1943, Hildebrand (in Van

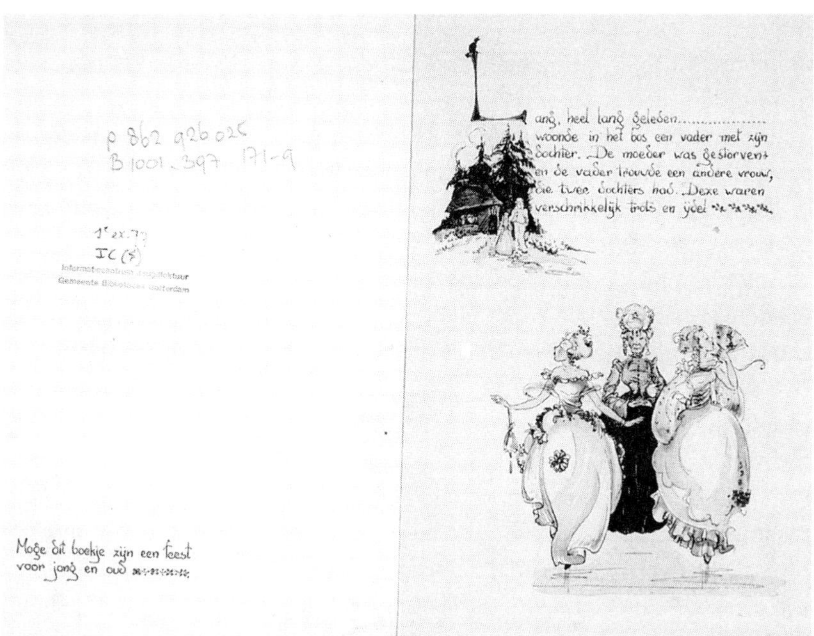

Van der Meer, Froukje. 1944. Assepoes: Het oude sprookje. Opnieuw verteld door Froukje van der Meer. 's-Gravenhage/Batavia: G. B. Van Goor Zonen.

Nieuwenhoven 1943) chooses "blank" (white), the adjective normally combined with "race." Like Cinderella, the stepsisters have blue eyes, an attribute that is explicitly called "beautiful": "Beautiful they were, the two daughters, they had a white skin and blue eyes, but in their hearts it didn't look so well. Inside they were black and bad."[8] In most illustrated Grimm versions, the stepsisters look anything but ugly, although their stuffed wigs symbolize their vanity. Here too, after 1980, they are often ridiculed by means of caricature and pictured in their underwear. Jo Blockerije (1984) shows one of them pulling faces while Cinderella tightens her corset. Asensio (1990) pictures them with huge noses and silly, colorful knickers.

In a few editions, the illustrations contrast with the text, bringing to the fore the tension between inner and outer self. In *Het mooiste sprookjesboek* (1993), Tatjana Hauptman gives the stepsisters an ugly face, although in the text, they have "a beautiful, fair face" (*een mooi, blank gezicht*). Their "gruesome black soul" (*akelig zwarte ziel*) shines through their makeup. Juan Ramon (1991), on the contrary, gives them rather pretty faces, although the translator states that they were "utterly hideous" (*foei-lelijk*).

The fate of the stepsisters at the end of the story differs substantially in the versions of Perrault and Grimm. Perrault stresses Cinderella's forgiveness and her stepsisters' repentance. Moreover, he adds two rhymed *moralités*, the first stating that graciousness is more important than beauty in a woman and the second that young people will not gain success without a rich godfather or godmother. Most of the studied Perrault versions underscore Cinderella's forgiveness just like the source text, but omit one or both of the *moralités*. Often, both text and illustration in this final scene have been strongly adapted to a young public.

At the end of *Asschepoester in het cirque Carré* (Anon. ca. 1875), Cinderella pardons her stepsisters and matches them to great lords of the court. The single moral lesson here is directly addressed to the young public: "So, sweet girls, be as modest, sweet and gentle as she is."[9] The final picture shows three carriages in a kind of circus arena. Huens (1950) pictures the prince, kneeling in front of Cinderella, while the fairy godmother raises her magic wand almost like a schoolteacher. Although in the text an explicit moral lesson is lacking, the message that goodness and humility are rewarded will be remembered by means of this final picture.

The anonymous illustrator of *Mijn mooiste fabeltjesboek* (1987) shows the stepmother and stepsisters, begging for mercy, all in tears. Not only the illustration but also the text has been adapted to children: "The wicked stepmother and her daughters asked for forgiveness, they had repented their unkind behavior. Cinderella forgave them and so all was well again."[10]

Juan Ramon (1991) opts for the romantic cliché, in the tradition of Walt Disney. The combination of the "adult" romantic kiss (in text and illustration) and the "childish" behavior of the stepsisters is remarkable:

> The stepsisters were furious! They stamped their feet and the stepmother turned bright red. But Cinderella laughed. She was brought to the palace soon. The prince embraced and kissed her and said, "You will be my wife." And they lived happily ever after.[11]

The Grimms' version (at least the one of 1857) ends much more horribly than that of Perrault: the oldest stepsister cuts off her big toe and the other her heel. As if that were not enough, the pigeons on Cinderella's shoulders peck out both of their eyes. As may be expected, these gruesome details have been left out or mitigated in many of the texts (sometimes the stepsisters lose only one eye). And the details are hardly ever depicted. It is not accidental that the scarce representations of these scenes were published after 1980, when many taboos were dropped in children's books (Vermeyen 1985; Holtrop 1989, 436) But even in those years in most versions the taboo is kept intact, as in two editions from 1990 (Asensio) and 2009 (Jean-Pol), in which the stepsisters only try to squeeze their foot in the shoe. They look all red, but there is no blood.

In just two editions, both of foreign origin, blood can be seen. Svend Otto (1984) still refrains himself. He only paints a bloodstain on the stepsister's shoe. Sylvie Chretien (1985), however, makes blood drip from the knife and out of the stepsisters' eyes. In the text, their evil characters are emphasized. The adaptor adds that they joined the wedding only with intent to murder Cinderella.

Translators and illustrators not only mitigated or eliminated the Grimms' cruel ending, in some instances they also added a scene. The version by Hildebrand and Van Nieuwenhoven, published during World War II (1943), is quite remarkable in this respect. The stepsisters are not blinded, but kicked out by the prince. He stresses that he normally respects handicapped people, but not these two, because they had tried to deceive him. A couple of paragraphs are added, telling how Cinderella and the prince became king and queen and had children and Cinderella went on visiting her mother's grave every day. Not only the text, but also the illustrations put the family in the picture, one of the keystones of the Third Reich.

Conclusion

With regard to the relation between illustrations and text, this study shows that in the Dutch and Flemish editions of Cinderella, the symmetrical and complementary/enhancing modes dominate. This confirms what Vanessa Joosen (2012, 165) already pointed out for the illustrations of Snow White. The illustrators mainly depict the story, they "repeat" in images what is told or described in the text. In doing so, they fill in the gaps with details that meet the readers' expectations. Even in the more innovative editions, text and illustrations are rarely contradictory. If there is some way of counterpointing, it means that the illustrations run counter to the readers' expectations, surprising them with original interpretations, such as a redheaded or sensual Cinderella or a black prince.

Because the texts offer very few details on the outer appearance of the characters, the illustrators are given the full freedom to fill in the gaps. A detailed investigation of the visual language makes clear that the way they visualize the fairy tale depends on shared stylistic conventions, rather than on personal style, although there is a clear evolution over time.

Initially, conventions are overwhelmingly present and most illustrators fall back on the same clichés. Most of the Dutch editions of Mother Goose before 1850 make use of the engraving of Simon Fokke from the first Dutch edition of 1754, showing Cinderella at the royal ball. In these illustrations, the emphasis is much more on the setting than on the expression of the characters.

After 1850 the personal style of the illustrator gains in importance, although the clichés persist. Not only do the same scenes recur time and again, but also the same attributes, settings, and postures: Cinderella near the fireplace with kettle and broom, helping her sisters, or lowering her gaze in the presence of the prince. Around 1880, in an increasing number of books, Cinderella is rendered in a sweeter and more childlike fashion. Both clichés of the modest and childlike Cinderella remain extremely powerful up until the present day and are insisted upon by commercial, international publishing houses especially. In doing so, the illustrators use figuration and expression, contrasting colors and visual symbols to strengthen stereotypical images of modesty, gallantry, or vanity. In order to ridicule this last vice, caricatures are often used. The first ones pop up at the end of the twentieth century, but even today, these funny distortions are a popular means to ridicule pride.

Around 1900 artists increasingly leave their stamp on the fairy tales, making a more frequent use of illustrative, formal, and graphic means in order to evoke emotions and create a specific atmosphere. There are manifest influences from various aesthetic movements, such as the British arts and crafts movement and the German *Kunsterziehungsbewegung* (De Bodt and Kapelle 2003; Van Coillie 2007, 22–24). Willy Schermelé (1943) and Froukje van der Meer (1944) are the first to achieve a real dialogue between text and illustrations, experimenting with lettering and decorative edges, mixing text and illustrations, or using speed lines. Nevertheless, these innovative illustrators, too, stick to the old clichés, focusing on Cinderella as a good housewife, a modest girl, and a helpful sister.

Since the end of the twentieth century more and more illustrators, experimenting with new techniques, deliberately contradict or simply do away with the clichés. First, parodies appear, such as *Prins Assepoets* (*Prince Cinders*) by the British illustrator Babette Cole (1992). Later on, artistic editions are published that offer alternative and often confronting interpretations.

The present study shows that the illustrated Cinderellas are indeed cultural texts, determined by and transferring culture-specific values. The ever-recurring clichés endorse the strength of the ideologies on which they are based, by materializing frames and images. The vast majority of the illustrations continue to reinforce the central message that humility and modesty will eventually be rewarded. As such they play a manifest role in the socialization of children, supporting the middle-class ideology in which virtue plays a central role.

From 1880 onward a change occurs, when the texts and illustrations are adapted to a new child image. The educational function becomes much less prominent, whereas the divertive and emotive functions gain in importance. Humor and caricature advance, together with sweetness and sentimentality. This child image is in line with new pedagogical ideas, promoted by the *Vom Kinde Aus* movement. By portraying the characters as children, their innocence is highlighted and violence and sensuality are banned.

Only in recent years illustrations have appeared that really shake the foundations of the predominant frames. Offering an image completely different from the popular clichés, they question the stereotypes and ideologies of which they are implicitly supportive. By picturing the prince in ordinary clothes, Heymans undermines his absolute power. By drawing him while he lovingly carries Cinderella in his arms, Thé offers a different perspective on the relation between man and woman than before. Sebastiaan Van Doninck most strongly unsettles the long-established frames: by depicting the prince as a black man, he confronts his public with their Western preconceptions.

At the beginning of the story, Cinderella is in dust and ashes. Provided illustrators go on granting her new looks and apparel in times to come, she will continue to rise from these ashes afresh like a fairy-tale phoenix.

Notes

1. "Les images dans notre tête qui médiatisent notre rapport au réel. Il s'agit des représentations toutes faites, des schèmes culturels préexistants, à l'aide desquels chacun filtre la réalité ambiante."
2. In the references, I mention the illustrator or "anonymous" if the illustrator is unknown.
3. This version is based on a theater performance of the fairy tale by Oscar Carré, played entirely by children (Buijnsters and Buijnsters-Smets 2001, 274).
4. *Cindercleana or Humility Rewarded.*
5. "Een nedrig kind ziet zich bemind."
6. "Deze waren verschrikkelijk trots en ijdel." (All translations of quotations in the text are my own.)
7. "Nu was er niet zoveel voor nodig om er mooier uit te zien dan Rosa en Agniet. De twee meisjes waren erg lelijk. Rosa had een dikke pukkel op haar neus en Agniet had twee enorme flaporen."
8. "Mooi waren ze, die twee dochters, ze hadden een blanke huid en blauwe ogen, maar in hun harten zag het er niet zo mooi uit. Van binnen waren ze zwart en slecht."

9. "Dus lieve meisjes! weest ook gij / Zoo needrig, lief en zacht als zij."
10. "De boze stiefmoeder en haar dochters vroegen om vergiffenis, ze hadden berouw over hun onaardige gedrag. Assepoester vergaf het hun en zo kwam alles weer goed."
11. "De stiefzusters waren woedend! Zij stampvoetten op de grond en de stiefmoeder werd knalrood. Maar Assepoester lachte. Zij werd gauw naar het paleis gebracht. De prins sloeg zijn armen om haar heen en kuste haar en zei: 'Jij wordt mijn vrouw.' En ze leefden nog lang en gelukkig."

References

Amossy, Ruth, and Anne Herschberger-Pierrot. 1997. *Stéréotypes et clichés: Langue, discours, société*. Paris: Editions Nathan.

Anonymous. [ca. 1851]. *Nieuwe gedichtjes op de vertellingen van moeder de Gans* Gedichtjes van Jan Schenkman. Amsterdam: G. Theod. Bom.

Anonymous. [1861]. *Oude sprookjes opnieuw verteld*. Tekst van J. J. A. Goeverneur. Schiedam: H. M. Roelants.

Anonymous. 1875. *Asschepoetster of Nederigheid beloond*. Text by S. J. Andriessen. Utrecht: I. de Haan.

Anonymous. [ca. 1875]. *Asschepoester in het Cirque Carré*. Translated by Jan Schenkman. Amsterdam: G. Theod. Bom.

Anonymous. 1893. *Asschepoetster* (Agatha's pantomime prentenboeken; no. 1). Text by Agatha. Amsterdam: Jacs. G. Robbers.

Anonymous. 1904. *Asschepoetster*. Verteld door mevrouw Van Osselen-Van Delden. Amsterdam: Allert de Lange.

Anonymous. 1913. *Asschepoester*. Verteld door Anna van Gogh-Kaulbach. Amsterdam: Allert de Lange.

Anonymous. [ca. 1915]. *Liesje in het droomenland*. s.l.: s.n.

Anonymous. [ca. 1985]. *Assepoester*. Aartselaar. Zuidnederlandse Uitgeverij.

Anonymous. 1987. *Mijn mooiste Fabeltjesboek*. Tekst van Ciny Peppelenbosch. s.l. Hemma.

Asensio, Agusti. 1990. *Assepoester: Oude sprookjes opnieuw verteld*. Opnieuw verteld door Jennine Staring. Gorinchem: De Ruiter.

Blockerije, Jo. 1984. *Sprookjes van Grimm*. Vertaald door Annemiek Jansen. Aartselaar: Deltas/Zuidnederlandse Uitgeverij.

Bruna, Dick. 1966. *Assepoester*. Utrecht: Bruna.

Buijnsters, Piet J., and Leontine Buijnsters-Smets. 2001. *Lust en Leering: Geschiedenis van het Nederlandse kinderboek in de negentiende eeuw*. Zwolle: Waanders Uitgevers.

Burgers, Hein J., and G. Kroon. 1865. *Asschepoester: Een sprookje uit de oude doos*. Op rijm gebracht door Jan Pieter Heije. Amsterdam: J. H. & G. van Heteren.

Chretien, Sylvie. 1985. *Assepoester*. Tekst van Bruno de la Salle. Doornik: Casterman.

Cramer, Rie. 1916. *Sprookjes van moeder de Gans*. Opnieuw bewerkt door Christine Doorman. Utrecht: W. de Haan.

———. [1925]. *Assepoester*. Bewerkt door Rie Cramer. Utrecht: W. de Haan.

Cole, Babette. 1992. *Prins Assepoets*. Leuven: Davidsfonds/Infodok.

De Bodt, Saskia, and Jeroen Kapelle. 2003. *Prentenboeken: Ideologie en illustratie, 1890–1950*. Amsterdam: Ludion.

Doré, Gustave. 1890. *Vertellingen van Moeder de Gans*. Vertaald door Jan Schenkman. Nijmegen: Cohen.

Drupsteen, Wilhelmina. 1907. *Asschepoester: Het oude sprookje*. Amsterdam: D. Coene.

Fahr-Becker, Gabrielle. 1997. *Jugenstil*. Keulen: Könemann.

Fokke, Simon. 1754. *Contes de ma mére l'Oye: Vertellingen van Moeder de Gans*. Den Haag: Van Os.

Freyberger, Regina. 2009. *Märchenbilder—Bildermärchen: Illustrationen zu Grimms Märchen, 1819–1945*. Oberhausen: Athena.

Gheeraert, T. "De Doré à Perrault: Conférence de Tony Gheeraert." *La Page des Lettres*. Académie de Versailles, January 3, 2007. www.lettres.oc-versailles.fr/spip.php?article782, August 27, 2015.

Hauptman, Tatjana. 1993. *Het mooiste sprookjesboek*. Verzameld door Christian Strich. Vertaald door Nannie Nieland-Weits. Weert: Van Reemst.

Heuninck, Ronald. 1984. *De mooiste sprookjes voor het slapen gaan*. Verteld door Ingrid Nijkerk. Aartselaar: Deltas/Zuidnederlandse Uitgeverij.

Hoeksema, Daan. 1907. *Asschepoester*. Opnieuw verteld door Christine Doorman. Amsterdam: J. Vlieger.

Heymans, Annemie. 1982. *Oude Bekenden*. Naverteld door Nienke van Hichtum. Amsterdam: H. J. W. Becht.

Hollindale, Peter. 1988. "Ideology and the Children's Book." *Signal* 55: 3–22.

Holtrop, Aukje. 1989. "De kleine grote wereld—De werkelijkheid in het kinderboek." In *De hele Bibelebontse berg: De geschiedenis van het kinderboek in Nederland en Vlaanderen van de middeleeuwen tot heden*, edited by Harry Bekkering a.o., 437–58. Amsterdam: Querido.

Huens, J. C. 1950. *Assepoester en andere sprookjes van Perraul*. Ingeleid en verteld door Jeanne Cappe. Nederlandse tekst Gaby Monden. Doornik: Casterman.

Iser, Wolfgang. 1974. *The Implied Reader: Patterns of Communication in Prose Fiction from Bunyan to Beckett*. Baltimore: Johns Hopkins University Press.

Jean-Pol. 2009. *Assepoester*. Schelle: Studio 100.

Joosen, Vanessa. 2012. *Wit als sneeuw, zwart als inkt: De sprookjes van Grimm in de Nederlandstalige literatuur*. Tielt: LannooCampus.

Kress, Gunther R., and Theo Van Leeuwen. 1996. *Reading Images: The Grammar of Visual Design*. London: Routledge.

Lakoff, George. 2004. *Don't Think of an Elephant!: Know Your Values and Frame the Debate*. White River Junction, VT: Chelsea Green Publishing.

López, Ana María Rojo. 2002. "Applying Frame Semantics to Translation: A Practical Example." *Meta* 47 (3): 312–50.

McCallum, Robyn, and John Stephens. 2010. "Ideology and Children's Books." In *Handbook of Research on Children's and Young Adult Literature*, edited by S. A. Wolf, K. Coats, P. Encisco, and C. A. Jenkins, 359–71. London: Routledge.

Münzer, Adolf. 1905. *Asschepoester*. Artistieke prentenboeken. Amsterdam: Van Holkema & Warendorf.

Nauwelaerts, Kris. 2008. "De fascinatie voor het esthetische prentenboek." *Literatuur zonder leeftijd* 22 (7): 63–74.

Nikolajeva, Maria, and Carole Scott. 2001. *How Picture Books Work*. New York: Garland.

Otto, Svend. 1984. *Assepoester en andere sprookjes van Grimm*. Vertaald door L. M. Niskos. Rotterdam: Lemniscaat.

Parlevliet, Sanne. 2009. *Meesterwerken met ezelsoren: Bewerkingen van literaire klassiekers voor kinderen, 1850–1950*. Hilversum: Verloren.

Parsons, Elisabeth. 2011. "Ideology." In *Keywords for Children's Literature*, edited by Philip Nel and Lissa Paul, 113–16. New York: New York University Press.

Ramon, Juan Lopez. 1991. *Assepoester: Mijn mooiste sprookjes*. Aartselaar: Deltas/Zuidnederlandse uitgeverij.

Robins, Alexandra. 1998. "The Fairy-Tale Façade: Cinderella's Anti-Grotesque Dream." *Journal of Popular Culture* 32 (3): 101–15.

Schermelé, Willy. 1943. *Asschepoester*. s.l.: s.n.

Scott, Carol. 2011. "Frame-Making and Frame-Breaking in Picturebooks." In *New Directions in Picturebook Research*, edited by Teresa Colomer, Bettina Kümmerling-Meibauer, and Cecilia Silva-Díaz, 101–12. London: Routledge.

Seago, Karin. 2008. "Proto-Feminist Translation Strategies? A Case Study of 19th-Century Translations of the Grimm Brothers' Sleeping Beauty." In *New Trends in Translation and Cultural Identity*, edited by Micaela

Muñoz-Calvo, Carmen Buesa-Gómez, and M. Ángeles Ruiz-Moneva, 165–84. Newcastle: Cambridge Scholars Publishing.

Serafini, Frank. 2011. "Expanding Perspectives for Comprehending Visual Images in Multimodal Texts." *Journal of Adolescent and Adult Literacy* 54 (5): 342–50.

Stephens, John. 1992. *Language and Ideology in Children's Fiction*. New York: Longman.

Thé, Tjong-Khing. 1996. *Grootmoeder, wat heb je grote oren . . . Klassieke sprookjes, opnieuw verteld voor jonge kinderen door Jacques Vriens*. Houten: Van Holkema en Warendorf.

Van Coillie, Jan. 2007. *Leesbeesten en boekenfeesten: Hoe werken (met) kinder- en jeugdboeken*. Leuven: Davidsfonds/Infodok.

Van der Meer, Froukje. 1944. *Assepoes: Het oude sprookje*. Opnieuw verteld door Froukje van der Meer. 's-Gravenhage/Batavia: G. B. van Goor Zonen.

Van der Pol, Coosje. 2010. *Prentenboeken lezen als literatuur*. Delft: Eburon.

Van Doninck, Sebastiaan. 2012. *Het Grote Grimm Boek*. Vertaald door Kristien Dreesen. Tielt: Lannoo, 2012.

Van Nieuwenhoven, Wim. [1943]. *Assepoester*. Naverteld door A. D. Hildebrand. Naarden: A. Rutgers.

Vermeyen, Annemarie. 1985. "Die Illustrationen zu den Kinder- und Hausmärchen in deutschsprachigen Ausgaben der Jahre 1945–1984." In *Brüder Grimm Gedenken*, edited by Ludwig Denecke, 193–268. Marburg: Elwert.

Warner, Marina. 1994. *From the Beast to the Blonde: On Fairy Tales and Their Tellers*. London: Vintage.

15

Imagining a Polish Cinderella

Monika Woźniak

It is a truth universally acknowledged (by scholars) that Perrault's "Cendrillon" and the Brothers Grimm's "Aschenputtel," the two most influential literary incarnations of Cinderella, are not quite the same character, being a product of different cultures, historical periods, and literary traditions. However, once the heroine began her dazzling ascent as one of the most beloved fairy-tale characters in Western culture, her identity became a more problematic matter. While it would probably be correct to say that in contemporary popular culture Perrault's fairy-godmother/pumpkin/midnight/glass-slipper version is a winner over the Grimms' hazel-tree/gold slipper/cut-off-toes-and-heels version (bearing in mind that Disney's 1950 movie is based loosely on the French text), most people do not really know (or care) much about the original literary sources of the tale.

Besides the wealth of textual transformations, there is an influential iconographic tradition related to them to consider. Starting with modest black-and-white vignettes, illustrations have enriched fairy tales since the very beginning of the publishing history of children's books, gradually gaining a more prominent role. While fairy tales definitely began their career in children's literature as text-centered stories, in which the illustrations played mostly a complementary or additional role, over time the dynamics of power between text and image have changed considerably. As both Perrault's and the Grimms' versions of Cinderella became the basis of more retellings, often freely merging elements and motifs from the two versions, visual repetition of key moments of the story—such as the escape of the heroine from the ball—embedded them in the popular imaginary and led to the consolidation of "signature pictures" (Cullen 2003) immediately and universally associated with Cinderella even out of the direct context of the tale. This process, already initiated in the second half of the nineteenth century, became even more pronounced with the massive development of picture-oriented children's books in the twentieth century, and in fact, as an icon of popular culture today, the Cinderella story seems to be based on visual rather than textual motifs, with the Disney movie and its innumerable by-products as the principal point of reference.[1] This chapter's aim, however, is not to examine general characteristics of the creation and evolution of the tale's iconographic wealth but rather to analyze its local, Polish variant in order to discover how visual representations of Cinderella may have influenced the reception of the tale in Poland and to see how and for what reasons they departed from consolidated international trends.

The Polish Visual Code in the Context of National History

There are numerous elements to be taken into consideration when examining a particular tale's visual representation in a particular cultural context. First of all, it is important to verify when and in what version it first penetrated into a given country and what impact it made.[2] For example, Bluebird never became a popular tale in Poland, and an iconographic repertory of the story is almost nonexistent. Second, one has to bear in mind the dynamics of the children's book market over time and its target audience. Another factor to take into consideration is the influence of famous, internationally recognized illustrators, such as Gustave Doré or Edmund Dulac in the nineteenth century, as well as the attitude toward illustration as an art and its embodiment in national artistic tendencies and fashions. Finally, extratextual pedagogical and ideological issues that may appear in a particular political or historical situation also have an impact on illustrators' artistic choices.

Of utmost importance are the peculiar vicissitudes of the Polish reception of Cinderella. Virtually unknown in the eighteenth century except for the few cultivated readers who may have read it directly in French, the tale first arrived in Poland in the early nineteenth century in the form of Gioacchino Rossini's opera *La Cenerentola ossia La bontà in trionfo*,[3] which in 1828 was staged in Kraków (albeit in German) and in 1829 in Lviv and Warsaw (Sandelewski 1972). A variant of Cinderella had been included in the collected volumes of national folktales created by Józef Wójcicki (1837) and Antoni Gliński (1853). Gliński's *Bajarz polski* (The Polish Story Teller), very popular in the nineteenth century and still in the first half of the twentieth, had a strong influence not only on subsequent Polish adaptations of Cinderella but also on the first visual representations of the heroine.

A dynamic development of the children's book market in Poland in the last three decades of the nineteenth century resulted in the first publications of the "classic" Cinderella tale, in collected volumes of fairy tales and as separate booklets. The first such publications were mainly based on Perrault's version, but these stories, published under their Polish authors' names, cannot be classified as translations or even adaptations, but rather as free rewritings, mixing elements from Perrault, Grimm, and Gliński. A common trait of all these rewritings was a strong tendency to polonize the tale to a degree that could vary from a moderate insertion of some Polish-related details to a radical transplantation of the whole story into a Polish context. Given this steady trend, it is probably less surprising that the first (more or less) faithful translation[4] of Perrault's fairy tales into Polish, made by a well-known author of children's books, Hanna Januszewska, appeared in Poland no sooner than 1961. Furthermore, it gained little favor with the reading public, and was soon overshadowed by a more liberal adaptation proposed by the same writer in 1968 (see Woźniak 2013).

The Grimms' name began to be associated with the Cinderella tale in Poland in the 1890s, but this does not mean that what was presented as the "Brothers Grimm" Cinderella was indeed a translation of the German text. Although marginally closer to the original source than earlier rewritings, these versions of the tale can at best be called adaptations. The only conscientious translation of *Kinder- und Hausmärchen*, by Zofia Kowerska, was published in 1896, but it was a modest, scholarly edition with no illustrations, which reached a very limited audience and had almost no impact on the Grimms' reception in Poland. An extensive compilation created in the 1920s by Marceli Tarnowski (1924), which became for many decades the most popular Polish version of the Grimms' tales, finally embraced the idea of translating (although without much philological rigor) rather than adapting the original texts, with one noticeable exception: that of Cinderella, which in the Tarnowski version seems more a fanciful variation on Perrault's plot than anything remotely related to the Grimms' tale. As a result, a text-based translation of "Aschenputtel" appeared in Poland only in 1956, in the first Polish postwar collection of the Grimms' *Märchen*.[5] Surprising as it may seem, up to the present day not a single critical edition of Perrault's or the Grimms' work has been published in Poland, and although recently rigorous translations of both versions of the tale finally became available,[6] it seems unlikely that they could indeed change the idea of Cinderella embedded in the Polish popular imagination on the basis of countless polonized versions of the tale.

This situation obviously had a huge impact on the development of the visual representation of Cinderella in Poland, especially in the context of other important extratextual factors, such as the low economic profile of the early Polish children's book market. The modest financial means of the first Polish publishing houses specializing in children's books, such as Arct (founded in 1887), and a limited demand for more luxurious editions, induced the publishers to cut down on costs and search for the cheapest solutions. A widespread practice was to buy inexpensive and colorful, if trivial, German illustrations and include them in the books, with no particular care taken regarding the correlation between text and image (Dunin 1991). It was a practice dictated purely by commercial interests, and initially Polish publishers were neither interested nor prosperous enough to invest in more sophisticated, artistic editions. The situation began to change at the beginning of the twentieth century, as a result of a growing demand for children's literature and an increasing general interest in the artistic potential of book illustrations among readers and artists alike (Lee 2007): the exhibition of printing art in 1904 in Kraków and the exhibition *Sztuka w życiu dziecka* (Art in the Life of the Child) in Warsaw in 1908 became a turning point in the history of Polish illustration for children.

This awakening of attention to the importance of good quality illustrations in children's books did not lead, however, to a significant boost in the importation of foreign works. On the contrary, criticism of imported illustrations, perceived as alien to Polish culture and spirit, resulted in a strong postulate for creating a national school of illustration, aimed specifically at the (perceived) needs and mentality of the Polish child (Lee 2007, 44–45). This tendency remained steady over the following decades and gave rise to the development of a highly original Polish school of children's illustration, which would flourish in the 1920s and 1930s, reaching its peak in the 1960s and 1970s. Although in the early decades of the twentieth century some publishers (in particular Jakub Mortkowicz, founded in 1903) occasionally risked printing sumptuous editions of fairy tales adorned by the illustrations of internationally recognized artists such as Dulac or Rackham, their impact was rather limited.

The predominance of Polish illustrations became even more absolute after World War II. Under communist rule the state took exclusive control of the publishing industry, pushing forward editorial choices compatible with the ideological and pedagogical ideas the regime promoted. For these and also for financial reasons foreign copyrighted illustrations would rarely be used in Polish children's books, with the exception of some classics, such as Tenniel's drawings for *Alice in Wonderland* or Shepard's *Winnie-the-Pooh* images. La Fontaine's *Fables* had several reprints with Doré's and Granville's out-of-copyright illustrations, but the visual representation of classic fairy tales, both radical retellings and more conventional adaptations and translations, was entrusted predominantly to Polish artists, who often continued stylistic practices initiated in the earlier period. The trend to draw inspiration from folk motifs, very visible in general (and children's) Polish book art in the 1920s and 1930s, was indeed encouraged and looked upon with much favor by publishing authorities. As a result the iconographic polonization of canonical fairy-tale characters such as Cinderella was further strengthened, also thanks to the excellent quality of many of the illustrations. In fact, children's book art became appealing to numerous eminent artists who found that it gave them more freedom of expression than other, more heavily censored, fields of creativity. The artistic originality of the Polish school of illustration was recognized internationally and resulted in many prestigious foreign awards for Polish illustrators. In the 1970s and 1980s the quality of illustration art declined slightly, due mainly to the general financial crisis of publishing houses and also their reluctance to accept new book art forms such as picture books, but it was the end of the communist regime in 1989 that brought radical change by opening Poland to the free market and the commercialization of the book industry. In the 1990s, the arrival of Disney movies and merchandising initiated the inevitable process (occurring much earlier in other European countries) of the Disneyfication of popular fairy-tale characters, Cinderella among them, in the collective imagination. The rapid growth of private publishing houses also resulted in the massive import of cheap foreign prints and bland, low-quality illustrations. However, in recent years the children's book market in Poland seems to have found a new, better balanced publishing policy, in which mass-market commercial publications coexist with more ambitious artistic projects.

The importance of the factors mentioned above emerges very clearly when we examine Polish representations of Cinderella, and they must all be borne in mind when analyzing particular characteristics of the tale's iconographic tradition in Poland.

Principal Components of Cinderella's Iconographic Tradition

Several aspects of Cinderella's visual canon are worth considering when we examine its creation and development. For instance, which scenes from the tale do the illustrators most frequently choose? It is only logical to expect that the scenes perceived as most representative, important, or emotionally engaging would be chosen. The process of selection may not be so crucial today, when e-books, apps, picture books, and single tale editions include numerous images, but it mattered more in times when a tale would be accompanied by few illustrations, often no more than one or two. The visual tradition of Cinderella usually skipped the beginning of the story, generally choosing an image of "poor Cinderella" as the opening illustration. Other favorite scenes included the magical transformation of the heroine (thanks to the intervention of the fairy godmother in Perrault and the magical tree in Grimm), the ball, the escape from the palace, and finally the trying on of the shoe, which often concluded the visual narrative of the tale. This is not to say that no one has ever tried to depict other moments of the story, such as the wedding of Cinderella or the evil sisters' preparations for the ball, but images of this kind are less frequent, while some scenes, such as the dying mother (in the Grimm version) talking to the heroine, or Cinderella being nice to her stepsisters during the ball, are practically absent from the visual code. Interestingly, while some of the images may be indicative as to which variant (Grimms' or Perrault's)[7] of the tale they refer to, more frequently they are not specific enough to make an immediate identification easy or indeed possible. It is, therefore, only logical to consider the emergence of the iconographic tradition of Cinderella as an important factor in the transformation of the heroine's identity to one that is image related rather than text related.

The solidification of Cinderella's visual tradition also involved the composition of canonical scenes from the tale. Naturally, the patterns of representation were changeable, up to a point; for example, early depictions of "poor Cinderella" often featured the girl sitting by the fire with her mocking stepsisters standing nearby, while subsequently it became more popular to show her alone. Some elements, however, such as Cinderella losing her slipper while running down a huge staircase, became universal and permanent, to the point of assuming the role of iconic symbol of the tale in popular culture.

The most complex and interesting aspect of Cinderella's iconographic tradition is the content of the images. Issues of interest include, among others, such questions as sex, gender, age, ethnicity, nationality, religion, ideals of beauty, clothing, and geotemporal setting. They are, however, less subject to standardization than the other components of the tale's visual patterns. In fact, they not only depend greatly on evolving aesthetic and ideological trends as well as on a variety of factors related to the immediate cultural context in which the illustrations are created, but also on the individual artistic preferences of a given illustrator. In any case, to wonder how a given issue has been addressed is not the only question worth asking while analyzing the content of Cinderella illustrations; another matter, at least as interesting, is whether it has been addressed at all in the context of a given national culture and literature.

Cinderella à la polonaise

Although the iconographic tradition of Cinderella in Poland encompasses a much shorter time span than in many other countries—beginning effectively only in the early twentieth century—over the decades it has undergone changes and variations that reflect the impact of external factors mentioned in the first part of this essay. However, since the aim of this chapter is to examine characteristics of Polish visual patterns of the tale as opposed to its images recurring on an international level, I will focus on persistent general trends in Poland, leaving aside a detailed diachronic survey. The corpus of tales examined for the purposes of this survey included all retrievable (several older prints, especially from the nineteenth and early twentieth century are sadly lost) single-tale editions and a majority of the tale collections that include the text of Cinderella,[8] up to 1989. As for the last two decades, the exponential growth of mass-market editions of fairy tales and the emergence of small private publishing houses with a very restricted distribution range, combined with a lack of exhaustive bibliographic data, has made it impossible to survey all the publications, therefore attention has been given primarily to the editions aspiring to quality and illustrated by Polish artists. On the whole, nearly one hundred illustrated Cinderella tales have been consulted, spanning from the 1890s up to the beginning of the 1910s.[9]

When considering three fundamental elements of the Polish iconographic tradition of Cinderella—selection, composition, and the contents of the images[10]—it is content where the peculiarity of the tale's visual representation is most evident. The selection and composition of images usually do not differ much from the general iconographic patterns, although they do bring some surprises. A few more unusual choices drew inspiration from radical retellings or adaptations, which were particularly frequent in the first half of the twentieth century. For example, a quite surprising image of the prince fighting a dragon for Cinderella's lost slipper refers to Janina Porazińska's *Kopciuszek* (Cinderella, 1929), a tale in verse that sees the heroine transplanted to medieval Poland, while Jan Marcin's (Szancer) version (1935, text and illustrations by the author) shows the stepsisters getting a perm at a hairdresser's. Nevertheless, most illustrators followed the conventional visual sequence, which includes poor Cinderella (alone or bullied by her stepmother)—mean stepsisters—magical transformation—ball—escape—trying on the slipper. This tendency became more and more marked over time, once the established cliché of Cinderella's visual representation came to be more widespread in Poland, especially since the beginning of the 1990s, when the Polish book market yet again was flooded with cheap

Janina Porazińska, *Kopciuszek* (1929), illustration by Stanisław Bobiński.

illustrations imported from other countries, especially from Italy. Despite this, unexpected images still occasionally pop up, such as Cinderella's father falling to his death from a horse in a recent, otherwise rather conventional retelling by Simon Messing, illustrated by Małgorzata Flis (2009).

The composition of the Polish pictures is usually conventional. The variations of the "poor Cinderella" introductory illustration show her alone in the kitchen or at the fireplace, with her stepmother ordering her around, or with her stepsisters intent on dilly-dallying while she is at work. All these images are part of the general iconographic tradition of the tale, as indeed are the most frequent takes on magical transformation in Polish books, which opt for Cinderella obtaining the dress from the tree (the Grimm variant), or, in Perrault-based adaptations, show a preference for the appearance of the fairy godmother in front of the crying heroine and the transformation of the pumpkin into a coach. The ball scenes generally focus on the iconic moment of the heroine's arrival or on her dance with the prince. There are, however, a few exceptions; for example, in Antoni Gawiński's "Kopciuszek" (1928, based on Perrault's version), the author and illustrator of the tale chooses to show Cinderella and the prince enjoying their dinner rather than dancing. Likewise, the trying on of the slipper illustrations dutifully follow the popular iconographic pattern, with the heroine sitting in the center, a messenger (or the prince himself) kneeling in front of her to put the slipper on, and the two disappointed or furious sisters in the background. The only particularity about the composition of Polish Cinderella illustrations concerns the escape scene, which often lacks the portentous staircase, so prominently featured in the tale's traditional visual canon (but then the escape scene is quite frequently omitted altogether in early Polish editions). One can only wonder whether this aversion could possibly have something to do with Polish architectural style, which has traditionally been horizontally oriented and has never cultivated a taste for grand staircases. The staircase does begin to appear more often in Polish Cinderellas from the 1970s, evidently under the influence of the international iconographic tradition, but even today it is not an obligatory element of Polish illustrations.

However, as mentioned above, it is the contents of the illustrations where the specificity of the Polish visual tradition of the tale manifests itself most clearly, in the selection of motifs and in the way they are presented. For example, Polish Cinderellas do not tackle a number of content-related matters, which have become increasingly important in visual representations in other countries. The issues of species, ethnicity, race, and gender are practically nonexistent in Polish visualizations of the tale. The fashion for intercultural (or multicultural?) Cinderellas has yet to arrive in Poland: other than Egyptian variant *Pantofelek pięknej Rodopis* (Fairy Rodopis's slipper, 1966) there have been no editions of Jamaican, American, Cambodian, Persian, or Middle Eastern Cinderellas, as can be found on the book market of many European countries. Poland still lacks animal or male Cinderellas[11] as well. Gender issues are also rarely addressed in Polish retellings of the tale, although in 2006 a very amusing version by Michał Rusinek (2006) appeared, which presents Cinderella as a frivolous bimbo, completely taken with tabloids and gossip press (in contrast to her serious stepsisters) whose fan girl infatuation with the rich son of a shady businessman almost brings her to a bad end. The illustrations for the book, by Małgorzata Bieńkowska, cleverly convey the erosion of the Cinderella myth by uniting "infantile" drawings with pieces from actual tabloids in a collage technique.[12]

In short, in many respects the Polish approach to the tale seems quite traditionalist. The lasting specificity of the Polish image of Cinderella stems, in fact, from two visual components: the strategy of presenting the heroine and the spatiocultural anchorage of the tale.[13] They took shape in an early phase of development of the tale's Polish iconography, and in spite of the growing standardization of Cinderella's image due to the influence of global visual clichés, are still at least mostly valid today.

The introductory illustrations of "poor Cinderella," which are as typical of the Polish visual narrative as they are of the international one, may seem in line with the general pattern concerning their function to show the hardships and sufferings of the heroine. There is, however, one substantial difference. The overwhelming majority of "poor Cinderella" images, from the oldest eighteenth-century vignettes to Ludwig Emil Grimm, from Gustave Doré to Edmund Dulac, Gustaf Tenggren, and up to the present day, show the heroine as *sitting* by the fireplace or in the kitchen, in illustrations of the Grimm version usually surrounded by pigeons or feeding them, more often than not just staring wistfully into the distance, her whole pose conveying that the housework is the last of her worries. While this image can claim to be true to the text of the tale, given that Perrault mentions that Cinderella "sat down in the cinders and ashes" by the chimney corner, and the Grimms write that she "had to sleep by the hearth in the ashes," both tales also emphasize that she used to do so after having done "hard work from morning until evening." By leaving aside the labor aspect,[14] the illustrators create an impression of a dreamy, languid girl, and this choice undoubtedly had a significant impact on the notion of Cinderella as a passive heroine, which would became so deeply fixed in the collective imagination.

By contrast, in the Polish tradition it is almost impossible to find an illustration of an idle Cinderella. The heroine is always busy and working hard: carrying water from the river, scrubbing the floor, looking after the cattle, carrying logs for the fire, or spinning. This last choice, frequent in older illustrations, is particularly interesting, because of the symbolism attached to the spindle and the activity of spinning, seen as the traditional occupation of a virtuous woman. In early twentieth-century illustrations, the insistence on the image of Cinderella as a hard-working girl was consistent

A typical Polish country manor in Hanna Januszewska's *Kopciuszek* (1987). Illustration by Bożena Truchanowska.

with the character of the adaptations they were related to. In fact, the majority of Polish retellings of the tale transformed the heroine into a peasant girl, living in a village. Antoni Gliński's story "O dziewicy Kopciuszku i o dębie złotolistnym" (1853, About virgin Cinderella and the golden oak leaves) from *Bajarz polski*, stylized as a Polish folktale, was still popular at the beginning of the twentieth century, and even many adaptations of the Grimms' and Perrault's tale tended to add some national flavor to the narrative. While few rewritings openly transplanted the story to Poland (such as was the case of Janina Porazińska's 1929 version mentioned above), several minor shifts would lead to the embedding of the tale into a Polish cultural context and mentality. All these tendencies found their reflection in the visual representation of the tale. The heroine is no longer a girl of noble origins fallen into disgrace, but a humble peasant girl living in a cabin, or in the best of cases in a small country house typical of the Polish architectural style. Similarly, details and accessories that appear in illustrations evoke associations with Polish home interiors (such as wooden floors, cozy rooms, small windows, animal skins on the walls), habits, and ways of life. However, the most prominent facet and indication of the heroine's Polish connection are her clothes.

The visual tradition of the tale has not established a specific dress code for Cinderella, besides the evident contrast between her modest everyday garments and gorgeous ball gown. An obvious choice for Perrault's version is the French fashion of the late seventeenth century, and indeed early illustrations tended to respect this implication.[15] However, Dulac and Rackham opted for the powdered wigs of eighteenth-century France, the Dalziel brothers chose Spanish Renaissance fashion, and later the Disney film featured mid-1860s crinolines. There have been medieval, Renaissance, baroque, rococo, Empire, Biedermeier, art nouveau, and art deco Cinderellas. Hardly any historical period has not been covered, although seventeenth- and eighteenth-century fashion seems dominant in illustrations of the Perrault version, while medieval costume, relatively less frequent, appears mainly in the Grimms' version of the tale. Then, of course, some illustrators, especially in modern times, do not always seek to be historically accurate and may mix the periods freely or go for creations born only from their imaginations (for example, in Arno's or Charlotte Gastaux's recent illustrations).

In Poland, the heroine's dress is usually modeled on the way Cinderella has been portrayed in early Polish adaptations. Transforming Cinderella into a poor village girl obviously implied showing her in peasant garments, but Polish traditional dress has acquired a marked ideological meaning over centuries, becoming since the nineteenth century a symbol of cultural and national identity.[16] It is not rare, therefore, to find an explicit mention of Cinderella's arriving at the ball in a national costume, or in "barwisty wieśniaczy strój" ("a colorful peasant dress," Jeżewska 1950, 12) as opposed to the other girls "bewitched by the foreign fashion" (Gensówna 1919, 6). The symbolism of the heroine's choice of dress is underscored by the powerful intertextual relation to the Polish national epic, *Pan Tadeusz* (1834), by Adam Mickiewicz. In his famous work, the author had his young heroine of noble origin, Zosia, refuse to dress in a fashionable outfit in favor of "wieśniaczy strój" (peasant dress) for her engagement party, emphasizing the unambiguous patriotic message of this choice.[17] The implications for the meaning of a similar preference in Polish Cinderella adaptations are quite clear, but just in case a distracted reader should miss them, some authors elucidate them even more plainly, for example by adding an interior monologue for the prince, who is wondering "Mam dziś żonę obrać sobie, / ale która będzie dobrą / dla narodu mego matką?" ("I need to choose my wife today / but which one will be a good / mother for my people?" Porazińska 1947, 26). As a result Cinderella became an incarnation of Polish female virtue: moral, responsible, caring, hard working, and patriotic, her beauty decidedly a secondary asset. Logically, the depiction of the stepsisters stressed not so much their mean behavior, pride, or ugliness (although they are invariably ugly in Polish adaptations), but their laziness. Accordingly, illustrations tended to show them spread on a sofa, sleeping, eating cakes, or simply yawning.

Polonization is less noticeable in the depiction of the prince and the castle. In Porazińska's *Kopciuszek* there is an explicit mention of Wawel—the royal castle of Kraków that was dutifully shown in various editions of the tale, while in the 1974 edition of Ewa Szelburg-Zarembina's "Kopciuszek," a lovely illustration by Jan Marcin Szancer shows the renaissance castle of Pieskowa Skała, but generally the prince's residence, if it appeared at all, tended to be presented in a generic fairy-tale-like fashion (with lots of turrets and spires). The prince himself sometimes was styled as a Polish nobleman in a *kontusz18* (Kawecka [1925]; Gawiński 1928; Jeżewska 1950), but more often than not he was presented just as a standard version of a fairy-tale prince charming, interchangeable with similar figures from Snow White, Sleeping Beauty, or other tales that involve a handsome male character of noble origin.

Although the postwar period saw a gradual shift from national adaptations toward more standardized versions of Cinderella (the last reprint of Porazińska's popular *Kopciuszek* dates to 1964) included in the Grimms' (1956) and Perrault's (1971) collections of tales,[19] some visual tendencies that early illustrations established turned out to be lasting, outliving their textual counterparts. A certain propensity to add a touch of "Polishness" to the heroine's surroundings is evident even today. Although Cinderella ceased to be presented as a peasant girl, and is no longer shown carrying buckets of water or logs for the fire (it is more likely that she is using a vacuum cleaner or washing the dishes), she has never regained her high social extraction from the original texts. Accordingly, Cinderella's house and all its contents usually still have a cozy and familiar look typical of the Polish decorative style. The same may be said about the heroine, at least as far as her "poor Cinderella" incarnation goes (the ball gown, once the issue of national costume faded away, became comfortably generic, not bound to a definite historical period fashion). Most important, however, is the fact that the contrast between the hard-working Cinderella and her lazy stepsisters is still underscored. As a result, even in contemporary iconography the heroine seems closer to the Polish model of the virtuous and laboring female than to the triumph of the sweet blond beauty glorified by Disney.

Conclusion

Considered on its own, the Polish visual code of the tale mirrors a complex approach to the story. Poland has not created its own national Cinderella

A peasant Cinderella goes to the ball at Pieskowa Skała Castle (Jan Marcin Szancer, 1974).

folk story, such as the Russian "Vasilisa the Beautiful," but instead has expansively appropriated the classic tale: even Antoni Gliński's "O dziewicy Kopciuszku," stylized as a Polish folktale, is in fact a free variation on the Grimms' version of the story (in Gliński 1924 [1853]). Similarly, Polish illustrators did not depart from the basic plotline, but brought it nearer to the national taste and mentality. Also, while the tendencies present in Polish retellings and adaptations of Cinderella had undoubtedly influenced the patterns of the heroine's visual representation, a complicated juxtaposition of several exterior circumstances—national, political, and other—seems to have had at least as much importance in the creation of the tale's iconographic tradition. What is more, the visual code outlasted the strategies of the textual adaptations. Even when nationally orientated retellings began to give way to more conventional Cinderella stories, illustrations continued to favor a Polish-like representation of the heroine and her surroundings, influencing, in turn, the way in which they are described in Perrault's and the Grimms' adaptations in Polish. For example, it became customary in Polish texts to refer to Cinderella's house as a "small cottage" or "little house" and to describe the heroine as "industrious" in addition to her other virtues.

Considered within the larger context of the recurring traits of the international iconographic tradition of the tale, the Polish way of representing Cinderella appears old-fashioned in some aspects while original and innovative in others. A patriotically oriented publishing policy at the turn of the nineteenth and twentieth centuries and the isolation in which the children's book market in Poland developed between 1945 and 1989 had both negative and positive consequences. On the negative side, a reluctance to experiment with different types of interactions and layouts between text and image should be noticed. Interactive prints, such as pop-ups, panorama, or theater books were remarkably rare, although not unknown, on the Polish book market, both before and after World War II.[20] As far as publications for small children are concerned, they have followed the traditional layout of illustrated books rather than picture books, and have rarely ventured into any unusual interplay between text and image. This conservative approach has been particularly evident in fairy-tale illustrations. On the other hand, Polish artists, unencumbered by any competition from the Disney influence and the foreign mass market, had the unique opportunity to develop their own individual style and interpretation of the tales. In the case of Cinderella, excellent artistic quality and the splendor of images created by such illustrators as Jan Marcin Szancer, Janusz Grabiański, and Bożena Truchanowska had a lasting impact on the young audience[21] and effectively contributed to the appropriation of the tale by the Polish culture.

After the political turn of 1989 brought the isolation of Polish children's illustrative art to an end, the situation changed radically. A plethora of colorful foreign illustrations and Disney-inspired mass-market products flooding the bookshops sidelined the earlier iconographic tradition and imposed new trends and conventions. One noticeable effect of this earthquake in the publishing industry was an accelerated standardization of textual and visual representations of most popular tales, Cinderella included. Some remnants of the Polish visual code of the tale still resist this tendency, but one has to wonder how long they will last against the inexorable progress of globalization.

Recently, however, positive aspects of the transformation of the children's book industry in Poland have also become more visible. Direct access to international trends and printing concepts encouraged Polish artists to try out new approaches to books for children and experiment with possible interactions between text and image. Furthermore, more and more publishing houses are developing an interest in innovative and original projects and are becoming more willing to undertake the risk of releasing experimental, sophisticated publications for a young audience. Although classic fairy tales seem to remain on the margins of these new trends, at least for now, and collective volumes that include Cinderella, as well as editions of the individual tale, still duly follow the traditional formula of illustrated text,[22] there are some signals that the situation could change. Beside the irreverent *Kopciuszek* by Michał Rusinek, mentioned above, there has been another very interesting take on Cinderella, proposed by the patriarch of Polish illustrators for children, Bohdan Butenko (Butenko 2008). In this version, the characters are coerced into fulfilling their canonical roles by the nagging fairy godmother. The author, who both wrote and illustrated the tale, engages the reader in a kind of metatextual dialogue, by commenting on the expected development of the plot and its triviality, mixing characters from different tales, changing protagonists' motivations, and making them self-aware that they are literary creations. The illustrations, which appear as a juxtaposition of different styles and techniques, develop a dynamic interaction with the text, underlining its eclectic, postmodern character.

To sum up, today's Polish iconographic tradition of Cinderella is clearly in a phase of transition, gradually abandoning its marked national traits and searching for new solutions and concepts. It is still too early to say whether in the future it will be able to retain its culturally specific character. However, given that Bohdan Butenko, one of the oldest active illustrators for children in Poland (born in 1931), was still able to surprise readers with a new conceptual approach to the textual and visual tradition of the

Interaction between text and image in Bohdan Butenko's "Kapciuszek" (2008). Courtesy of the author.

well-known tale, perhaps artists of younger generations will also be able to give a new, unique look to the Polish Cinderella.

Notes

1. The deep impact of Disney's 1950 *Cinderella* is discussed at length in the introductory essay to this volume.
2. For example, in Italy, Perrault's *Cendrillon*, translated by Carlo Lorenzini (Collodi) in 1872 and reprinted frequently in the following decades, in some cases with Gustave Doré's illustrations, had gained a neat advantage on Grimm's variant, first published and translated, partially, only in 1896. This fact was also reflected in the iconographic tradition of the tale.
3. The libretto, by Jacopo Ferretti, is loosely based on Perrault's tale.

4. In fact, the very concept of a "faithful" translation is problematic, and by certain standards Januszewska's version doesn't qualify as one because of its rather liberal approach to semantically loaded terms such as "douceur," "grâce," or "humeur" and even more so because of its particular historical stylization, which gives it a flavor of the typical Polish literary style of the eighteenth century.
5. In fact, even this translation was not completely faithful to the letter of the original text, since it had been based on a censored DDR edition from 1954, which, in the case of Cinderella, cut out the final four sentences of the tale (Cinderella's wedding and the stepsisters having their eyes pecked out by pigeons).
6. A new collection of the Grimms' tales published by Media Rodzina in 2009 and 2010, in the translation of Eliza Pieciul-Karmińska and a volume of Perrault's tales by Barbara Grzegórzewska, issued by Librone in 2010; both editions are aimed at a child audience.
7. Naturally, the German iconographic tradition of Cinderella would be mainly related to the Grimms' variant, while French illustrations almost exclusively developed depictions of Perrault's tale.
8. Illustrations of Cinderella are not to be found in all fairy-tale collections, even if the tale is included in the volume; on the other hand, sometimes illustrations in the reprints released by the same publishing house may differ, which makes creating a complete repertory of images complicated.
9. Only the editions quoted in the text have been included in the references list.
10. There are other issues that could be addressed in an analysis of Cinderella's iconographic tradition in Poland, such as techniques used in illustrations, chromatic preferences, layout of the text and image on the page, and so on. They are, however, less pertinent to the matter of culturally specific characteristics of the tale's visual patterns, and are therefore not considered in this analysis.
11. The only "masculine" take on Cinderella I have been able to find is an episode from the popular animated series about two boys *Bolek i Lolek* (1963–1986, English title: *Bennie and Lennie*). In the episode titled *Pantofelek Kopciuszka* (1971, Cinderella's slipper), Lennie masquerades as Cinderella at a costume party. Bennie falls for him thinking he is a girl, and when Lennie loses his (very big) slipper escaping from the party, Bennie searches for the mystery girl, only to discover in the end that he was a victim of his friend's joke.
12. See Bieńkowska's illustration included in Sandra Beckett's essay in this volume.

13. The modality of the heroine's representation may be considered a compositional issue, but since the two issues are strictly related, for the benefit of the analysis I decided to treat it as a content characteristic.
14. The few images that depict Cinderella at work, usually related to Perrault's version, show her sweeping the floor in a leisurely manner, combing her stepsisters' hair, or adjusting their dresses.
15. Perrault describes the fashionable ball gowns of both stepsisters in great detail, which is rather unusual in fairy tales.
16. The importance attributed to traditional dress is better understood when contemplated within the political context of the Poles' long struggle to preserve their national identity in the period between 1795 and 1918, when Poland was erased from political maps of Europe.
17. For the English translation of Mickiewicz's poem and the description of Zosia's dress, see (Mickiewicz 1917 [1834], 298–99), http://archive.org/stream/pantadeuszorlast00mick#page/298/mode/2up/search/let+us+love.
18. The *kontusz* was a long robe, usually reaching to below the knee, with a set of decorative buttons down the front. It was a traditional male garment worn by the Polish nobility since the sixteenth century.
19. Both volumes became very popular and had numerous reprints. Although not exactly a faithful translation (especially Perrault's tales, adapted by Hanna Januszewska) they were far closer to the original texts than previous retellings.
20. Some Vojtěch Kubašta pop-ups published in the 1960s and 1970s were practically the only interactive children's books ever published in Poland under communist rule (1945–89).
21. As testified by nostalgic opinions expressed on many Polish Internet forums, such as http://forum.gazeta.pl/forum/f,16375,Ksiazki_dzieciece_mlodziezowe.html or http://forum-ksiazki.kei.pl/index.php.
22. Interestingly, some recent collective fairy-tale volumes, especially those that claim to offer faithful translations of the Grimms' tales, have been published with old illustrations by Otto Ubbelohde (Grimm and Grimm 2010) or Philipp Grot Johann (Grimm and Grimm 2012).

References

Burlingham, Cynthia. 1997. *Picturing Childhood: The Evolution of the Illustrated Children's Book, Illustrated Children's Books from University of California Collections, 1550–1990.* https://archive.org/stream/picturingchildho00burl#page/n5/mode/2up.

Butenko, Bohdan. 2008. *Krulewna Śnieżka*. Illustrated by the author. Warsaw: Nasza Księgarnia.

Cullen, Bonnie. 2003. "For Whom the Shoe Fits: Cinderella in the Hands of Victorian Illustrators and Writers." *The Lion and the Unicorn* 27 (1): 57–82.

Dunin, Janusz. 1991. *Książeczki dla grzecznych i niegrzecznych dzieci: Z dziejów polskich publikacji dla najmłodszych*. Wrocław: Ossolineum.

Gawiński, Antoni. 1928. "Kopciuszek". In *Bajki Staroświeckie*. Illustrated by the author. Warsaw: Arct.

Gensówna, Franciszka. 1919. *Kopciuszek: Bajka na scenę w 7 odsłonach*. Warsaw: Brzeziński.

Gliński, Antoni Józef. 1924 [1853]. *Bajarz polski: Baśni, powieści i gawędy ludowe*. Illustrated Jerzy Hoppen. Vilnius: Lux.

Grimm, Jacob, and Wilhelm Grimm. 1930 [1924]. *Bajki*. Translated by Marceli Tarnowski. Łódź: Fiszer.

———. 1956. *Bajki*. Translated by Marceli Tarnowski. Illustrated by B. Truchanowska. Warsaw: Nasza Księgarnia.

———. 2010. *Baśnie dla dzieci i dla domu*. Translated by Elwira Pieciul-Karmińska. Illustrated by Otto Ubbelohde. Poznań: Media Rodzina.

———. 2012. *Wszystkie baśnie i legendy*. Translated by Róża Skiba (from Russian). Illustrated by Philipp Grot Johann. Warsaw: Rea.

Januszewska, Hanna. 1987 [1969]. *Kopciuszek*. Illustrated by Bożena Truchanowska. Warsaw: Nasza Księgarnia.

Jeżewska, Kazimiera. 1950. *Kopciuszek*. Illustrated by Eugenia Różańska. Kraków: Kot.

Kawecka, Zofia. [1925]. *Kopciuszek*. Illustrated by L. Perfecki. Kraków: Salon Malarzy Polskich.

Kopciuszek. 1973. Illustrated by Vojtěch Kubašta. Prague: Artia.

Lee, Jiwane. 2007. "Polska szkoła ilustracji." PhD thesis, Uniwersytet Adama Mickiewicza, Poznań.

Messing, Oscar. 2009. *Kopciuszek*. Illustrated by Małgorzata Flis. Kraków: Marketing Room Poland.

Mickiewicz, Adam. 1917 [1834]. *Pan Tadeusz; or, the Last Foray in Lithuania*. Translated by George Rapall Noyes. London: Dent.

Nikolajeva, Maria, and Carole Scott. 2006. *How Picturebooks Work*. London: Routledge.

Perrault, Charles. 1971. *Bajki*. Adapted by Hanna Januszewska. Illustrated by Janusz Grabiański. Warsaw: Nasza Księgarnia.

Porazińska, Janina. 1929. *Kopciuszek*. Illustrated by Stanisław Bobiński. Warsaw: Nasza Księgarnia.

———. 1947. *Kopciuszek*. Illustrated by Stanisław Bobiński. Warsaw: Nasza Księgarnia.

———. 1951. *Kopciuszek*. Illustrated by Ludwik Maciąg. Warsaw: Nasza Księgarnia.

Rusinek, Michał. 2006. *Kopciuszek*. Illustrated by Małgorzata Bieńkowska. Poznań: Santarski.

Sandelewski, Wiarosław. 1972. *Rossini*. Kraków: Polskie Wydawnictwo Muzyczne.

Schwarcz, Joseph H. 1982. *Ways of the Illustrator: Visual Communication in Children's Literature*. Chicago: American Library Association.

[Szancer], Jan Marcin. 1935. *Kopciuszek*. Illustrated by by the author. Warsaw: Arct.

Szelburg-Zarembina, Ewa. 1974. *Bardzo dziwne opowieści*. Illustrated by Jan Marcin Szancer. Lublin: Wydawnictwo Lubelskie.

Weinstein, Amy. 2005. *Once Upon a Time: Illustrations from Fables, Primers, Pop-Ups, and Other Children's Books*. New York: Princeton Architectural Press.

Wójcicki, Kazimierz. 1974 [1837]. *Klechdy, starożytne podania i powieści ludu polskiego i Rusi*. Warsaw: Państwowy Instytut Wydawniczy.

Woźniak, Monika. 2013. "When (and Where) Do You Live, Cinderella? Cultural Shifts in Polish Translations and Adaptations of Charles Perrault's Fairy Tales." In *Textual Transformations in Children's Literature: Adaptations, Translations, Reconsiderations*, edited by Benjamin Lefebvre, 87–100. New York: Routledge.

———. 2014. "Polishing the Grimms' Tales for a Polish Audience: *Die Kinder- und Hausmärchen*." In *Grimms' Tales around the Globe*, edited by Vanessa Joosen and Gillian Lathey, 39–58. Detroit: Wayne State University Press.

Zdzitowiecka, Hanna. 1966. *Pantofelek pięknej Rodopis*. Illustrated by Antoni Boratyński. Warsaw: Nasza Księgarnia.

16

Cinderella in Polish Posters

Agata Hołobut

Introduction

My essay presents an overview of posters designed in twentieth- and twenty-first-century Poland to advertise theater, opera, ballet, and film adaptations of the Cinderella tale. Working on the assumption that poster art employs graphic abbreviation to achieve maximum visual effect with minimal resources, I analyze pictorial metaphors and metonymies Polish designers use to convey an idea of *Cinderella-ness*, filtered through their individual sensitivities and reflecting the sociocultural atmosphere of the time.

In the first section I discuss the main functions of the art form and its evolution in Poland, focusing on the emergence of the Polish Poster School and its influence on contemporary design. I then outline a cultural background for my analysis, commenting on the variety of Cinderella adaptations in Polish opera venues, playhouses, and puppet theaters. The following sections present selected Cinderella posters, centered on social, personal, and finally metatextual aspects of the story. Inspired by different media (film, opera, ballet, puppet theater) and directed at specific groups of addressees (adults and children, respectively), these art forms offer rich iconological material that can be analyzed from different critical perspectives. The posters can be analyzed as intersemiotic transpositions of particular productions, adjusted to their audience through the techniques of design. Or they can be viewed as indicators of evolving artistic trends, marketing strategies, and ideological approaches to the subject matter. In the present article, however, my emphasis will be on the content of the works, treated as self-sufficient visual representations of the Cinderella story. Hence, their referential function, that is, their relation to specific literary and musical models, shall be treated as subsidiary to their imaginative function, that is, the posters' ability to reinterpret the tale visually and enrich its iconography. Put side by side, the examples feature a wide array of pictorial metaphors of social advancement, humility rewarded, and beauty triumphant. They also illustrate an intriguing evolution of metonymic representations of the heroine's adventures from glass slippers to detergents, feather dusters, and stilettos.

Functions of Poster Work

Allusive, alluring, and ephemeral, the event poster announces an upcoming performance, film, or concert and encapsulates its message, trying to attract the potential audience. It reveals artistic and ideological aspirations of the commissioning party (that is, theater producers, film distributors) and reflects the socio-aesthetic beliefs of the designer, documenting his/her interpretation of a given theme or aspect of the tale and its production. If successful, it also teases the brain and pleases the eye, combining utility with artistry.

In a word, the poster can perform all the functions distinguished by Roman Jakobson in his classical model of communication (Mathiot and Garvin 1975, 150). By definition, all posters are *phatic*, *conative*, and *referential*, because they aim at establishing contact, arousing the viewers' interest, and conveying information. Displayed in the street and noticed in passing, they must be eye-catching and communicate the message quickly, making an immediate but memorable impression (Ansell and Thorpe 1984, 7–8; Boczar 1984, 18). This power lies in a clever combination of verbal and visual imagery, the latter often dominated by metaphor, metonymy, or symbol.

Nonetheless, the poster is not only intended to transfix and inform. It also expresses the artist's attitude to the theme and its sociocultural context, revealing an *emotive* potential. Personalized, it immediately gains in *poetic* and aesthetic value as an independent work of art, fit for galleries and private collections (Byrne 1901, 154). Finally, the poster can also perform a *metalingual* function. By respecting or subverting the dominant artistic and social conventions, it comments on the history of graphic design and its relation to other arts. As the art scholar Danuta A. Boczar observes:

> The poster is continually revitalized by its contacts with the fine arts, literature and cinema. By condensing artistic styles into the required communicative graphic terms, [it] familiarizes and challenges the public with new artistic ideas. (1984, 24)

Thus it can cater to popular tastes, shape them or caricature them, becoming "an artistic barometer of society" (Ansell and Thorpe 1984, 7), which gauges the aesthetic, intellectual, and ideological pressures within a given cultural community.

Poster Art in Poland

Expressive power, poetic value, and interart complexity have come to characterize the Polish poster, widely acclaimed for its "brash wit" and "strength of gesture" (Boczar 1984, 16).

Its beginnings date back to the 1890s, when Poland was still partitioned among Russia, Prussia, and Austria. The first poster advertisements and playbills appeared in Kraków and Lviv, created by painters, illustrators, and stage designers. In 1898 the first international poster exhibition was held in Kraków, which gave momentum to the evolving medium and helped to formulate its principles. According to the curator Jan Wdowiszewski, the poster ought to combine artistic and utilitarian value and be equally suitable for gallery walls and poster pillars. It should function as a democratic art form, presenting a critical view of reality (Dydo and Dydo 2008, 17).

These guidelines were to define Polish design for the years to come. Before World War I, poster art was shaped by the Młoda Polska artists, who combined art nouveau decorativeness with Polish vernacular motifs, introducing painterly technique into applied arts (Boczar 1984, 16). The interwar period saw the painterly give way to the architectural, as the center of graphic design moved to Warsaw Technical University. Professors and graduates of the Department of Architecture set the tone in poster design and perfected it into an advertising medium "based on sophisticated humour, a maximum of synthesis and a masterly use of colour" (Dydo and Dydo 2008, 21).

Paradoxically, the Polish poster reached new heights of creativity with the advent of communism, lending color to the gray streets and outsmarting censorship with subtle wit. After World War II, the pro-Soviet regime monopolized cultural patronage in Poland, commissioning propaganda posters and favoring Socialist realism aesthetics. Yet its prefabricated triumphalism waned in the 1950s, giving way to more abstract surreal and expressionistic poetics, truer to the spirit of the postwar trauma (Boczar 1984, 18–19). As the centrally planned economy staunched consumerism, the poster turned into "a visual rather than an advertising vehicle," which promoted ideological and cultural messages and was hence assessed "not in terms of sales but in terms of design" (ibid.). State publishers popularized political, public service, and industrial messages, while cultural institutions, such as film production units, theaters, operas, and museums, commissioned their own event posters, printed by in-house publishers. This decentralization of control over the commissioning of posters allowed this art form to evade the party's "cultural arbiters" and resist cultural totalitarianism (Crowley 1994, 193–94). The sheer presence of censorship, however, turned Polish designers into escape artists, accomplishing feats of mental agility to break free of aesthetic and ideological constraints.

This was especially visible in film and theatrical posters, which stimulated aesthetic invention. In the 1950s, such talented painters and architects as Henryk Tomaszewski, Jan Lenica, Wojciech Fangor, Roman Cieślewicz, Jan Młodożeniec, and Franciszek Starowieyski used the event poster as a vehicle for social commentary and formal experimentation. In their announcements of new films and plays they evolved a "novel, unconventional approach to the subject," employing graphical shortcuts, symbols, metaphors, or allegories to synthesize the story and convey its atmosphere (Dydo and Dydo 2008, 25). They avoided a "literal transcription of the plot" (Boczar 1984, 20), transposing the general mood or capturing key motifs. Consequently, the poster lost its informative transparency and assumed the role of an "interpreter" and "commentator" revealing the artists' attitudes to a given subject (Schubert in Dydo and Dydo 2008, 25).

These distinctive developments in poster art, initiated in the 1950s, came to be known as the Polish Poster School. It combined expressive freedom with painterly technique, drawing on texture and vibrant color. Each author developed his/her own signature style. As technological deficiencies, such as poor quality ink and paper, had to be compensated for, designers searched for in-depth insight, individual poetics, and manual execution (Górowski 2009, 39). As Boczar concludes, the Polish poster contributed to contemporary graphic art by creating a new understanding between the artist and the audience built on emotional and intellectual involvement. Confronted with the "far-reaching conceptual abbreviation based on association and metaphors" the recipients were invited not to look at the picture, but to interpret it (Boczar 1984, 24).

Many designers of the younger generation have upheld the legend of the Polish Poster School, following the paths of their predecessors. According to Kristinn A. Rzepkowski, in many contemporary designs one can still recognize "a distinctly personal gesture" and "an underlying dig at some aspect of society," suggestive of the artists' and viewers' dissatisfaction with the status quo (Rzepkowski 2000). Other commentators, however, point to the Westernization of poster art in Poland, which became enamored of digital technologies (Górowski 2004, 69) and dominated by its commercial advertising role (Fryc 2006, 18).

Cinderella on the Polish Stage

The overview of posters presented below, though selective and eclectic, documents the enormous popularity of the story of Cinderella adapted for theatrical and operatic stages in Poland. The Zbigniew Raszewski Theater Institute in Warsaw, which preserves the largest theater documentation in Poland, records on its website[1] 147 opera, ballet, and theater performances of Cinderella staged in Poland since the beginning of the twentieth century, the earliest dating from 1906[2] (see table below). As one of the posters announces an even earlier performance, the actual list of productions might have been longer.[3]

The most popular textual version of Cinderella seems to be the Polish poet Jan Brzechwa's playful rhyme for children, adapted for the stage (by Zdzisław Rej or Bohdan Radkowski) and performed twenty-two times. For example, the second prevalent version is Evgeny Shvarts's play *Zolushka* (1938), presented in a few alternative Polish translations. The earliest documented performance (1954) used Maria Malicka's rendition, while Tadeusz Czyżowski's subsequent majority of productions were based on the translation by Irena Lewandowska and Witold Dąbrowski. Both plays appeared in puppet theaters all around the country and were addressed specifically to children.

Other theatrical adaptations of the story held dear by Polish producers were inspired by the Grimms' version of the tale. These include classical pieces by the actors and directors Adolf Walewski and Stanisław Płonka-Fiszer, as well as plays authored by dramatists Ludwik Świeżawski and Irena Prusicka. Several productions were also inspired by Charles Perrault, although only six adaptors have openly acknowledged these obvious allusions.

Among the musical versions of the story, Sergei Prokofiev's ballet has dominated the Polish stages, with Strauss's and Rossini's *Cinderellas* appearing sporadically in opera houses and dance theaters. One of the most popular musical interpretations of the tale, created by Giorgio Madia, is a hybrid production combining ballet with Rossini's music. Apart from these internationally acclaimed adaptations, there appeared musical pieces by the Polish composers Stanisław Gerstenkorn, Janusz Baca, and Marian Lida.

The remaining productions listed in the following table document other adaptations of the fairy tale, prepared predominantly for puppet theaters and designed specifically for young viewers.

Cinderella adaptations on the Polish stages in the years 1906–2013.

Author Credited	No. of Stagings	First	Last
Jan Brzechwa	22	1967	2012
Evgeny Shvarts	19 [20]	1954	2007
Sergei Prokofiev	18	1953	2012
Brothers Grimm	10 [13]	1958	2013
Stanisław Płonka-Fiszer	11	1948	1978
Irena Prusicka	10	1977	2007
Adolf Walewski	9	1906	1996
Gioacchino Rossini	8	1970	2010
Ludwik Świeżawski	8	1987	2003
Stanisław Gerstenkorn	4	1979	2001
Maciej K. Tondera	3	2002	2008
Marta Guśniowska	2	2010	2012
Janina Kilian-Stanisławska	2	1948	1949
Dorota Stępień	2	2004	2007
Johann II Strauss	2	1998	2008
Wanda Żółkiewska	2	1960	1962
Janusz Baca [Perrault]	1	2010	
Liliana Bardijewska	1	2011	
Tatiana Gabe	1	2009	
Kazimiera Jeżewska, Stefania Kornecka-Cybulska	1	1953	
Iwona Kusiak, Cezary Żołyński [Grimm]	1	2010	
Marian Lida	1	1995	
Henryk Lotar	1	1970	
Ireneusz Maciejewski	1	2008	
Andrzej Malicki: *Kopciuszek. Historia możliwa* [Perrault]	1	2010	
Charles Perrault	1 [6]	2002	
Beata Pejcz [Grimm, Perrault]	1	2005	
Janina Porazińska	1	1966	
Krzysztof Rau: Kopciuszek czyli magia koła	1	1999	
Jan Vladislav	1	2004	
Oleg Żiugżda [Shvarts, Grimm, Perrault]	1	2009	

Given the number and variety of performances, based on different sources and executed in various media, I selected the posters on the grounds of their importance in Polish visual culture, their current relevance (playbills advertising recent productions), or their outstanding artistic value (works by renowned poster designers, documented in albums, poster libraries, and galleries).[4] I approached them as visual representations of the Cinderella story, disregarding the peculiarities of respective stage adaptations. Hence, I ignored the works' potential appeal to a child audience, touching upon the subject only in my concluding remarks. I also neglected any adjustment to the aesthetic and ideological intentions of the advertised production. Instead, I focus on the iconic and symbolic potential of the posters, that is, their ability to shape and enrich the popular iconography of the fairy tale.

I conducted a qualitative analysis of forty-six posters, created over a period from 1903 to 2013, in order to find out which motifs caught the artists' attention; how these motifs were presented; what aesthetic and ideological attitudes toward beauty, romance, social, and gender roles they exposed; and what changes in design conventions they signaled. As it turned out, certain themes have dominated the artists' interpretation of the story. The posters can be therefore grouped into three broad categories: those treating Cinderella as a pretext for social, personal, or cultural commentary, as illustrated below.[5]

Cinderella as a Tale of Social Inequality and Advance

Interestingly, the earliest representations of the story in my collection focus on the motif of social stratification and inequality. Tadeusz Rychter's theatrical poster of 1903 (see color insert, plate 10), announcing the performance of the "Fairy Tale Fantasy Titled Cinderella" in the Municipal Theatre in Kraków, demonstrates an illustrational approach to the theme, typical of its epoch. The author was a stage designer, who created complementary playbills for his productions.

The poster presents a narrative sequence of images. The first one portrays a shabby, inconspicuous silhouette in a dark kitchen; the second one—the same inconspicuous silhouette trying on a golden slipper. The shadowy figure contrasts sharply with her illustrious companions: the king in red and his ladies-in-waiting, clad in pastels. Both pictures exude an unreal, supernatural aura, with the white doves fluttering and the golden slipper aglow. Although the sequence vaguely suggests that fortune will finally smile on the heroine and that solitude and ostracism will give way to social interaction, she remains a grimy, faceless servant girl, outshone by colorful high society. It is indeed her persistent facelessness, her nonbeauteous anonymity, and destitution that strike the viewer as a compositional constant, provoking empathy and self-identification. In a crowd blessed with individual features she is the only one deprived of a face. It is the recipients' task to provide her with one, projecting on the heroine their sorrows and fantasies and thus regaining faith in social justice.

Another design that focuses on class distinction, presenting it in a different light, is Roman Szałas's poster of 1947, advertising the Soviet musical film *Cinderella*, written by Evgeny Shvarts and directed by Nadezhda Kosheverova and Mikhail Shapiro. Unlike the original Soviet poster,[6] which celebrates the romance between a dressy damsel and her princely suitor, the Polish design plays on the social and aesthetic contrasts that underpin the story. It juxtaposes two figures belonging to two different worlds: a simple Slav peasant girl and a foppish western European prince. Each element of their encounter, including costumes, props, scenery, and choreography, emphasizes class division. He wields a sword and she wields a loaf of bread; he wears court shoes and she wears clogs; he makes an elegant bow, while she remains seated. The chimney wall and the shaft of light from the fireplace clearly divide them. Both figures resemble cutouts superimposed on the humble background, so we perceive their encounter as more provisional than the divide between them, bridged by the film title. Interestingly, in contrast to the previous poster, it is the courtier who looks awkward and out of place in the picture, surrounded by wood paneling and stone walls.

A complex interpretation of the fairy tale, which touches on its socioeconomic aspects, was offered by an eminent poster artist, Mieczysław Górowski, in his poster for Evgeny Shvarts's *Cinderella* at the Ludwik Solski Theater in Tarnów (see color insert, plate 11). Contrary to conventional rags-to-riches stories, this rendering focuses on rags. While the previous examples were clearly illustrational, capturing specific memorable moments, Górowski's poster invites metaphorical interpretations with its intricate composition and painterly technique. The image is divided into three planes. In the foreground, to the far right, a tattered, faceless child appears, praying, whispering, or perhaps crying. She leans against a cracking wall, which dominates the entire scene. The wall catches the eye with its texture and emptiness. It appears as a hybrid of stone, parchment, and a lunar surface, only to transform into a strip of dark clouds in the upper-left corner of the poster. From behind, an ominous horse-drawn carriage emerges, moving in the girl's direction. Can it be real? Or is it only imagined?

The unusual composition of the poster elicits various responses, and the organization of space is open to metaphorical interpretations. If we focus on the depth of the image, the three planes may present three modes of existence: the foreground standing for external reality (the girl's physical experience); the middle plane standing for internal reality (the girl's psychological experience); and the third plane—for virtual reality (the girl's dreams). Within this reading, the wall seems to represent the child's state of mind, sorrow and despair gradually giving way to escapist visions of a different life. This requires a synthetic rather than sequential reading of the multilayered composition: the depth of the planes perceived as evocative of the depth of human experience. Such an interpretation corresponds to Górowski's poetics, the artist being known for his preoccupation with questions of truth and un/reality (Krupiński 2004, 12).

However, we can also focus on the horizontal organization of the picture, associating space with time. Within this reading, the composition implies a sequence of events. The heroine is up against the wall, yet her fate is about to change. The nature of this change depends on our interpretation of the girl's pose. If we treat it as indicative of utter despair, her plight will be miraculously eased. If we assume she is simply playing hide-and-seek,[7] with her face covered while she is counting, the change of fortune will come as a long-awaited advancement. She will soon open her eyes to a new reality, represented metonymically by the carriage.

Górowski's vision is characteristically reflective and ambiguous. As he claimed in one of his essays, "theatre is emotion; human comedy and drama; interpersonal conflicts and internal dilemmas." The poster must explore them, looking for "the most pertinent point of the play" (Górowski 2004, 69; trans. A. H.). Depending on our interpretive perspective, the point emphasized in the poster may be the forces of destiny or the power of imagination to transform the most desperate human condition.

Jerzy Kolecki's poster for Jan Brzechwa's *Cinderella*, performed in 1987 in the Rabcio Puppet Theater in Rabka-Zdrój, projects a different metaphorical interpretation of the story. The tale is reduced to the motif of social advance, evoked by the orientational metaphor UP IS GOOD, which underlies the image of red-carpeted stairs. Shown from a low angle, they allude to the heroine's prospective social success. For the time being, she is metonymically symbolized by a splendid golden slipper. Her aspirations, by contrast, are conveyed by another metonym, a golden crown, associated with power and opulence.

Apart from portraying Brzechwa's *Cinderella* as a tale of courtly dreams come true, Kolecki's poster encourages reflection on the role of theatrical fiction in vicariously fulfilling our emotional needs. The first step of the stairs transforms into a stage, while the beige frame resembles a curtain.

Jerzy Kolecki. Jan Brzechwa's *Cinderella*, 1987. In the collection of Academy of Fine Arts Central Library in Kraków.

The red carpet seems to connect the world of the audience with that of dramatic characters; their aspirations externalize ours.

An interesting variation on the same visual motif is Dariusz Panas's poster announcing Ireneusz Maciejewski's recent puppet production of *Cinderella* at the Kubuś Puppet and Actor Theater in Kielce.[8]

The central image is a hybrid of a golden slipper and a steep stairway. The heroine must have only just run down the steps and out of the picture: we can still see her left foot extended in the air. The image is a visual paradox: the hybrid condenses Cinderella's shoe-less flight with her subsequent shoe-centered reward. Ironically, the size of the shoe surpasses its owner. This carries humorous undertones, characteristic of the stage production concerned.

Renowned satirical cartoonist Edward Lutczyn's playbill for Irena Prusicka's *Cinderella* at the Comedy Theater in Warsaw[9] focuses on the reversal of power relations in the shoe-test scene. The poster presents a horde of female rivals competing for courtly splendors, symbolized by the golden slipper. Reduced to bare feet, the rivals are all materially equal. Still, one contestant (presumably Cinderella) seems qualitatively superior to the others, because she is blessed with a very small foot. Needless to say, the podiatric attractiveness of competitors seems directly proportional to their inner beauty; and the configuration of toes is expressive of the contestants' determination or reserve.

The above posters foreground the social aspects of the story: some focus on the human condition, others focus on class divisions and advancement. The fairy tale, however, not only inspires reflection on rags and riches, mistreatment and reward. It also poses metaphysical and aesthetic questions of the relationship between the material and the supernatural, between the tragic and the playful, between sumptuousness and simplicity.

Cinderella as a Tale of Femininity

Confronted with the theme of Cinderella, many artists focus on the main protagonist, so as to explore the issues of feminine identity, women's alleged dreams about life, and men's alleged dreams about women. This is shown in Jan Młodożeniec's poster for Rossini's *Cinderella* at the Grand Theater in Warsaw, created in 1979.[10]

One of the most eminent representatives of the Polish Poster School, Młodożeniec is known as a master of a synthesizing, poetic approach to the subject matter, which combines childlike and folk-like naïveté with great sensitivity to color (Gorządek 2005). Here, he presents Cinderella's story as a game of appearances. The picture comprises three planes, which impose a hierarchical order on their components. The composition puts the costume in the foreground, while its owner is relegated to the background. The woman appears beautiful and feminine, but her gray face is outshone by the geometrical patterns on her gown. Altogether, Młodożeniec's rendition stresses the role of costume in shaping Cinderella's identity.[11]

Another pictorial representation of the story centered on the main character was created by contemporary poster artist and painter Leszek Żebrowski in his playbill for the Pleciuga Puppet Theater in Szczecin. The artist often allows large motifs to fill the entire visual field. In this monochrome composition, he presents a portrait of a girl (possibly a doll or a marionette), who hypnotizes viewers with a direct gaze. Her appearance brings out the tension between artificiality and naturalness. The girl's photorealistic face looks three dimensional and palpable, the chiaroscuro effect contributing to the illusion of realism. At the same time, the head is completely out of proportion and apparently severed from the rest of the body, like a broken doll's. Her hair, along with flowers and ribbons, by contrast, is rendered in a painterly fashion, probably by hand. Surprisingly, it strikes the viewer as more natural and organic than the photorealistic face. There is a mystery to this picture, which alludes to the paradox of Cinderella's story: with its fantastic exuberance, it is not of this world, yet as a representation of human dreams, it is primeval and elemental. The effect is reinforced by the texture of the background, which resembles a blend of lace with microscopic pictures of plants, a fusion of a human artifact with the work of nature.

Ten years later, the same artist created a poster for the ballet production of Cinderella at the Kraków Opera, in which the heroine's image gained a completely new significance. The portrait is crowned with an unusual turban—a collage of sweepers, mops, tea towels, and detergents, not to mention an extravagant pink stiletto with a golden lining. It combines two visions of femininity. The oil-painted profile, which brings to mind Renaissance Italian paintings, represents classical ideals of beauty as timeless and unchanging. The turban, composed of photographic metonymies of household chores, sets the vision in a contemporary frame. The poster explores the duality of a woman's role in the twenty-first century: a nymph and a kitchen maid, aspiring toward ethereal beauty, yet burdened with down-to-earth responsibilities.

Another memorable image of the heroine can be found in Rafał Olbiński's iconic poster for Rossini's *Cinderella* production at the Cincinnati Opera. The author, an eminent Polish artist working in the United States, has won international acclaim for his surreal style reminiscent of René Magritte's visual enigmas. The image presents a young woman "dressed in night." This complex pictorial metaphor brings out the heroine's secret identity, unknown to her family. She towers above the horizon only to blend

Leszek Żebrowski. Evgeny Shvarts's *Cinderella*, 2000.

with it, as her gown ("night") transforms into a night sky over a royal carriage. We can imagine the girl inside, a small nocturnal Cinderella hidden inside her larger diurnal self. The image foregrounds the motif of mystery, indicating a tension between the visible and the invisible.

Intriguingly, the visual pun depends on the reversibility of the figure/ground alignment. In order to appreciate what is hidden "inside," we need to disregard the main figure and perceive her as a ground for other pictorial elements. This process indirectly alludes to an important strand in Rossini's opera: Cinderella's ability to see the inconspicuous, contrasting with her family's disregard for others.

Seven years later, the same author created another memorable image of Cinderella, to announce the production of Johann Strauss's ballet at the Opera in Wrocław. Since the play is set in a department store, the poster presents a contemporary young woman who has turned her back on the viewers to rest her legs on a crescent moon. Engrossed in thought, she sits in a wooden chair on the shore of a lake. This unusual setting triggers a contextual metaphor (Forceville 2013): with her legs stretched diagonally upward, the figure symbolizes control and independence. She is a girl who can reach for the stars.

Another design celebrating the expressive power of legs is a recent poster for Prokofiev's *Cinderella* production at the Baltic Dance Theater. The

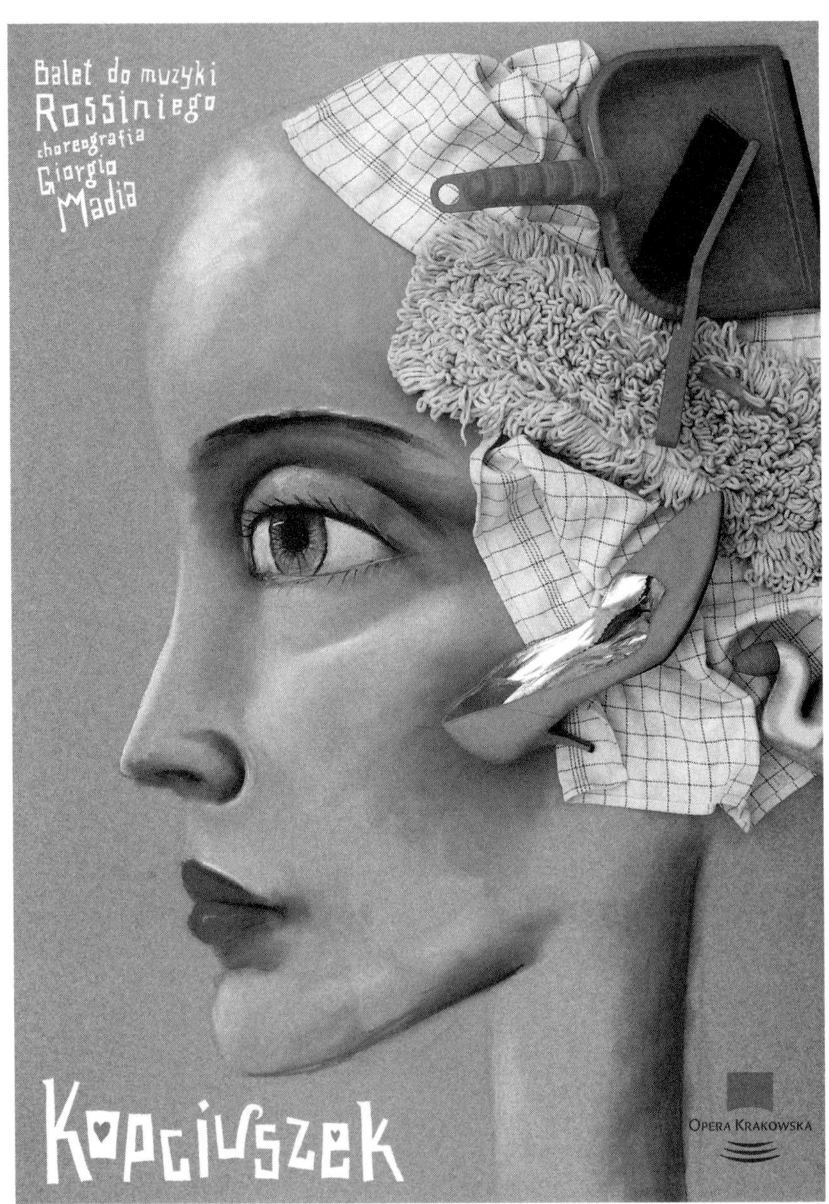

Leszek Żebrowski. Cinderella. Giorgio Madia/Gioacchino Rossini, 2010.

Rafał Olbiński. Rossini's *Cinderella*. 2001.

Rafał Olbiński. Johann Strauss's *Cinderella*, 2008.

performance, set at the turn of the 1930s and 1940s,[12] presents the heroine as a factory worker. The same convention governs the poster's industrial aesthetics: the image of an aluminum bucket and a dirty rag on terrazzo flooring. These props are not the only visual metonymies used in the poster: it focuses on the bare legs of a cleaning lady, who seems to have nothing on except a pair of golden slippers. The slippers, demonstrably out of place, trigger a contextual metaphor. A person working physically in ballroom shoes evokes the concepts of transformation and social advancement from rags to riches.

Yet certain aspects of the picture composition provoke feelings of unease. Judging by her pose, the heroine is supposed to appear as pert and independent, which was the choreographer's express intention.[13] However, with her legs bare, she seems reduced to a sexual object. This may strike the viewers as inconsistent with the other elements of the picture, yet it certainly attracts attention.

This industrial vision of Cinderella may seem rather gloomy if we compare it to the poster advertising Giorgio Madia's ballet production of *Cinderella* at the Grand Theater in Łódź.[14]

Presented against a baby-pink collage of floral wallpaper and a clock, a figure of a retro pin-up girl appears in a seductive pose, toying with her pink stiletto. This stylization alludes to the costumes and stage design prepared for the performance, set in the 1950s. What attracts most attention, however, is the girl, who resembles a coquettish bimbo with her hair elegantly coifed and her mouth wide agape. The poster appears as a deliberate conglomerate of various Cinderella clichés. Its sugary form emphasizes the unwavering pop-cultural appeal of the story and its vulnerability to kitschy reworkings and spin-offs. It is for the viewer to decide whether the poster perpetuates or mocks these stereotypes, although Giorgio Madia's personal involvement in the design clearly suggest the latter, echoing the choreographer's humorous adaptation of the story inspired by Walt Disney's classical production.[15]

Cinderella's cultural iconicity is also the focus Edward Lutczyn's 1978 poster for Evgeny Shvarts's play at the Groteska Theater in Krakow.[16] Another example of contextual metaphor, the image presents an orphan child perched on a gigantic, shiny glass slipper. The maltreated heroine, dressed in red rags, flashes a bright smile, as if posing for a photo shoot or beaming at her admirers. The huge glass slipper transforms into a platform from which she greets her fans. The poster offers a self-reflexive commentary on Cinderella's popularity in contemporary culture, which the advertised production only confirms. Similarly to the previous design, Lutczyn's

Łukasz Gawroński / Marek Weiss / Piotr Białas. Prokofiev's *Cinderella*. 2011.

Cinderella behaves as a self-confident celebrity who enjoys interaction with her audience.

Each of the above posters revealed a different vision of femininity, highlighting chosen aspects of Cinderella's story. Some implicitly commented on social and aesthetic expectations concerning women, while others emphasized conflicts between submission and independence, coquetry and self-reliance. Several artists reflected on the universalism of the motives of reward and dream come true present in the story.

Cinderella as a Cultural Construct

Some designers foreground the medium in which the story is represented. These posters emphasize the medium-specific qualities of particular productions, such as ballets and puppet theaters. The best illustration of this interpretive approach is Marian Stachurski's film poster of 1965, advertising a film adaptation of Prokofiev's ballet, directed by Heide Draexler-Just.[17]

Stachurski visually condenses the ballet to the scene of an encounter between two pairs of legs that stand for two historical periods and aesthetics. The figure to the right, presumably the prince, resembles a jester in pointed poulaines, ornate breeches, and a castle-shaped belt. The figure to the left, possibly Cinderella, looks contemporary in her white stockings, psychedelic skirt, and ballet shoes. Both bring to mind two traditions in the fairy-tale iconography, the former standing for folklorization (archaization) and the latter for modernization.[18] Consequently, the film is presented as a confrontation of two equals and two aesthetics, a combination of conservatism and innovation. A particular emphasis is placed on ballet as an important medium in which the Cinderella story has been popularized.

A similar approach is found in Piotr Żerdzicki's poster for Prokofiev's *Cinderella* at the Grand Theater in Poznań, created in 1984. The image is dominated by the motif of a ballet dancer's foot, spinning and fluttering with shawl-like ribbons. Its manner of presentation triggers figurative interpretations. The form of the foot evokes an integrated metaphor of a human being, assuming human features (Forceville 2013). Personified, the foot transforms in viewers' imaginations into a dancing figure with prominent hips and spine, a symbol of fairy-tale magic.

Representative of a younger generation of Polish artists, Adam Żebrowski offers a different perspective on *Cinderella* as a text of culture (see color insert, plate 12). In his poster for Prokofiev's ballet production at the Grand Theater–National Opera in Warsaw, he evokes a contextual metaphor. A shiny ballet shoe appears in a transparent plastic bag, presumably

Piotr Żerdzicki. Prokofiev's *Cinderella*, 1984.

a piece of evidence in a police investigation. Consequently, the story of Cinderella is relocated to the twenty-first century, with the motif of the heroine's disappearance singled out as the most important thread in the entire plot. This brilliant visual abbreviation is rich in intertextual allusion; the viewer starts reflecting on the condition of contemporary culture and the wide popular interest in criminal stories and police procedurals.

The posters discussed in this section put an emphasis on the artistic form in which the story was presented to the audience. As such, they invited the viewer to reflect on their creative and interart implications.

Concluding Remarks

Posters offer invaluable material for intersemiotic and cross-cultural analysis. Aimed at visual synthesis, they summarize on-stage and on-screen dramas with striking visual motifs, images that "enter our visual vocabulary and become important cultural icons" (Ansell and Thorpe 1984, 8). Some of the works analyzed in the previous sections have already secured their place in the history of Polish graphic art; others capture ephemeral artistic, cultural, and ideological trends. Yet they all enrich the Cinderella iconography, forming new links in a chain of adaptations, with literary texts of culture being adjusted for the stage and screen by playwrights, composers, or scriptwriters and then rendered by directors, designers, and performers.

Implicated in complex interart relationships, posters invite many critical approaches. I have adopted a thematic perspective, analyzing the dominant Cinderella motifs selected by the artists, regardless of the advertised type of production and the target audience. These included class inequality, social advancement, and the complexity of women's roles embodied by the heroine: a domestic helper, an ethereal beauty, an idealist dreamer. Viewed diachronically, the selected posters seem to demonstrate the artists' decreasing interest in social injustice and their growing preoccupation with cultural stereotypes, although the corpus is too small to support generalizations.

Since the collected playbills allude to different types of film and theatrical productions, these factors might have influenced the visual content. It seems, however, that ballet is the only narrative medium consistently integrated into poster imagery. Except for Leszek Żebrowski's and Rafał Olbiński's renditions, other playbills, designed by Marian Stachurski, Piotr Żerdzicki, and Adam Żebrowski convey metatextual allusions to dance, using podiatric imagery to illustrate the tale. Still, this is not surprising, as the lost slipper is probably the most recognizable metonym related to

Cinderella, used in other designs, too, especially those by Kolecki, Panas, and Lutczyn. The remaining types of theatrical productions—opera, musical theater, puppetry, and drama—are hardly identifiable in poster iconography. For example, it would be difficult to guess that Górowski, Kolecki, Panas, and Żebrowski have all been inspired by puppetry performances.

There is one aspect of the advertised performance, however, that clearly affects the chosen iconography: the intended audience. Unlike theatrical productions, posters are usually available to the general public. Yet the ones announcing productions for children are often characterized by dual address. They fire the children's imaginations by using visual cliché (such as the image of opulence in Kolecki's design), caricature (such as the representations of wild-toed feet and celebrity Cinderella in Panas and Lutczyn's posters), and presenting empathy-evoking child protagonists, as illustrated by the orphaned girls in Górowski, Żebrowski, and Lutczyn. Simultaneously, these playbills affect the adult viewers with their implicit irony, detectable in the naive representations of success (the staircases in Kolecki and Panas's posters or the celebrity Cinderella in the latter of Lutczyn's designs) and exaggerated images of competition (Lutczyn). They also appeal to mature audiences by revealing layers of metaphorical meaning, particularly prominent in Górowski's and Żebrowski's designs. Posters created specifically for an adult audience, by contrast, are more oriented toward subversion (in Gawroński/Weiss/Białas, and Madia's design) and paradox. They also refrain from presenting child protagonists.

Obviously, these general remarks refer to a small corpus of posters, and it would be interesting to verify them using a more extensive sample, illustrating the evolution of Cinderella representations in Poland over the last century. Since playbills "tell us as much about society as they do about art" (Ansell and Thorpe 1984, 8), they certainly offer promising research material not only for semioticians and art critics but also for sociologists, cultural anthropologists, and literary scholars.

Notes

1. Available at: http://.e-teatr.pl (last accessed November 27, 2013).
2. Available at: http://.e-teatr.pl/realizacje/lista.html?nazwisko=&tytul+Kopciuszek&rok=&Submit+szukaj (last accessed November 26, 2013).
3. Several performances documented in the Theatre Institute archives are credited with double authorship. The author of the literary source (Perrault, Brothers Grimm) is mentioned along with the scriptwriter (Baca, Kusiak, Żołyński). To signal these intricacies, I have provided additional

information in square brackets, revealing the literary sources if mentioned in the credits.

4. I wish to thank the director of the Academy of Fine Arts Central Library in Kraków for her invaluable assistance and her kind permission to use the photographs of works preserved in the poster collection.
5. I would like to express my sincere gratitude to Maciej Górowski, Jerzy Kolecki, Rafał Olbiński, Dariusz Panas, Marek Weiss, Adam Żebrowski, Leszek Żebrowski, Piotr Żerdzicki, and the directors of the Grand Theater in Łódź for their kind permission to reproduce the posters. I also wish to thank Piotr Bożyk for his invaluable support and Szymon Zaremba, Hanna Grabowska, Tomasz Graczyk, and Olimpia Schneider for their kind help.
6. Available at http://sovietmovies.blogspot.com/2010/04/nadezhda-kosheve rova-mikhail-shapiro.html (last accessed March 15, 2014).
7. I am grateful to my student, Bartosz Lorek, for this insightful suggestion.
8. Available at http://www.wici.info/Kalendarz,kopciuszek,22888.html (last accessed March 15, 2014).
9. Available at http://www.e-teatr.pl/pl/realizacje/16181,szczegoly.html (last accessed March 15, 2014).
10. Available at http://galeriagrafikiiplakatu.pl/pl/plakaty/46/Jan-Mlodozeniec /492/ (last accessed March 15, 2014).
11. For an in-depth commentary on the relationship between Cinderella's attire and her identity, see Dutheil de la Rochère (2013).
12. Scigliano, Eugenio. 2001. Premiera "Kopciuszka" w Operze Bałtyckiej. Available at http://www.e-teatr.pl/pl/artykuly/128116.html (last accessed November 30, 2013).
13. Ibid.
14. Available at: http://www.e-teatr.pl/pl/realizacje/40728,szczegoly.html (last accessed March 15, 2014).
15. Available at http://www.operalodz.com/spektakl.php?id=47 (last accessed May 23, 2014).
16. Available at http://www.e-teatr.pl/pl/realizacje/25353,szczegoly.html (last accessed March 15, 2014).
17. Available at http://galeriagrafikiiplakatu.pl/pl/plakaty/218/Marian-Stachur ski/13121/Kopciuszek/?&imagpos+0 (last accessed March 15, 2014).
18. I wish to thank Martine Hennard Dutheil de la Rochère for this observation.

References

Ansell, Joseph, and James Thorpe. 1984. "The Poster." *Art Journal* 44 (1): 7–8.

Boczar, Danuta A. 1984. "The Polish Poster." *Art Journal* 44 (1): 16–27.

Byrne, A. G. 1901. "Suggestions on Poster Designing." *Brush and Pencil* 9 (3): 154–60.

Crowley, David. 1994. "Building the World Anew: Design in Stalinist and Post-Stalinist Poland." *Journal of Design History* 7 (3): 187–203.

Dutheil de la Rochère, Martine Hennard. 2013. *Reading, Translating, Rewriting: Angela Carter's Translational Poetics*. Detroit: Wayne State University Press.

Dydo, Krzysztof, and Agnieszka Dydo. 2008. *PL 21: Polski plakat 21 wieku*. Translated by Teresa Bałuk-Ulewiczowa. Kraków: Galeria Plakatu.

Forceville, Charles. 2013. "When Is Something Pictorial Metaphor?" Available at http://semioticon.com/sio/files/forceville-metaphor/cforceville2.pdf (last accessed November 29, 2013).

Fryc, Herman. 2006. "Review of Anna Agnieszka Szabłowska's *Tadeusz Gronowski: Sztuka plakatu i reklamy*." *2+3D* 19 (2): 18.

Górowski, Mieczysław. 2004. "Plakatowa globalizacja." *2+3D* 1: 68–69.

Górowski, Mieczysław, and Agata Hołobut. 2009. *Drzwi do plakatu: Mieczysław Górowski rozmawia z Agatą Hołobut*. Kraków: Universitas.

Gorządek, Ewa. 2005. Jan Młodożeniec. Available at http://culture.pl/pl/tworca/jan-mlodozeniec (last accessed November 29, 2013).

Krupiński, Janusz. 2004. "A Question of (un)Reality. Sketches on the Art of Mieczysław Górowski." Translated by Teresa Bałuk-Ulewiczowa. In *Mieczysław Górowski: Posters*, edited by Maciej Pawłowski, 8–47. Kraków: Rzecz Piękna.

Mathiot, Madaleine, and Paul L. Garvin. 1975. "The Functions of Language: A Sociocultural View." *Anthropological Quarterly* 48 (3): 148–56.

Rhodes, Gary D. 2007. "The Origin and Development of the American Moving Picture Poster." *Film History* 19 (33): 228–46.

Rzepkowski, Kristinn R. 2000. "Polish Poster Art: Distinctly Personal Gestures." Available at http://info-poland.buffalo.edu/classroom/poster/poster.html (last accessed November 10, 2013).

17

On the Evolution of Success Stories in Soviet Mass Culture

The "Shining Path" of Working-Class Cinderella

Xenia Mitrokhina

"Cendrillon ou la petite pantoufle de verre" by Charles Perrault was available to the Russian aristocracy in the eighteenth and nineteenth centuries in the original French version, due to the fact that Russia's elites were bilingual at the time. French was the language of diplomatic ties, social interaction, and correspondence. Far more than just a means of communication, French was a Russian's cultural window to Europe, the medium for the acquisition of a European mentality and philosophy.

Nevertheless, the first Russian translation of Cinderella saw light as early as 1768 (in *Skaski o volshebnitsakh*, a collection of eight fairy tales by Charles Perrault). The book was intended for high society (the translator, Lev Voinov, dedicated it to Naryshkina, a lady-in-waiting at the royal court), became popular and was reprinted several times. This and subsequent translations were very close to the original, except for the heroine's name: until the mid-nineteenth century, it was translated as "Gryaznushka" or "Zamarashka," both meaning "slattern" (including in Ivan Turgenev's 1866 translation).[1] The better-sounding version, "Zolushka," which evokes a parallel with "zola," meaning "ashes," and with "zolotse," meaning "goldie," was found in the 1840s by a translator who, sadly, remained unknown. In 1857 "Sandriliona" was chosen as the name for one of the earliest magazines on practical housekeeping published in Russia (Lisovskij 1995 [1915], 554). This proves that the story was popular and the respective mythologem, that of a modest hardworking girl who magically achieves happiness, was already well established.

Around the same time, Russian philologist Alexander Afanasyev, inspired by the oeuvre of Jacob and Wilhelm Grimm, started traveling to Russian villages to collect folklore. A collection he first published in 1855–63 includes a folktale called "Chernushka," meaning "The Blackie" (Afanasyev 1985 [1863–64], tale 293). In it, we find the cut-off finger and the poked-out eyes of the wicked sisters. The fairy godmother is missing; instead, doves help the heroine. There is also the festival at the prince's palace, and a shoe that gets stuck to some resin that the prince has his servants spread on the stairs. This text is very similar to the Grimms' version of Cinderella, but the Grimms' volume had not yet been translated into Russian. Was it a genuine Russian story? There is insufficient data to rule out or prove this possibility.

Around the same time, another folklore collector, Ivan Khudyakov, wrote down a fairy tale called "Zamarashka" ("Slattern") in the city of Kazan (Khudyakov 1860). It is in many ways similar to Afanasyev's "Masha the Blackie" but has significant differences: the heroine is not orphaned on her mother's side but a "simpleton" (which brings her close to a key archetype). The helper is her godmother; doves are not mentioned. It is tempting to believe this suggests an influence of Perrault's fairy tale, descended to the grassroots by word of mouth, but again, data are not sufficient.

The first complete Russian translation of the Grimms' folktales was published in 1863–64. Alexander Afanasyev reacted with an emotional publication in *Knizhny Vestnik* (Book Newsletter), welcoming the translation but harshly criticizing the translator (unnamed, as often happened) for inaccuracy and a superficial attempt at localization (Afanasyev 1864, 379). The 1870 translation edited by N. Polevoy is much better and is now considered a classic.[2] The *Brothers Grimm Tales* have been invariably popular with the Russian reader; however, subsequent interpretations of Cinderella in Russia did not follow the German tradition but the French one, with its happy end uncomplicated by revenge. Its numerous versions published before the 1917 Bolshevik revolution represented practical adaptations of the plot, for example, for puppet shows, children's theater (Kazanskij 1906; Sobolshikov-Samarin 1906; Selivanova 1913), or silent film (Shaghinian 1916), and such, without any changes of the plot.

When looking at the Soviet era, it is essential to understand the way fairy tales—whether folklore or not—functioned within the ideological system of the time.

Just four years after the Bolshevik revolution, in 1921, an official censorship body was established, called Glavlit (General Management on Literature and Publishing). It would ban and confiscate books, both classical and modern, that it judged to contain "dangerous counter-revolutionary approaches" (Blum 2000b 53), "flotsam of bourgeois morality," "bourgeois mumbo jumbo" (Blum 2000a). Here is how the head of Glavlit, Pavel Lebedev-Polyanski, viewed his mission:

> We must apply the party line to every sphere of practical activity and all realms of our ideology, including sociology, history, philosophy, medicine, agriculture, fiction, and children's literature. (Blum 2000a, 48)

When it came to fairy stories, Glavlit banned and confiscated the ones that were declared to be ideologically harmful atavisms of the old social system, aiming to distract children from reality by means of fantasy and fiction. In 1926–27, two rhymed fairy tales by Korney Chukovsky, *The Crocodile* and *Barmaley*, were banned on the grounds of being "unacceptable from an educational viewpoint" (Chukovsky 1963; Blum 2000a). In his diaries, Chukovsky quotes a propaganda poem about a good Soviet boy who rejects a fairy's gifts with the words, "It's all lies that you say, ma'am. We have no more need, lady, for your magic tablecloth" (Chukovsky 1963).

At the same time, the Commission of the People's Commissariat for Education circulated a letter recommending "removing the fairy tale from the educational process." It also instructed nursery staff "to manufacture dolls resembling public actors, leaders of the proletariat, the workers and the farmers" (Goldovsky 2007).

One of aspects of this campaign was the rewriting of classical folklore and children's classics in accordance with current ideological requirements. Quite a few novels were produced within this trend, starting from Alexey Tolstoy's remake of Carlo Collodi's *Pinocchio* under the name of *The Golden Key or the Adventures of Buratino* (1936) and all the way to Alexander Volkov's *The Wizard of Emerald City* (1939), loosely based on Frank Baum's *The Wonderful Wizard of Oz*. There is great variety among the remakes and the authors' reasons for producing them. The intensity of the ideology also varies strongly from volume to volume.

In the meantime, Bolshevik propagandists used catchy popular fairy-tale and folklore forms, filling them with revolutionary content. From the 1920s to the 1950s, a large number of fairy tales styled to look like folklore were published about Lenin, Stalin, and other leaders (Piaskovskij 1930; *Svetlyj put': narodnye skazki o Lenine i Staline* [Folktales about Lenin and Stalin] 1938; Kriukova and Popov 1938; Ghippius 1938; Gorky and Mekhlis 1939). In reality, the "folk stories" were written by authors, hired for the job, working independently or in collaboration with popular storytellers representing the numerous ethnic groups resident in the USSR (Alpatov 2003). The resulting fairy stories, ballads, and songs either placed the Soviet political leaders within a paradigm of mythical characters (within which, ironically but predictably, there was again room for exaggerations and miracles) or recounted recent events in the style of ancient epic chronicles, thereby creating a kind of communist folklore.

In the Soviet remakes of old fairy tales, realistic incentives often replaced magical incentives. A highly illustrative example is a novel by Lazar Lagin first published in 1938, called *Old Khottabych*,[3] described as a "Soviet fairy-tale novel" (this hybrid definition of the genre is interesting per se), telling the story of a genie who renounces his archaic and absurd magical abilities and learns to be a useful member of Soviet socialist society. This makes perfect sense if we remember that the whole nation had been singing the "Aviators March" since 1922:

> We are born to make fairy tales come true,
>
> To overcome wide open space

Cinderella was one of the stories that underwent striking transformations during the early Soviet years, when its plot was reshaped into a model scenario for "victory of the proletariat." Looking back, it is fascinating to realize that these very special interpretations had originally stemmed from a purely verbal coincidence.

One of the still remembered catchphrases of the 1917 revolution was a slogan attributed to Vladimir Lenin, "Every cook can govern." The phrase became much more than just a slogan; spread far and wide, it resounded like a mantra of the socialist transformation of society. In reality, this catchphrase represents an inaccurate quotation from a 1917 article by Lenin, "Can the Bolsheviks Retain State Power?" (Lenin 1917). However, it is in this modified form that the phrase became popular and has remained so for almost a century.

The "cook" in this catchphrase is a metaphor for all lower classes. This metaphor was common at the turn of the twentieth century; apparently it had existed for some time. The July 1, 1887, law of the Russian Empire "On the Reduction of Gymnasium-Level Education,"[4] which abolished the right of the lower classes to secondary education, was thus popularly known as "The Circular on the Children of Cooks." The objective of the law was to prevent—or at least stall—the upward social mobility that had led to a rise of revolutionary trends in the Russian Empire.

Meanwhile, there was the universally known fairy tale of Cinderella—basically, a success story of upward social mobility by means of magic. What's more, its characters had apparent relevance to the social types of the epoch.

The result was a merger of the fairy tale, the Bolshevik catchphrase about the cook, and another, perhaps equally popular catchphrase, "Who was nothing will be everything." The phrase came from the Russian translation of "The Internationale," a popular left-wing anthem of French origin. The French lyrics were slightly different; that particular line read, "Nous ne sommes rien, soyons tout"—"We are nothing, let us be everything."[5] Just like the slogan about the cook, this one, too, painted the picture of a magic social transformation that did not require any analysis of one's potential or assessment of available means to achieve success.

In Cinderella, the familiar children's story became a metaphor for upward social mobility in the Soviet Union. The social practices of the early USSR were very much in line with this interpretation. The Soviet state discriminated against members of all the social classes that used to be privileged in the Russian Empire, replacing them throughout with members of the working class and farmers. It was in this spirit that Soviet author Viktor Ardov rewrote Cinderella in the late 1930s, placing the protagonist in the industrial setting that was at the time almost obligatory for literature in the USSR. The result is a rather unpretentious story, full of sketchy humor, about a sweet girl and a happy romance. The protagonist, Nastya, is a housemaid who has just recently moved to a small town from a village. With her mistress, Anna, she lives in a small hotel right next door to a male engineer, Lebedev; she works at a weaving plant, and the female head of the plant's communist party headquarters is Maria Sergeevna Pronina, who also lives next door. Ms. Pronina combines working-class sincerity with the authoritative manner of a senior administrator. "Not for a second does she stress belonging to the 'weaker sex'" (Ardov 1940, 21). Pronina represents an obvious Soviet analogy to the fairy godmother. Later, already as a famous weaver, Nastya jokes, "I have a religious adviser and it's you, Maria Sergeevna!" (Ardov 1940, 129).

Nastya falls in love with Lebedev at first sight, and he nicknames the shoe-polish-smudged housemaid "Cinderella." Her mistress also takes an interest in the handsome engineer, invites him to dance ("the ball to which Cinderella was not invited"), and strikes up an affected conversation about the paintings on display at the city museum. Nastya has a row with her mistress and moves in with Pronina. The kind-hearted communist functionary helps the girl to get a job at the weaving plant. Nastya gets a room in the plant's dorm, works at the plant, enrolls as a student and attends additional engineering classes in the evenings. To become worthy of her engineer prince, she grabs every opportunity to improve her education and manners, and to become a professional. As a result, she ends up as a Hero of Labor and a celebrity, far ahead of her prince on the social ladder.

In the last scene, the comedy goes full circle. Six years later, Nastya, her former mistress, and engineer Lebedev meet at a hotel in Moscow. The mistress has remained a bored provincial lady. She fails to recognize Nastya who has undergone a "magical transformation." Nastya tells her story and shows a photo of herself on the front page of a newspaper. Her former mistress points out that Nastya's nose in the photo is straight, not turned up as in real life. Nastya explains that the photographer has retouched the photo. Meanwhile, engineer Lebedev keeps trying to get Nastya's attention, but she is too busy. Her phone rings every minute with invitations to presentations, meetings, and ceremonies; a photographer fusses over her all the time. Finally, Lebedev manages to tell Nastya that he has been in love with her for a long time.

> If you are Cinderella, he says, then I am probably the prince . . . because all I have been doing for quite a while is look for you. (Ardov 1940, 139–40)

The characters embrace and call for room service. However, the dishwasher who comes to take their order cannot write it down because she is illiterate. Lebedev says: "What if this girl is another Cinderella?" Nastya laughs out loud. The dishwasher looks at her and smiles. The story ends (Ardov 1940, 144).

The comedy was not a big success. At present it is hard even to find it in a library. However, it rose to fame when filmmaker Grigori Alexandrov used it as the basis for the screenplay of *The Shining Path*. At the time, Alexandrov was already famous and a big favorite with Stalin. He had recently produced two major box office hits: a jazz comedy, *Cheery Guys*, and a character comedy, *Volga-Volga*, both with a strong ideological bias. Stalin recommended that his next film should depict "the hero of our times." To achieve this, Alexandrov took Ardov's comedy and, as the author admitted, rewrote it beyond recognition, reducing the original text to a "shriveled corpse" (Khort 2007). He gave Nastya some of the traits of a real-life heroine, the record-breaking weaver and People's Deputy Dunya Vinogradova. He also filled the narrative to the brim with propagandist pompousness and symbolism, making it arguably the most vivid example of ideological tampering with a classical fairy tale.

The film's working name had been *Zolushka* (*Cinderella*) but Stalin requested a change (Khort 2007). The main character was played by Alexandrov's wife, the Soviet film diva Lyubov Orlova. The most vivid Soviet composer of the day, Isaac Dunayevsky, wrote the music. Furthermore, the film contained an assortment of innovative filming and comedy tricks, and full compliance with the party line. Its success was overwhelming. It became a landmark in Soviet cinema and Soviet mentality.

Let us briefly point out some of its special characteristics.

The characters and the plot begin by being very similar to those in Ardov's comedy. Hardworking and cheerful Tanya is a lot like Nastya; she falls in love with the engineer next door—an alien from a glorious world far beyond who nicknames her "Cinderella." The female communist functionary next door is also there. "Not a young fairy but a middle-aged comrade," as Tanya will later define her Soviet equivalent of a fairy godmother. When the middle-aged comrade fairy encourages Tanya to sign up for a literacy course, we hear the characteristic ting-a-ling that was used back then and is still used in children's films to mark miracles and magic transformations. This genuinely postmodernist touch is just one of the brilliant features of this highly original and professional film.

The filming involved everyday interaction with censors whose approval was needed for each little detail. The director recalls that since Pronina's role in the film was essentially a Soviet incarnation of a fairy, she needed to look the part. Alexandrov reported this as such:

> It took a long time to decide how many blouses can Pronina, a Communist party functionary, change over the ten years of her life shown in the film, from 1930 until 1940. I decided it should be ten, one per year, but the planning people insisted on three. After many months of discussions, the Committee on Cinematography approved of a number right in between: six. (Alexandrov 1940)

When Tanya the cook is dismissed and kicked out into the street by her landlady, the Communist Party functionary takes her in. Fast asleep in her bed behind a screen, Tanya sees a dream. The camera zooms in to the silhouette of Moscow's skyline, Tanya's communist guardian takes her hand and leads her inside through the majestic gate. The scene of the dream is left incomplete. In those years, miracles and magic were purged from art as atavisms of the religious worldview; the ways in which the authors of this film work around the ban on magic are quite spectacular.

Actress Lyubov Orlova as Zolushka (Cinderella) in *Svetlyj Put'* (The Shining Path, 1940).

The communist functionary enrolls Tanya in a literacy course and then helps her get a job at the weaving mill as a cleaner. Tanya learns to read and write with enthusiasm, and then makes great efforts to train as a weaver so she can operate a loom and join the cheerful crowd of girls in overalls. It's worth mentioning here that manual labor at a factory or a construction site was the central theme of Soviet cinema, arguably because it combined the idea of literally "building" socialism with the supreme values of collective labor and belonging to a large class of similar-minded people.

The storyline of the "royal ball to which Cinderella is not allowed to go" is also present and remade with great originality. Amid New Year celebrations in the town, the local club is ablaze with light. Tanya can hear the sounds of music, laughter, and dancing as she sits alone on a bench in a snow-covered public park. This is when she gets to meet her "prince" again: the factory engineer whose photograph she has kept at her bedside ever since their encounter at the Grand Hotel. However, he ruins everything by trying to kiss her right away; she sees this as a sign that he doesn't respect her or take her seriously, and turns him down. The love story is interrupted again, all the way until the very end of the film. It is, however, noteworthy that at this stage, the heroine's relationship with her prince becomes one of greater social equality. The engineer no longer descends from a magical world out of her reach; they now both work at the same mill and are on an equal footing.

The subsequent personal growth of the heroine takes place very rapidly. Tanya learns to operate weaving looms and eagerly joins the Stakhanovite movement for overachievement at the workplace (just like Nastya and her real-life prototype, the weaver Dunya Vinogradova), in which workers set records for producing many times their daily quota. Tanya thus learns to operate 150 looms instead of eight. Newspapers publish reports about her and interview her.

The social climbing of Nastya in Ardov's comedy ends at this point, whereas the story of Tanya, "the heroine of our times," goes on. Very soon, she becomes a member of the Supreme Soviet (the Soviet parliament), a celebrity, and an engineer.

The climactic scene in the film shows Tanya being awarded the Order of Lenin. Apparently taking place in the Kremlin, this scene is shown by means of a blown-up image of the heroine's face, wearing an expression of excitement verging on religious ecstasy—a high point of held-back joy. It is hard to say what is more impressive: the novel shooting technique or the extent of patriotic emotion in Tanya's eyes. The next episode provides the key to understanding the film. Tanya, wearing a white dress and ballet slippers, is dancing round and round in a richly decorated hall in the Kremlin, an obvious reference to the royal palace. She sits down in front of a huge mirror and starts to go over her entire life in her mind; she looks into it —and sees herself as kitchen help in a shabby coat, then as a factory worker in overalls. Together with her reflection, she sings about her country, where fairy tales come true. Then a magical figure in symbolic ethnic dress appears in the mirror, an apparent projection from the future. Tanya asks her what the future will be like, and the image takes her inside the mirror. Together they fly over Moscow in a car, singing, "every way is open to us." (The director reportedly wanted female factory workers to fly in neat rows of airplanes all around the car and sing in a choir, but this wasn't possible at the time.)

This feels like the final scene, but it isn't. Proletarian Cinderella's triumph takes a new turn; the film's main message is enhanced by repetition. In the next scene, Tanya is invited to Moscow to speak at the opening ceremony of a new pavilion at the Exhibition of Achievements of the National Economy—the biggest trade show in the USSR. The setting is another exact, albeit ideologically doctored, parallel to a royal palace. We are shown a magnificent palatial interior with columns, electric lights, carpets, and, to top it all, a gigantic dais shaped as a weaving loom. Speaking from this tribune is our heroine—radiant, dressed in an elegant suit, a true member of the new Soviet elite. We can see the head of the Communist Party cell and the foreman from the mill (clearly standing for her godparents) applauding her triumph. Their guileless admiration emphasizes the film's message: here is a working-class girl rising to fame, she is one of many, you can do it too. In the end, the heroine sings a song that would top Soviet charts for decades to come, and was frequently played at ceremonies and official events. The original title of the song was "The March of the New Man"; it was subsequently renamed "The March of the Enthusiasts," and it goes:

> Are we the ones to stay put?
>
> In our darings we are always right!
>
> . . .
>
> We meet no barriers at sea or on land.

The "we" in the chorus is extremely characteristic. This is a call for action: the song encourages listeners to follow in the heroine's footsteps and rise to glory as she did. As such, the lyrics of the song stress the programmatic nature of the life scenario outlined in the film.

The final scene is a love confession. Respectful and affectionate, the engineer is shown walking next to the girl of his dreams. Behind the couple, we see bas-reliefs depicting the glorious present and brilliant futures of liberated labor. The heroine's self-education, hard work, and perseverance are rewarded by personal happiness.

Although it is hard to avoid irony when faced by the straightforward ideological message of *The Shining Path*, it is undoubtedly a great cinematographic achievement. In terms of its genre, it is a lyrical comedy—light, breezy, and colorful. With its numerous eye-catching original sets, the film is well made and conveys, despite all the ideological clutter, a genuinely fairy-tale atmosphere of magic and joy.

Nonetheless, it is especially interesting to have a closer look at the symbolic "editor's wastebasket," that is, at what had been deleted from the classical story, and what had been inserted into it—by the authors and the time. Since, unlike Ardov's comedy, this film enjoyed immense popularity and influence, and represents the next evolutionary step in terms of Soviet transformation of the classical plot, it makes sense to analyze it in greater detail.

First, the transformation of Soviet Cinderellas has been reinterpreted in social rather than personal terms: at the start of the plot, the servant girl is abused and scolded by her lazy employer, not her stepmother. The conflict no longer involves family members, but members of two different social classes. After making the right choice, the heroine makes a breathtaking social climb. Characteristically, her original place of work, the Grand Hotel, is conspicuously old-fashioned, and even the scenery around it is archaic, making the place look like a comic remnant of the old world. From this world of samovars and galoshes, she makes a jump first into the world of shining industrial equipment (the factory), and then the world of style, education, and palatial decor (the Soviet trade fair). In some of its aspects, this spectacular rise to glory makes one think of time travel, thereby creating a metaphor of the entire country's travel toward the "shining socialist future." Within this metaphor, the freckled village girl who wipes her nose with her hand transforms first into a slim modern proletarian in overalls, and soon afterward, into an incredibly elegant, confident, fashionably dressed, and happy celebrity.

Second, the means of traveling along the "shining path," that is, the method of achieving good fortune, has been strongly modified in this film interpretation of Cinderella. The fairy-tale Cinderella achieves happiness and moves into the royal palace thanks to her sweet disposition (and because she is conveniently passive), a magic helper, and a fortunate sequence of almost chance occurrences. At any rate, the success scenario in the original fairy tale is ambivalent and can hardly be regarded as a set of practical guidelines. Contrastingly, in the iconic Soviet film, the path to glory is described step-by-step, with great vividness and topicality.

Third, the driving force of the heroine's magical transformation has been radically changed. The magical element has been deleted; Tanya's transformation is her reward for trying hard, persevering, and being a good team worker. No fairies are involved—her only helpers are her older, more experienced comrades. At the end of the film, they exclaim: "What miracles people can achieve!"

Just as in the marches quoted above, we find that the main concepts of the story are replaced with new politically correct ones. "God is a lie," the interference of magical assistants is also a lie and a thing of the past. In the new world, there are new kinds of miracles: the patriotic deeds and industrial achievements of the new Soviet people. In a radio recital of *Old Man Khottabych*, the choir sings a cheerful song: "You know very well that the world is full of miracles but it's the people who make the miracles happen."

Interestingly, the reward remains unchanged: Tanya's triumph is structurally identical to that of a classical Cinderella. Everything is there: a palace (the Pavilion of the Textile Industry), music, a festive crowd, beautiful clothes (adapted to the needs of a professional woman), a prince, and an imminent wedding. What we are missing is retribution for the wicked half-sisters: first, because Tanya is, as befits a heroine of the new socialist world, an orphan, and second, because happiness is charitable. But the most emotionally loaded scene in the film is not the romantic happy end but the part where the Soviet Cinderella is awarded an order of the state. Everything that follows is a reverberation of the happy ending; the love of the "prince" comes as a bonus, not as the main achievement.

In the movie, we watch the Soviet Cinderella undergo a complete transformation: from the clumsy village girl to the proletarian in overalls, and finally to the famous and awesome lady. The pattern of the transformation is repeated in the scene in front of the mirror. The metamorphosis appears consistent; however, it represents a big lie. The transformation from village girl to factory worker is feasible and realistic: a whole army of former farmer girls joined the Soviet industrial workforce. However, once they became muscular workers, they normally remained that way. There were numerous female members of the Supreme Soviet, decorated Heroes of Labor—clumsy, masculine, and ideological to the point of being grotesque.

The contrast with the feminine, refined, and socially graceful Tanya is striking. The reformed Tanya has all the charms and graces of Soviet star Lyubov Orlova, whose background is anything but that of a Soviet Cinderella. Orlova came from an old aristocratic family; Leo Tolstoy was her relative and Fyodor Chaliapin was a friend of her parents. And yet millions of viewers believed in this transformation.

Lyubov Orlova was popular beyond belief. In 1941, the German troops came very close to Moscow, and the city was in panic. The local authorities pasted huge posters all over the city announcing Orlova's concerts, and the panic subsided. “If our beloved actress is still here and even giving concerts, the situation must be under control” (Khort 2007).

The film's societal impact was so powerful that it is even reflected in Soviet demographics (Stishova 1997, 98–107; Andrusenko 2012; Klotz 2012). Identifying with the heroine and dreaming of following in her footsteps, dozens of thousands of village girls rushed to the capital city so they, too, could be wooed by a handsome lover next to a gigantic fountain. They were looking for self-fulfillment in work; as their reward, they expected to get a happy romance, because this was how it worked in the movie. It is indeed noteworthy that in *The Shining Path*, glory and happiness come as a reward for hard work and perseverance—things that are not normally present in romantic stories. “If you are a good worker and teammate, if you join the ranks of industrial laborers and fully identify with them, you will become a beauty and marry a good man.” This substitution of one motivation for another was what made the film a huge success and turned its star into an icon of the Soviet woman.

Even a very superficial comparison between *The Shining Path* and Walt Disney's *Cinderella* (also regarded as a metaphor for upward social mobility) makes it clear how special the interpretation of the Soviet movie is. Teammate and hard worker, the heroine is just feminine enough so as not to be confused with a man (her equal in every other respect); in place of a ball, she attends an opening ceremony of an industrial pavilion; instead of an evening dress and touching little glass slippers, she wears a business suit. Her austere and dignified image is, however, crafted with great skill.

> The plan to transform women was largely implemented by the late 1940s. . . . Cinderella was forgotten. Soviet cinema did not revisit the ideological myth it once created for the sake of propaganda. Of course, the archetype of Cinderella remained buried deep in the culture. The mutating gene of *The Shining Path* was latent for a while. Once it awoke, it abruptly changed its trajectory. Cinderella got lost in

> the ideological jungle and tried to find her way by following familiar signs, like Hop-o'-My-Thumb. (Stishova 1997, 105)[6]

An interesting "interlude between the two epochs—the mythological and the anti-mythological" (Stishova 1997, 106) was a film directed in 1947 by Nadezhda Kosheverova, based on a screenplay by Eevgeny Shvarts. Stripped of any ideology, brimming with a "Philosophy of Good," the new Cinderella won the hearts of several generations, throwing *The Shining Path* and even the classical fairy tale into the shade (Pritulenko 1997, 95). Subsequently, other film directors questioned the ideological mythologem of *The Shining Path* by contrasting it with reality, for example, in Gleb Panfilov's *The Beginning* made in 1970 or the 1979 film by Nikolai Obukhovic' called *Our Mom Is a Hero*.

In *The Office Romance*—a brilliant 1977 lyrical comedy by Eldar Ryazanov—we watch a female director of a statistical bureau, a spinster who chose her career over a love life many years ago, entirely transformed by a love affair with one of her subordinates. In Vladimir Menshov's *Moscow Does Not Believe in Tears*, a melodrama that was also made in 1979 and won an Oscar in 1981, another almost sexless female general manager meets Mr. Right. Although socially he is beneath her, his personality and charisma enable him to play the leading role in their relationship.

Finally, in the last days of the USSR, during the Perestroika—a time of high hopes, economic decline, and criminal anarchy—we observe the emergence of a fallen Cinderella, a victim of the harsh times who sells sex to rich foreigners for hard currency. It is among her clients that she finds her prince, a well-off westerner who marries her and takes her away. However, her convoluted life story culminates in tragic death rather than a happy end (*Intergirl*, a 1989 film by Pyotr Todorovsky).

The Shining Path veered the Soviet Cinderelliana in an unexpected direction: the story of hardworking Cinderella, the Fairy Godmother, and Prince Charming was transformed into a hyperbolic saga of social success. Seen today, the film's ideological drive appears almost comical. Nevertheless, this film marked the emergence of the Soviet narrative about the meaning of a woman's happiness, hopes, and disappointments. All subsequent references to Cinderella speak to *The Shining Path*, arguing with it, deflating its socialist mythology, and offering, in its stead, a more realistic and human storyline.

Notes

1. Available at: http://fantlab.ru/work165585 (last accessed August 7, 2014).
2. Some other early translators: S. Snessoreva (1870), A. Tereshkevic', V. Andreevskaja, E. Peskovskaja (1880–90s), A. Fiodorov-Davydov (1900), F. Anderson (1901), A. Frideman (1903), etc.
3. English translations of the title include "Old Man Khottabych" and "Old Genie Khottabych."
4. Available at http://school-collection.edu.ru/catalog/res/cf7d38ef-a636-46a6-afdb-aa159e58a1ed/ (last accessed August 7, 2014).
5. First three quatrains translated by A. J. Kotz in 1902 became the Soviet national anthem (1918–44).
6. All translations from the Russian are by Nina Iskandaryan.

References

Afanasyev, Aleksandr. 1985 [1863–64]. *Narodnye russkie skazki: Sobrannye A. N. Afanasyevym* [Russian folktales by A. N. Afanasyev]. 295 (2): 316–17. Moscow: Nauka.

Afanasyev, Aleksandr (signed I.M-k.). 1864. "O russkom perevode skazok Grimmov" ["About the Russian translation of the Grimms' tales"]. *Knizhnyj Vestnik* 19: 379–82.

Agafonova, Nadezhda. 2010. "Skazka lozh da v nej namyok" [Tale of sense, if not of truth]. Available at http://knigozavr.ru/2010/07/23/skazka-lozh-da-v-nej-namyok (last accessed June 13, 2014).

Alexandrov, Grigori. 1940. "Zametki o komedii" ["Notes on Comedy"]. *Pravda* 2 (2).

Alpatov, Serghej. 2003. "Stalin i folklor" ["Stalin and the folklore"]. *Pervoje sentiabrja. Literatura* 9. Available at http://lit.1september.ru/article.php?ID=200300905 (last accessed June 13, 2014).

Andrusenko, Elena. 2012. *Lift dlja Zolushki* [*Elevator for Cinderella*]. Available at http://rus.ruvr.ru/2012/01/18/64101646.html (last accessed June 10, 2014).

Ardov, Viktor. 1940. *Zolushka*. Moscow: Iskusstvo.

Blum, Arlen. 2000a. "Burzhuaznaja Kurochka-Riaba i pravoslavnyj Ivan-durak" [The bourgeois Riaba the Hen and the orthodox Ivan the Fool]. *Rodina* 3. Available at http://www.istrodina.com/rodina_articul.php3?id=276&n=10 (last accessed August 7, 2014).

———. 2000b. *Sovetskaja Tsensura b epokhu bolshogo terrora* [The Soviet Censorship during the Great Terror]. Saint Petersburg: Akademicheskij proekt.

Available at http://www.opentextnn.ru/censorship/russia/sov/libraries/books /blium/?id=522 (last accessed August 7, 2014).

Chukovsky, Kornei. 1963. *From Two to Five* [Ot dvukh do piati]. Available at http://www.chukfamily.ru/Kornei/Prosa/Ot2do5/Ot2do5.htm (last accessed September 7, 2014).

Eimermacher, Karl. 1998. *Politika i kultura pri Lenine i Staline* [Politics and culture under Lenin and Stalin]. Moscow: AIRO-XX.

Ghippius, Evghenij, ed. 1938. *Narodnye pesni o Lenine i Staline* [Folk songs about Lenin and Stalin]. Moscow: Iskusstvo.

Goldovsky, Boris. 2007. *Istoriya dramaturgii teatra kukol* [The History of Dramaturgy at the Puppet Theater]. Moscow: Anastasia Chizhova Gallery.

Gorky, Maksim, and Leonid Mekhlis, eds. 1939. *Krasnaja Armija: Pesni o Lenine, Staline I Krasnoj Armiji* [Red Army: Songs about Lenin, Stalin, and the Red Army]. Moscow: Voenisdat.

Kazanskij, Veniamin. 1906. *Zolushka*. Moscow: Teatralnaja biblioteka.

Khort, Aleksandr. 2007. *Liubov' Orlova*. Moscow: Molodaja Gvardija. Available at http://www.lubov-orlova.ru/roles/svetliy-put.html (last accessed June 13, 2014).

Khudyakov, Ivan. 1860. *Velikorusskiye Skazki* [Tales of Russia Major]. Moscow: Soldatenkova i Schepkina. Available at http://ru-skazki.ru/khudyakov-great-russian-tales.html (last accessed August 7, 2014).

Klotz, Alisa. 2012. "Svetlyj put'": Institut domashnikh rabotnits kak migratsionnyj kanal i mekhanism sozial'noj mobilnosti epokhi stalinisma" ["The Shining Path": Fenomena of housekeepers as migration channel and social mobility mechanism in the Stalinist era"]. *Novoje literaturnoje obozrenie* 117. Available at http://magazines.russ.ru/nlo/2012/117/k7.html (last accessed June 13, 2014).

Kriukova, Marfa, and Viktorin Popov, eds. 1938. *Saga o Lenine* [Lenin's saga]. Moscow: Sovetskij pisatel'.

Krupskaja, Nadezhda. 1928. "O 'Krokodile' K. Chiukovskogo" [About K. Chiukovskij's Crocodile]. *Pravda*, January 2, 1928. Available at http://www.chukfamily.ru/Kornei/Proetcontra/Krupskaia.htm (last accessed August 7, 2014).

Lagin, Lazar. 1938. *The Old Genie Hottabych* (in English). Available at http://www.lib.ru/LAGIN/hottabych_engl.txt (last accessed at June 10, 2014).

Lenin, Vladimir. 1917. Mogut li bolsheviki uderzhat' vlast'? ["Can the Bolsheviks Retain State Power?"]. Available at http://www.marxists.org/ archive/lenin/ works/1917/oct/01.htm (last accessed August 7, 2014).

Lisovskij, Nikolaj. 1995 [1915]. *Bibliografija rossijskoj periodicheskoj pechati, 1703–1890* [Bibliography of the Russian periodical press, 1703–1890]. Moscow: Literaturnoje obozrenije.

Mitrokhina, Xenia. 1996. "The Land of Oz in the Land of the Soviets." *Children's Literature Association Quarterly* 21 (4): 183–88.

Nachalo [The Beginning]. 1970. Directed by Gleb Panfilov. Moscow: Mosfilm.

Nasha mama—gheroy [Our Mom Is a Hero]. 1979. Directed by Nikolai Obukhovic. Leningrad: Lenkinokhronica.

Perkhin, Vladimir. 2011. *Russkaja Zolushka elizavetinskikh vremen* [The Russian Cinderella from the time of Elisaveta"]. *Moskva* 12: 166–70.

Petrovskij, Miron. 2006. *Knigi nashego detstva* [Books of our childhood]. Saint Petersburg: Ivana Limbakha.

Piaskovskij, Anatolij, ed. 1930. *Lenin v russkoj skazke i vostochnoj legende* [Lenin in Russian Tales and Oriental Legends]. Moscow: Molodaja Gvardija.

Pritulenko, Valentina. 1997. "Zolushka na vse vermena" [Cinderella at all times]. *Iskusstvo kino* 31. Available at http://kinoart.ru/archive/1997/03/n3-article16 (last accessed August 7, 2014).

Selivanova, Elena. 1913. *Zolushka: Khrustalnye bashmachki: Muzykalnaja skazka* [Zolushka: Little Glass Slippers: Musical]. Moscow: Gramakova.

Shaghinian, Marietta. 1916. *Zolushka, secret dobrodeteli. Kinopovest* [Zolushka, the Secret of the virtue: Filmscript]. Moscow: Universitetskaja biblioteka.

Sluzhebnyj roman [The Office Romance]. 1977. Directed by Eldar Ryazanov. Moscow: Mosfilm.

Sobolshikov-Samarin, Nikolaj. 1906. *Zolushka*. Moscow: no data.

Stishova, Elena. 1997. Prikliutchenija Zolushki v Strane bolshevikov" ["The Adventures of Cinderella in the bolshevik's State"]. *Iskusstvo kino* 5: 98–107.

Svetlyj put': narodnye skazki o Lenine i Staline, kolkhoznye pesni i chastushki [The Shining Path: folktales about Lenin and Stalin, *kolkhoz* songs and couplets]. 1938. Stalingrad: OKI.

Svetlyj Put' [The Shining Path]. 1940. Directed by Grigori Alexandrov. Moscow: Mosfilm.

Tolstoy, Alexey. 1936. *Prikliuchenija Zolotogo kliuchika* [The Adventures of Buratino]. Leningrad: Detghiz.

Turghenev, Ivan. 1866. "Zamarashka." Available at http://fantlab.ru/work165585 (last accessed August 7, 2014).

Volkov, Alexandr. 1939. *Volshebnik Izumrudnogo goroda* [The Wizard of Emerald City]. Moscow: Detghiz.

Yanovskaya, Elvira. 1923. *Skazka kak factor klassovogo vospitanija* [The fairy tale as a factor of class education]. Khar'kov: n.e.

Zolushka. 1947. Directed by Nadezhda Kosheverova. Leningrad: Lenfilm.

18

The Triumph of the Underdog

Cinderella's Legacy

Jack Zipes

Cinderella has come a long way—from riches to ashes to riches and a marriage to a charming prince in his magnificent palace. Who would have thought that this abused young woman, orphaned by her mother and abandoned by her father, would have had a chance against a vicious and conniving stepmother and two spiteful stepsisters? But fortune has always been on her side throughout history, and it has taken various forms: a fairy godmother, her reincarnated mother in the form of helpful animals and birds, magic plants, and helpful men. And she has also been driven by her own indomitable spirit and desire to claim her rightful place in the world. Although she has often been portrayed as a meek mouse, she is not a wimp. Cinderella is a survivor par excellence, and she has assumed various guises from persecuted stepdaughter to feisty orphan and underdog. Indeed, there are a multitude of Cinderella types, and this large variety makes it extremely difficult to explore the filmic discourse about her tale of woe and happiness, for it is not based on one or even two hypotexts.

Cinderella is probably the most popular fairy tale in the world. There are thousands of oral and literary versions. Indications are that the tale may have originated in ancient China or Egypt. The shoe or slipper test may have been connected to a marriage custom in which the bridegroom takes off the bride's old shoes and replaces them with new ones. But this thesis has never been completely verified, and depending on the society and customs, shoes are used in many different ways in marriage celebrations and tests to determine authenticity. In the various literary and oral versions the shoes are leather, gold, silver, and glass. Charles Perrault invented the glass slippers in 1696 most likely as an ironic joke since a glass slipper was likely to break if it were to fall off a foot. What most of the tales, oral and literary, have in common is the conflict between a young girl and her stepmother and siblings about her legacy. Cinderella must prove that she is the rightful successor in a house in which she has been deprived of her rights. She is to be tested in a kind of initiation ritual common to many cultures, as Vladimir Propp (2012) has explained in his posthumous book, *The Russian Folktale*. She receives help from her dead mother in the guise of doves, fairies, and godmothers. Belief in the regeneration of the dead who can help the living in the form of plants or animals underlies one of the key motifs of the fairy tale. In the European literary tradition, which first began with Bonaventure des Périers's *Les Nouvelles Recréations et Joyeux Devis* (*New Recreations and Joyous Games*, 1558), it is clear that Giambattista Basile's "La Gatta Cenerentola" (1634) played a role in influencing Charles Perrault's "Cendrillon ou La Petite Pantoufle de verre" (1697) and Marie-Catherine d'Aulnoy's "Finette Cendron" (1697). They, in turn, had some effect on the Grimms' "Aschenputtel" of 1812, as did Basile. Significant in Basile's tale is the active role that Cinderella plays in determining her future: she kills her first stepmother (only to be exploited by her second one) and stops her father's ship from returning from Sardinia. Some of this activism, in contrast to Perrault's narrative, can be seen in the Brothers Grimm's version of 1812.

Since there were so many different versions by the time the Grimms composed their Cinderella—for instance, they may have also been influenced by the Bohemian version "Laskopal und Miliwaka" in *Sagen der böhmischen Vorzeit aus einigen Gegenden alter Schlösser und Dörfer* (*Legends of the Bohemian Early Period from Some Regions of Old Castles and Villages*, 1808)—it is difficult to establish one source for their work in particular. Clearly, many different literary and oral tales fostered a huge Cinderella cycle in the East and the West. Alan Dundes's *Cinderella: A Casebook* (1982) provides valuable background information and discussions about the cycle and different interpretations (see also Cox 1967; Ting 1974; and Booth 1980). The early literary work of Basile, d'Aulnoy, Perrault, and the Grimms certainly played a role in the creation of nineteenth-century plays and musical adaptations, such as Nicolas Isouard's popular fairy opera, *Cendrillon* (1810), as well as in the equally successful operas, *La Cenerentola ossia la bontà in trionfo* (1817) by Gioacchino Rossini and Jules Massenet's *Cendrillon* (1899), not to mention the various vaudeville and melodramatic *féerie* adaptations and children's plays produced during the nineteenth century.

The cinematic discourse of Cinderella was closely connected to the theater and to the texts of Perrault and Grimm, sometimes an amalgamation of Perrault and Grimm.

Perrault endowed his heroine with innate qualities, while the Grimms' young girl must earn these qualities. They are both well born, that is, they come from well-to-do homes. Perrault made no reference to a god, while the Grimms "Christianized" a secular tale that had no reference to a dear Lord in their own original manuscript. Whatever the case may be, both tales entered the civilizing process of Europe to set a model of comportment: girls are to be gentle, pious, and good, and their beauty and happiness depend on their spiritual qualities. Although they are not total orphans, they become complete orphans due to the ineptitude of their fathers or their unwillingness to protect their biological daughters. As a result the Cinderellas of Perrault and the Grimms are viciously treated and brutally attacked by their stepmothers and stepsisters. The only defense of these poor rich girls is their virtuous behavior, patience, and tenacity. Ultimately, they are rewarded by a higher power, and they *regain* their status in life through marriage to a prince. Neither the Perrault tale nor the Grimms' tale is a rags to riches story. Both belong to the category of didactic and moralistic fairy-tale exemplars that set models for girls of the upper class who need to show off their beauty and docility to win the appropriate mate.

The fairy-tale films of the twentieth century seek to alter the plot while following the traditional patriarchal narrative. That is, most of them discard fathers who enable their second wives to maltreat a stepdaughter; most of them omit the fact that Cinderella was born into a well-to-do family; most of them dispense with religious connotations. They patch up the narrative in response to the changing role of women, but they still insist that Cinderella use her talents and beauty in a public spectacle so that she can impress a young man and wed him. The major shift in the majority of the films beginning with Georges Méliès's two versions in 1899 and 1912 is to create an underdog survivor, whose kind demeanor attracts a fairy, who intervenes on her behalf so that she can move away from her persecutors to marry a rich man.

The other tendency is to create a savvy heroine who outwits her stepmother and stepsisters and determines her own fate without the help of some higher power. At the bottom of the conflict in most of the films is the unspoken biological disposition of parents to devote more time, emotion, and attention to promote their own offspring rather than care for their nonbiological children, and this disposition, common throughout the world, explains the popularity of the tale, and it helps explain the competition among siblings who are not born of the same parents. In this regard, the morality of the Cinderella films, that is, the triumph of the "good" Cinderella is designed to demonstrate in its narrative how a child, who has the odds stacked against

Georges Méliès's *Cinderella* (1912).

her, must develop strategies for dealing with the brutal treatment by stepmothers and stepsisters, who test her. Her magnanimous triumph at the end of her predictable rise to fortune does not put an end to the real social problem of unjust treatment and discrimination, but films, just like their literary and theatrical forbears, can pose alternatives to object relations in families that no longer resemble the so-called norm of the bourgeois nuclear family. Put another way, many films propose that discrimination that stems from social and biological forces can be cured by culture or cultivated differently in the civilizing process.

Since there were well over 130 different kinds of Cinderella films made during the twentieth and early part of the twenty-first centuries, it would take a book to examine how the cinematic Cinderella discourse has evolved. Consequently, I want to examine mainly those films that have "punctuated" the discourse in original and innovative ways and shed light on how and why the narratives that stem largely from Perrault and the Grimms have been transformed in response to cultural changes, especially in light of gender formation and family conflict. For the most part, the transformations tend to be modern remakes with a faux feminist touch. I shall begin first by discussing a few silent films, followed by an analysis of cartoons, musicals, and live-action films.

Melodramatic and Modern Cinderellas

The brilliant Georges Méliès was the first to adapt Cinderella in two different cinematic versions in 1899 and 1912. Neither film is exceptional with regard to transforming the Perrault narrative, but each demonstrates particular tendencies that become clearer in most of the silent film versions of Cinderella. In both of Méliès's films, the father is totally eliminated from the plot, and the girl's true test is whether she will live up to the fairy's expectations, overcome the oppression that she suffers, and find some kind of happiness. Her stepsisters do not taunt her in Méliès's 1899 film; only in the second film is she slapped and maltreated. The setting is more nineteenth century than it is seventeenth in both films, and they also feature love at first sight and a lost slipper followed by a slipper test. The character of the prince plays a negligible role. Although there are delightful comic antics in the first film, Méliès was more interested in creating a melodrama in both films that was to move viewers to shed a few tears for the persecuted heroine and to smile when she triumphed in a grand finale. Méliès was too fixated on recapturing the traditional Cinderella story in hyperbolic form with his usual antics of sexy women and mischievous imps than to explore deeper meanings in the story.

It is this emphasis on melodrama that marks almost all of the Cinderella silent films that followed Méliès's productions. For instance, one of the notable early films, James Kirkwood's *Cinderella* (1914), starring the great actress Mary Pickford, strengthens the plot by emphasizing the moral goodness of Cinderella in an overly didactic way. In the initial scene, the stepmother and stepdaughter refuse to give alms to a poor old woman (who incidentally is dressed in black and resembles a witch) outside their mansion. Soon after, the sweet Cinderella appears and provides the old woman with something to eat. All at once, the woman turns into a tall, beautiful fairy who will protect Cinderella throughout the film. Then, when Cinderella, dressed in elegant rags and high heels, meets the prince in a forest, they fall in love, but they cannot consummate their love. He returns to his castle, she, to her large mansion where she is mercilessly maltreated by her stepmother and stepsisters. Little does she know, however, that she has won the favor of the fairy godmother, who continues to help her at crucial times without making herself visible. Cinderella also continues to show her pious nature by praying and turning the other cheek. When a ball is organized by the prince to find a wife, Cinderella is, of course, cruelly treated and prevented from attending. In a comic scene, the stepsisters see a fortune-teller, who announces that one member of the family will marry the prince, and they mistakenly believe it will be one of them. After they depart for the ball, Cinderella is surprised by the visit of the fairy godmother, and the plot basically follows the Perrault script. At the end, when Cinderella, despite being a poor maid, wins the prince, he tells her that he would like to behead her stepsisters, but Cinderella rejects the idea. Then, the fairy appears to bless her and her prince.

Kirkwood tries to remain true to the spirit of the Perrault text, and thanks to the length of the film (52 minutes), he can expand the love story and exaggerate the trials and tribulations of his heroine. Typically, she is the kind and dutiful orphan, whose pure soul glimmers through her rags. Both the fairy and the prince recognize this purity, and Cinderella, as the good, untarnished virgin, is blessed for more or less *not* speaking out against her victimizers. But, in 1914, times were about to change, and a new woman was on the horizon.

Aside from the usual melodramatic re-presentations of the Perrault text in the silent-film era, there were also several films with the same title that indicated the re-presentation of a different Cinderella: Percy Stowe, *A Modern Cinderella* (1908); J. Stuart Blackton, *A Modern Cinderella* (1910); J. Searle Dawley, *A Modern Cinderella* (1911); Eleuterio Rodolfi, *A Modern Cinderella* (1913); John Adolfi, *A Modern Cinderella* (1917). There were also others, such as C. J. Williams's *A Reluctant Cinderella* (1913), Sidney Morgan's *A Lowland Cinderella* (1922), and John Daumery's *Naughty Cinderella* (1933). They all served notice that women were coming into their own and becoming more independent thanks to the women's suffrage movement, World War I, and the modern industrial transformation that opened up new opportunities for women in the workforce, including Hollywood itself. Cinderella began to take destiny in her own hands, and only here and there did she need a little help from friends.

One of the most interesting films during this period was *Ella Cinders* (1926) directed by Alfred Green and starring Colleen Moore and Lloyd Hughes. The film was based on a syndicated comic strip written by Bill Conselman and drawn by Charles Plumb that originated in 1925 and ended in 1961. It featured a wide-eyed pert girl with black hair in a Dutch-bob haircut named Ella, who must carry out all the housework in a dysfunctional family run by the tyrannical Myrtle "Ma" Cinders and her two nasty daughters, Lotta and Prissy Pill. Although not beautiful, Ella wins a beauty contest, and the prize enables her to leave the small town of Roseville with her kid brother Blackie and head for Hollywood, where she discovers that the film company that had sponsored the contest no longer existed. However, she stays in Hollywood and endeavors to make a name for herself during the next thirty-five years in all sorts of comic-strip adventures in the West and a marriage to a young man named Patches, who has his own sort of amusing experiences. In the process of producing a comic strip over so many years the core Cinderella story was dropped in favor of a series of brief tales depicting a smart young woman who would fall into and out of trouble.

In contrast, Green's *Ella Cinders*, a feature film, retains the core Cinderella plot transformed into an exceptional farce that focuses on class differences and reinforces the personality of Ella as a young woman with determination, a great sense of humor, and pride. Green discards the brother as best friend in favor of Waite Lifter, who is a handsome iceman/fairy godfather. Although Ella knows how to fend for herself, she does need some protection and encouragement from Waite to enter the beauty contest. When she must submit a picture to the judges, her photographer submits one in which she makes a funny face. The reason she wins the contest is because the down-to-earth judges value personality and humor above beauty. They are also apparently critical of the pretentious class climbers represented by Ma Cinders and her daughters. There is no love lost between Ella and her stepmother and stepsisters. They do not part on good terms. But it is clear that she and Waite are in love with each other as he drives her to the train station and she departs for Hollywood. Shortly thereafter, we learn that Waite is actually from a very rich family and the star of the Illinois football team. He rebels against his father and follows Ella to Hollywood, where we see her sneaking into a Hollywood film studio, determined to become a star even though she has no connections. In an amusing scene in which she busts through the gates of a studio and interrupts the shooting of a film, Ella shows her acting talent and becomes a "discovered" young star. In another amusing scene, Waite arrives to rescue her from what he thinks is her impoverished existence, and he, too, interrupts the shooting of a scene to propose to her.

There are no miraculous transformations in this fairy-tale film. Instead, we have fortunate accidents that enable a young woman from the lower classes to discover her profession and to find a young man who accepts her for what she is: frank, funny, forceful, and talented. It is true that she abandons acting for marriage and a family, but she makes the decision to follow her heart. The "modernization" of Perrault's tale and the adaptation of the comic strip are effective. Green does not dabble in melodrama. The action combines elements of Méliès's burlesque humor with a touch of Chaplinesque comedy, especially when the gifted actress Colleen Moore makes faces at the camera. Indeed, she brought a new face to Cinderella.

As I have already mentioned, there were other silent films that "modernized" Cinderella. Two others of note are Herbert Brenan's *A Kiss for Cinderella* (1926) and King Vidor's *The Patsy* (1928). Although Brenan does not depict a "new woman," his film, based on J. M. Barrie's play, does feature a servant maid who realizes her dreams of becoming Cinderella in wartime London. In King Vidor's comedy, based on a play written by Barry Conners, Patsy, played by the famous actress Marion Davis, is the younger mistreated daughter, who must do all the chores in the house, even though her father favors her. She is in love with her older spoiled sister's boyfriend, and eventually, after the boyfriend gives her advice on how to catch a man, she catches him. Vidor does not bother following the plot of any traditional Cinderella story. For him, as for many other filmmakers from the 1930s onward, the association of a disowned, downtrodden, maltreated lower-class female (and sometimes male) was enough to recall the Cinderella fairy tale. The traditional plot would be stretched out of shape, but not entirely. It was up to the cartoons to challenge and distort the conventional narrative, and they began doing this in the 1920s.

Unfettered Cinderellas

While it is true that live-action silent films were the first to introduce Cinderellas with new faces and personalities, the cartoons kept pace and were quick to let her take away her bonds and reveal herself/himself in preposterous and provocative ways. Three early animated films indicate that the traditional manner of telling the Cinderella story had to be challenged: Bud Fisher's *A Kick for Cinderella* (1924), Lotte Reiniger's *Aschenputtel* (1922), and Walt Disney's *Cinderella* (1922). All three films are exceptional experiments and twist and turn the plot of the traditional fairy tale in original ways. Fisher's film is based on the comic strip characters of Mutt and Jeff. The tall Mutt decides to give a Charleston exhibition and leaves the desolate Jeff at home before a fireplace. As he weeps, a fairy appears and gives him magic slippers and a limousine that drives through the wall of the house to take him to the dance hall.

He is warned that he must return by midnight. Once he appears, he dances solo and outdoes Mutt, who had made a grand impression on the audience. As he is showing off, however, Mutt ties his coattails to a large plant, and Jeff sees the clock about to strike twelve. He springs onto the clock and struggles to prevent it from moving. He loses, and he also loses his clothes to his embarrassment. Then, all at once, he is struggling with a

Bud Fisher's *A Kick for Cinderella* (1924).

pillow in front of the fireplace. He had been dreaming, and Jeff appears to call him a sap!

Not only is the cartoon unusual because the main character is a male, but also because it ends abruptly with a disappointed "Cinderella man," who does not realize his dreams. And there is certainly no marriage on the horizon. Unlike many early cartoons, there are no chase scenes. The adroitly drawn characters dance in a delightful way, and their facial expressions reveal their jealousy and competitive spirits. However, Fisher's film pales when compared to Lotte Reiniger's silhouette animation. She based her film on an adaptation of the Grimms' fairy tale, and the black-and-white figures are all uniquely cut to express the personalities of the figures. The film plays upon the motif of cutting, "snip snap," and Reiniger introduces an estrangement effect by having the scissors first cut the figures before they are animated. The screen is predominantly black-with-white boxes opening as if they were stages to reveal the story of Cinderella with a touch of humor. The fat stepmother and the spindly stepsisters are comic figures while Cinderella is shaped as a noble, graceful character. Reiniger eliminates the father figure and gives the doves a major role in helping Cinderella. At the ball the prince is so much in love with Cinderella that he kisses her, falls on his knees, and proposes to her. However, she must flee in her coach that shrinks when she arrives at the tree where her mother is buried. The prince follows but does not recognize her. When he returns to the

Walt Disney's *Cinderella* (1922).

palace, he sends out some droll messengers who fail to do anything. So, the prince returns to Cinderella's house, where the sisters cut off parts of their feet to fit the slipper. In the end, Cinderella triumphs, and the stepmother is so distraught and angry that she splits herself in half.

Reiniger's humor was always subtle, just as her Cinderella is silently and gracefully strong. In contrast, Disney's reworking of Cinderella is raucous and delirious. He sets his story in America of the 1920s and quickly introduces the characters in different contexts. For example, Cinderella works in the kitchen with her only friend, her cat. Incidentally, Disney's major characters, Cinderella, the cat, the dog, the prince, and the king, had already been drawn with more or less the same traits in his remarkable *Puss in Boots* of 1922. The difference here is that the prince is much more active and has a dog as a friend, not a cat. He is first pictured on his horse hunting a bear. To show his mock heroism, Disney has him gallop to a cave where the bears had merrily been playing music, and the prince manages to capture them all and drag them back to his palace. Next we are informed that there will be a ball on Friday the thirteenth. In another comic scene in the kitchen, a fairy godmother who looks more like a witch than a fairy appears and provides Cinderella with a dress and a limousine driven by her cat.

She appears at the ball dressed as a flapper, and the prince immediately falls in love with her. The bearded king dressed in shorts and a gown approves. (He had been the tyrannical villain in *Puss in Boots*.) In addition, the dog falls in love with Cinderella's cat and dances with her. As usual, Cinderella must flee at midnight, and as usual the prince discovers who she is and embraces her in the end. Of course, the dog also embraces the cat. Disney's upbeat film that favors the underdog was characteristic of all his early cartoons and later feature animated films. Here the modern Cinderella is confident that she will win the prince, and the storyline does not disappoint her expectations or those of the viewers.

In Dave Fleischer's *Poor Cinderella* of 1934, the expectations are also fulfilled but gently mocked at the same time. Betty Boop stars in this film and begins by singing a sweet melodramatic song that will be repeated throughout the cartoon:

> I'm just a poor Cinderella.
> Nobody loves me it seems.
> And as I am the poor Cinderella,
> I find my romance in dreams,
> for that's where I meet my prince charming.
> I'm just a poor Cinderella,
> but I'll be a princess some day.

Since Betty, who is not very sexy or provocative in this film due to a more vigorous enforcement of governmental censorship, is the star of the film, there is no mean stepmother, nor do the nasty stepsisters play a role. A charming blue fairy sets her on her way. Her horses sing her theme song. Cupid must hit the prince over the head with a hammer. Betty's foot glides into the lost slipper and she is driven off in a coach with a "just married" sign.

This whimsical cartoon is untypical of the more provocative cartoons that deliberate the fate of Cinderella. In the Terrytoon production of *The Glass Slipper* (1938), the film begins with Cinderella speaking on a phone with a New York accent to her friend Sadie. Dressed in rags, Cinderella recounts how a fairy dressed like the sexy Mae West appeared and sent her to the prince's ball in royal clothes. The people at the ball are dancing to jazz music. The prince resembles a clown and gallops to Cinderella. In the end, when he goes searching for the young woman whose foot will fit the slipper, he visits Sadie, who hangs up the phone expecting to become a princess. However, the fairy Mae West appears and steals the prince, concluding the film with her famous line: "I always get my man."

The explosion of audience expectations—always a critique of sentimental love—is characteristic of two cartoons directed by Tex Avery: *Cinderella Meets Fella* (1938) and *Swingshift Cinderella* (1945). Both films show Avery at his controversial best. In *Cinderella Meets Fella*, he depicts the heroine alone as a tiny doll-like creature dressed in rags. When the clock strikes nine, she becomes irate, picks up the phone, and yells at the police in a harsh voice to go and search for her fairy godmother, who is late for their appointment. The police pick her up. She is drunk and makes mistakes when she uses her magic wand. Cinderella, now in an elegant gown, must drive to the ball in a western coach driven by a cowboy. The prince turns out to be the tipsy Egghead, who appears in other Avery cartoons. They dance to an overly sentimental tune of "Boy Meets Girl," and as the hands of the clock approach midnight, a bird tries to stop them from striking twelve. Before Cinderella dashes off, she purposely drops a slipper right before Egghead's eyes. When he arrives at her house illuminated by fluorescent lights, he finds a note saying that Cinderella got tired of waiting and went to the movies to see a Warner film. Egghead rushes to the movie house and is pictured on a screen with Cinderella in the audience. She then jumps into the screen and drags Egghead back into the audience so that they can watch a newsreel together.

Avery typically uses every technique possible to estrange the audience from the story, especially to prevent viewers from identifying with any of the characters. The viewers must be conscious that they are watching something artificial and are sharing the jokes that nevertheless will surprise the viewers because anything is possible in an Avery cartoon. In *Swingshift Cinderella*, loosely based on his *Red Hot Riding Hood*, the film begins with the wolf chasing a tiny bratty Red Riding Hood until the wolf realizes it is the wrong character. So, he ditches Little Red Riding Hood, transforms himself into a debonair gentleman, and drives to Cinderella's house. Cinderella is a voluptuous blonde, and he attempts to invade her house. She calls upon an older grandma fairy godmother to protect her. Eventually, Cinderella goes off to perform in a nightclub, and the fairy godmother tames the wolf and brings him to the nightclub where Cinderella, reminiscent of Red Riding Hood in *Red Hot Riding Hood*, struts and sings, "All the little chicks are in love with a groovy wolf. Oh, Wolfie, Oh Wolfie!" In the end, she escapes, returns home, and changes into factory clothes for her swing shift. When she boards a bus, she thinks she is free of the wolf, but the passengers all turn out to be wolves who ogle her.

Avery's Cinderellas are cunning, strong, and feisty young women. Marriage is far from their minds. Even in cartoons in which Cinderella marries, it is clear that she refuses to be a wimp. In *Cinderella and the Glass Huarache* (1964), directed by Hawley Pratt, Cinderella becomes a sexy Spanish dancer and marries the handsome son of Don Miguel. In this cartoon that features an unidentified cowboy in a saloon, who tells the "sad" story of

Tex Avery's *Swingshift Cinderella* (1945).

Cinderella, we learn that the story is sad because the storyteller had married the mean stepmother. Of course, irony is key to two versions of Cinderella that appeared as fractured fairy tales in the Rocky and Bullwinkle TV series: *Cinderella* (1960) and *Cinderella Returns* (1960). In both films Cinderella must sign a contract with a short plump fairy godmother before the woman agrees to help her. In the first cartoon, Cinderella, who must sell pots and pans if she is to marry a rich prince, is unaware that the prince is broke and wants to marry a rich heiress. In the end, he turns into a Fuller Brush man, selling brushes from door to door. In the second film, the prince wants to marry a commoner and leave the castle, and Cinderella pretends to be rich and beautiful and ignores the fairy's warnings that she should be her common self. Here, too, Cinderella loses the prince. This time, to the fairy godmother.

It is due, in great part, to the cartoon tradition that the wishes and dreams of Cinderella are made to seem ridiculous or are never fulfilled in the way that Cinderella hopes. Even though she fails in winning a prince, Cinderella is more often depicted as an assertive and opportunistic young woman than a passive servant. She senses deep down that she has the wits, charm, and determination to change herself and her status. Yet some filmmakers question whether it is better for her to be so independent or whether she should assume the role of a demure, humble, and helpless victim. Kindness, piety, and purity, so many a young woman has learned, are the good girl's way to success and marriage.

Glorification of the Good Cinderella through Music

In the postwar years, the pious victimized Cinderella has been celebrated in musicals by the Walt Disney Company, Rodgers and Hammerstein, the Sesame Street Studio, and repeat performances of Rossini's *Cenerentola* and Prokofiev's ballet *Zolushka* (1945). Indeed, it is important not to underestimate the role of theater, vaudeville, and opera in the development of the cinematic discourses of particular fairy tales. In addition, the adaptations made for television and the market for DVDs are also significant. However, it would be misleading to lump all the different kinds of musical "Cinderellas" together, because many of the repetitive productions of the same opera, play, or book adaptation interpret the libretti and scripts in diverse ways. Nevertheless, there is a dominant sentiment in the filmic representations of Cinderella that echoes throughout the history of the adaptations—poor Cinderella as stereotype of the persecuted heroine who *cannot* take charge of her life and who needs the help of magic powers and men to bring her happiness in the form of marriage. Almost all the musical versions follow in Perrault's tradition, which extolled the model of the pious, good-hearted young woman.

Although Rossini's libretto of *La Cenerentola* (1817), written by Jacopo Ferretti, brought about great changes in Perrault's plot and characters, it basically upheld the conservative role that women were to play in society. As is well known, Ferretti introduced a stepfather as villain and replaced the fairy godmother with the philosopher Alidoro, the prince's tutor. In addition, the prince is disguised as his own valet, and the valet, as the prince. The opera is livened by a series of mistaken identities and the prince, who falls in love with Cinderella from the time he catches a glimpse of her. It is her pure heart that wins the day, and the prince rescues her from a life of drudgery. Prokoviev's ballet of *Zolushka* was much more traditional than Rossini's opera and basically reproduced Perrault's tale through a remarkable musical score. The major change that he made was to introduce the fairy as a beggar at the beginning of the play, something that Kirkwood also did in 1914. Otherwise, Cinderella was to dream and dance her way into the prince's heart.

However, the musical adaptation of Perrault's tale that truly ignited filmgoers' hearts was Disney's animated *Cinderella* (1950), followed much later by two direct-to-video film sequels *Cinderella II: Dreams Come True*

(2002) and *Cinderella III: A Twist in Time* (2007). It is difficult to understand why this film, which resuscitated the Disney production of fairy-tale films in 1950, had so much success.[1] The music is mediocre; the plot is boring; and the themes are trite; the character of Cinderella, who loses both her parents within minutes of the beginning of the film is that of embodied sweetness and helplessness. If it were not for the animals, the two cute mice Jaq and Gus, the wonderfully mean cat Lucifer, and the loyal dog Bruno the Bloodhound, not to mention the bumbling king, who dreams of his son marrying a beautiful princess and looking after his grandchildren, the film would not be worth mentioning in the Cinderella discourse. However, it is important to note because it contributed to the development of the musical melodramatic tradition that stems from the féerie of the nineteenth century. The Disney corporation tried to rectify the mistakes made in the original *Cinderella* with its two sequels by making Cinderella more active. For instance, in *Dreams Come True*, Cinderella plays a sort of matchmaker and tries to help her stepsister, Anastasia, who has fallen in love with a common baker. Once again, the mice steal the show in their conflict with Lucifer. The stepmother and stepsisters are incorrigibly nasty. In *A Twist in Time*, Cinderella and the prince celebrate their first wedding anniversary when Lady Tremaine, the evil stepmother, steals the fairy godmother's wand and uses it to send everyone on a trip back in time before Cinderella married the prince. Lady Tremaine wants to redo everything so that her daughter Anastasia will be chosen to marry the prince. However, the mice save the day again; the prince blocks the wand's power; Anastasia has a change of conscience, takes the wand from her mother, and gives it to Cinderella, who then returns it to the fairy godmother, who restores order and enables Cinderella and her prince to remarry. Although Cinderella is more active in this film, about the only thing the film really wants to do is to recreate interest in other Disney films about Cinderella and to pull on the purse strings of children and adults.

The goals of other musicals are about the same: to create sweet and hollow entertainment. A classic example of live-action trash is the Richard Rodgers and Oscar Hammerstein made for a TV production of 1957. This film features a mousy Cinderella, who constantly looks at the prince with goggle-eyes, and a prince, who stiffly rides a horse and wards off his parents who want him to marry a wealthy princess. The major shift in emphasis regards the prince. Almost all the post-1950 films to the present seek to develop a prince who is much more democratic and aware of his sentiments for Cinderella, whom he meets accidentally at the beginning of the film. In the Rodgers and Hammerstein musical, the plot is so artificial and contrived, and the songs, so mushy and saccharine, that one wonders why such an adaptation has been reproduced two other times on television in 1965 and 1997.

In contrast, *The Slipper and the Rose*, a 1976 British musical, directed by Bryan Forbes, is a delightful farce that raises some serious questions while mocking social prejudices in England and spicing the Cinderella story with whacky humor. The film takes place in the tiny kingdom of Euphrania during the seventeenth or eighteenth century, and the bumbling king and his lord high chamberlain are intent on arranging a marriage for the prince to a princess of a powerful nation to protect Euphrania. However, Prince Edward will have nothing of this. Indeed, the film is more about him than about Cinderella, who is cruelly sent to the kitchen cellar after her father dies. Once again, we have a poor waif, who is helped by a witty godmother. If it were not for her humor and the many comical scenes that reveal how the prince is revolted by his father's plans, and how his father and his stupid courtiers foul up their plans, the film would be totally boring. In contrast to the bland American musicals that take the sentiments of a meek Cinderella seriously, this British musical, despite the grand finale of a happy ending, rescues itself by not taking itself seriously and transforming the Cinderella story into a vaudeville play.

The most hilarious vaudeville musical, however, is the Sesame Street version, *Cinderelmo* (1999), directed by Bruce Leddy. Perhaps it should be called a "mock Cinderella," for the hero is the downtrodden, easygoing, redheaded Elmo, who dreams of dancing with the princess. In typical Sesame Street tradition, the film mixes humans with Muppets as though a multicultural, multiethnic, and animistic world were normal. Most of the familiar Muppets from the Sesame Street TV show are in this film, and role reversals are the rule. Elmo's stepbrothers are Muppets and his stepmother a human played in burlesque style by Kathy Najimy. Princess Charming, who is turning eighteen, must marry by the end of a ball, otherwise her parents will lose the kingdom. She, too, is human and takes everything in stride with good humor. Since she has never found anyone she would like to marry, her parents agree to invite everyone, including monsters, to the ball. Elmo receives the help of a gentle but clumsy godfather, who turns the dog into a prince and the dog's bowl into a coach. After much commotion at the ball, Elmo dances with the princess and impresses her. When he loses his silver slipper, she pursues him and discovers that he is much too young to marry—he is only three-and-a-half—but the fluffy dog is retransformed into a prince at the end, and it appears that he might fit into this bizarre kingdom. The song and dance routines are lively and are part of the jests.

Throughout the film, transformations and mutations and mistakes provide opportunities to see the Cinderella story anew without melodrama and a sentimental ending. The humor that borders on the ridiculous is in tune with the cartoon depictions of the Cinderella tale, but here, in contrast to the cartoons, the humor is always gentle.

One other semimusical worth noting is the black-and-white Russian film *Zolushka* (1947), which has become a classic. The film features a cute diminutive Cinderella, whose father adores her but is too weak to help her confront the tyrannical stepmother. The most interesting character is a bumbling king who keeps losing his wig as he does his best to find a perfect young woman for his son, the prince. The songs, mainly sung by Cinderella, are melodic, and the dancing is entertaining. In the final analysis, however, the film is nothing but a traditional melodrama that must have lightened Russian hearts after the devastation of World War II.

Diverse Postwar Cinderellas in Europe and America

Numerous melodramatic live-action Cinderella films continued to be produced after World War II, and they reflect shifting cultural differences with regard to the character of Cinderella, that is, the role young women were and are expected to play, and cultural attitudes toward the traditional tales. In Europe, there was a strong tendency to stick closely to the narrative of the Grimms' version. Strange to say, Perrault's version was rarely adapted, even in France.

During the 1950s Fritz Genschow directed a series of fairy-tale films in West Germany that were directed at young audiences. In 1955 he filmed a live-action cute if not kitschy *Cinderella*, in which a very meek and persecuted young girl is helped by a fairy godmother, who springs from a tree planted at her mother's grave, and by a collective of real animals. A male voiceover storyteller narrates the film, and there is a comic forest spirit, who assumes different guises to liven the film. The father is kept alive in this version only to absent himself when his new wife and stepdaughters mistreat his daughter. Cinderella is a pious child, who never speaks back to her victimizers and spends more time at her mother's grave than in the house. Ultimately, her piety wins the day, and after her stepsisters cut off a toe and a heel in a vain attempt to win the prince, Cinderella is asked how they should be punished. Instead of having their eyes pecked out by pigeons, she sentences them to one year of hard labor so they can realize what it is like to be a serf. While the acting is at times condescending to children, the film is well made and is an endeavor to keep the legacy of the Grimms' version alive and well in West Germany. The difficulty with this depiction of a staid young Cinderella is that it continued to foster myths about fixed gender roles in West Germany that oblige marriageable girls to silent observance.

Short mention should be made about the animated Russian film *Cinderella* (1979), directed by Ivan Aksenchuk and produced by the Soyuzmultfilm Studio. Short because the film, though in color, is a drab imitation of the Disney plot and structure, despite the Cold War. In this film a totally passive young girl watched over by the dark portrait of her dead mother lets everyone boss her around or push her to her destiny. She is dressed according to standard—a patched dress and clogs with blonde hair and blue eyes. The drawings are black line cartoons with sweet music. If there was a feminist movement in the Soviet Union during the 1970s, this film certainly contributed to its setback.

The same could be said about the German/Czech *Aschenputtel* (1989), directed by Karin Brandauer, which more or less repeated the Genschow literal interpretation of the Grimms' tale, though Cinderella appears to be a bit more active. This may be due to the fact that her father is a total fool and refuses to recognize how badly his new wife and stepdaughters treat his daughter. Yet, out of reasons of respect—one does not talk back to one's brutal stepmother—Cinderella cannot contradict her stepmother in front of her father. Once again we have a pious daughter looked after by a tree and pigeons. Her visits to her mother's grave and a few prayers enable her to win a prince. In both the German films, the prince is basically a handsome appendage, as he is in the Grimms' tale. He functions basically as the "pretty" reward that is due to Cinderella once she passes the test of obedience and fidelity.

The only European film that resists conforming to the Grimm hypotext of Cinderella is Václav Vorlíček's *Three Wishes for Cinderella* (1974). The title in Czech is *Tři ořišsky pro Popelku* or "Three Hazel Nuts for Cinderella," and the film is based on a fairy tale written by Božena Němcová, one of the great Czech writers of folk and fairy tales in the nineteenth century. Vorlíček, the most prolific Czech director of fairy tales, spiced this dynamic tale with clear feminist ingredients in his film that corresponded to the changing role of women in postwar Czechoslovakia. Moreover, he was fortunate to find the talented actress Libuše Šafránková to play Cinderella. She brought a charming rebellious spirit to her role and was so captivating that the film became a cult classic in Europe.

True, the film, which takes place in eighteenth-century Bohemia, does not break greatly with the melodramatic tendency in the Cinderella filmic discourse, but it does display a modern Cinderella, who takes destiny in her hands with alacrity. (In part, this may be due to Němcová's text, which was imbued with an unusual ideological impulse. (She herself was a socialist, who struggled against oppression in her country.) In the film, Cinderella is an orphan who has undeservedly been cast out of her family mansion on a large estate by a greedy stepmother and her nasty plump daughter and forced to work like a serf. Nevertheless, the spritely Cinderella shrugs off the maltreatment and is supported by all the workers on the estate, along with her dog Casper, her horse Nicolas, and an owl named Rosalie. Indeed, she has a love for nature and loves to spend a great deal of time in the forest. Moreover, she is an expert rider and hunter, thanks to her dead father, and when she first meets the prince in the forest, she embarrasses him by preventing him from shooting a deer. In another instance, disguised as a forester, she defeats the prince in a shooting contest. Baffled, the egotistical prince, who is somewhat a rebel himself, wants to become better acquainted with her, but she outwits him and always manages to escape his grasp. Still, it is apparent that the prince, who does not want to wed, is similar in spirit to Cinderella. When he is finally forced by his well-meaning parents to find a wife, a ball with beautiful women is held, and of course, Cinderella, aided by three magic hazel nuts given to her by a coachman, charms him. The rest is history.

Vorlíček's film, though sentimental, succeeds because he does not force the humor of mistaken identities, nor does he use magic tricks to create a false sense of enchantment. For instance, there are no rats, mice, lizards, or pumpkins. Cinderella rides to the ball on her own horse. The scenes at the country estate, the palace, and the forest are stark and realistic. The images of nature are contrasted with the cluttered courtyard and artificiality of the palace. Cinderella and the prince are free spirits. Cinderella receives help from friends and animals because they naturally respond to her courage and good will, not because she is helpless. Their help also signifies that one talented individual cannot succeed alone. At times the music is schmaltzy, and the shots of Cinderella galloping through the snow with her prince are overly romantic. But overall *Three Wishes for Cinderella* is a contentious film that challenges traditional assumptions about Cinderella as a poor helpless waif. She will wed out of love not out of necessity, and it is clear that she has come into her own.

Whereas most European directors—perhaps because they are more historically inclined—have chosen to set the Cinderella story in the baroque period, American and British filmmakers have tended to adapt Cinderella stories and novels for the screen in innovative ways to use the story as a vehicle for some well-known actor or actress, and to relocate the action to a more modern setting and attract teenage audiences by showcasing a teenage star as representative of girl power. In almost all the films, the emphasis is not so much on Cinderella's claim to her legacy but on the maltreatment by nonbiological stepmothers and stepsiblings. In every case the underdog triumphs against odds with or without the help of friends. In the worst cases—and there are many—the fairy tale is transformed into melodramatic spectacle for the spectacle's sake.

The cinematic adaptations of prose works are among the most interesting if not the most creative interrogations of underdogs in the modern Cinderella cinematic discourse. For instance, Babette Cole's idiosyncratic picture book *Prince Cinders* (1987) was adapted and made into a highly amusing animated film by Derek Hayes in 1994. The film is a close rendition of the book, which concerns a skinny, hardworking boy exploited by his three muscle-bound brothers. Turned into a goony ape by an incompetent fairy, Prince Cinders accidentally wins the heart of a down-to-earth princess while his brothers are turned into fluttering winged fairies who must do household chores. In another made-for-TV British miniseries, *I Was a Rat* (2001), Philip Pullman's delightful 1999 novel provides another original twist to the Cinderella tale. This time a page boy who appears at the door of an aging couple explains that he had once been a rat and that the fairy had not retransformed him after Cinderella had married and become Lady Ashlington and then Princess Aurelia. The couple takes him in, name him Roger, and send him to school, but he continues to behave like a rat. The head of the school wants to beat him because of his disobedience, but Roger escapes and is portrayed as dangerous vermin by the mass media. The film set at the beginning of the twentieth century expands upon the novel set in the second half of the twentieth century, and the director, Laurie Lynd, adds a touch of Charles Dickens's social realism mixed with fairy-tale motifs and some slapstick humor. For instance, Roger is captured by the police and taken to a royal medical laboratory where experiments are done to determine whether he is a monster and should be exterminated for the good of the people. Only Princess Aurelia, who knows the truth about his background, can save him and reveal the stupidity of the people and the press that want to persecute a simple boy. The film explores the entire question of identity and whether it is better to remain a simple kitchen maid or a rat rather than to rise in society. The figure of Cinderella is an auxiliary in this instance, but the film does raise the questions about the manipulation of identity at a time when the media spreads more "myths" about people than truth.

In another more serious film made for American TV, *The Confessions of an Ugly Stepsister* (2002), Gregory Maguire's complex and riveting 1999 novel is transformed into an equally compelling film about a Dutch Cinderella viewed from the perspective of a mute ugly stepsister. Actually, the story is less about a Cinderella type and more about a complicated stepmother. Maguire set his story in the small city of Haarlem in seventeenth-century Holland, and he has a great eye for capturing the customs and living conditions of the time. The film follows suit and produces a nuanced historical portrait of the times; the images do not form a magical enchanting tale. The narrative concerns the return of the widow Margarethe Fisher from England with her two daughters, Ruth, an awkward but gentle mute, and Irene, a plain but gifted and compassionate girl. Fierce in her determination to protect her daughters and to provide a livelihood for them, Margarethe finds a job as a servant for a master painter and then as head of the wealthy van den Meer household, where Irene is giving English lessons to a beautiful and anxious girl named Clara, who had been abducted and saved from her kidnappers when she was a child. Eventually, her mother Margarethe takes over the household and marries Cornelius van den Meer after the death of his wife. From this point on she rules the domestic affairs of the house with an iron fist. Ruth's "confession" is a true story mainly about her mother and her ambitious striving to make sure that her own genetic daughters would have a better life. She acts out of desperation and tries to overcome poverty by any means she can just as the Dutch merchants ruthlessly deal with one another in the town of Haarlem. It is a dog-eat-dog world that the film depicts, and it is no surprise that the crude and domineering Margarethe is not punished in the end but lives on to represent the indomitable will not just of stepmothers, but of mothers obsessed with protecting their daughters.

While the cinematic adaptation of Maguire's work remained close to the original novel, this is not the case with *Ella Enchanted* (1997), written by Gail Carson Levine. The book, which won the esteemed Newberry Award, is a straightforward fairy-tale novel about a young girl named Ella, who lives in the Kingdom of Frell and is granted the gift of obedience by a fairy named Lucinda. This gift creates grave problems for her when she turns fifteen and her mother dies. At the funeral she makes the acquaintance of Prince Charmont (Char), and they become friends. But Ella is now sent to a boarding school, and two nasty sisters, spoiled daughters of Dame Olga, take advantage of her after learning about her spell of obedience, which is more a curse than a gift. To break the spell Ella goes in pursuit of Lucinda, who refuses to rescind the gift of obedience. Ella is almost killed by ogres but is saved by Char. In the meantime, Ella's father, who is in debt and needs a rich wife, marries Dame Olga, and when her father leaves to conduct some trading business, Ella's life becomes hell. Her only hope is to marry Char, who proposes to her. She refuses because her curse of obedience would endanger his kingdom. Now the fairies Lucinda and Mandy come to her rescue and enable her to attend a ball, break the curse, and agree to marry Char.

This convoluted plot is made even more convoluted in the film by the addition of an evil uncle named Sir Edgar, who rules Frell as regent and has a vicious snake. Edgar wants to kill Char, whom Ella more or less saves. There are all sorts of struggles involving ogres, giants, and elves. In the end, however, Ella gets her man, and the film, which stars Anne Hathaway, is fluff entertainment that adds a touch of feminism to make it more fashionable.

Cinderella films have often been used as vehicles for celebrities or potential celebrities to charm and delight audiences while seemingly probing the meaning of assumed Perrault and Grimm hypotexts. A good example is Frank Tashlin's *Cinderfella* (1960), which stars Jerry Lewis as a goofy innocent heir to millions and Ed Wynn as a fairy godfather, who explains to him how women have taken advantage of simpletons like himself for centuries. Tashlin, who worked as an animator in cartoons before turning to live-action films, directs Lewis in song and dance numbers that enable Lewis to show off his slapstick routines. While amusing, the film is more notable for its stupid misogyny than anything else.

The "celebrity" film that may have caused a rash of other sentimental films, such as *Cinderella* (2000), featuring Kathleen Turner as a vicious femme fatale, *A Cinderella Story* (2004), featuring Hilary Duff as a victimized waitress in a diner, and *Another Cinderella Story* (2008), featuring newcomers Selena Gomez and Andrew Seeley as dancing Cinderella and prince, is undoubtedly *Ever After* (1998) with its star-studded cast of Jeanne Moreau, Drew Barrymore, Angelica Huston, and Dougray Scott to name but a few of the stellar actors. This film directed with great craft by Andy Tennant awakened a new interest in the Cinderella story, I believe, not only because of its box-office success, but, like *Three Wishes for Cinderella*, because it was also intent on displaying a tomboy young woman with power who could control her own destiny, and in this case, pursue her utopian dreams. Both films—and there is an apparent influence of the Czech film on *Ever After*—were designed to speak to the problematic condition of late twentieth-century young women, who no longer need men to save them while they must still abide by conventions and conditions set by men.

Ever After has a particularly clever frame. The initial shots show the Brothers Grimm arriving at the home of the elderly Grande Dame of France played appropriately by the great actress Jeanne Moreau, the grande dame of late twentieth-century French cinema. She has invited them to her elegant mansion to tell them a "true" story about her great-great-grandmother, Danielle, and to correct their version of Cinderella. There is also an implicit critique of Perrault's version. She begins her tale as the brothers admire a beautiful oil painting of a young woman. The Grande Dame indicates that there is a story behind the painting. The brothers' curiosity as been piqued, and of course, the audience is curious, too, but is aware that a few games are being played when the Grande Dame begins her "true" story because we all know that there is no authentic Cinderella tale.

According to the Grande Dame, however, Cinderella's real name was Danielle De Barbarac, and she narrates in a flashback what actually happened in the seventeenth century. The plot that incorporates motifs and characters from previous Cinderella films, albeit from a much more pronounced "feminist" perspective, can easily be recapitulated: Danielle is raised solely by her father after her mother's death (which accounts for her tomboy attributes); when she becomes a young woman, her father surprises her by marrying a baroness with two comely daughters, one nasty, the other kind; the father unexpectedly dies from a heart attack; the Baroness Rodmilla De Ghent takes over the household and reduces Danielle to the status of a maid; Danielle accidentally meets and embarrasses Prince Henry of France in a field; Danielle pretends to be a comtesse; Danielle rescues Henry from gypsies; the baroness keeps treating Danielle in a mean-spirited way and plans to have her nasty daughter marry Prince Henry; the king and queen, desperate to create a line of heirs, want Prince Henry to marry a Spanish princess; Prince Henry refuses but agrees to choose a bride at a masquerade ball; Danielle is almost prevented by her stepmother from attending the ball, but servants help her to appear at the ball; however, Danielle is humiliated when her stepmother reveals that she is not of noble blood; Prince Henry deserts her; Leonard da Vinci, the great painter, reprimands him; Danielle is sold to a sinister nobleman; Prince Henry decides to break off his marriage to the Spanish princess and save Danielle from the sinister nobleman only to find that Danielle has freed herself; Prince Henry apologizes and proposes to Danielle; the stepmother and one of her daughters are sentenced to work in the royal laundry; the kind stepsister is given a position at the court; Danielle and Henry wed and supposedly live ever after; Leonardo da Vinci reveals a painting that he has made of Danielle.

There are other events in this finely acted film shot as a period piece. In the end, the Grande Dame has the final word and displays the glass slipper that Danielle had worn to the masquerade ball. The brothers are bedazzled and convinced. They ride off and appear to have been taught a true historical lesson on the screen, while people in the audience can delight in being part of a joke that has been played on the poor brothers. Of course, spectators can also be delighted in having watched images of a headstrong young woman, who reads Thomas Moore's *Utopia* as a bible and fights for the liberation of slaves and indentured servants.

But can they? In one of the more insightful critiques of the film, Christy Williams declares:

> *Ever After* assumes a feminist stance, but offers a mass-mediated idea of feminism in which individual women can be strong and achieve equality through personal actions that do not, however, work to challenge or change the underlying patriarchal structure of society. And these heroines can still be (sexually) desirable and marriageable in doing so.[2] (Williams 2010, 101–2)

Although I agree with many of Williams's arguments, I believe that she exaggerates the extent to which *Ever After* is complicit in furthering misogynistic tendencies in contemporary society. If anything, the film, I believe, tends to problematize feminist aspirations and reveal how undependable male love and dedication are when confronted with a young woman with unabashedly democratic ideals and a zest to make social reforms. Moreover, the very frame of the film raises important questions of authenticity and narrative appropriation that Williams appears to misinterpret. The Grande Dame summons the Brothers Grimm to *her* space, where she reappropriates the Cinderella story, told from a female perspective. Or, in other words, she wants to recapture her legacy and confronts the Grimms and history by talking about the accomplishments of her great-great-grandmother. In the face of the evidence, the Grimms do not protest. Rather, they ride off and are apparently jostled by the "truth." In this respect, *Ever After*, while showing the limits of the second wave of feminism, destabilizes the traditional patriarchal narrative while also showing the compromises that young women still make (or must make) to take part in a socioeconomic system that will not allow them to act radically in a political or personal way if they want to be part of the ruling hierarchy. The best that they can hope for is minimal reform, and *Ever After* shows this by making the stepmother and her daughter complicit with the sinister nobleman. They are not the real villains in history though they may be portrayed as the villains in the film. As we know, the real cads in history were men like Prince Henry and his successors, and the real heroines were never Cinderella-type young women, eager to marry well.

What is relevant always depends on who gets to tell his or her story, who is authorized to make his or her film, and who controls the distribution of stories and films. For instance, another film that rivals *Ever After* in its "feminist" significance, one that raises issues rather than proposes a complete answer, is *Ashpet*, directed and produced by Tom Davenport. During the 1980s and 1990s Davenport made original use of the fairy tale and film to enhance viewers' understanding of storytelling, politics, and creativity. One of his best endeavors is his 1990 film, *Ashpet: An American Cinderella*. This cinematic version is about a young white woman named Lily, who learns to reclaim her rights and heritage through the help of a wise black woman whose sense of history and knowledge of oppression empowers the "enslaved" Lily to pursue her dreams. The action takes place in the rural South during the early years of World War II, when people were making sacrifices and forced to separate because of the military draft. But Lily manages to find the strength to overcome isolation and exploitation by piecing together a sense of her own story that her stepmother and stepsisters had taken from her. Consequently, Davenport's Cinderella story is no longer history in a traditional male sense, that is, no longer the Grimms' story, or a simple rags-to-riches story. Nor is it a didactic feminist interpretation of Cinderella. Instead, Davenport turns it into an American tale about conflicts within a matrilineal heritage in the South, narrated from beginning to end by a well-known Afro-American storyteller, Louise Anderson, who plays the role of Dark Sally, the magical conjure-woman and fairy godmother. The focus of the film becomes Dark Sally, and it shows how her storytelling can lead a young woman to recover a sense of her history and give her the strength to assert herself, as many women are doing today.

Mounting and Dismantling Cinderella

The question of voice, control of the narrative and the camera, and representations of ideological conceptions of success and happiness are crucial in the creation of all fairy-tale films, especially those with heroines similar to Cinderella. *Ashpet* was made during the late 1980s, when the first phase of the feminist movement had made its mark, and the second phase (of many more to come) was in the process of solidifying gains and also receiving a backlash. Some of the gains and losses are reflected to a certain extent in three mainstream Hollywood films with "Cinderella-like" protagonists: Howard Deutsch's *Pretty in Pink* (1986), Mike Nichols's *Working Girl* (1988), and Gary Marshall's *Pretty Woman* (1990).[3] Each of these films depict the travails of lower-class women, all white, who use their elbows, cunning, and sensitivity, to scramble to the top. In *Pretty in Pink*, Andie, a working-class teenager in Chicago, falls in love with a rich preppie named Blane McDonough. Their class differences lead to class conflicts, but Andie eventually gets his man at the school prom when he exhibits a love that helps him rise above class arrogance. In *Working Girl*, Tess McGill, a working-class secretary from Staten Island, seeks to become an executive in a Wall Street firm, but she is victimized by her female boss, Katharine Parker, who steals one of her wonderful business ideas to raise her own prestige. However, while Katharine is cooped up due to a skiing accident, Tess accidentally meets her boss's fiancé, Jack Trainer, an executive at another corporation, pursues her business idea with success, and falls in love with Jack at a wedding party. When she is seemingly exposed as a fraud, Jack sticks up for her, and Tess gets her man and a promotion to an executive position. In *Pretty Woman*, which takes place in Los Angeles, Edward Lewis, a ruthless New York corporate executive, arrives to take over and exploit a family business. He accidentally meets a good-natured prostitute, lower-class Vivian Ward, who helps him find his way to his hotel. At first Edward does not realize that Vivian is a prostitute, and when he does, he decides to employ her so that he can help him in a business deal. She learns manners and culture in the process, and he learns how to soften. After some misunderstandings and an attempted rape by a business associate, Edward makes a decision to give Vivian what she wants, which is "the fairy tale."

All three films are loaded with super Hollywood stars: Molly Ringwald, Melanie Griffith, Harrison Ford, Sigourney Weaver, Alec Baldwin, Joan Cusack, Richard Gere, and Julia Roberts. Typically Hollywood, these films are not works of art but vehicles for the actors to attain more celebrity and commodities for the producers to increase their profits in the film industry. All three were directed by male filmmakers who used male cinematographers to realize their male fantasies. The sites of the films cover America's dream cities: Chicago, New York, Los Angeles. The plots that drip with sentimentality and conventionality are predictable: lower-class struggling girl (Cinderella) meets wealthy cultivated male (prince); lower-class girl wants to find a place in the opulent world of the rich and famous; she needs helpers (fairy godmothers) to show her the way to her goal; she passes various tests and overcomes obstacles to show that she is worthy of moving up in the world; she claims her prince as trophy.

It is ridiculous to try to salvage these films for contemporary feminism by analyzing how the Cinderellas in these films demonstrate their talents and are active, humane, thoughtful, and assertive, as some critics have done. Such "salvation" merely rationalizes the sequence of demeaning behavior that the female protagonists must exhibit: they must obsequiously learn the male rules of the game to attain status and wealth, while believing they are making a stand for women's souls. A true rebellion is out of the question. They mount their male trophies while being mounted themselves as complicit in ways males fantasize about new kinds of Cinderellas.

However, can a Cinderella girl act any differently in a socioeconomic system that lays traps for them in every game situation? Can a filmmaker depict other valid possibilities other than complicity? These are the questions asked by Ericka Beckman, an independent filmmaker, in her highly experimental and provocative short film, *Cinderella* (1986). In the process she dismantles the traditional nineteenth-century and Hollywood narratives of Cinderella and positions a young working woman on the verge of self-discovery. There will be no closed happy end in this film.

Beckman's story gives the girl Cinderella and the tale itself a total remake. Before the title is flashed on the screen, we see a farmer heading toward a small wooden building with FORGE written in large letters. Then the title appears indicating that we are to view a Cinderella story. Indeed, we shall see a forgery of the traditional Cinderella that will be forged before our eyes, but the forgery will ironically lead to the forging of a new Cinderella, truer to the position of women in the contemporary Western world, for this forgery is a woman's appropriation of male fantasizing and an assertion of a female, if not feminist voice. Inside the forgery there is an accordion player chanting and squeezing a papier-mâché accordion while a couple of blacksmiths are working in tune to the music and chants. Cinderella, dressed in working clothes, pumps papier-mâché bellows fanning the fire in the glowing furnace. Suddenly a voice is heard that announces: "Cinderella. Now's the hour. From the fire comes your power!" Soon a gift-wrapped box comes tumbling out of the furnace. Once Cinderella opens the box she discovers a green satin dress with a crinoline. Female voices sing that the game is about to begin and that she must use the dress to win the prince. However, no sooner does she wear the dress than the chorus accuses her of being a robber and announces that she must be put in her place. Then Cinderella is pictured in her work clothes back at the bellows. A few moments later, another gift box appears, and it now becomes clear that Cinderella is being tossed into a computer-generated game on a grid that, at times, resembles a spider's web as does the crinoline frame of her dress. She is fired up, so to speak, and enticed. If she wants to win the game and the prince, she must learn the right moves, and as she tries three times, she is taunted and also instructed by the chorus what she must do to become the perfect player. As a "Greek" chorus, the voices can be likened to the messages of corporate America that sets the standards for marketing and consumption. To rise from her working class and to succeed, Cinderella is expected to conform to these standards.

In many respects, Beckman's film can be likened to a Brechtian learning play without the didacticism of Brecht. The startling images of Cinderella's repeated endeavors to win the game, which is really a game of entrapment, are closer to surrealism than to the social realism of Brecht. An animated clock jostles and intimidates her and sounds warnings. She is frightened into minting money. Robots and machines appear to test her as if she were a laboratory guinea pig. Yet the images that dissolve into one another meld structures and space. Indeed, Cinderella is like a lovely Victorian Alice in wonderland that makes no sense, but this time it is a contemporary working-class Cinderella caught in a computer game, and as she unravels the grid and the straitjacket of the crinoline, she begins to sing for herself and the film ends on a strident note:

Let me set the record straight,
How I played it differently.
If I can't change what I see,
Change it in my memory.

I see there's no end to this game.
When it's over, it starts up again.
Lift up your skirts. He's attracted to you.
He'll give you money for a copy or two.
The company will tell you what to do.
Residuals are too good to be true!

Listen to the record, spinning like a top,
I can put my finger down. I can make it stop.

I feel something rising up,
rising, rising through the cracks.
Pushing it's way to the top.
Nothing's going to hold me back!

A song is rising, rising from the cracks.
It's been tied down so long,
it's striking back!
NO NO NO . . .

All these circles, these tattoos,
my skirt records what I live through.
I'm rising up, I'm turning round.
My skirts will never be let down!

NO, NO, No . . .

Although produced in 1986, Beckman's brilliant film is still very topical and definitely more significant for the Cinderella filmic discourse than the other faux "feminist" Cinderella films of the 1980s and 1990s. The dreams of underdogs, whether they are female or male, who seek to liberate themselves from the oppression of wicked stepmothers, stepsisters, and dysfunctional fathers and from an "evil" social system, are both real and valid. The interference and intercession of helpers are also necessary if an underdog is to understand how games work. Yet if the oppressed do not want to join the wealthy upper class to become oppressors, they must learn how to resist conformity while maintaining their integrity. As Beckman's film demonstrates, there's no end to the game as it is played now, and resistance is the first step toward recreating a Cinderella tale with the possibility of self-definition.

Resistance and self-definition are the keys to understanding the unusual film, *Year of the Fish* (2007), directed by David Kaplan, another independent filmmaker, who used rotoscopic animation to depict the desperate situation of a young Chinese woman, Ye Xian, in a massage parlor in New York's Chinatown. The rotoscopic process involves tracing over live-action film that gives the pictures the effect of a watercolor painting and a graphic novel. It also creates an estrangement effect that is perfect for the narrative perspective: an estranged young woman viewing a strange "new world." After her mother's death, Ye Xian, who can barely speak English, has been sent to New York by her impoverished father to help support him and his family. Misled by relatives, Ye Xian believes that she will be working in a professional studio of some kind. However, once she signs a contract with Mrs. Su, the owner of the parlor and the "wicked stepmother," she soon realizes that she is supposed to be a sex worker. But Ye Xian refuses to pleasure men and is thus forced to work as a maid in the parlor to pay back the money. Mrs. Su, who is called Mama by everyone in the parlor, mistreats her and tries to force her to marry her degenerate brother. As Ye Xian tries to make sense out of the strange "culture" in Chinatown, she meets a bizarre "fairy godmother," Auntie Yaga, who has traits of a bag lady and the Russian witch Baba Yaga. This eccentric woman appears and disappears throughout the film. In her initial meeting with Ye Xian, she offers the young woman a goldfish as a good luck charm and later helps her after Mrs. Su kills the goldfish and serves it as a meal to her family of sex workers. Ye Xian also encounters a seemingly demented old man, who mysteriously instructs her and helps her find her way through the morass in Chinatown. At the same time that all this is happening, she falls in love with a young musician named Johnny, her "prince." Attracted by his accordion music, she keeps bumping into him on her errands in Chinatown. Eventually, after they meet at a celebration of the Chinese New Year, he helps her escape the massage parlor.

While Kaplan follows the linear narrative of the traditional Cinderella story, he probes the tale and deepens its significance by relating it to the experiences of a young immigrant woman trying to make sense out of strange signs and customs in an unfamiliar culture. The Chinese world in which she lands in New York is not what she expected. Prostitution, sweat factories, and a vicious employer are what she encounters. Yet she has a remarkable spiritual resolve so that she remains true to herself and protects her integrity at every step toward her freedom. Kaplan focuses entirely on the honest and strong moral character of Ye Xian. The camera reflects the world as she sees it and feels it. She is saved by herself and helped by a few kind people who understand her plight. But the happy ending is, as Kaplan hints, just the beginning of a new life in a Chinatown, which will not change. Like Beckman's Cinderella, however, Ye Xian has learned what kinds of exploitative games people want to play with her, and her resistance to such manipulation can only become stronger.

The Fate of Cinderella in Film

Is the Cinderella character, whether based on Perrault's or the Grimms' tale, doomed perpetually to suffer persecution and to triumph happily in cinematic history in a wedding with a charming prince? Are attempts to change her fate and character more along feminist lines, as in the case of Beckman's *Cinderella* or Tennant's *Ever After*, an indication of changing attitudes toward women in the film industry, or are they merely cosmetic touches intended to appeal to a larger female audience?

In a recent book, *Fairy Tale and Film: Old Tales with a New Spin* (2014), Sue Short writes: "A fraught critical area of critical debate is the question of how feminism has informed our understanding of fairy tales and whether they offer suitable role models. Critiques of the 'innocent persecuted heroine,' relying on marriage to a prince, have led to claims that we should either extend the examples discussed beyond the usual trinity ('Cinderella,' 'Snow White,' and 'Sleeping Beauty') or rewrite these figures to give them greater contemporary relevance" (Short 2014, 15–16). Short is of the opinion that there has been and should be a vigorous re-presentation of the meek Cinderella figure. In her introduction, she states: "Examples such as *A Cinderella Story* (Mark Rosman, 2004), *Never Been Kissed* (Raja Gosnell, 1999) and *My Big Fat Greek Wedding* (Joel Zwick, 1992) are discussed as inspiring new versions of 'Cinderella' with ambitions that attest to feminism's positive impact" (Short 2014, 15–16). At the same time she makes these claims, she expresses some caution as to whether these romantic comedies will really lead to major changes in the manner that women in Cinderella roles will be depicted in films.

If the recent *Cinderella* (2015), directed by Kenneth Branagh, is any example, Short's hopes for a feminist transformation will be disappointed as well as her overly optimistic interpretations of romantic comedies. Branagh based his live-action film, produced by the Disney Studios, on the original 1950 Disney animated film, and the result is a pathetic unoriginal adaptation of a film that was already a trivial, somewhat sexist interpretation of Perrault's fairy tale. Typical of Hollywood, Branagh loaded his film with celebrity actors such as Cate Blanchett, Lily James, Richard Madden, and Helena Bonham Carter and dressed them as Barbie and Ken dolls with flashy costumes in spectacular sets, and then he blithely directed them to imitate the insipid plot of the 1950 Disney film without the humor and music of that film. He did at times "strengthen" his Cinderella by making her somewhat more active, but for the most part, Branagh drilled a message that if Cinderella were kind and courageous, she would be rewarded for her behavior. Indeed, to nobody's surprise, she is rewarded with a prince, and most reviewers of the film chirped in admiration. However, there were some notable exceptions such as Steve Persall of the *Tampa Bay Times*, who wrote: "After he [Branagh] dehydrated the pulpy fun from a Marvel superhero and Tom Clancy spies, you can imagine how Branagh mishandles Cinderella, so reverent and corny when a touch of mockery wouldn't hurt. We don't expect a rollicking fairy tale spoof like *Enchanted* or an abomination like *Snow White and the Huntsman*. But this *Cinderella* is achingly old-fashioned, with scant humor, a regressive heroine and godmother effects that aren't special. Branagh's *Cinderella* is an outdated Disney princess, from a time before Ariel and Belle redefined femininity in 'toons. Plenty of assertive, ambitious women have been drawn since. The trend toward live-action fairy tales gives them even more backbone" (Persall 2015).

Whether or not Cinderella's fate in film is made stronger and more spectacular, it is clear that the message of this underdog in all its iterations has become somewhat hackneyed, and it may be time to reconsider a total remake in keeping with the changing role of women in society or to abandon her story altogether.

Notes

1. For a comprehensive analysis of the film's production, see Ohmer (1993).
2. Williams remarks further:

> The problems identified in second-wave feminism are simplified, emptied of radical critiques of gender inequality, and marketed to young women. This limited version of feminism, which draws on girl power and liberal feminism, reinforces patriarchal authority by its focus on individual achievements and by isolating one woman, the heroine, as an exception to standard feminine behavior. To denaturalize the idea of feminism *Ever After* projects, I will focus on the limited power of Danielle's action within the film's dynamics of narrative authority, the highly gendered representations of Danielle, the reversal of the damsel-in-distress plot, and the re-gendering of the fairy godmother as male. The fragments of the "Cinderella" tale that are maneuvered most consistently in *Ever After*—the phrase "once upon a time," the dress, the rescue, and the godmother—placate a late twentieth- and early twenty-first-century audience's expectations of popular feminism, but fail to move the "Cinderella" story beyond the structural misogyny bound up in the tale's plot. (102)

3. For an informative article, which deals mainly with *Working Girl* and *Pretty Woman*, see Zhao (1996).

References

Booth, Anne Birgitte. 1980. *The Cinderella Cycle*. New York: Arno Press.

Cox, Marian Emily Roalfe. 1967. *Cinderella: Three Hundred and Forty-Five Variants of Cinderella, Catskin, and Capo'Rushes, Abstracted and Tabulated with a Discussion of Medieval Analogues, and Notes* [1893]. Introduction by Andrew Lang. Nendeln, Liechtenstein: Kraus Reprint.

Dika, Vera. 1987. "A Feminist Fairy Tale." *Art in America* (April): 31–33.

Dundes, Alan, ed. 1982. *Cinderella: A Casebook*. New York: Garland.

Greenhill, Pauline, and Sidney Eve Matrix, eds. 2010. *Fairy Tale Films: Visions of Ambiguity*. Logan: Utah State University Press, 2010.

Grimm, Jacob, and Wilhelm Grimm. 2003. *The Complete Fairy Tales of the Brothers Grimm*. Edited and translated by Jack Zipes. 3rd ed. New York: Bantam. 79–83.

Ohmer, Susan. 1993. "'That Rags to Riches Stuff': Disney's Cinderella and the Cultural Space of Animation." *Film History* 5: 231–49.

Perrault, Charles. 1989. "Cinderella or the Glass Slipper." In *Beauties, Beasts, and Enchantments: Classic French Fairy Tales*. Edited and translated by Jack Zipes. New York: Meridian. 25–30.

Persall, Steve. 2015. "Not Much Magic to Disney's New 'Cinderella.'" *Tampa Bay Times*, March 11. http://www.tampabay.com/things-to-do/movies/review-not-much-magic-to-this-cinderella/2220867.

Propp, Vladimir. 2012. *The Russian Folktale*. Edited and translated by Sibelan Forrester. Detroit: Wayne State University Press.

Short, Sue. 2014. *Fairy Tale and Film: Old Tales with a New Spin*. Houndmills, Basinstoke: Palgrave Macmillan.

Ting, Nai-Tung. 1974. *The Cinderella Cycle in China and Indo-China*. Helsinki: Suomalainen Tiedeakatemia.

Williams, Christy. 2010. "The Shoe Fits: *Ever After* and the Pursuit of a Feminist Cinderella." In *Fairy Tale Films: Visions of Ambiguity*, edited by Pauline Greenhill and Sidney Eve Matrix, 99–115. Logan: Utah State University Press.

Zhao, Wuming. 1996. "Cinderella in Eighties' Hollywood." *CineMagaziNet* 1 (Autumn): 1–18. http://www.cmn.hs.h.kyoto-u.ac.jp.

Cinderella Filmography

Cinderella (1898)
Director: George Albert Smith

Cinderella (*Cendrillon ou La petite pantouffe de verre*, 1899)
Director: Georges Méliès

Cinderella (*Cendrillon*, 1907)
Director: Albert Capellani

Cinderella (1907)
Director: Lewis Fitzhannon

A Modern Cinderella (1908)
Director: Percy Stowe

A Modern Cinderella (1910)
Director: J. Stuart Blackton

A Modern Cinderella (1911)
Director: J. Searle Dawley

Cinderella (1911)
Director: George Nichols

A Cowgirl Cinderella (1912)
Producer: David Horsely

Cinderella (*Cendrillon ou La petite pantouffe de verre*, 1912)
Director: Georges Méliès

Cinderella (1912)
Director: Colin Campbell

Cinderella (1912)
Director: Arthur Melbourne Cooper

Cinderella (1912)
Director: Arthur Cooper

Lord Browning and Cinderella (1912)
Director: Van Dyke Brooke

A Modern Cinderella (*Cenerentola*, 1913)
Director: Eleuterio Rodolfi

Cinderella's Gloves (1913)

A Southern Cinderella (1913)
Director: Burton King

Cinderella and the Boob (1913)
Director: Dell Henderson

A Reluctant Cinderella (1913)
Director: C. J. Williams

An Awkward Cinderella (1914)
Director: Otis Turner

Mr. Cinderella (1914)
Director: Eugene Moore

Cinderella (1914)
Director: James Kirkwood

Cinderella (*Aschenbrödel*, 1916)
Director: Urban Gad

A Cripple Creek Cinderella (1916)
Director: Ulysses Davis

The Cinderella Man (1917)
Director: George Sloan Tucker

A Modern Cinderella (1917)
Director: John Adolfi

A Kentucky Cinderella (1917)
Director: Rupert Julian

A Studio Cinderella (1917)
Director: Matt Moore

Cinderella and the Magic Slipper (1917)
Director: Guy McDonell

Daddy Long Legs (1919)
Director: Marshall Neilan

Cinderella Cinders (1920)
Director: Frederick Ireland

A Kitchen Cinderella (1920)
Director: Malcolm St. Clair

Cinderella's Twin (1921)
Director: Dallas Fitzgerald

A Rural Cinderella (1921)
Director: Erle Kenton

Cinderella of the Hills (1921)
Director: Howard Mitchell

The Irish Cinderella (1922)
Features Emralila, poor Irish girl

A Lowland Cinderella (1922)
Director: Sidney Morgan

Cinderella (1922)
Director: Walt Disney

Cinderella (*Aschenputtel*, 1922)
Director: Lotte Reiniger

The Lost Shoe (*Der verlorene Schuh*, 1923)
Director: Ludwig Berger

A Kick for Cinderella (1924)
Director: Bud Fisher

Cinderella (1924)
Director: Herbert Dawley

The Comediennes (1924)
USA silent comedy. Contains *Cinderella Cinders* with Alice Howell.

A Kiss for Cinderella (1925)
Director: Herbert Brenon

Cinderella (1925)
Director: Walter Lantz

Ella Cinders (1926)
Director: Alfred E. Green

Mr. Cinderella (1926)
Director: Norman Taurog

A Bowery Cinderella (1927)
Director: Burton King

The Patsy (1928)
Director: King Vidor

The Bush Cinderella (1928)
Director: Rudall Hayward

Cinderella (1930)
Directors: Manny Gould, Ben Harrison

Cinderella Blues (1931)
Directors: John Foster, Harry Bailey

The Jazz Cinderella (1930)
Director: Scott Pembroke

Cinderella Blues (1931)
Directors: Harry Bailey, John Foster

A Modern Cinderella (1932)
Director: Roy Mack

Cinderella (1933)
Director: Frank Moser

Naughty Cinderella (1933)
Director: John Daumery

Cinderella's Fella (1933)
Director: Raoul Walsh

Poor Cinderella (1934)
Director: Dave Fleischer

Hollywood Here We Come (1934)
Director: Archie Gottler

Mister Cinderella (1936)
Director: Edward Sedgwick

A Coach for Cinderella (1936)
Animation: Frank Goldman

Cinderella (*Cendrillon*, 1937)
Director: Pierre Caron

Steve Cinderella (1937)
Director: Roland Davies

A Ride for Cinderella (1937)
Director: Max Fleischer

Farewell to Cinderella (1937)
Director: Maclean Rogers

Cinderella Meets Fella (1938)
Director: Tex Avery

Campus Cinderella (1938)
Director: Noel Smith

The Glass Slipper (1938)
Director: Mannie Davis

Vasillisa the Beautiful (*Vasilisa Prekrasnaya*, 1939)
Director: Alexandr Rou

Midnight (1939)
Director: Mitchell Leisen

Princess Cinderella (*Cenerentola e il signor Bonaventura*, 1941)
Director: Sergio Tofano

Cinderella Goes to a Party (1942)
Directors: Frank Tashlin, Bob Wickersham

Swing Shift Cinderella (1945)
Director: Tex Avery

Cinderella Jones (1946)
Director: Busby Berkeley

Clun Brown (1946)
Director: Ernst Lubitsch

Cinderella (*Zolushka*, 1947)
Directors: Nadezhda Koshevrova, Mikhail Shapiro

Sepia Cinderella (1947)
Director: Arthur Leonard

Cinderella (*Cenerentola*, 1948)
Director: Fernando Cerchio

Cinderella (1950)
Directors: Wilfred Jackson, Hamilton Luske, Clyde Geronimi

April in Paris (1952)
Director: David Butler

Sabrina (1954)
Director: Billy Wilder

Cinderella (*Aschenputtel*, 1955)
Director: Fritz Genschow

Glass Slipper (1955)
Director: Charles Walters

Cinderella (1957)
Directors: Ralph Nelson, Roland Vance, Clark Jones

Cinderfella (1960)
Director: Frank Tashlin

Cinderella (*Khrustalnyy bashmachok Zolushki*, 1960)
Directors: Aleksandr Rou, Rostislav Zakharov

Cinderella Returns (1960)
Directors: Gerard Baldwin, Frank Braxton, Pete Burness, Sal Faillace, Paul Harvey, Jim Hiltz, Bill Hurtz, Lew Keller, Ted Parmelee, Gerry Ray, Dun Roman, Bob Schleh, George Singer, Ernie Terrazas, John Walker, Rudy Zamora

No Biz Like Show Biz (1960)
Directors: William Hanna, Joseph Barbera

Cinderella (1960)
Directors: Gerard Baldwin, Frank Braxton, Pete Burness, Sal Faillace, Paul Harvey, Jim Hiltz, Bill Hurtz, Lew Keller, Ted Parmelee, Gerry Ray, Dun Roman, Bob Schleh, George Singer, Ernie Terrazas, John Walker, Rudy Zamora

The Bolshoi Ballet in Prokofiev's Cinderella (*Khrustalnyy bashmachok Zolushki* 1961)
Directors: Aleksandr Rou, Rostislav Zakharov

Slippery Slippers (1962)
Directors: Joseph Barbera, William Hanna

Cinderella on the Left (1962)
Director: Donald Brittain

Señorella and the Glass Huarache (1964)
Director: Hawley Pratt

The New Cinderella (*La nueva Cenicienta*, 1964)
Director: George Sherman

Cinderella (1964)
Rodgers and Hammerstein musical
Director: Charles Dubin

Sinderella and the Golden Bra (1964)
Directors: Loel Minardi, Lowell Terry

How Now Cinderella (1965)
Directors: William Hanna, Joseph Barbera

Hey Cinderella! (1969)
Director: Jim Henson

Cinderella (1969)
Director: John Vernon

Cinderella (1972)
Directors: Arthur Rankin Jr., Jules Bass

Three Wishes for Cinderella (*Tři Oříšky Pro Popelku*, 1973)
Director: Václav Vorlíček

Chickenrella (1975)
Directors: William Hanna, Joseph Barbera

The Slipper and the Rose: The Story of Cinderella (1976)
Director: Bryan Forbes

Cinderella 2000 (1977)
Director: Al Adamson

Cinderella (1977)
Director: Michael Pataki

Cindy (1978)
Director: William Graham

Cinderella (1979)
Director: Mark Hall

Cinderella (1979)
Director: Ivan Aksenchuk

The Cinderella Wearing Sabots (*Kigutsu No Cinderella*, 1979)
Director: Yuji Endo

The Tender Tale of Cinderella Penguin (1981)
Director: Janet Perlman

Cinderella '87 (*Cenerentola '87*, 1983)
Director: Ricardo Malenotti

Cinderella (*La Cenerentola*, 1983)
Director: John Cox

Cinderella (1985)
Director: Mark Cullingham

Girl with the Diamond Slipper (*Mo deng xian lu qi yuan*, 1985)
Director: Jing Wong

Cinderella? Cinderella! (1986)
Director: Charles Nichols

Cinderella (1986)
Director: Ericka Beckman

Pretty in Pink (1986)
Director: Howard Deutsch

Maid to Order (1987)
Director: Amy Jones

Ashpet (1988)
Director: Tom Davenport

Working Girl (1988)
Director: Mike Nichols

Cinderella (*Aschenputtel*, 1989)
Director: Karin Brandauer

Pretty Woman (1990)
Director: Gary Marshall

The Magic Riddle (1991)
Director: Yoram Gross

My Big Fat Greek Wedding (1992)
Director: Joel Zwick

Prince Cinders (1993)
Director: Derek Hayes

Cinderella (1994)
Producers: Ken Cayre, Stan Cayre
Studio: Jetlag Productions

Cinderella Frozen in Time (1994)
Director: Sterling Johnson

A Tale of Cinderella (1996)
Directors: Patricia di Benedetto Snyder, Tom Gliserman

Cinderella (1997)
Director: Robert Iscove

The Shoe (*Kurde*, 1998)
Director: Laila Pakalnina

Tale of Cinderella (1998)

Ever After (1998)
Director: Andy Tennant

Never Been Kissed (1999)
Director: Raja Gosnell

Cinderelmo (1999)
Director: Bruce Leddy

Cinderella: Single Again (2000)
Director: Kellie Ann Benz

Are You Cinderella? (2000)
Director: Charles Hall

Cinderella (2000)
Director: Beeban Kidron

Cinderella (*Aschenputtel*, 2000)
Directors: Gary Blatchford, Jody Gannon, David Incorvaia

The Adventures of Cinderella's Daughter (2000)
Director: Scott Zakarin

I Was a Rat (2001)
Director: Laurie Lynd

Mr. Cinderella (2002)
Director: Ahmad Idham

Cinderella II: Dreams Come True (2002)
Directors: John Kafka, Darrell Rooney

Confessions of an Ugly Stepsister (2002)
Director: Gavin Millar

Ella Enchanted (2004)
Director: Tommy O'Haver

A Cinderella Story (2004)
Director: Mark Rosman

Cinderella (2006)
Director Man-dae Bong

Cinderella III: A Twist in Time (2007)
Director: Frank Nissen

A No Fairy Fairytale: The Cinderella Nightmare (2008)
Director: Annika Pampel

Another Cinderella Story (2008)
Director: Damon Santostefano

A Scrooge Meets Cinderella Story (2009)
Director: Andrea Litto

Cinderella (2015)
Kenneth Branagh

Contributors

Daniel Aranda is a lecturer and researcher in French language and literature at the University of Nantes. He lectures at the University Institute of Technology of La Roche-sur-Yon and is a tenured faculty member of the Centre for Educational Research of Nantes. His research focuses on characters in fictional narratives: character recurrence in fictional series and characters in folktales, children's literature, and popular fiction. In 2012, he published a collective book titled *L'Enfant et le livre, l'enfant dans le livre* (L'Harmattan). He is currently conducting studies on the representation of child soldiers in French literature from 1914 to 1918.

Cristina Bacchilega, professor of English, teaches fairy tales and adaptations, folklore and literature, and cultural studies at the University of Hawai'i at Mānoa. She coedits the journal *Marvels & Tales: Journal of Fairy-Tale Studies,* and she is the author of *Postmodern Fairy Tales: Gender and Narrative Strategies* (1997); *Legendary Hawai'i and the Politics of Place* (2007); and *Fairy Tales Transformed? Twenty-First-Century Adaptations and the Politics of Wonder* (2013). Her recent essays appear in *Marvelous Transformations: An Anthology of Fairy Tales and Contemporary Critical Perspectives* (2012), *Channeling Wonder: Fairy Tales on Television* (2014), and *The Cambridge Companion to the Fairy Tale* (2015). She serves as an editorial board member of the journal *Folklore* and has long been involved in the International Society for Folk Narrative Research.

Sandra L. Beckett is a professor in the Department of Modern Languages, Literatures, and Cultures at Brock University (Canada). She is a member of the Royal Society of Canada and a former president of the International Research Society for Children's Literature. She has authored numerous books, including *Revisioning Red Riding Hood around the World: An Anthology of International Retellings* (2013); *Crossover Picturebooks: A Genre for All Ages* (2011); *Crossover Fiction: Global and Historical Perspectives* (2009);

Red Riding Hood for All Ages: A Fairy-Tale Icon in Cross-Cultural Contexts (2008); *Recycling Red Riding Hood* (2002), *De grands romanciers écrivent pour les enfants* (1997); and three books on the French novelist Henri Bosco. She is also the editor or coeditor of several books, including *Beyond Babar: The European Tradition in Children's Literature* (2006); *Transcending Boundaries: Writing for a Dual Audience of Children and Adults* (1999); and *Reflections of Change: Children's Literature since 1945* (1997).

Ruth B. Bottigheimer is research professor in the Department of Cultural Analysis and Theory at Stony Brook University, State University of New York, and a leading historian of European fairy tales. Her recent publications include *Magic Tales and Fairy Magic: From Ancient Egypt to the Italian Renaissance* (2014); *Fairy Tales Framed: Early Forewords, Afterwords, and Critical Words* (2012); *Fairy Tales: A New History* (2009); *Gender and Story in South India*, edited with Lalita Handoo and Leela Prasad (2007); and *Fairy Godfather: Straparola, Venice, and the Fairy Tale Tradition* (2002).

Cyrille François is a senior lecturer at the School of French as a Foreign Language (University of Lausanne), and he successfully defended his PhD thesis from the same university in June 2015. His research focuses on narrative strategies in the fairy tales of Perrault, the Brothers Grimm, and Andersen, as well as in their translations. He is the author of several articles and scientific reviews of fairy-tale-related books.

Martine Hennard Dutheil de la Rochère is a professor of English and Comparative Literature at the University of Lausanne (Switzerland) and former associate dean of the Humanities. She has published on Dickens, Conrad, Rushdie, Donoghue, Hopkinson, and Carter, the fairy-tale tradition from Antiquity to the present, and literary translation (practice, theory, reception). She is the author of *Reading, Translating, Rewriting: Angela Carter's Translational Poetics* (2013); coeditor of *Des Fata aux fées: Regards croisés de l'Antiquité à nos jours* (2011); and she guest edited *Angela Carter traductrice—Angela Carter en traduction* (2014). Her fairy-tale-related work has appeared in *Fairy Tales Reimagined*, *The Conradian*, *Palimpsestes*, *JSSE*, *Gramarye*, and *Marvels & Tales*.

Kathryn A. Hoffmann is a professor of French at the University of Hawaiʻi at Mānoa. She is the author of *Society of Pleasures: Interdisciplinary Readings in Pleasure and Power during the Reign of Louis XIV* (1997) and various articles and book chapters on interdisciplinary approaches to literature, history, and museology in seventeenth- and eighteenth-century France. She is currently preparing a book on the female body, including glass casket themes in fairy tales, reliquaries, and anatomical museums.

Agata Hołobut holds a PhD in Linguistics. She works as a lecturer in Translation Studies at the Institute of English Studies, Jagiellonian University in Kraków and cooperates with the Academy of Fine Arts in Kraków. Her main areas of interest include cognitive linguistics, visual arts, and translation studies. She has published several articles on literary, audiovisual, and intersemiotic translation, as well as a book-long interview with a renowned Polish poster designer, Mieczysław Górowski, titled *Drzwi do plakatu* ("A door to a poster," Universitas, 2009).

Roxane Hughes is a PhD student in the English Department at the University of Lausanne. She is preparing a dissertation on "Writing the Chinese Bound Foot: A Literary Encounter between China and America."

Gillian Lathey is Senior Honorary Research Fellow at the University of Roehampton, London, where from 2004 to 2012 she was director of the National Centre for Research in Children's Literature. She is the author of *The Impossible Legacy: Identity and Purpose in Autobiographical Children's Literature Set in the Third Reich and the Second World War* (1999); *The Role of Translators in Children's Literature* (2010); and *Translating Children's Literature* (2015). She has edited *The Translation of Children's Literature: A Reader* (2006) and coedited with Vanessa Joosen the volume *Grimms' Tales around the Globe: The Dynamics of Their International Reception* (2014).

Mark Macleod is a senior lecturer in English at Charles Sturt University (Australia) and an award-winning publisher, writer, speaker, and television presenter. A former New South Wales state president and then national president of the Children's Book Council of Australia, he won the CBCA Lady Cutler Award in 2001 and the Australian Publishers Association Pixie O'Harris Award for distinguished services to children's literature in 2003. He is the executive editor of *International Research in Children's Literature*.

Rona May-Ron teaches English as a Foreign Language at the Hebrew University of Jerusalem. She is in the last stages of writing a PhD dissertation, also at the Hebrew University, on the recurrent subversion of the Cinderella tale in the novels of Margaret Atwood, under the supervision of Shuli Barzilai. She is particularly interested in feminist theory and literature and in the way they intersect with the cultural and literary study of fairy tales.

Xenia Mitrokhina works as a lecturer in the History of European Literature (Middle Ages and Renaissance) and as a lecturer in the History of Culture at the Institute of Journalism and Literary Creation, Moscow, Russia.

Jennifer Orme has published in *Marvels & Tales: Journal of Fairy-Tale Studies* (2010, 2015), *Transgressive Tales: Queering the Grimms* (2012), and *Beyond Adaptation* (2010). She has taught at Ryerson University's Chang School for Continuing Education in Toronto and online distance courses for the Women's and Gender Studies Department at the University of Winnipeg.

Ashley Riggs is a postdoctoral researcher and lecturer at the Faculty of Translation and Interpreting in Geneva, where she successfully completed her PhD, titled "Thrice Upon a Time: Feminist Fairy-Tale Rewritings by Angela Carter and Emma Donoghue, and Their French Translations," in June 2014. She contributed an article on Carter's rewritings of Little Red Riding Hood to *Angela Carter Traductrice—Angela Carter en traduction* (2014), edited by Martine Hennard Dutheil de la Rochère. Ashley also translates professionally.

Jan Van Coillie teaches Dutch and children's literature in translation at the Faculty of Arts of the KU Leuven, campus Brussels and was acting chairman of the Belgian Centre for Children's Literature. He has published widely on children's poetry, fairy tales, and children's literature generally. From 1999 until 2004 he was editor in chief of the *Encyclopedie van de jeugdliteratuur.* He is also active as a translator, especially of picture books and children's poetry.

Talitha Verheij is a PhD student at the University of Utrecht, the Netherlands. Her research is part of the project *Popularisation and Media Strategies (1700–1900).* The aim of this project is to analyze how processes of selection and adaptation of popular stories in songs and catchpenny prints have interacted with the motives and strategies of producers, distributors, and consumers.

Monika Woźniak is associate professor of Polish Language and Literature at the Sapienza University of Rome. Her research has addressed several topics in literary translation, children's Literature and translation, as well as audiovisual translation. She has published widely in Polish, Italian, and English, was guest editor of the special issues of *Przekładaniec: Journal of Literary Translation* (Kraków) on audiovisual translation (2008) and on fairy tales in translation (2010), and is coauthor and editor in chief of a monograph on the history of Italian-Polish and Polish-Italian translations for children, *Przekłady w systemach małych literatur* (Translation within the context of minor literature, 2014).

Jack Zipes is professor emeritus of German at the University of Minnesota, translator, editor, and author of several books devoted to the literature and culture of childhood, and the history of the fairy-tale tradition. He has published and lectured on the subject of fairy tales, their evolution, and their social and political role in civilizing processes. He is author of numerous books that are foundational to the field of fairy-tale studies, among which are *Fairy Tales and the Art of Subversion: The Classical Genre for Children and the Process of Civilization* (1985; reprint 2011); *Sticks and Stones: The Troublesome Success of Children's Literature from Slovenly Peter to Harry Potter* (2000); *Why Fairy Tales Stick: The Evolution and Relevance of a Genre* (2006); *Enchanted Screen: The Unknown History of Fairy Tale Films* (2010); *The Irresistible Fairy Tale: The Cultural and Social History of a Genre* (2012); and recently of the complete first edition of the *Kinder- und Hausmärchen* in English (2014) as well as *Grimm Legacies: the Magic Spell of the Grimms' Folk and Fairy Tales* (2014).

Index

Page numbers in italics refer to images.